Words and Music

"I think most fans will be able to relate to one or more of the experiences presented here, myself included (even to the extent of getting thrown out of a sound-check through someone else's daft behaviour). It is also good to read a book which tries to get some sort of perspective and insight into what rock music actually means to a lot of people, rather than yet another tome which just hangs on the every word of a rock star."

Simon Robinson, Deep Purple Appreciation Society

"Quite simply this is an astonishing piece of work. A remarkable undertaking . . . well argued and presented. The attention to detail is quite mesmerising. The sections relating to Twelfth Night are accurate, incisive, and revealing. As articulate and eloquent as Geoff himself: no higher praise! The chapter where the author compares Black Sabbath to Geoff Mann is both striking and fascinating, So much more than a compelling comparison of 'God's music' and the 'Devil's music'!"

Brian Devoil, Twelfth Night

"Very interesting! I enjoyed it immensely."

Lucy Jordache, Marillion Communications Manager

"When first contacted about this book I was extremely excited to read it as Michael is first and foremost a music lover, a rock fan. To get his perspective was going to be an interesting one. I have to say that everything I hoped for is here. It's a jolly enjoyable read. It's very strange reading about The Reasoning but very humbling and we are honoured to be a part of this. Michael has written something that you can feel a part of. A must read for all music fans."

Matt Cohen, The Reasoning

"Michael's book is a mixture of anecdotes and analysis which together combine to bring meaning to what rock music means to fans. Those of us who have closely followed some of the bands mentioned in the book will find much to relate to and interest them."

Anne Bond, The Web UK (Marillion Fan Club)

Words and Music

Excursions in the Art of Rock Fandom

Michael Anthony

First published in Great Britain in 2012 by Celtic Mist Publications
celtic.mist@btinternet.com

Copyright © Michael Anthony, 2012

ISBN 978-0-9572528-0-6

Cover art and chapter icons by Antonio Seijas, www.antonioseijas.com

Typeset by JCS Publishing Services Ltd, www.jcs-publishing.co.uk
Printed and bound by CPI Group (UK) Ltd, Croydon, CR0 4YY

Contents

Acknowledgements   ix

1 Rock and Roll Ain't Noise Pollution   1

2 Evie and the Essence of Rock and Roll   15

3 This One Sacred Hour   53

4 Truly, Madly, Deeply   93

5 God and the Devil   131

6 Hippy, Heavy, Horny, Happy   175

7 Morrison Hotel   205

8 Blood on the Tracks   247

9 Islands are Mountain Tops   291

10 High Voltage Rock 'n' Roll   337

Notes   351

Permissions   361

Index   369

Dedicated to the memory of Raymond Power

Friend and rocker

It's built to please true music lovers
It stays with you a lifetime

Bigelf
'Gravest Show on Earth'/'Counting Sheep'

Acknowledgements

Thanks to all the great artists, performers and writers whose work, discussed here, has enriched my life beyond measure, and to the friends and fellow fans, too numerous to list, with whom it's been my privilege to share music.

Special thanks to Antonio Seijas, Lucy Jordache, John Helmer, Brian Devoil, Jane Mann, Damon Fox, Matt Cohen, Simon Robinson and Anne Bond, and to the kind licensing folk who assisted with the copyright permissions.

Thanks to Alys, Anwen, Chrissy and Frances for love, inspiration and support.

Last but by no means least, thanks to Steve Williamson of JCS Publishing Services for service and friendship way beyond the call of duty. God bless you mate!

Michael Anthony is a Cardiff-based rock fan and writer.
He has never played bass for Van Halen.

Rock and Roll Ain't
Noise Pollution

Blowing my own Horn(by)

In his enormously enjoyable book, *Hell Bent for Leather: Confessions of a Heavy Metal Addict*, Seb Hunter describes his experiences with 'heavy metal', both as a fan and as a hopeful and ambitious young rock musician. In words that will strike a chord with many a rock fan the world over, Hunter describes his discovery of AC/DC at a school disco as "the only real eureka, blinding-light moment I've ever had".[1] As he started to explore the AC/DC back catalogue with a friend, he soon discovered "their 1979 masterpiece" *Highway to Hell*. "As we cued-up the record for the fiftieth time," writes Hunter, "I realised that this wasn't just a passing phase – this was the real deal, *the meaning of life.*"[2]

For many of us, music is a powerful force in our lives – whether we play it, write it, perform it or just listen to it. Music excites, it adds colour, it attaches itself to moods and times and memories, it changes the way we look at things, the way we feel about things, the way we approach things, the way we see ourselves, and, indeed, the way we present ourselves to the world. Seb Hunter is by no means alone in finding meaning in AC/DC and a range of other bands who, broadly, are part of the same rock tradition.

In the early and mid-1980s most of the bands discussed by Seb Hunter – including Led Zeppelin, Deep Purple, Black Sabbath, Aerosmith, Iron Maiden, Judas Priest, Kiss and Hanoi Rocks – were generally referred to as 'heavy metal'. Today, most of them would be described as 'classic rock'. I'm not one for definitions, but something does need to be said about this term 'classic rock', which seemed to emerge from nowhere in the late 1990s. What exactly is 'classic rock'? This very question is a perennial hot topic among readers of *Classic Rock* magazine no less, with many, including Deep Purple singer Ian Gillan, expressing some reservations about its use. The concern relates to the connotations of the word 'classic', where this might be taken to suggest that classic rock is music of the past, music that might be of historical curiosity but which has had its day – music, in other words, that has lost its currency, its value and its relevance. The magazine itself sees things rather differently and puts the matter very nicely in its September 2010 edition: "At CR we tend to define 'classic rock' in two ways. The first and most important is any 'rock music that endures' – rock that people will listen to forever – be it prog, punk, blues rock, metal, grunge, whatever. The second is any new rock music that references a 'classic rock' sound/aesthetic."[3]

Music that endures? Music that people will always listen to? Music that will always have value? I can run with that, and the facts appear to be on the magazine's side. There has been an extraordinary resurgence of interest in 'classic rock' in recent years– so much so that I shall now stop putting the term in inverted commas. As noted above, the classic rock label comfortably embraces a broad range of rock genres and musical styles, and *Classic Rock* magazine has proudly reported that it is currently the biggest growing music magazine in the UK, outselling long-established publications such as the *New Musical Express* (*NME*). What's more, the popularity and appeal of artists like Led Zeppelin, Iron Maiden, AC/DC, Deep Purple, Black Sabbath, and others not mentioned above, such as the Doors and Bob Dylan, remains undiminished, and, if anything, is enjoying a new period of growth. In 2009, for example, Bob Dylan released *Together Through Life* and achieved his first No. 1 album on both sides of the Atlantic since the early 1970s. In 2007 Led Zeppelin reformed for a one-off gig in London to pay tribute to Atlantic Records guru Ahmet Ertegun, and caused general astonishment at the overwhelming demand for tickets. In the same year Robert Plant released the *Raising Sand* album with Alison Krauss – to widespread critical acclaim. In 2008

AC/DC released *Black Ice* and enjoyed considerable success with both the album and their subsequent tour. Metallica had a good year in 2008, with their *Death Magnetic* album rescuing their reputation among current rock fans and re-establishing them as a giant of the modern era. Iron Maiden's 2008 world stadium tour saw them mobilise and build on their already considerable fan base, playing to enormously enthusiastic audiences in stadia across the world. Deep Purple have continued to tour extensively throughout the last decade, undertaking lengthy world tours and playing to appreciative audiences across the globe. The Ronnie James Dio-fronted version of Black Sabbath also reformed and toured under the Heaven and Hell moniker. Their 2009 – and sadly Dio's last – album, *The Devil You Know*, proved to be the finest studio outing associated with either Dio or Sabbath for nigh on a quarter of a century. In 2006 the Doors released the *Perception* box set, and 2010 saw the release of yet another Doors film on DVD. I could go on.

For the first time, we live in an age where a 40–50 year tradition has produced several generations of rock bands, each inspired by the preceding generation, and we now have rock stars who are performing well into their sixties (and in some cases beyond). Some bands from the 1960s and 1970s have kept going throughout the entire period. Others have reformed in recent years as the success of new young bands and tribute bands inspired by them has rekindled interest and popularity. Elsewhere, the development of the internet has inspired novel DIY approaches that have enabled bands like Marillion to find new ways of communicating with their audience and take control of their own affairs, ensuring that not only can they survive in the new millennium, but with sufficient musical and business creativity they can even start to flourish again.

The classic rock tag would therefore seem an appropriate catch-all for the kind of music I want to talk about, though I often find it more natural to simply use the term 'rock music'. I should warn the reader now, however, that having established that point, I have no further interest in trying to define rock music, classic rock music, nor any other musical label, in ways that might limit the scope of this work. In fact, you will quickly notice that I use the terms 'rock', 'classic rock', 'heavy rock', 'rock 'n' roll', and even 'heavy metal' pretty much interchangeably throughout. To those who like everything in their world to be categorised and ordered in lots of tiny linguistic boxes, I make no apologies for this but ask that on this occasion you put your desire for order to one side and simply go with the flow.

I am, you may have gathered, rather suspicious of labels, and in this context, I am very taken with something that Deep Purple keyboard player Jon Lord says in the sleeve notes to the 1999 release *In Concert with the London Symphony Orchestra*. Reflecting on the chequered history of his *Concerto for Group and Orchestra*, which he first composed in 1969, and his own motivations in writing it, Lord says: "I still believe, and always will, to the depths and heights of my soul, that music, shorn of labels and standing alone, when it is conceived, composed and performed with love and integrity, can elevate us all."

Arguably music is always "shorn of labels" at the point at which the listener connects with it. "Any musical endeavour can only ever really be said to succeed," writes Vincent Budd, "in terms of its emotional effect on those willing enough to experience it."[4] As simple and primitive as rock music can sometimes be, it seems to me undeniable that it can be "conceived, composed and performed with love and integrity" and that it often succeeds in inducing powerful emotional experiences. Rock music can inspire and enrich us, it can put us in touch with higher and better things and it "can elevate us all". I am far more interested in the power of the music to do this than I am in labels.

Given that this is so, I'd like to share one of my ongoing frustrations with you. Whatever you want to call the kind of music that I like, from as early as I can remember, much of it has been criticised and ridiculed by whoever the current arbiters of taste happen to be. In the early years of high school, they laughed because I liked Neil Diamond. (A guilty pleasure? Well, have you heard his original *Hot August Night* album?) Then, when I discovered rock music, I found that punks, ska devotees and new romantics were not only utterly dismissive of rock music but also of each other. When it comes to music, it always takes two – the listener *and* the music, the *listeners* and the music. But when music becomes too bound up with fashion and the mood of the time, the sacred bond between the listener and the music is broken, and the music becomes something else. It becomes a tool used by the prevailing orthodoxy to exercise a social pressure that is as destructive to the spirit of creativity and human difference as it is discriminatory towards those who happen to like something else. My own taste has not changed but has broadened over time. I've never understood those whose taste appears to be entirely determined by whatever is most fashionable or cool at any given moment. Nor do I understand it when people who've taken pleasure in ridiculing rock music over the years suddenly tell me they like The Darkness, for example, or Steel Panther, because they're 'ironic'. And what about the snipes and jibes of those absurdly tyrannical music journalists who subscribe almost ideologically to the doctrine that so-called 'heavy metal' is music made by old men for young boys? Or the seemingly endless procession of musical snobs who use the name 'Spinal Tap' as an adjective which they believe has sufficient power to summarily dismiss nearly half a century of rock tradition as flippantly as you like. Music should be respected as music, and if it moves you and makes your life better or clearer in some way, then that's good – and if other people are moved by music that doesn't move you, then that's good too because it suggests variety and richness and colour; it gives you things to think about and talk about and swap and share. Where music is concerned, variety is, indeed, the spice of life.

In his book *31 Songs*, Nick Hornby reveals himself to be a man of extraordinarily broad taste – and all power to his elbow. But, much to my surprise, even he seems to have swallowed and regurgitated some of the more obvious mainstream objections to heavy rock. While recognising "the traditional interpretation of boys and their infatuation with heavy (or nu-, or rap) metal", Hornby does, in inimitable fashion, set himself apart from other infatuated boys: ". . . I suspect that there is a musical, rather than pathological, explanation for my early dalliance with Zeppelin and Sabbath and Deep Purple," he says, "namely that I was unable to trust my judgement of a song." As his faith in his own ability to judge grew, he says, he had less need for "loud, distorted electric guitars".[5] His recent discovery that "the rock riff is nutritionally essential" to a balanced musical diet, and that only Led Zeppelin could satiate the hunger for it, served only to show Hornby that Zeppelin "can no longer be comfortably accommodated" into his life.[6] He writes:

> The culture with which I surround myself is a reflection of my personality and the circumstances of my life, which is in part how it should be. In learning to do that, however, things get lost, too, and one of the things that got lost . . . was Jimmy Page. The noise he makes is not who I am any more, but it's still a noise worth listening to; it's also a reminder that the attempt to grow up smart comes at a cost.[7]

What then of those of us who believe that we have 'grown up smart' but still find more than "loud, distorted electric guitars" in the music of Led Zeppelin, Black Sabbath and Deep Purple? What then of those of us who, despite having married, taken on responsible jobs, and – in my case as in Hornby's – learned to care for a child with a chronic condition, still *can* comfortably accommodate Zeppelin and Sabbath and Purple into our lives? These are some of the bands I want to write about. They still mean as much to me now as they did when I first heard them. And I know I am not alone. Indeed, these are some of the bands I *must* write about. Why? Well, for one thing, because Nick Hornby doesn't.

So what makes *me* so qualified to write? Plenty of others have been to more gigs, bought more albums, read more books and spent more time hanging around bands than I have. My answer is that this is not a book about being a 'superfan' or a musical anorak (although there's nothing wrong with that). Anyone who has been moved by music can write the kind of thing I've attempted here, irrespective of how many albums they own, how many gigs they've been to and which bands have moved and inspired them. What I have written is about the way music – in this case rock music – can weave its way into the fabric of a life, a very ordinary life, and do extraordinary things there.

As a teenager I was often inclined to be critical of people who liked to 'lose themselves in a good book'. "No wonder the world's in such a mess," I used to think, "when people prefer to turn a blind eye and flee to some fictional world than face up to things." Some people seemed to use books in the way others used drugs or alcohol – as necessary escapism. Yet I conveniently overlooked the fact that even works of fiction can be full of wisdom, can open doors for us and can show us things that, quite simply, are best expressed in that way. I also failed to recognise the extent to which I found my own meaning in music – losing myself in albums as others lost themselves in books, trying to collect music to match every emotion, and turning to albums as one might turn to old friends.

In 2007 I took my daughter to the Hay-on-Wye Literature Festival. There, I heard the writer and former Children's Laureate Michael Morpurgo say that when someone finishes one of his books he wants them to feel that the world he has created is as real as the 'real world' outside the book. It struck me that in my youth certain records used to make me feel that way. I did not regard retiring to my room to listen to music as a form of escapism at all – at least not usually. Just as life inspires art, so we can learn from art, and art inspires life. Most of my favourite music seemed to capture something important and hold it still a while for me to experience – and so I often turned to music when I felt the need to immerse myself in 'real life'. Whether we are talking about books, or paintings or music, art is not something that exists apart from 'real life'. Rather, for those who are moved by it, it is something integral to their lives, something that is woven into their thoughts, their activities and their characters in ways that are often difficult to disentangle and describe.

As far as I'm concerned, *anyone* who has actively taken music into their life is qualified to write – about the music, about the way in which it has inspired them, and about the role it has played in shaping their character and bringing them together with others. And yet, while anyone is qualified to write, so few people do, and even fewer seem to write in this way about the kind of music that matters to me.

⟡ Words and music ⟡

In choosing a title for what I have written, I was looking for something that would convey a sense of journey, exploration and artistic endeavour, and I hope I have found something that does that.

It is no doubt true that our music choices say a lot about who we are and are an important part of that journey. Though in some senses we can't choose what music moves and inspires us or what music we like, there are other clear senses in which we do choose. We choose what albums we buy, which ones we keep, which bands we explore further, and how often we listen to them. What we do with music and how we take it into our lives *is* something we choose – and for rock fans making such choices is almost an art in itself.

Writing about music is also an art and there are, I have discovered, some very good biographies, autobiographies and writers out there. In almost all cases in what follows I have only cited work that I have found interesting, informative and engaging. Even where I disagree with an expressed opinion, I would have no hesitation in recommending to you any of the various books, articles and magazines that I have cited in my text.

In considering a title, I also wanted something that would draw attention to the difference between 'words' and 'music' while giving each their due. When one chooses to write about music one is self-consciously choosing one medium to try to convey something about another, and I think it is important that both author and reader alike recognise the tension and limitations of using the written word to convey an experience of a quite different kind. Music must be *heard*, and however well one writes, the written word is no substitute for the real thing.

This point clearly applies to the work of writers and music journalists, who take a step back and describe bands, performers, the music they create, and their experience of it from afar, as it were – from *outside* the music itself. But something also needs to be said about the relationship between words and music *within* rock music. Most, though not all, rock music makes extensive use of vocalists and lyrics, and often, when rock music moves us, words and music work together to produce this effect.

When Geoffrey Cannon reviewed Bob Dylan's *Self Portrait* album in the *Guardian* newspaper (26 June 1970), he wrote: "It's human context, not verbal dexterity that lets words, especially words of love, work."[8] Similarly one might argue that *musical* context is often necessary for rock lyrics to work. Though lyrics often appear as 'just' words on album sleeves and booklets, it is important to remember that typically they are sung and performed. Pulled out of their natural home and presented starkly on a page they can lose their magic and charm and look so very ordinary. Commenting on a few quoted lines of one of Dylan's most striking lyrics ('Idiot Wind' from the *Blood on the Tracks* album), Paul Williams (writer and founder of the American rock magazine *Crawdaddy!*) says: "I notice if you read these lyrics without hearing the music, the melody, the chords that go with 'em, it's not the same; music and words *have* to be experienced together."[9]

I recognise that my own presentation and discussion of lyrics within these pages is limited in this very way. Nevertheless, I hope I can say enough to inspire you, or at least encourage you, to go and listen to the words of the songs I describe in their natural home – that is, in the musical context that gives them life.

Another kind of limitation (if 'limitation' is the right word) of what I have presented here lies in the need for interpretation. On the bonus DVD that accompanies the limited edition of Magnum's 2009 album *In the Valley of the Moon King*, songwriter Tony Clarkin refuses to talk about the meaning of his songs.[*] There must be room for interpretation, suggests Clarkin – if I tell you what the song means, there's no space for it to work its magic on you, or for you to respond to it at a personal or individual level.

What I present in my discussions of music below is, self-consciously, interpretation: it is *my* interpretation. I try to make you see and feel

---

* One assumes that his tongue was firmly in his cheek when he penned the album title!

something of the music I discuss and what it means to me. But who am I? I am one listener among many thousands. There is and always should be room for interpretation, disagreement and discussion – and once again I hope that when you read what I have written you will want to explore for yourself not just the music I have described but other music too. I hope you will want to return to the music with fresh eyes and fresh ears and become alive, if you're not already, to the possibilities it holds.

Excursions in the art of rock fandom

This is a book about rock music. More specifically it is a book about the value of rock music and the meaning it can have in people's lives. In addition to this introduction there are nine chapters. Each has a theme which is illustrated by my response in some way to particular bands or albums. I wanted to write about *albums* and *bands*, rather than songs, because for the most part it's through albums and bands that I have experienced music. What's more, I believe this is how all those whose taste largely approximates to mine experience music. Relating to a whole album or the entire output of a band requires considerably more effort than relating to a song. Relating to music in this way has implications for the kind of significance you attach to it, the place it has in your life, and what you might want to say about it.

Taken as a whole, the book describes the journey of someone who has listened to and been inspired by rock music over the last 30 years or so. The text moves from the excitement of discovery, through the joy of sharing and belonging, to a much more introspective, private and personal way of listening to music when that early idealism shatters. Finally, matters come full circle with the rediscovery, through music, of much of my initial spirit of optimism. I believe that my experience is very common. I hope that many others will recognise their own experiences in my account and I hope that you will derive both pleasure and sustenance from the journey I have described.

'Evie and the Essence of Rock and Roll' takes as its starting point a conversation I had with a friend who works in the music industry. It explores the connection between the meaning that people can find in rock music and what one might call the 'rock 'n' roll lifestyle'. The phrase 'sex, drugs and rock 'n' roll' has a wide currency these days, but scratch beneath the surface of popular usage and it's soon obvious that despite tendencies towards promiscuity and substance abuse by those who live and breathe rock 'n' roll, the rock 'n' roll lifestyle isn't one thing. As always, common phrases and labels mask a wide range of attitudes and behaviours. What's more, however integral drug use and general decadence are to the histories of some of the great rock bands, it is clear that the music itself can never be reduced to, or explained away by, some of the more hedonistic and destructive tendencies of those who create it. Whatever the source of musicians' motivation, inspiration and life choices – and these sources themselves are varied – the music, once created, has a life of its own. As fans we respond to this music in an even greater variety of ways. The same bands, songs and albums hold different places and have different significance in the lives of different people. This realisation – which shouldn't really come as a surprise – opens up vast vistas of human experience that are often ignored, trivialised or ridiculed by the mass media and mainstream popular culture. 'Evie and the Essence of Rock and Roll' is an attempt to create the 'conceptual space' within which some of this experience and significance can be explored.

'This One Sacred Hour' tries to illustrate something of the power of the live gig experience to move large numbers of people in potentially life-changing ways. It does this by presenting recollections of some of the finest and most memorable gigs I have been to. Of course, my own experience is inevitably very limited and barely scratches the surface of what rock gigs have to offer. Whether you have had similar experiences with the same or different bands, or gig experiences of a quite different kind, I hope you will find much here to which you can relate and with which you will engage.

'Truly, Madly, Deeply' seeks to explore the way rock music can contribute to personal development and growth, not just through a connection with some of rock's great lyrical themes but through an emerging sense of personal identity and group belonging. Once again it seeks to tap into a common well of experience, this time looking not at the live gig but at what is usually the rock fan's primary connection with music – namely music in its recorded form. One can listen to recorded music alone, or one can share and swap it with friends. For the rock fan, music can become an important way of learning about oneself *and* relating to other people.

'God and the Devil' explores the recurring tension between Christianity and claims of 'Satanism' in rock music. Settling on this metaphysical theme, it looks at the way rock music can help people to think through and develop views on issues of personal and common significance. It does this through a consideration of the work of two artists who, it might be thought, occupy opposing extremes on the rock spectrum: namely Black Sabbath and ex-Twelfth Night vocalist and ordained vicar Geoff Mann. In reality, these artists have far more in common than the casual observer or the uninitiated might expect – and both offer considerable support to lost but knowledge-hungry listeners keen to find their place in the world via reflection on some of life's 'big questions'.

The integration of the more personal and introspective aspects of rock fandom with its more social and communal dimensions is, I think, part of what makes rock music such a powerful and all-embracing force in people's lives. But what happens when the balance tips too far in either direction? What happens, for example, when we get so immersed in social or "communal revelry"* that we lose our grip on what's going on around us? What happens when we realise that we have drifted away from the shared values that once gave our social activities their drive and energy? 'Hippy, Heavy, Horny, Happy' is a pivotal chapter, exploring, as it does, a kind of breakdown and fragmentation of the early idealism that characterised my love of rock music – an idealism that rock music itself fuelled and inspired.

'Morrison Hotel' looks at one possible result of this fragmentation – a sense of detachment and isolation and a swing to intense introspection. In the absence of like-minded individuals, there is always a tendency for us to look to an appropriate idol for support and guidance. When, as a rock fan, you find a band or an artist to help guide you through such a dark period of your life, you can but hope that you have chosen a reasonable guide. Of course, in reality, choice has little to do with it. The experience of finding an artist whose music and outlook completely takes over your whole being is truly intoxicating. It can provide both hope and validation as one comes to identify ever more closely with the public persona and musical output of the artist. But there are clear dangers to personal growth when one becomes spellbound to the point of imitation,

---

* To borrow a phrase of Paul Wilkinson's from *Rat Salad: Black Sabbath the Classic Years 1969–1975* (Pimlico, 2007), p.2

subservience, or obsession. When one's idol is Jim Morrison, and one is already feeling lost and cut adrift, the dangers are particularly stark, with the hero-worship directing the fan to any number of doors that it's probably wiser (or at least safer) not to open. The relationship between rock stars and their fans, and the forms the relationship takes, has always fascinated me, ever since I first saw those old black and white film reels of young girls screaming hysterically at the Beatles. The psychology of the rock star/rock fan relationship is interesting, and the dynamic can quickly become unhealthy for both parties. Jim Morrison, of course, is dead: the relationship can't do him any more harm.

'Blood on the Tracks' continues the introspective theme, but presents such introspection through rock music in a more sober, wider-ranging and helpful context. This is a chapter about balance, about restoring one's equilibrium, about keeping one's influences in perspective, learning from them and using them to grow. This is also a chapter about the genius of Bob Dylan. Dylan at his best is simply peerless, whether he's commenting on social or political issues, reflecting on love and relationships, or engaging in playful self-mockery and subverting his own art form and public image. Dylan is a man of many masks. You can't catch him. You shouldn't even try. But he has created a body of work that is simultaneously rousing and edifying, sad and joyful, personal and impersonal: a body of work that sits somewhere in the gap "between despondency and hope". Nowhere is this more true than on the masterful *Blood on the Tracks*, an album which contains little of the anger and protest for which Dylan is still perhaps best known, but which is the most perfect and timeless rock album I know. It is an album that grows with you and invites you to grow with it. I could not have written a book about being a rock fan without acknowledging its greatness.

'Islands are Mountain Tops' brings us full circle and in one sense – we are, after all, nearing the end of the book – completes the journey. As one gets older, one hopes one becomes wiser and better able to integrate all aspects of what it means to be a rock fan – the thought-provoking contemplation, the social bonds and the communal revelry, and just the sheer pleasure and entertainment – into a stable, happy and rewarding life. How wonderful if you find a band who enable you to draw the personal and social aspects of your love for music together in a way that not only sits comfortably with your adult life, but helps you rediscover the enthusiasm and idealism of your youth. Rediscovering Marillion in 2004 brought much of that early idealism and enthusiasm for music back into my life. This time, however,

I *am* older and wiser and, I think, better able to recognise the limitations of rock music as a vehicle for social change. 'Islands are Mountain Tops' describes some of the joy and 'elevation' I've experienced recently, through the work of a band on whom I'd once given up. Of course, the journey isn't really at an end. As long as we draw breath, there is no end point – we go on living and learning, opening ourselves to new experiences and looking to share them with others. "Happiness", as they say, "is the road." And the road, as we all know, is long and winding.

Rock music, or classic rock music, may not always be fashionable. It may not always achieve appropriate mainstream acknowledgement and respect, but it continues to evolve just out of sight of 'respectable society' and its audience has never really gone away. 'High Voltage Rock 'n' Roll' attempts to demonstrate this point by focusing on the 2010 High Voltage Festival, which brought together many of the bands and people who feature in this book in one astonishing event. The Festival was also notable for a special one-off performance by Heaven and Hell to celebrate the life and music of Ronnie James Dio who sadly lost his battle with stomach cancer in May 2010. When Ronnie James Dio left Black Sabbath and re-emerged with his own band, I was much taken with the distinction he liked to make in his album credits between those who create, those who labour and those who support. If the High Voltage Festival showed anything, it showed that many of those who labour and those who create are still out there, entertaining us, inspiring us, uncovering possibilities of meaning, and doing their utmost to communicate these possibilities and the sheer joy of music to the rest of us – those who listen.

For those about to rock

Ultimately any writer has to write for him or herself – to satiate the need for expression, and to release that pressure that builds and builds until getting words down on paper becomes the most urgent and pressing demand on your time. I thank all of those who've put up with me on a daily basis during the writing period. I hope that I have repaid their patience and tolerance by producing something that is both readable and enjoyable. I hope too that my teenage daughter will read it and understand why her 44-year-old father still gets feverishly excited about buying CDs and still disappears for the odd night every now and then to go and see a band.

The author and publisher Kevan Manwaring once advised me to "write the book you want to read." That is what I have done. I see rock fandom as one 'big discussion', and this book is my contribution to that discussion. In it I have done my best to capture moments from my own life – and the lives of some of those with whom I've discovered and shared rock music – in a way that will be familiar and speak to all rock fans. The people in these pages are real and the power of rock music in our lives has been very real. I hope that those friends and acquaintances I have written about are able to recognise themselves in what I have written, and I hope that they are happy with the way my memories have allowed me to portray them.

Inevitably, much of what I have written here is personal. The responses to the music I describe are mine. The accompanying anecdotes are based on my recollections. And yet, I believe that my experience is common. I hope that what I have written will remind you of your own experiences with music – different bands and different gigs and different moments to be sure, but experiences that carry the same sense of excitement at hearing a stunning new album for the first time, or rekindle the sense of awakening that rock music can sometimes inspire, that feeling that something is being revealed, that the world is somehow opening out before you. I hope that what I have written will stir memories of the power and awe of your first rock gig, or the thrill and warmth of any good rock gig come to that. I hope that what I have written will help you to recall a time when music first became a part of your life – not just a 'soundtrack' but a *part* of your life, a time when music first became a part of you and who you are, part of what you shared with friends, part of your thinking and the way you saw the world, part of what you wanted from life and, if you're lucky, part of what your life is now. If you're reading this then potentially you're someone whose relationship with rock music has followed the same, or a similar path, to my own. Welcome and enjoy. For those about to rock, I salute you!

2

Evie and the Essence of Rock and Roll

"It was great," I said. "There were whole families there – three generations of the same family in some cases, children Alys's age and people the same age as my Mum and Dad."

I was talking to my friend Evie, who works in the music industry. Evie works on the promotions side, securing publicity for a portfolio of bands in support of tours and album releases. By all accounts she's very good at what she does. Alys is my daughter. She was nine years old at the time of this conversation.

It was early spring 2007. I had recently been to a Marillion Weekend in Port Zelande, Holland. Almost 3,000 Marillion fans from all over the world had descended on a Center Parcs resort on a remote part of the Dutch coast for a four-day celebration of all things Marillion. There was a full line-up of support bands, a pub quiz, a signing session, a Marillion museum, and full and exclusive use of the resort facilities. What's more, the band themselves stayed on site and played a completely different two-and-a-half-hour set each night.

It was a truly international affair. In fact people from 40 different countries were there. I found myself speaking with Americans at Amsterdam airport, lunching with Swedes on arrival, chanting with Spaniards during Saturday night's covers and rarities set, and waving a flag with a Mexican on Sunday. I renewed my acquaintance with my Greek Cypriot friend Antonis – whom I first met in the front row at one of the Astoria gigs on the *Marbles* tour – and I marvelled at both the enthusiasm and height of the Dutch contingent. In the 1980s, fading rock stars would always claim to be 'big in Japan' and have a live album to prove it. Well, Marillion are certainly 'big in Holland' – though if success is measured by creativity, artistic integrity, endurance and core-fan loyalty their star can hardly be said to be fading.

I mentioned to Evie that the Center Parcs people in Port Zelande had initially been wary of agreeing to book their entire resort out to 3,000 rock fans. Indeed, there had been countless warnings about good behaviour and the resort's strict 'zero tolerance' drugs policy. In the event, everything went so well that the resort management wrote to the band offering two lucky families a free weekend break: "Your fans really are just one big happy family," the letter had enthused.

"Well, no offence to Marillion," Evie replied, "but they're not very 'rock 'n' roll' these days are they?"

"What do you mean?"

"Well, 'rock 'n' roll' is 'sex and drugs and rock 'n' roll' isn't it? When you hear '3,000 rock fans' you expect sex and drugs and rowdiness, but it's not like that with Marillion is it? They're not like a new young band, or even like one of the older bands who still live the rock 'n' roll lifestyle."

I sighed, inwardly and deeply. There is a not uncommon view that rock and roll is simply an attitude, and is all about rock stars doing the kind of decadent, dangerous, wild and irresponsibly hedonistic things that the rest of us secretly want to do but, for whatever reason, can't or don't. The music and the lifestyle fit together like a hand fits a glove, so the view goes, and it is this that makes rock music and 'rock stars' rebellious and exciting, stirring in us desires and compulsions that are almost as deeply repressed and powerful as those attributed by Freud to Oedipus. We expect our heroes to live the lifestyle to the max. We live our fantasies through them. Following their fortunes is car crash TV for the soul. Evie knows lots of musicians and media people. She spends her life cavorting with rock stars and music industry folk. She understands very well the difference between 'rock 'n' roll' as a type of music and 'rock 'n' roll' as an attitude. But my conversation with Evie got me thinking . . .

♂ Sex, drugs and rock 'n' roll ♀

It's not that I don't understand what people mean when they say that something is 'very rock 'n' roll' or when they talk about 'the rock 'n' roll lifestyle'. And, of course, it would be absurd to deny that sex, drugs and outlandish behaviour are common and often highly visible features of the way many rock musicians choose to live. So what's my problem?

My 'problem', as it were, is that 'rock 'n' roll' – by which I mean rock music – means something different than this to me. Whatever images the phrase commonly evokes, and whatever the lifestyle choices of those who create it, rock 'n' roll for me is first and last and always . . . *music*. Once it is 'out there', on CDs, DVDs and computer discs, and in concert halls and arenas around the world, it takes on a life of its own. My point would hold even if all rock stars who ever lived and recorded ended up as sex-crazed drug fiends (or drug-crazed sex fiends) – the music would still have a value of its own and a significance that goes beyond the lives and habits of its creators. Of course, not all rock musicians do end up sex-crazed, drug-crazed or just plain old crazed. How musicians conceive of their art and how musicians choose to live their lives varies tremendously. There is no *essential* attitude or set of behaviours by which the music can be explained, or to which the music can be reduced. And of course, it would be very hard to argue that conformity to some stereotypical 'rock 'n' roll lifestyle' could, in and of itself, be any kind of measure of the value of a band's musical output.

I also think there is room to doubt the received wisdom that there is a *necessary* connection between rock and roll and a particular *kind* of 'rebellion'. While it is true that excessive drinking, rampant promiscuity, substance abuse, and wild, lewd, raucous and inappropriate behaviour are perhaps the most obvious ways in which large numbers of rock musicians have chosen to thumb their noses at 'respectable society', these are not the only, nor indeed the most interesting, ways in which rock music or rock musicians can, and have, opposed the status quo, rejected conventional attitudes and rebelled. In fact, there's a real sense in which drinking yourself into a stupor, snorting coke and trashing your hotel room is no longer, in any meaningful way, rebellious at all.

The connection between the rock and roll stereotype and the kind of rock music I love is not something that you often see challenged. But as you will have gathered from what I've said above, I think it should be. Not because I'm on a moral crusade of any sort, or because I don't recognise the prevalence of such stereotypical behaviour among both rock stars and certain kinds of fans, but simply because the assumed connection between the more decadent features of the lifestyle, on the one hand, and the music, on the other, seems to me to obscure the very *possibility* of someone finding the kind of joy and meaning in the music that I have found. And so here I am, at 44 years of age, trying to create a bit of 'conceptual space' for myself to explain why this great musical tradition (the classic rock tradition, if you like) has had such a profound influence on my life, and the lives of many, many others. For years our experiences have been trampled under the feet of a disapproving popular culture, aided and abetted, it must be said, by the excesses of some of our own heroes and the foolishness of second or third division 'rock stars' who have come to mistake the trappings and distractions of artistic success for success itself.

The reference here to *artistic* success is important, and, indeed, the idea that rock music can be conceived of as art, and that those who create it can be driven or inspired by many different things, is a powerful one. It opens the door to a potentially limitless number of possibilities, all of which free the artist and the listener from the conceptual constraints imposed by the rock and roll stereotype. Recognising this, and opening yourself up to some of these possibilities, can be a very exciting and liberating experience.

Few have done more to connect rock music and art in the minds of fans and critics than Bob Dylan, and even fewer have been able to produce a back catalogue that rivals Dylan's in terms of both size and range. A feature of Dylan's work is its challenging nature, as, chameleon-like, he has frequently taken off in new directions, leading his audience to places they never imagined they would go. Of course, there have been a few wrong turnings and dirt-tracks *en route*, but Dylan has always re-emerged sooner or later, with a renewed sense of purpose and new stories to tell. In his film, *Rolling Thunder and the Gospel Years: A Totally Unauthorised Documentary*, Joel Gilbert asks Joel Selvin, rock reporter with the *San Francisco Chronicle*, if he felt that Bob Dylan was someone who needed to discover new inspiration to "re-energise his art from time to time"? Selvin replied:

> After *John Wesley Harding* and *Nashville Skyline* you could feel [that with] each record this guy was further and further away from whatever

source of inspiration had . . . whatever crucible had forged those songs that he had written so many of. 'If Dogs Run Free'? OK, you know, I mean did Irving Berlin suffer because his life had moved in different directions, or did he just keep cranking out pop songs? And is that the difference between the pop song writer and the rock song writer who's using his own life as material, his own experiences as the metal, the content that he's fashioning?[1]

I do not want to suggest that Selvin has defined *the* difference between rock and pop music, but he has, nonetheless, put his finger on something that matters to a lot of rock fans – namely that rock musicians often draw on their own experiences for inspiration and are somehow 'in' the music in a way that more frothy, chart-orientated performers are not. If we accept this, then it is not surprising that sometimes even serious artists write about touring, life on the road, their experiences with women (or men) and their experiences with drugs, regardless of their attitudes towards these things and whatever else they write about.

In particular, the relationship between drugs and music is an interesting one. While everyone has their own take on the matter, it is always possible to find musicians who would argue that drugs are an *essential* part of the creative process. In an interview with *Playboy* magazine in March 1978, Bob Dylan was asked why 'grass' had been so prevalent in the jazz and folk clubs of his youth. He replied:

Being a musician means – depending on how far you go – getting to the depths of where you are at. And most any musician would try anything to get to those depths, because playing music is an immediate thing – as opposed to putting paint on a canvas, which is a calculated thing. Your spirit flies when you are playing music. So, with music, you tend to look deeper and deeper inside yourself to find the music.

At the same time, it is interesting to note that there are other drugs of which Dylan does not speak so fondly. Asked whether psychedelics had a similar effect on him, he says:

No. Psychedelics never influenced me . . . When psychedelics happened, everything became irrelevant. Because that had nothing to do with making music or writing poems or trying to really find yourself in that day and age . . . People were deluded into thinking they were something that they weren't; birds, airplanes, fire hydrants, whatever. People were walking around thinking they were stars.[2]

It would be wise, I think, to avoid making general assumptions about the relationship between drugs and musical creativity. Just as there are different people, so there are different drugs, and different people approach different drugs (if they approach drugs at all) in different ways. It would not be difficult, for example, to find opinions on LSD use that are different to those expressed above by Bob Dylan. Rather than making easy generalisations, it is perhaps more instructive to pay attention to particulars: looking to see what particular musicians say about particular drugs and their influence on their music at particular times. Sometimes such accounts can be interesting and illuminating. At other times the claims made by musicians can turn out to be one-sided, deluded and overstated, just as the claims of other drug users can. I remember an occasion, for example, when a friend persuaded me to sit in a park with him for an afternoon while he dropped acid. He claimed he was capable of the most amazing philosophical insights while under its influence but could never remember them afterwards. So we sat surrounded by deliciously coloured flowers, lush green grass and myriad summer sounds and . . . we waited. I had with me my pen and notebook, ready to capture and preserve his acid-tinged jewels of wisdom. But I'm sorry to report that very few words emerged at all, let alone insights likely to revolutionise the world of academic philosophy. Similarly, those learning a second language often claim that they converse better after a few pints. Invariably the truth of the matter is that despite their subjective perceptions, and an apparent growth in confidence, most learners don't speak better – they just speak more!

As for Bob Dylan, it is pertinent at this point to wonder what influence he felt his drug taking had on his own creativity. In an interview with Jann S. Wenner for *Rolling Stone* magazine in November 1969, Dylan claimed that given the rigours of endless touring and recording, he needed to take drugs in the mid-sixties simply to keep going. "Did taking drugs influence the songs?" asked Wenner. "No, not the writing of them," replied Dylan, "but it did keep me up there to pump 'em out."[3]

In his editorial to *Classic Rock* magazine, issue 110 ('the Drugs Issue'), Editor-in-Chief Scott Rowley quotes American comedian Bill Hicks:

> If you don't believe that drugs have done some good things, then do me a favour: go home tonight and take all your albums and all your CDs and all your tapes and *burn* 'em. Cos you know what? All the musicians that

made all that great music that's enhanced your life throughout the years? They were *real* high on drugs.

Rowley comments:

> Bill Hicks was funny – but was he right? It's not that drugs weren't a part of all those records, but drugs didn't *make* the records – people with talent did. C'mon, drugs don't make you more creative (wouldn't the housing estates of Britain be bursting with budding songwriters, novelists and artists if they did? Wouldn't hair metal be pretty damn good?), at best they just give creative people stuff to write about: euphoric highs, crushing lows, moments of clarity, stories of chaos . . .
>
> The poet William Blake grandly claimed that 'the road of excess leads to the palace of wisdom.' But if the truth be told, the age-old combo of sex and drugs and rock 'n' roll usually leads to disaster. Or, as that other great Romantic poet, Axl Rose, put it after visiting Jim Morrison's grave: 'The road of excess leads to a dirt plot in a foreign land that people pour booze and piss all over.'[4]

It's refreshing to read such a sober analysis, particularly from the editor of a magazine that regularly features bands associated with rock and roll excess. While it is beyond dispute that many rock musicians have used drugs, and that some have used them very extensively, ultimately the relationship between drugs and musical creativity remains an uneasy one. All too often those who felt that drugs did aid the creative process have ended up in the grip of a grim addiction, losing almost all sense of creativity, short-changing themselves and their fans, and, in some cases, losing their lives.

☉ *Breaking on through?* ☉

Scott Rowley's references to William Blake and Jim Morrison inevitably bring the Doors to mind. The Doors are, in many ways, the example *par excellence* of a rock band who used drugs for creative purposes, only for the drugs to bite back hard. The Doors took their name from a William Blake line quoted by Aldous Huxley at the start of his influential work *The Doors of Perception*:

> *If the doors of perception were cleansed, everything would appear to man as it is, infinite.*

The Doors were of their time, and were certainly not alone in using LSD to try to cleanse "the doors of perception". It was not uncommon at the time for a certain kind of drug use to sit comfortably alongside an interest in Eastern philosophy, meditation, and other practices designed to tap into the 'universal mind'. Certainly at the start of their career, the Doors' use of drugs was at least partly an intellectual and spiritual pursuit rather than a reckless desire for pleasure or a means of escape. Drugs were one way of achieving the kind of vision that they sought – an altered state of being that would unlock some of the human mind's untapped potential. The band's musical prowess, their sense of drama, and Ray Manzarek and Jim Morrison's love of film and performance, gave them a powerful way of reaching hundreds of thousands if not millions of people, ostensibly with a manifesto of liberation. Liberation meant freedom. It meant giving people a sense of themselves and freeing them from unnecessary constraints. It meant encouraging them to wake up and to see their lives differently. It was about opting-in rather than opting-out. The Doors, in this respect, were on a journey that was entirely different to the squalid, hedonistic nihilism that characterises the drug use of so many other rock bands, and that, in fact, came to characterise the drug use and early demise of their own troubled and charismatic singer.

One can doubt the 'egalitarian' nature of the Doors' vision. Did they intend it for everyone? Did they expect to be able to influence a new social order? If the rest of the band ever saw themselves as radicals in this sense, then, in retrospect, Morrison seems to have forgotten to buy in or, at least, to have cancelled his subscription at some point. In an era of 'flower power' and 'free love', the Doors came to represent something darker in the culture. Unwittingly perhaps, they developed a form of individual pessimism that owed as much to Morrison's reading of Nietzsche, and, through Nietzsche, of Ancient Greek philosophy and mythology, as it did to the Vietnam War, the Cold War, political corruption, and the emerging power of corporate America. Morrison's sensual but bleak erudition was, without doubt, a powerful influence on the way the Doors' increasingly fragmented 'artistic vision' was expressed. Indeed, some might argue that with his own death Morrison simply took his growing disillusionment to its logical conclusion. The Doors could start mini-revolutions at gigs and in teenagers' bedrooms, but, with Morrison at the helm like a drunken sea-captain, what could they really offer beyond the chaos of their incendiary studio and stage performances? Ultimately, despite his sensual prowess and his intellectual and artistic finery, Morrison went the same way as other high-profile and notable contemporaries – Brian Jones, Janis Joplin, Jimi Hendrix. The stark frustration of his personal pessimism is apparent at the start of the live version of 'Roadhouse Blues' that is included on the posthumous poetry album *An American Prayer*. Having raised with his audience the subject of star signs and astrology, and exposed the sycophantic nature of a yearning female fan in the process, Morrison makes it clear that he doesn't believe in astrology and, indeed, has little faith in the future. Whatever happens, he tells the crowd, he's going to make sure he gets his kicks before the whole world (his and ours) comes to an explosive end.

☉ Stairway to heaven? ☉

If Scott Rowley is right that "the age-old combo of sex and drugs and rock 'n' roll usually leads to disaster", then he is also right in implying that it is easy to overstate the role that drugs play in artistic creativity. Whichever way you look at it, drugs (which is to say, particular musicians' drugs of choice) are, *at best*, only one part of a whole that, in the case of the great rock bands, is invariably greater than the sum of its parts. I think the point can be well illustrated by a cursory look at any selection of great rock bands. So I'd like to have a look at a few more, starting with the band who are often credited with having written the rule book on rock excess and bad behaviour – Led Zeppelin.

The documented history of Led Zeppelin is littered with stories of drug abuse, drunkenness, hotel-trashing antics, general mayhem and exploits with groupies. In his book *When the Levee Breaks: The Making of Led Zeppelin IV*, Andy Fyfe notes that: "Before the massive success of the fourth album, Led Zeppelin's frolics had been fuelled by youthful exuberance – they were kids from a relatively socially-repressed country being let loose in the candy store of America."[5] It was only after the massive sales of *Led Zeppelin IV*, says Fyfe, that "the mayhem within the Led Zeppelin camp . . . increased exponentially . . . and gradually . . . took on a darker, more violent aspect."[6] Stories were to emerge, for example, of an alleged drink-fuelled attempted rape of an air stewardess, of alleged threats of violence towards journalists who witnessed 'reportable' antics, and of manager Peter Grant and tour manager Richard Cole's conviction for assaulting an over-zealous security guard.

The Zeppelin juggernaut appeared to generate a momentum of its own, and it rolled on relentlessly through personal tragedy for Robert Plant and through Jimmy Page's developing drug addiction. It was finally brought to an abrupt halt by the tragic drink-related death of drummer John Bonham.

The Led Zeppelin story is undeniably a story of rock 'n' roll excess which few bands can rival, and Jimmy Page has since said explicitly that for him "drugs were an integral part of the whole thing, right from the beginning, right to the end."[7] But even with Zeppelin, one should be wary of assuming too much about the nature and extent of the reported debauchery, including any alleged drug taking, and its influence on the music. It's worth noting, for example, that in many cases the reported bad behaviour is attributable to the crew and other members of the entourage rather than to the band themselves. Robert Plant has noted that the Led Zeppelin myth was often propagated by others, and not the musicians. As he told one interviewer: "We had a lot of mercenaries around us, bathing in reflected glory . . . We tried to fire them as often as we could." [8] It's also worth noting that the general decadence around the band was tempered by what Andy Fyfe calls "Plant's down to earth hippie ideals"[9] and by what John Paul Jones refers to as the "funster" side of their characters.[10] Plant, again, has noted that where there was "tomfoolery, occasionally, it was almost always indulged with an air of mischief and bonhomie".[11] The decadence was also tempered by the more family-orientated off-the-road home lives of three of the band, and by the relative quietness and level-headedness of Jones for whom, according to Fyfe, success "meant a life of peace and security for his family."[12]

What then of the relationship between drug use and the making and content of *Led Zeppelin IV*, the album regarded by Fyfe as something of a turning point and by many others as the band's greatest achievement? To what extent can that album be explained by, or reduced to, the band's use of drugs? According to long-time tour manager Richard Cole there were no "serious drugs" around the band during their time at Headley Grange recording *Led Zeppelin IV*, "just dope and a bit of coke". "Mostly," says Cole, "we had an account at a shop in the village and we'd go down there regularly and collect huge quantities of cider."[13] Given Cole's tendency to exaggerate the tales of decadence that could be attributed to the band, a tendency exposed by both Robert Plant and John Paul Jones in recent times, there seems no reason to doubt this particular claim.

Of course, some people would regard "dope and a bit of coke" as "serious drugs", and it would be hard to argue that there is no drugs influence on *Led Zeppelin IV* at all. For example, Fyfe notes an account Plant gave of the writing session for 'Black Dog', a track brought to the sessions by John Paul Jones, and concludes that "it's probably fair to say that large quantities of hash were . . . playing a role in the writing process."[14] Fyfe also points out that 'Misty Mountain Hop' "features Plant's only lyrics to deal specifically with drugs", as the singer recounts an experience in which he engages with a group of hippies in a park and yearns for a place people are able to free their spirits.[15] Fyfe further notes the psychedelic influences evident on both 'Four Sticks' and 'When the Levee Breaks', claiming of the latter that "its phased guitars and backward loops and echo on the harmonica [replicate] the phased vision usually experienced during acid trips."[16] I have no idea whether Fyfe could substantiate the latter claim, but I don't think it affects the point that in so far as drugs were part of the heady brew that is *Led Zeppelin IV*, they were just one ingredient among others. For example, as Fyfe demonstrates well elsewhere in his book, opener 'Black Dog' is a deceptively complex track. Any song which reportedly contains 98 time-signature changes clearly requires considerable musical understanding and dexterity in both its writing and performance, as well as cool and clear heads at the arrangement and production stages. *Led Zeppelin IV* is a monumental album, and there is far more going on across every one of its eight tracks than a simplistic 'drugs hypothesis' might lead one to believe. If you really want to understand *Led Zeppelin IV*, you have to acknowledge the breadth of musical influences on the band, their sheer love of music, and even non-musical (and non-drug) influences such as singer Plant's reading of Tolkien and Celtic history. *Led Zeppelin IV* is one of the biggest selling and most influential albums of all time. The sales alone, estimated by Fyfe, conservatively perhaps, to be somewhere in the region of 40 million worldwide,[17] suggest that from the listener's perspective you don't need to take drugs to appreciate either the magic or the power of this great album and this great band. Although drug use and drug experiences may have contributed to the form and content of parts of the album in some way, ultimately, to echo Scott Rowley's words, it was the talent and unique combination of four exceptional musicians – not drugs – that produced *Led Zeppelin IV* and, indeed, the rest of the immense Led Zeppelin canon.

◑ *Masters of reality?* ◑

To some extent the same holds true of the original Black Sabbath. Over time Sabbath became well known for their 'interest' in illicit substances, an interest that, at times, they seemed only too happy to publicise. 'Sweet Leaf', for example, from the *Master of Reality* album (1971), is the band's paean to marijuana, while 'Snowblind', from *Volume 4* (1972), explored the world of cocaine use. And Sabbath were clearly in no mood to be coy when they famously, and without subtlety, gave thanks to "the great COKE-Cola Company of Los Angeles" in the *Volume 4* album credits. However, while drugs clearly had some kind of influence on Sabbath's music, just as clearly drugs, again, were only one influence among others. Sabbath's unique contribution to rock music was to fuse industrial working-class anger and blues rock influences with darker musical themes designed to unsettle and disturb. The results went far beyond anything that drugs *alone* could have inspired. In *Black Sabbath* (February 1970) and *Paranoid* (September 1970), they had two classic albums under their belts *before* they were reportedly introduced to cocaine on their first tour of the United States. It could be argued with some plausibility that the blueprint for their success, and their distinctive contribution to rock music, was laid down well before they discovered hard drugs, and that artistically the form, style and content of those early albums had little to do with the influence of illegal substances. Indeed, 'Hand of Doom' from the *Paranoid* album appears to be a chilling warning of the dangers of a certain kind of drug use, with later lyrical allusions to the 'hand of doom' image – in 'Sabbath Bloody Sabbath' (1973) and 'Back Street Kids' (1976) – offering a sobering reminder of the grim picture of addiction painted by that early track.

The development and refinement of Sabbath's sound beyond the first two albums produced some great music, reaching, for me, a creative high point with *Sabbath Bloody Sabbath* (1973) and *Sabotage* (1975). The more experimental and sophisticated direction gradually taken by the band is often attributed to guitarist Tony Iommi's growing musical ambition, though while Iommi's songwriting showcased the bands talents to stunning effect on the aforementioned albums, the last two studio albums with original singer Ozzy Osbourne – *Technical Ecstasy* (1976) and *Never Say Die* (1978) – divided critical opinion and led to division within the band. Personally I am a fan of both albums, though it is clear from Sabbath biographies that drug and alcohol abuse was starting to take its toll on the mental and physical health of various band members. As the 1970s wore on, drugs became a problem for the band rather than an inspiration. Far from helping them produce great records, drug abuse conspired with 'musical differences' to bring the original, creative force that was Black Sabbath to an end.

◑ Get your wings ◑

American giants Aerosmith are an interesting case. The band achieved notable success in the 1970s, particularly in their home country, releasing a string of classic albums, including the impressive *Toys in the Attic* (1975) and *Rocks* (1976), and counting Jon Bon Jovi and Guns N' Roses among the ranks of those who claim to have been influenced by them.

Singer Steven Tyler and guitarist Joe Perry have both said that during this time they took drugs, at least initially, to enhance their creativity, with Perry commenting that for a long time he didn't think he was capable of producing anything of note without them. Listening to those albums now, it's very hard to spot a drugs influence as such on the music. It's not like listening to an obviously drug-inspired band like Gong, and nor is it music of startling and unexpected originality. This is straightforward rock. It's cool and sassy and delivered with a swagger, sure, but it doesn't really push any boundaries, musically or lyrically. Listening to Aerosmith's 1970s output in this context, one can't help but think that most rock musicians are not, after all, tortured artistic geniuses grappling with astonishing musical innovation that cannot quite be delivered unless or until they have dropped another tab, had another snort or smoked another joint. Neither are they typically brave and fearless thinkers sacrificing personal health and sanity for some form of 'altered state' wisdom that will benefit mankind. While there may be artists, musicians, poets and painters like this, most rock musicians are on a quite different trip. Indeed, the simplicity of rock music is often its strength. You shouldn't *need* drugs to play or appreciate blues scales or basic rock songs. Or at least, if you do, you've got real problems.

And Aerosmith certainly did develop problems. Whatever the motivation behind their initial drug taking, it soon became a habit, a trapping of success made possible by the income their music sales generated. 'Trapping' is indeed the right word. Tyler and Perry, the so-called "toxic twins", lived on the edge for some time, as drugs sent them spiralling down, got in the way of the music and threatened to destroy the band. At one point Perry even quit.

Somehow Aerosmith survived – as both a creative and a commercial entity – but they had to give up the drugs to do it. In fact, having given up drugs they emerged as a tighter and *more* creative unit. For me, the run of albums from *Permanent Vacation* (1987) through *Pump* (1989) and *Get a Grip* (1993) to *Nine Lives* (1997) represents Aerosmith at the absolute top of their game. It's a personal view I know, but for me each of these albums is immeasurably superior to almost anything the band put out in the 1970s. Each one of these albums was recorded *after* they had cleaned up their collective act. No drugs required.

◑ *Masters of puppets?* ◐

Far from using drugs to discover themselves or get their creative juices flowing, the challenge facing many musicians who choose to use drugs is, in modern parlance, to achieve a 'work–life balance' that prevents their recreational drug use from getting in the way of their ability to write, play and perform. Of course, when one is dealing with addictive and illegal substances of questionable purity, safety and origin, achieving such a 'balance' is no easy matter – and rock history is littered with tragic examples of those who have tried and failed. Not that the tragedies stop others from trying. The point about recreational drug use is that often no claims are made for its impact on musical creativity– it is simply an accompanying and (until addiction hits) optional lifestyle trait. The point is perhaps well illustrated with reference to a band not often associated with drugs – Metallica.

In his book *Justice For All: The Truth About Metallica*, Joel McIver quotes drummer Lars Ulrich on the subject. Speaking in 1997, Lars said:

> Everybody apart from James [Hetfield] dabbles a little bit on a recreational level . . . It's possible to dabble in something without it having become something that takes over your life, whatever it is – alcohol, drugs, any-thing. It doesn't have relevance in our daily lives and isn't anything to worry about, because if there's anyone who's at the top of the game in terms of doing what we're doing and being professional about it, it's us.[18]

In an interview that ran in *Playboy* magazine in March 2001, both Lars and guitarist Kirk Hammett elaborated further. Kirk confessed to having developed a "bad coke problem" on the . . . *And Justice For All* tour but added that he had managed to overcome the problem after realising that his drug use was just depressing him. He also admitted: "I tried smack once. I was so thankful that I hated it." In a similarly candid manner, Lars told the interviewer: "I tried acid once; I was shit-fucking scared. The only drug I've ever really engaged in is cocaine. It gave me another couple of hours drinking. A lot of people use it as a way to get closer to you, and you fall for that. I go through cycles where I say, OK, I'm going to pull away for a while. And then I take six months away."[19]

For those of us who followed the band's early career through their vinyl releases and the UK music press, these admissions are perhaps surprising. While Metallica's rise to international stardom was fuelled by sufficient quantities of alcohol to earn them the nickname 'Alcoholica', their attitude to harder drugs appeared to be as uncompromising as their music, and this attitude seemed to stretch beyond the music to the themes of their lyrics. On *Master of Puppets*, for example, Metallica literally raged against anything that seemed to them to remove personal choice and control or suppress the individual. This included drugs, state-ordered war, institutionalisation, and organised religion. *Master of Puppets* is both an angry and a liberating album, and although its concern with individual freedoms is very American in tone, there is much in the lyrical content to which teenagers in 1980s Britain could relate. The title track itself has a strong anti-drugs message and, perhaps embarrassingly for Lars and Kirk, explicit references to drug habits that implicate cocaine users in particular. As vocalist and rhythm guitarist James Hetfield explained to *Thrasher* magazine: "'Master of Puppets' deals pretty much with drugs. How things get switched around: instead of you controlling what you're taking and doing, it's drugs controlling you."[20]

It is not clear if the experiences described by Lars and Kirk relate to the *Master of Puppets* period at all (*Master of Puppets* is the album before . . . *And Justice For All*), but then, perhaps occasional, sporadic, recreational drug use is perfectly consistent with the theme of 'Master of Puppets'. The underlying message is that as an individual you should avoid situations where your free will and personal choice are compromised. You must stay in control, and do your utmost to prevent anyone, or anything, from taking over your life and becoming your master. The album sleeve itself presents a powerful reminder of where you're likely to end up if you do allow others to pull your strings, with a giant pair of puppeteer's hands presiding over an 'unknown soldier' type graveyard. An army helmet and dog-tag hanging off one of the tombstones clearly broaden the message beyond the drug slavery of the mighty title track. The geometry of the crosses seems to suggest that even in death, these unfortunate souls fall into neat rows, conforming to a pre-determined pattern that is mapped out for them.

Despite the recreational confessions of Lars and Kirk, it seems extremely unlikely, given the strong message of 'Master of Puppets' and Ulrich's comments about the band's professionalism, that the band were (in Bill Hick's words) "*real* high" when they wrote, conceived and recorded either *Master of Puppets* or any of their other immensely powerful and influential albums. Similarly, while their excessive recreational alcohol use eventually took its toll on singer and rhythm guitarist James Hetfield, it seems highly unlikely that his admission to a rehabilitation facility in July 2001 had anything to do with any other kind of substance abuse.* Thankfully Hetfield was soon to re-emerge and the band set about unravelling years of inner tension and recording a new album. The trials and tribulations of the period are captured in Berlinger and Sinofsky's fascinating and revealing documentary *Some Kind of Monster*.

◑ *No Class* ◔

One problem with discussing the impact of drug use on both lifestyle and musical creativity is that 'drugs', as noted earlier, are not one thing. The term 'drugs' covers a range of 'controlled substances' which can vary greatly in their costs, risks and effects. Indeed, the very existence of drug classification systems suggests that both the State and the Courts recognise that in *general* terms some illegal substances are comparatively less harmful than others. In the UK, the Home Office website carries information on the division of illegal drugs into Classes A, B and C. At the time of writing it stated:

---

* As noted by McIver, (Ibid., pp.309–10) who cites former bass player Jason Newsted in support of this view. Newsted speculated that Hetfield might be "drunk . . . with sadness, tense things or stress", and that a number of personal issues might have caught up with him all at once.

Class A drugs are the most dangerous, and the legal penalties related to them are the most serious. Class B drugs are considered less dangerous, and the legal penalties are lower. Class C drugs are considered the least dangerous illegal drugs.[21]

Heroin, cocaine, LSD and ecstasy all fall into the Class A group, as do crack, magic mushrooms and amphetamines in cases when they are prepared for injection. Other forms of amphetamines sit in the Class B category, as does cannabis, which was reclassified from Class C to Class B in January 2009 to reflect the fact that "skunk, a much stronger version of the drug now dominates in the UK." Class C drugs include tranquilisers, some painkillers, GHB (the so-called 'date-rape' drug) and ketamine. While 'slippery slope' arguments prevail among those who would take a tough line on the use of all illegal substances, in the minds of many, the moderate recreational use of cannabis has been, and probably remains, a world away from physical and psychological addiction to more obviously damaging 'harder' Class A substances.

Perceived differences between drugs often show themselves in the attitudes of rock musicians too, and, as the Dylan comments I quoted earlier demonstrate, one finds opposition to the use of certain drugs in the most unlikely of places. In a 1986 interview for *Creem*, Ozzy Osbourne told Sylvie Simmons:

> I know a lot of people who've taken cocaine, including myself, a lot of people who've smoked dope, including myself, a lot of people who've taken a lot of things – but I've never really taken heroin . . . Everybody I know that's taken heroin is either a mental case or dead. Or they end up zombies. Even if you stop taking it, you never return to the person you were before; you end up screwed up for the rest of your life . . . Heroin *is* awful. Look what happened to poor old Phil Lynott.[22]

Lemmy of Motörhead is another man renowned for his drug and alcohol consumption, and, in his autobiography *White Line Fever*, he is remarkably frank about his appetites and lifestyle. Lemmy, it should be remembered, is the man who claims he was sacked by Hawkwind because he was "doing the wrong drugs" (speed not acid);[23] and even the name of his own band, Motörhead, is, apparently, "the American slang for speedfreak".[24] "I don't especially recommend my lifestyle," says Lemmy, "it would slaughter the average person."[25] He recounts the story of the time he visited a doctor with the intention of having his blood changed, a process Keith Richards is said to have gone through. After carrying out tests, the doctor informed him that not only would 'pure' blood kill him, but that his own blood was now so toxic that it would be deadly to the average human being.[26] Elsewhere, in his book, however, Lemmy provides a powerful account of the time in the late sixties when he "learned to hate heroin". He writes:

> I knew this guy, Preston Dave – he wasn't even a junkie. He was get-ting there, but not quite. And a bunch of us were sitting with him at a Wimpy Bar, the early English attempt at, say, Burger King. It was in Earls Court Road and was open all night. Preston was shaking and shit, and so he went off to Piccadilly – where you went to score heroin. So he came back and went to the toilet. A few minutes later, he came lurch-ing out backwards. His face was black and his tongue was sticking out. Somebody had sold him rat poison – took his money, smiled at him and sold him certain death. I thought, "Hell, if that's the kind of people who are hanging around with heroin, you can fucking have it." And I also saw people doing horrible fixes with old, blunt needles that would really fucking mess their arms up. You'd see people with embolisms in their arms the size of a cricket ball. And they'd be selling their asses for a fucking shot. It always looked like misery to me. No fun at all.[27]

Lemmy's book contains other sad stories of heroin tragedies, and his views on the matter have not changed over the years. He has felt it appropriate to deal with the issue in songs such as 'Dead Men Tell No Tales' from Motörhead's *Bomber* album, and he has also, despite reservations about their value and effectiveness, played at anti-heroin concerts.

When men with the track records and experience of Lemmy and Ozzy Osbourne tell you that heroin is bad shit, you sure as hell know you should listen. This thought, or one very much like it, is no doubt what motivated the rather aristocratic Conservative politician William Graham to invite Lemmy to the National Assembly for Wales building in Cardiff to speak to Welsh politicians and the Welsh media on the matter. BBC Wales journalist Adrian Masters reported that Lemmy was so keen to have his say that he even booked and paid for his own taxi. However, as they faced the cameras together, Mr. Graham looked surprised and a little uncomfortable when Lemmy suggested that one possible solution to the problem of heroin would be to legalise it so that addicts could receive proper treatment and have their drug use properly regulated. Nothing else seems to have worked, said Lemmy, so why not give it a try? An embarrassed Mr. Graham was quick to point out that this was not Welsh Conservative Party policy. Nevertheless, the National Assembly for Wales' official Record of Proceedings shows that on 23 November 2005, several days after Lemmy's visit, the Welsh politicians formally discussed the matter further, with William Graham himself leading a short plenary debate entitled: 'Heroin – Is Lemmy Right?'

For those who like to look at an issue from all sides, '*The Singer from Deep Purple*', Ian Gillan, presents a typically idiosyncratic view in his report of an encounter with a Russian who tried in vain to persuade him to sign a 'Rock Against Drugs' petition. Gillan refused – not, he says, because he's in favour of drugs, but because he didn't think that a petition was the best way to deal with the matter. He writes:

> I tried to tell him that the day you ask a Scotsman not to have another whiskey; the day you ask a German not to drink another beer – or a Frenchman not to have another glass of wine; the day you ask a Russian not to have Vodka; that's the day I'll ask a Jamaican not to smoke his ganja; a North American not to touch hashish; the Bolivian not to chew his coca leaves. The arrogance of one society to judge the customs of another society as uncool just astounds me. But having said that, I have seen close friends come to grief because of drug abuse.
>
> I do not condone the use of opiates, heroin, coke and all that shit that gangsters are trying to get people into. Also, I have no intention of sticking a needle in myself and hate to hear of situations where food, drink or cigarettes have been interfered with. It's a subject I can deal with best in my music, and 'No Easy Way'* is an example. It looks at the tragic end of two friends of mine – one a hooker, the other a junkie.[28]

As for "poor old Phil Lynott" (to return to Ozzy's example of where heroin might get you), the effects of his death (in January 1986) still clearly ripple on. In November 2007 I managed to catch both Motörhead and Thin Lizzy live. Motörhead were playing on the same bill as fellow rock stalwarts Joan Jett and Alice Cooper, and, during an excellent set, dedicated a cover of 'Rosalie' to the former Lizzy frontman. "We'd like to dedicate this to Phil Lynott," Lemmy told the crowd, "he was our friend." Similarly, the John Sykes/Scott Gorham version of Lizzy that toured in 2007 were (as always) highly respectful of their former main man, and were clearly proud to be up there on stage propagating his musical legacy. In the period immediately

---

* A track from the Gillan album *Glory Road*

following Lynott's death, however, not everyone responded in quite the same way. Outspoken American loudmouth Ted Nugent rather belatedly chastised Lynott for ruining his life with drugs and squandering his talent. Nugent further accused Lynott of extreme selfishness and an appalling lack of regard for the feelings of those who cared about him. Most famously, he claimed he'd like to "piss on his grave". Nugent is, of course, better known for his verbal shock tactics and his right wing political tendencies than his tact and sensitivity, but he has since explained his comments in a manner that suggests that his chosen words were, at least, well intentioned. Reflecting on his original *Kerrang!* outburst in the October 2007 edition (issue 111) of *Classic Rock* magazine, he said:

> Oh, I remember my disparaging words about Phil after he died. Well, later on I met his mother, Philomena, we hugged and she thanked me for those words, believe it or not. Because if you don't condemn the abject mistakes of an individual then those who purport to be influenced by said individual may end up dead too.
>
> Phil was a gifted genius of a musician. When he died he joined a long line of people who suffered similar fates. People like Keith Moon, John Belushi, Jimi Hendrix and Janis Joplin. Having all those corpses in front of you is inexcusable. It's absolutely condemnable. I stand by the statement I made.

Poignantly, Philomena Lynott reports that her son may well have recognised and regretted his folly. "Merciful Jesus, what have I done to you, Ma?" he is reported as saying from his hospital bed.[29] It was the last time he spoke to her.

O▸ Smoke without fire ▸O

In the light of the Ian Gillan comments I quoted above, one might wonder what can be said in this context about the connection between drugs and creativity in the work of Deep Purple? Well, despite the extra-curricular activities of Glenn Hughes and Tommy Bolin as the Mark IV line-up hurtled towards dissolution in the mid-1970s, it is clear that through the efforts of the hardworking Mark II line-up of Ritchie Blackmore, Ian Gillan, Roger Glover, Jon Lord and Ian Paice that toured and recorded between 1969 and 1973, Purple built their reputation not on substance abuse and rock 'n' roll excess but on exciting music. Above all, it should be recognised that

Lord and Blackmore in particular were, first and foremost, consummate and dedicated musicians. While Lord admits to having had "a little flirt" with cocaine at some point in the mid-1970s, he also told *Classic Rock* magazine that even at a time when "the whole world and his mother was doing Charlie" Blackmore and Paice were never interested.[30]

According to unofficial Blackmore biographer Jerry Bloom, Ritchie once told an interviewer:

> It's funny when you're talking about the so-called drugs period, everyone says, "Oh the Sixties". I still don't recall the Sixties as being any different to any other time. The drugs I never took. Until this day I've never taken cocaine. I want to be the only musician in the world who has not taken cocaine. That's my ambition. Okay, I drink. But LSD, cocaine, all that nonsense, I don't take, and I've never touched it – I was too nervous. I never needed LSD; it's not needed in the way that I think. I would have gone mad. I was lucky for that. I think I have had very stable parents. They did not even drink, and mainly my thoughts against drugs came from my parents.[31]

It's also clear from Ian Gillan's autobiography that illegal substances played no part whatsoever in his own life during (and before) the Mark II line-up's most creative period. Speaking of some of the songs on *In Rock* (1970), Gillan writes:

> 'Flight of the Rat' . . . began as a joke when 'Flight of the Bumble Bee' was mentioned, and Jon started doing variations around it. In fact 'the rat' was a drug habit – we'd often play with words that way. 'Into the Fire' was also a drug-associated song, so with a collection of songs of this kind, including 'Blood Sucker', everybody presumed we did drugs. Whenever we protested not, the stock reply was, "Well, you would say that, wouldn't you?" and so we gave up arguing about it. I admit to dabbling with drugs, but that was later and will be dealt with then.[32]

As promised, later in his book Gillan describes in humorous fashion his first, almost inadvertent experience with an illegal substance – which turned out to be a marijuana and opium joint given to him by fellow travelling musician Buddy Miles to help him sleep. Help him sleep it did, giving him "this incredible . . . recurring dream of immense sexuality and dignity" involving an exotic sounding "Amazonian-looking woman." "When conscious", writes Gillan, "my condition was extremely painful, and I had to play four shows with a hard-on." It's not clear from his account whether this last part actually happened or whether it was itself part of the dream,* but whatever the status of Gillan's erection, this is the only experience of the kind he reports in his book. Most notably, it happened *after* the recording of the seminal albums *In Rock* (1970), *Fireball* (1971) and *Machine Head* (1972). Wherever Mark II Purple's inspiration and creativity came from, it seems it wasn't 'drug enlightenment'.

◑ *The Number of the Beast* ◑

For as long as I've been interested in rock music, Iron Maiden have had an excellent reputation among rock fans. In the early days they were generally known as a group of good-hearted East End boys who loved their music, loved their football ('Up the 'Ammers!') and liked a pint or two in the Ruskin Arms or one of their other East End haunts. As they began to establish themselves as a Championship rock outfit, they were, of course, exposed to the same temptations as any other group of young men at large in the early 1980s, but by the time they had achieved the stable line-up that delivered promotion to the Premier League – namely Harris, Murray, Smith, Dickinson and McBrain – they were a highly professional and disciplined outfit. How else could they have sustained the phenomenal effort that, on the World Slavery Tour, for example, saw them play 300 gigs in 28 countries over a gruelling 13 month period? Anyone who has ever seen Iron Maiden live is aware of the commitment and dedication that goes into every single gig. Maiden's work ethic and determination to deliver for the fans is legendary and second to none. "As for the sex and drugs," says biographer Mick Wall, they didn't really fit with the work ethic and in Maiden's early years "they cost at least two members of the band their jobs".[33]

One of those members was original vocalist Paul Di'Anno. As Maiden main man and bassist Steve Harris explains:

> Someone who's singing has got to look after their voice, and you can't be staying up all night smoking yourself stupid and taking speed and what have you. You've got to look after yourself, and Paul wasn't, and so, at the end of the day, we ended up cancelling gigs because of his

---

* See pp.101–2 and try to figure it out for yourself!

problems, and that's one thing, if you know me, I just can't tolerate. I'm not into drugs myself, never have been, but I'm not against other people doing what they like, as long as it doesn't fuck up their gig. Well, Paul was letting it fuck up his gig.[34]

Di'Anno's autobiography, *The Beast*, presents a catalogue of explicit and sordid antics which show the full extent to which, even after leaving Maiden, Di'Anno continued to allow his "excessive rock 'n' roll lifestyle" to "fuck up his gig". In fairness to Di'Anno he's very upfront as a writer and he sets out his stall early. In his Foreword he says:

> If you're one of those Bible-bashing herberts who think rock musicians are the sperm of the devil, sent to this world to pollute the minds of impressionable teenagers, this book will probably provide the proof you've been looking for. If the thought of impressionable young girls getting it doggy-style from drug-addled rock stars offends you, well, you'd better put this book down now, love . . . On the other hand, if you're one of those sickos who's just reading this because you want to hear disgusting, depraved tales of booze, drugs and sex, well you'd better pull up a chair old son, 'cos you're definitely in the right place.[35]

Di'Anno is, we are told, "the man who makes Led Zeppelin look like a bunch of convent girls". I'll spare you the details – but you can seek them out yourself, if you are so inclined, because Di'Anno is as honest as the day is long and certainly doesn't try to hide any of them from us. Bizarrely, he still appears to be unfeasibly proud of *most* of his antics, which were performed, we are told, "under the influence of enough Jack Daniels to float a small yacht, and enough cocaine to finish off an entire country".[36] And lest you think ill of Mr. Di'Anno from the way I have presented him here – oh, the responsibility of the writer – let me reassure you that however dangerous, decadent and damaging his antics became, they were always performed with the good cheer and aplomb of a man who remained "full of cockney charm". The cheeky chappy!

As noted above, Di'Anno is *very* clear about the nature and content of his book. So clear, in fact, that even the front cover has the following "WARNING" stamped across it:

> This book is thoroughly obscene. If you are elderly, of a nervous disposition, or just plain boring, do yourself a favour and buy a nice Nick Hornby book.

Well, as you may recall from my introduction, I have read some Nick Hornby myself, and have thoroughly enjoyed the experience. Arguably all of Nick Hornby's books have greater literary merit than Paul Di'Anno's autobiography, but none illustrate the point I am trying to make quite as well: namely that Di'Anno's particular form of rock and roll excess became incompatible with his role as the singer and front-man of a hard-working heavy rock group destined for the very top.

If I may go back to Mick Wall's biography briefly, comments made by Maiden manager Rod Smallwood make a useful contribution to our discussion by casting further light on the mind and attitude of Steve Harris. Smallwood says:

> Steve won't touch drugs. He never has, and the reason is that he's scared what they'll do in his mind. He's already got a very creative and open mind. He doesn't need any other stimulation in that department. Some of his songs, like 'Twilight Zone', are based on out-of-body experiences. 'Number of the Beast' was a dream. If your head does this anyway, you don't need drugs. If anything, he likes something to cool him down, and a few beers will do that for him.[37]

Tea drinkers from Barnsley

Saxon, who were contemporaries of Iron Maiden, are another band who, seemingly, had little interest in drugs. Despite being one of the driving forces of the harder, more aggressive music that characterised the New Wave of British Heavy Metal (NWOBHM) in the early 1980s, and despite writing songs about motorbikes and other fast vehicles, Saxon were famously uninterested in the alternative kind of 'speed'. The title track of their third album *Strong Arm of the Law* tells the tale of the police pursuing them after a gig, pulling them over and stripping down their vehicle, convinced that because they were a loud rock band they *must* be carrying drugs. "Where is the gear that we know that you use?" asks a disgruntled policeman. "The only speed we use is our car," quips singer Biff.

In *White Line Fever*, Lemmy recalls an early Motörhead tour for which Saxon provided support: "We did something like fifty-three gigs with two days off before having a break. On our dates through England we had

Saxon supporting us. They were nice guys, but kind of weird because they didn't drink or smoke. They had a tea urn in their room. We found that odd."[38] Odd or not, Saxon became very well known for the huge quantities of tea bags they used to take on tour with them, even bragging about it in the 'tour data' section on the sleeve of their live album *The Eagle Has Landed*. Indeed, 'Tea-drinkers from Barnsley' was a memorable clue in an early *Kerrang!* magazine crossword puzzle.

I also remember an exchange in the pages of the now defunct British music weekly *Sounds*. It was *Sounds* journalists in fact – editor Alan Lewis and scribe Geoff Barton, who first coined and used the term 'New Wave of British Heavy Metal' to characterise the post-punk emergence across the UK of a number of new, raw, more aggressive heavy rock bands. (Clearly there was something in the water.) *Sounds* had supported these bands with features in the paper, and indeed, the self-professed 'Bible of Heavy Metal' itself, *Kerrang!*, started life as a *Sounds* special. Anyway, someone had written into *Sounds* suggesting that despite their leathers and their love of motorbikes, Saxon couldn't really be regarded as a bikers' band because they eschewed drugs. It was left to Moz Morris, then organiser of the Saxon fan club (*The Militia Guard*) to respond by pointing out the foolishness of drug use and reiterating the band's right to choose a more positive and less destructive way of life.

♬ Impeckable ♬

While Welsh rock band Budgie released their first album in 1971 and enjoyed some success with a string of very good albums through the early and mid 1970s, they are perhaps best known to modern rock fans through covers of their songs by others, including Metallica (who recorded heavy versions of both 'Breadfan' and 'Crash Course in Brain Surgery') and Iron Maiden. Yet there is plenty to explore in a back catalogue that is characterised by a cluster of unusual and entertaining song titles such as 'Nude Disintegrating Parachutist Woman', 'Hot as a Docker's Armpit', 'In the Grip of a Tyrefitter's Hand', 'You're the Biggest Thing Since Powdered Milk', the exquisite 'Napoleon Bona Parts One and Two', and the more recent, but no less eccentric 'I'm Compressing the Comb on a Cockerel's Head'. At the start of the 1980s, Budgie enjoyed a kind of second coming when guitarist 'Big' John Thomas joined original bass player and vocalist Burke Shelley and drummer Steve Williams. Riding on the wings of the New Wave of British Heavy Metal, they released an EP, *If Swallowed Do Not Induce Vomiting* (1980) and three solid albums, *Power Supply* (1980), *Nightflight* (1981) and *Deliver Us From Evil* (1982*)*, and even headlined the Friday night of the Reading Rock Festival in 1982. In 2006, with Simon Lees occupying the guitar berth, Budgie capitalised on a series of live and archive releases, and the general resurgence of interest in classic rock music, with the release of a new studio album: *You're All Living in Cuckooland.*

The band's longevity can be at least partly explained by the focus and determination of main man Burke Shelley. In the sleeve notes to the excellent Budgie collection *The Definitive Anthology: An Ecstasy of Fumbling* (1996), Shelley shares with rock journalist Chris Welch his secret for surviving life on the road. He says:

> It never wore me out because I used to go training every day. I wouldn't eat food from three o'clock onwards, so by the time I got on stage I was hollow and it was easy to sing. I'd go jogging and swimming and take breathing exercises, so I was always tip top and I was never much of a drinker. You see rock casualties now, who can barely form their words. Pop and rock music seems to be the road to the Betty Ford Clinic. But it was my kick to see if we could keep up standards. I actually got a thrill out of being on the road. I loved preparing for a gig, the sound check, the tuning up. Everyone else would be in the hotel bar, but I'd stay in the dressing room.[39]

⊙ *Misplaced Childhood* ⊙

And what about Marillion, the band at the heart of my exchange with Evie which triggered this entire discussion? Well, if the sleeve notes to the re-mastered versions of their EMI albums are to be believed, in their early days they were certainly no strangers to intoxicating substances and the occasional walk on the wild side. Certainly this is true of original frontman Fish, a seeker of wisdom and would-be poet in the James Douglas Morrison tradition. In fact, Fish always seemed a bit too eager to drop big hints about his substance abuse – something which, at times, he appeared to romanticise, alongside his legendary alcohol intake, as part of his rock star inheritance. The bedsit squalor and angst of Marillion's excellent debut album *Script for a Jester's Tear* is augmented by the drug song 'He Knows You Know', while the chemically tinged experience of *Fugazi*'s 'She Chameleon' will have you either wishing you had been there or feeling relieved that you weren't, depending on your inclinations. According to Fish, the concept for the band's biggest selling album, *Misplaced Childhood*, came to him during a particularly harrowing trip following his ingestion of "a tab of very strong acid" sent to him through the post by a former girlfriend (*not* 'Kayleigh', in case you're wondering). During the experience he was "visited" by the presence of a child, and inspired to produce "a large scrawl of prose", within which "were the diamonds and structure on which would hang the entire [*Misplaced Childhood*] concept."[40] *Misplaced Childhood* itself was recorded in Berlin at a time when the Berlin Wall still stood. The band's sleeve notes on the EMI two-disc remaster provide a fascinating insight into the intensity and uniqueness of their Berlin experience. While careful to protect almost everyone's identity but his own, Fish offers what he calls "a tantalising taste of the debauchery" of the time, promising a true exposé in a later autobiography – a book for which, as far as I'm aware, the world is still waiting.

After *Misplaced Childhood*, there was to be only one more studio album with Fish. He formally resigned from the band in September 1988, to be replaced in the early part of the 1989 by Steve 'h' Hogarth. Despite the success of their first album with Hogarth, *Season's End*, and a run of minor chart hits drawn from this and the lighter, more commercial *Holidays in Eden*, Marillion album sales started to show a decline. If anything, the decline was hastened by 1994's dark, bold and utterly compelling *Brave*, and 1995's *Afraid of Sunlight*. Since then Marillion have taken the 'indie' route, first signing to Castle Records for a run of albums that encompassed *This Strange Engine* (1997), *Radiation* (1998) and *marillion.com* (1999), and, thereafter, taking complete control of their music and their finances via the development of an internet fan base and a model of working which relies heavily on those fans. Coinciding with the introduction of this new 'business model', the band has hit a creative purple patch in recent years, with the stunningly different *Anoraknophobia* (2001) and the masterful *Marbles* (2004) in particular showcasing some of their strongest material ever. Clearly comfortable with the creative side of their lives, the band have continued to nurture the 'special relationship' they enjoy with their fans, all of which contributes to the wonder of the multi-national event that is a Marillion Weekend.

It is something of a standing joke between band and fans that all Marillion's songs are about 'death' and 'water'. In reality, the band's songs cover a much broader range of human interest and relationship-based topics. Even with Hogarth in the band, there are occasional drug references (see, for example, the lyrics to 'The Party' or the drug sequence and vision of desperate squalor that is part of the story told by the both the musical and film versions of *Brave*), but there is not much evidence of any kind of 'drug influence' on their output these days.

☉ *Rebel with a cause* ☉

In arguing above that once created, music can take on a life and meaning of its own regardless of the lifestyles, peccadilloes and weaknesses of those who create it, I'm not trying to 'sanitise' rock music. Many rock stars are more than happy to be associated with rock 'n' roll excess, and there can be no doubt that some of rock's most influential icons have chosen a path of decadence and self-destruction. It's not surprising therefore that well-meaning parents often worry about what their children are getting into, when all they know of rock music are media portrayals of rock's saddest, most foolish and most senseless tragedies.

The point extends to sexual activity and promiscuity too. Writing of his experiences soon after joining Deep Purple, Ian Gillan says:

> Groupies featured highly in the culture of rock 'n' roll, and they willingly helped to create the basis for a lifestyle with which no self-respecting parent would wish their daughters to associate. Come to think of it, not many self-respecting parents were that keen on their kids, male or female, becoming musicians either, but over the years there would be many brilliant occasions when the girls would enhance our lives – and that of the roadies and assorted crew.

While adopting a fairly liberal attitude himself ("what's wrong with a bit of sexual enjoyment, fiddling about here and there, or grabbing the occasional tit?"), and feeling aggrieved by the 1960s women's movement ("who chose to represent the whole of their sex on such matters"), Gillan comments: "I know it's wrong to try and justify it all under cover of rock 'n' roll, and I also accept that the whole prospect probably horrifies some people and might even put off some parents letting their kids go to a show". On the other hand, he muses, "it doesn't happen to the entire audience. Well, not every night."[41]

As I noted earlier, rock music is often strongly associated with a certain kind of rebellion – the kind that invariably involves reckless pleasure seeking and a good deal of nose thumbing at authority. Rock music provides plenty of role models for those inclined to go in this direction, and, in this respect, it often appeals to 'hemmed-in teenagers' who are looking to discover themselves by kicking against whatever they perceive to be the world of their parents. One doesn't have to go down this path though. There is more than one way of 'sticking it to the man' (the professed mission of Dewey Finn, the character portrayed by Jack Black in the rather touching film *School of Rock*). As rock music has evolved, each new generation of bands has played louder and faster than its predecessors, or taken some other unexpected turn in attitude or image which has shaken the security of those who are comfortable only with the sounds and images of their own youth. Sometimes, if the intention is to bewilder, irritate or worry one's elders, liking the music is enough!

As for those who do choose the 'sex and outrage' route, it has to be said that some of the fundamental behaviour traits of a lifestyle that once represented such a shocking departure from moral norms and acceptable standards are now so widespread that, if anything, they have become the new orthodoxy. To convince yourself of this, take a look around the clubs or a walk down the high street of any UK city on a Saturday night and look at what is going on around you. Excessive drinking, casual sex, drug use, and wanton destruction and vandalism appear to be fairly common features of many a young person's night out. The behaviour has become predictably conventional, now engaged in by large numbers of young people in a sheep-like and unthinking manner. (It's almost braver and shows more character for young people to rebel against their peers these days, than against their parents.)

This 'insight' isn't new, and shouldn't really come as a surprise to anyone. Herd-like hedonism was a growing part of the image-obsessed nightclub culture that was popular with my own peers in the 1980s, and it was given a new lease of life, and a more mainstream appeal, in the 1990s by the emergence of 'rave' culture and new drugs such as ecstasy. Back in my own youth, the 'rebellion' extended to the so-called 'alternative' music scene, where it was always in danger of taking a

more violent form. I remember, for example, going to see a band called
The Cramps at Cardiff's Top Rank club. At the time The Cramps pulled
an audience which provided a pretty representative cross-section of
Cardiff's 'alternative' music fans. There were 'indie' fans in either
cooler-than-thou or mock-horror apparel, psycho-billies with flat-tops
(a look I quite liked, actually), and anarcho-punks absolutely brimming
with frustration and aggression. In terms of dress code, anything was
acceptable as long as it was some shade of black – the more macabre
and bizarre the outfit the better – though the prevailing darkness was
offset by the peacock-like hair displays of some of those present. As
the evening wore on I saw more and more clearly that the scene didn't
offer much of an 'alternative' at all. People got drunk, fights broke
out, glasses were smashed, and the whole 'rebellious' shebang was
carefully managed and controlled by the respectably dressed security
men who stalked the perimeter of the dance floor and intervened only
when they absolutely had to. This was no revolution! In fact, for me it
was a thoroughly depressing experience, and one that stayed with me. I
remember wandering home ruminating on the 'stage-managed rebellion'
I had observed, grudgingly acknowledging the business acumen of those
who had made a bob or two through venue hire and bar takings. I had
a few friends who were active on the alternative scene at the time, and
the more people I met, and the more parties I went to, the more my
views were reinforced. Karl Marx was wrong. It's not religion that's the
opiate of the masses, it's . . . er . . . opium and cannabis and alcohol and,
indeed, anything else that keeps you in an unthinking and non-critical
daze while others get rich off your habits and apathy. This is the kind
of thing I had in mind earlier when I said that there is a sense in which
drinking yourself into a stupor, snorting coke and trashing your hotel
room is not, in any *meaningful* way, rebellious at all. Not only is the
'rebellious' behaviour generally contained and managed, but in fact it's
all become rather conformist and somewhat *passé*.

In this connection I am very struck by comments that Lemmy makes
towards the end of his autobiography. He writes:

> One thing I am very glad of is that I went through the sixties. People
> who didn't really don't know what they missed. We pushed a certain
> consciousness, a way of life and it was exciting – no AIDS, people
> weren't dying so much from drug abuse and it was truly a time of

freedom and change. The only time I've seen any rebellion was in the
fifties, sixties and early seventies. The rest of it you can keep. The kids
now have attitudes more like the parents we were all trying to fight![42]

It's certainly not difficult to see where Lemmy is coming from. For all
the concern parents may show for their children when they start to dabble
in the mainstream sex, booze and drugs culture, many of them have been
there too. And, since the 1980s at least, the hedonism of youth culture has
not been accompanied by "a certain consciousness", but instead seems to
have been part of the general shift towards a self-seeking individualism
that has characterised the mood of the times. What's more, for all the
disgust, dismay and discomfort this 'rebellious' behaviour might invoke
in older generations, it doesn't actually change anything. It seldom offers
any kind of alternative, and is rarely constructive.

But rock music *can* be constructive. With clear artistic purpose many
rock musicians have expressed themselves in ways which *can* enhance
awareness, encourage change and, on occasions, promote and inspire a
more real and positive kind of rebellion. In what ways then has this been
done?

First, as a medium that can be powerful, moving and exciting, rock
music is well placed to communicate themes and images that are both
stimulating and thought provoking. Interviewed for Penelope Spheeris's
film *The Decline of Western Civilisation Part II: The Metal Years*, shock
rocker Alice Cooper says:

Rock and roll should corrupt kids enough to [make them] think. There's
nothing wrong with thinking.

On the evidence of the film itself, 'thinking' was the exception rather than
the rule on the American 'hair metal' scene that was dominant at the time,
but nevertheless Alice makes a strong point. There is plenty of rock music
that makes you think. Or, at least, there is plenty of rock music that makes
me think – and that's the way it should be.

In many cases, the encouragement to think comes from lyrics that focus
the listener's attention on particular issues or provide a new perspective.
One doesn't need to look too far to find examples of songs that draw
attention to issues of topical significance, or that question some aspect
of conventional or received wisdom. Some bands, like U2, have strong
reputations in this direction, but there are plenty of excellent examples

in the back catalogues of bands already mentioned in this chapter. Black Sabbath's 'War Pigs', Metallica's 'Disposable Heroes' and Saxon's 'Broken Heroes' all offer particular takes on war; Ozzy Osbourne's 'Revelation (Mother Earth)' deals not just with war but with man's ability to destroy the planet, its biblical overtones adding to the drama; Marillion's 'Forgotten Sons' offers reflections on the problems Northern Ireland faced in the early 1980s; more recent Marillion songs like 'Last Century for Man' and 'A Voice from the Past' focus attention on Western excess and Third World poverty; Budgie's *Deliver Us From Evil* album reflects anxieties at a time when Cold War tensions were running high; Gillan's 'Mutually Assured Destruction', a top 40 hit, focuses on the possibility of these tensions leading to nuclear war; Deep Purple's 'No One Came' is a fine study of the often superficial nature of success in the music industry, while a slightly later song, 'Mary Long', offers a humorous take on censorship; Motörhead's rather grim 'Don't Let Daddy Kiss Me' deals with child abuse ("The worst crime in the world"); Alice Cooper's 'Only Women Bleed' deals poignantly with the issue of domestic violence; and even Iron Maiden's 'Run to the Hills' offered a radical take, for its time, on the way the United States has treated Native American Indians. And let's not forget Bob Dylan, who, in his early years, was widely regarded, in the words of Joan Baez, as "a leader of dissent and social change."[43]

I have focused in the preceding paragraph on lyrics, but, of course, music itself has a tremendous power to 'speak' to people. Music shorn of lyrics has its own kind of profundity and can take us places and show us things we'd never dreamed existed. The significance that rock fans attach to the *music* and musicianship (rather than *just* catchy tunes and vocal hooks) is another way in which rock often sets itself apart from mainstream pop. Rock fans like to hear musicians play, and place great stock in the ability of their idols to surprise and delight. So much can depend on the 'riff' to set the tone and drive tracks forward, but much also depends on song structure, solo work and the interplay between musicians. While in pop music everything is built around the looks, moves and voice of the singer/s, in rock music *all* the musicians are respected and revered, with guitarists in particular – like Hendrix, Clapton, Blackmore, Page, Iommi, May and Beck – gaining a prominence that in many cases leads to them becoming household names. It is true, perhaps, that the 'showmanship' in rock sometimes undermines the music's desire to be taken seriously ("It's such a fine line," in the combined words of Spinal Tap's David St

Hubbins and Nigel Tufnell "between stupid and clever"), and it is true too that the anger and aggression at the heavier end of the rock spectrum is not to everyone's taste, but there is no doubt that musical expression is as central to a good deal of rock music as it is to other serious (and often more sophisticated) musical forms.

Given the power of words and music to stir the soul, it almost goes without saying that rock music can be at its most powerful when words and music combine perfectly to either drive home a message or, in less direct fashion, create a mood that provides a glimpse of some aspect of human life or some way of being not previously appreciated. Adopting such a 'total' approach to communicating a mood, an experience or a way of life, can be the one of the most subtle but most enduring ways in which rock music can show us something important and inspire us. Those familiar with *Led Zeppelin III* (1970) will recall the following sleeve note:

> Credit must be given to Bron-y-Aur, a small derelict cottage in South Snowdonia for painting a somewhat forgotten picture of true completeness which acted as an incentive to some of these musical statements.

Clearly the cottage and the hills of Snowdonia had a profound impact on Page and Plant, who repeated the credit on their 1994 album *No Quarter*. Zeppelin fans will further recall the appearance of the Page-penned instrumental 'Bron-yr-Aur' on 1975's *Physical Graffiti*. But just as the cottage and the surrounding area inspired the music, so in turn the music manages to capture and convey something of the "picture of true completeness" that Page and Plant experienced. I would urge anyone who doesn't understand what I mean to get hold of *Led Zeppelin III* and make time to sit down and really listen to it. What does it say to you? Where does it take you? Or, if you would prefer, listen to 'The Rain Song' from *Houses of the Holy* (1973). This is perhaps the most perfect example in the entire Zeppelin canon of words and music combining to present possibilities of meaning that seem to transcend everyday experience.

Of course, not everyone will be moved by Led Zeppelin in the way I've just described, but most rock fans will be able to relate to one band or another in this kind of way. It would not surprise me if those nurtured on 1990s britpop found something similar in Welsh band Gorky's Zygotic Mynci, while those who grew up in the early 1960s might well point to The Beatles as a band whose very *zeitgeist* encouraged young people to think

about themselves and their lives differently. Speaking about the music of
The Beatles and the influence it had on *his* life, Ozzy Osbourne has said:

> It was something magical, almost a spiritual experience for me. Of course,
> my dad hated it. Way back then, The Beatles were revolutionaries and their
> music was revolutionary music. You know, they were considered to be a
> bad influence because they gave the kids ideas, the ideas to do something
> else with their lives rather than waste it in factories or become plumbers.
> For adults, it was a dangerous thing. But for us, they were heroes.[44]

Often the potential for rock music to have a positive impact on people's
lives is most evident through a reaction (and sometimes a *shared* reaction)
to a live gig experience. It is not an exaggeration to say that for some the
'live' experience can be not just life-enhancing but life-changing. Such
an experience is not easy to describe and for that reason its impact on the
thinking and lifestyle choices of those moved by it is often missed despite
its very real and radical nature. Conceivably, any gig experience can have
this kind of effect – and I'll explore this further in the next chapter – though
my comments may put some readers in mind of events like 1985's *Live
Aid*; an event described by writer Nigel Williamson as "pop music's most
powerful collective humanitarian response to suffering and injustice".[45]

The *Live Aid* phenomenon was, of course, an event of global significance. Huge concerts were staged on both sides of the Atlantic bringing
together an astonishing array of the biggest selling pop and rock acts of
the day in an effort to raise sufficient sums of money to combat famine
in Africa. Among the many acts who appeared, there were performances
from bands and musicians of considerable rock and blues pedigree including Bob Dylan, Neil Young, Paul McCartney, Eric Clapton, Mick Jagger,
David Bowie, Queen, Status Quo, Judas Priest, The Who, U2, Dire Straits,
Tom Petty, Albert Collins, B.B. King, Bo Diddley, and George Thorogood
and the Destroyers. The American concert in Philadelphia was also the
scene of two remarkable heavy rock reunions, as first the original Black
Sabbath line-up and then the three surviving members of Led Zeppelin
took to the stage. Zeppelin felt the need to replace John Bonham with
not one but *two* drummers, as Tony Thompson of Chic and Phil Collins
took on sticks duties for the occasion. While discussing the Led Zeppelin
reunion, Andy Fyfe comments: "For one day, rock music was no longer
about rebellion: it was about conscience and doing the right thing, raising
millions around the world for famine relief."[46]

It is easy to be cynical about *Live Aid*, especially given its role in ushering in the age of the 'celebrity rock star' as some of rock music's oldest and biggest stars were embraced by, and became part of, the very establishment that *Live Aid*, to my mind, was supposed to be rallying against. Many of those who took part found that participation in *Live Aid* raised their public profile and gave a welcome boost to their careers. The point was not lost on anarcho-punk band Chumbawamba who produced a thought-provoking album in response called *Pictures of Starving Children Sell Records*. Their satire and exposure of rock star hypocrisy was biting and hard-hitting. What was needed, argued Chumbawamba, was sustained awareness and real systematic change, not charity for a day, and who could argue that they were wrong about that? Nevertheless, I don't imagine that anyone in Africa who needed help at the time would have been overly concerned about the motives, habits or lifestyles of those who raised some much needed cash on their behalf.

The main point I want to make here though, is that to my mind Andy Fyfe's characterisation of the event is entirely misplaced. 'Conscience' and 'doing the right thing', are not alternatives to 'rebellion'. In fact they are often what motivate and inspire rebellion. Actively speaking out and campaigning against a political and economic system that creates injustice and extremities of wealth might be seen by some as the very stuff of rebellion. But whether participation in *Live Aid* itself was 'rebellious' or not, even the cynics and sceptics would have trouble denying that, at the very least, events like *Live Aid* show the power of music to unite large numbers of people in a common cause and point to the latent potential of music to help inspire change.

Rock music can be life-affirming. It can wake us up and make us feel alive. It can offer positive alternatives to people either through direct messages, or by showing us new possibilities of meaning. Rock music can challenge us, stretch our understanding and provoke both thought and action. In all of these ways rock music has the power to defy convention, enhance people's lives and bring about change for the better. None of these things have much to do with a 'sex, drugs and rock 'n' roll lifestyle', not explicitly or *necessarily* anyhow, but all of them can help us to decide what kind of people we want to be and how we want to live. In fact, one of the most valuable things that music can do for people is to give them a sense of themselves.

❂ *'Everything is what it is and not another thing'* ❂

I know from my days studying philosophy that the philosophical search for the essence of a thing is often a fool's quest. One of the most memorable things I learned from reading the great twentieth-century philosopher Ludwig Wittgenstein is that things that look the same are often different. So central was this insight to Wittgenstein that he considered using a line from Shakespeare's King Lear – "I'll teach you differences" – as a motto for his later work.[47] According to biographer Ray Monk, Wittgenstein also considered using Bishop Joseph Butler's wonderful phrase: "Everything is what it is, and not another thing."[48]

On the back of this influence, I wish to make the following points. First, a label can suggest a false unity and hide a variety of subtle, and not so subtle, differences between things. Secondly, these differences are often more interesting than whatever it is that things have in common. And thirdly, whether things called by the same name all have something in common or not, there is often a variety of responses to them that can be just as interesting to explore as the things themselves. Let me explain what I mean.

People who profess to be vegetarians may be vegetarians for different reasons. One may be a vegetarian for moral reasons – "it is wrong to kill animals for food." Another may take a more pragmatic self-interested view – "I don't trust the food industry to provide me with safe nutritious meat." I've met both types of people, and I'm sure you have too. One can't even assume that people who are vegetarians on moral grounds are the same. One may hold a principle around 'the sanctity of life'. Another may connect their vegetarianism more explicitly with religious concepts like 'karma'. Others may offer a more basic, visceral response as the foundation of their vegetarianism, while others again may hold views developed in moral philosophy that animals – at least the adult ones – qualify as 'persons' and "it is wrong to kill persons." So, despite the common label, vegetarianism is not one thing. Is there something that all vegetarians have in common – an essence of vegetarianism? Well 'not eating meat' is probably as close as we'll get (though some people who call themselves vegetarians eat fish) – but defining vegetarianism thus tells you very little about any *individual* vegetarian. Definitions can obscure differences, and the differences often mean as much or more to people than the thing we are tempted to call the 'essence'.

Now, consider a football match that is watched by a large number of people. To the uninitiated, uninterested spectator, it might just look like a bunch of people running around chasing a ball. My wife struggles to see football as any more than this. To those who understand more of the game, the subtleties of team organisation and tactics (4-5-1 versus 4-4-2, for example) are more apparent. The uninitiated and the expert watch the game through different eyes. They see and take different things from the game. And there are varying degrees of knowledge and interest between these two extremes. The team manager sees more of the game's technical and strategic subtleties than the players – that is why he is the manager. The players understand more of the subtleties than I do. In turn I see more of the bigger picture than my young daughter. Some of those watching are there solely for entertainment. Some focus on the aesthetics of the game. Some are interested in the all-round quality of their team's performance. For others the result of the game is a matter of overwhelming psychological importance – closely connected, perhaps unhealthily so, with their sense of self-worth and well-being. It's the same game – but there are very many ways of watching and reacting to it. This sort of variety is present every time a group of people gather to watch a football match. And of course, every match is different. It involves different players, different teams, and different officials, for example, and the rules of the sport allow different games to take radically different courses. If we restrict ourselves to say, Premiership and Football League matches in England, all the games will have some things in common: for example, both teams will start with eleven players, there will be a referee and two assistant referees, the pitch will conform to size regulations, and only approved balls will be used. However, as far as the spectators are concerned these shared features are simply taken for granted in this context – they are conditions of the games going ahead rather than matters of interest in themselves, forming part of the background against which the features of the game that really excite people are viewed.

Let us apply these points to rock music. 'Rock' is indeed a weighty label which masks huge variety in terms of both sound and musical style. Pretty quickly too, it divides into a number of genres and sub-genres: hard rock, heavy rock, progressive rock, blues rock, folk rock, jazz rock, country rock, southern rock, pomp rock, melodic rock, indie rock, stoner rock and punk rock, to name a few. Consider the following admittedly selective list: The Rolling Stones, The Who, Bob Dylan, the Doors, Jimi

Hendrix, Deep Purple, Led Zeppelin, Black Sabbath, Alice Cooper, Free, Genesis, Yes, Pink Floyd, AC/DC, Kiss, Jethro Tull, Fairport Convention, Aerosmith, Journey, Rush, Lynyrd Skynyrd, Queen, Scorpions, Van Halen, Iron Maiden, Bon Jovi, U2, Metallica, Nirvana, Pearl Jam, R.E.M. and the Red Hot Chilli Peppers. These artists are all indisputably giants of the rock world – but they are all, to my ears, very different. If there is something they all share in common, an 'essence' as it were, it must be something so general or technical that it is completely uninteresting. For example, that they all have drummers, guitarists and bass players (as do many bands who are clearly not 'rock' bands) or, I don't know, that they all use identifiable 'rock' beats or guitar riffs in their music in some way or at some point. (The 'essence' can't lie in a certain 'attitude', because as we've seen above, attitudes across and between musicians vary and do not respect the borders imposed by linguistic tags.) It's far more exciting and instructive to be alive to the musical and lyrical *differences* between bands, to subtleties of style, to differences in the way each band perceives itself and presents its music. The differences are far more interesting than the similarities. That there are differences, and that these do matter to people, shows itself in the fact that different bands have different (if sometimes overlapping) sets of fans. There are bands I have included on the list above that I do not care for particularly, even though I own albums by all of them. There are other bands on the list who, along with others not featured here, have had a big impact on my life and my character and who I like very much. But if you sit 25 rock fans in a room with such a list and ask them to rank the bands in order of preference you'll almost certainly get 25 differently ordered lists. If you ask the same rock fans to explain the reasons for their rankings, you'll start to draw forth a wide range of responses and opinions. Taken together, these responses would form a rich tapestry of experience that would demonstrate very clearly how much rock music means to people and how important a part it has played in their lives. If it is true that there is great variety in rock music, then it is also true that there is even greater variety in the way that listeners and fans respond to that music. Rock music means different things to different people. I'd like to tell you more about what it means to me.

3

This One Sacred Hour

By the time I discovered rock music at the end of the 1970s, it already had a history. There was already a tradition that one become part of simply by loving the music. There was a great sense among British rock fans at the time that the music transcended everything. "It's the music that matters," BBC Radio 1 *Friday Rock Show* DJ Tommy Vance* would tell us. There was something almost Nietzschean about the value we attached to music. We knew that some of our heroes were flawed characters, but the music they made mattered more than their personal foibles and failings.

For rock fans, the live celebration of the music – the gig – has come to take on great significance. Gigs pass quickly. You wait for them with great anticipation for weeks, months even, and then, before you know it, they are over. But what happens in that hour or two gives them a weight that can anchor them for years in our individual and collective memories. The great gigs exist as 'perfect moments'. They have to be *experienced*. And once we've experienced them we live our lives in their afterglow, doing what we can to hold on to the joy, togetherness and power of the experience and extend it to other parts of our lives.

Going to a gig is a social experience. It is something that you do with other people. Even if you go alone, you become part of a group as soon as you enter the venue. Queen guitarist Brian May is reported to have said that a rock concert is like a football match where both sets of fans are supporting the same team. It's not a perfect analogy, because at rock

---

* The sadly deceased Tommy Vance – "TV on the Radio!"

gigs there is only one team so to speak, but it makes the point very well: everyone is on the same side and is there to *share* something special. (The analogy was repeated by Iron Maiden's Steve Harris in an interview that appeared in *The Guardian* newspaper the week before Maiden's *Somewhere Back in Time* Twickenham gig in July 2008.)

Other influential rock musicians have made comments on the special nature of the gig and what it means to them. Rock warhorse Lemmy tells us that: "The first time you break through to an audience and they all go nuts, that's better than screwing, you know, that's better, that's the best."[1] Ozzy Osbourne, who, like Lemmy, is well known for the occasional hedonistic indulgence, goes further than this, recognising the experience as something that goes beyond personal gratification: "If you got a gig that's going great," he says, "there's no sex, drug, drink or award that can beat that feeling . . . And you know what? That is God given. That is the nearest thing to spirituality that I've ever come across."[2]

The reference to spirituality is not misplaced. Others have made similar remarks. Iron Maiden manager Rod Smallwood, for example, has drawn attention to the sense of 'oneness' and belonging that gigs can generate: "The great gigs," he says, "are when the band feel inspired by the occasion and the hearts of the crowd, the love of the audience. That feeling of identity and loyalty with the band is quite inspiring." Referring to some of Maiden's biggest gigs, Donington in 1988 (attendance: 107,000), Rock Am Ring in 2003 (75,000) and Rock in Rio in 2001 (250,000), he continues: "It is strange when an audience that size becomes one whole animal, when hands all the way to the back are all raised, all being involved. It's an almost religious feeling."[3]

Of course, not all live performances carry this sort of significance. Variables include the ability, attitude and performance of the band, the quality of the material, the nature of the occasion and response of the fans. Every single gig is a unique combination of all these things and more. But there are times when chance and good fortune bring all relevant factors together in ways which have the power to move and affect people deeply. The communal nature of this experience is significant here. As noted above, these are experiences you share *with others*. The bonds created give a sense of belonging and worth. That is why music can be such a positive and cohesive social force, and that is why the music and occasion come to have a value and significance that transcend the feelings of any one individual.

¡O¡ Heavy Metal Thunder: Sophia Gardens, Cardiff ¡O¡
26 November 1980

There's never anything quite like your very first gig. You tend to remember the first time, and thankfully my first experience was a very good one, courtesy of Helen, the girl next door, and Biff and the boys. Along with a school friend called Hawkeye, I had a ticket to see Saxon on their *Strong Arm of the Law* tour. I was 13, and a very small 13-year-old at that. Although my parents were somewhat reluctant to let me go, they were reassured when my next door neighbour Helen and her friends, who were all a school year older than me (and who looked a good three or four years older than that), agreed to take me with them. So off I set on that cold winter's night for an experience that would influence my musical taste and social 'orientation' for many years to come.

Despite my sense of excitement, it wasn't entirely without trepidation that I mingled with the denim and leather brigade and tried to feel myself one of them. I had chosen to wear what I considered to be the most suitable jacket in my wardrobe – a black part-wool bomber jacket with a white collar. I didn't really look the part and I knew it. Would it cause me any problems? Would people point at me and laugh? Would some big hairy biker guy come and pick me up and throw me out of the hall? I really had no idea what to expect – it was like stepping into another world. Inside the venue the atmosphere, scented with a mixture of smoke and patchouli, crackled with expectancy. Helen and her friends headed for the bar and the big hairy bikers. Hawkeye and I checked out the merchandise stall and generally wandered about doing our best to look natural and feel at home. And then the lights dimmed, and the growing crowd cheered. We stood about two-thirds of the way back from the stage, slightly to the right. The support band, Limelight, struck their first chords, and I remember a feeling of utter terror as the awful sound permeated my entire body. I had never experienced anything like this. It was, frankly, almost too much to bear. I endured it for as long as I could and then retired to the café at the back of hall. The volume reduction was minimal, but at least I could sit down and pull myself together. I looked closely at some of the people around me. What was I doing here? Did I really belong? What if someone saw me and took a dislike to me? What if they picked on me and force-fed me drugs? Such were the irrational thoughts going through my head. Slowly but surely I began to acclimatise to the volume and relax.

I wandered back to watch the band and even started to appreciate them a little. I remember the rather dramatic pose struck by the guitarist, who, bathed in green and purple light, crouched down with one leg extended sideways, and rocked gently as though riding the music that he and his band-mates were creating.

With Limelight gone, the crowd breathed out for a few minutes, before the mood again turned to one of expectancy. The bar and cafeteria started to empty, people started jostling for position, excitement and impatience intermingled, the buzz was electric. You just knew something special was about to happen. The chant went up: "Saxon" . . . clap, clap, clap . . . "Saxon" . . . clap, clap, clap . . . "Saxon" . . . clap, clap, clap. The lights dimmed, the crowd roared, and there they were, in the flesh, smiling, punching the air, getting off on the music and the crowd's reaction, with the crowd, to borrow Lemmy's words, going nuts.

I don't remember the setlist with any certainty, though it was drawn from the debut album *Saxon*, the excellent *Wheels of Steel*, and the new album, *Strong Arm of the Law*, which I didn't yet own. A number of highlights remain in my memory. '747 Strangers in the Night' already threatened to become a classic of the genre, and was mesmerising. 'Wheels of Steel' (the track) offered audience-participation possibilities that made it a memorable feature of Saxon's early shows. 'Motorcycle Man', a high-speed, high-octane thriller from *Wheels of Steel* was delivered with gusto and enthusiasm. They also played a curious track from the new album, which was notable for the quirky-sounding chorus which I found it hard to get hold of first time around. But I heard it soon after on a Friday Rock Show session and quickly came to know it as 'Heavy Metal Thunder'. It didn't take me long to get the hang of the *sound* of the chorus, though even now, all these years later, the lyrics still puzzle me. The first line is no problem:

> *Throw your head back, throw your hands high,*
> *shake your body (body, body)*

But what about the next line? It sounds like:

> *If it's too loud and your groin hurts*
> *Fill your heads with heavy metal thunder*

Why, I have wondered many times, would excess volume make my groin hurt? Biff's stage apparel certainly did its best to draw attention to that part of his anatomy, but is he really singing about 'groins'? And assuming that my groin was hurting, how exactly would filling my head "with heavy metal thunder" improve my predicament? But listen again carefully and some possible alternatives emerge. Could he be singing:

- *shake your groin up* (more fun than your groin *hurting*, but just as nonsensical);
- *come and join us* (possible, but "if it's *too* loud" why would you join the people who are making the noise?); or
- *and your brain hurts* (possible, but again, if excess volume is making your brain hurt, how would exposing yourself to more of it help?).

Whatever the 'missing' phrase, it is a strong and exciting track that's tailor-made for live performance. At the time I was more than willing to "fill my head with heavy metal thunder" whether it helped my groin (or my brain) or not.

Another highlight of the show was the final encore, 'Machine Gun'. If 'Motorcyle Man' had the guitarists sounding like twin exhausts, by the end of the show they were firing like Gatlin guns. The climax of the song had to be seen to be believed, as the Hendrix-inspired Graham Oliver set his guitar alight and left it swinging from the ceiling amid swirling smoke and sirens. As the stage cleared the giant eagle – the centre piece of Saxon's stage show – shone brightly to mark another triumph. Saxon moved on to the next town. They took no prisoners.

On the face of it, it's hard to say what attracted me to Saxon. I wasn't really into motorbikes or any of the other forms of transportation (planes, trains and automobiles) that Saxon liked to write about in apparent 'Boy's Own' style. But dig a bit deeper, and it's not that hard to see the appeal. Their songwriting frequently showed a keen interest in both modern history and more obvious matters of human significance. 'Dallas 1pm', for example, is a song about the assassination of President Kennedy that focuses on the human aspect of the tragedy, ("The world was shocked that fateful day/A young man's life was blown away.") while 'Suzie Hold On' is a rather sensitive lyric about someone struggling to hold on to life in the face of adversity and illness. "I wish I had a fortune," sings Biff, "I'd take the pain away." There was a hard-edged 'working-class underdog' feel to the band that I really liked and felt I could identify with. The *Wheels of Steel* album seemed to bear this out. The front cover features a stark, but compelling 'eagle' design which was simplicity itself. The back cover showed the band sitting in dark and dingy surroundings looking like a bunch of regular guys, one or two of whom could do with a good scrub. Not for them opulent hotel suites, fancy clothes and scantily clad chicks. Not yet anyway. The cover complemented the music perfectly. The production had a live, raw feel, with the pristine clarity and dirty riffing of the twin guitars augmented by the rolling thunder of the rhythm section and Biff's sometimes guttural, sometimes shrill vocal delivery. Echo effects, selectively applied to some of the vocals, create a sense of space, speed and movement, which suit the song's themes very well: motorbikes, plane disasters, street fighting, and encouragement to be yourself and to 'Stand Up and Be Counted'. Saxon in 1980 were an unpretentious band with a passion that seemed borne of necessity. They had risen from relatively humble origins. They were excited by their music and the fact that they were able to play it live to a hungry and welcoming audience. Saxon were an honest and sincere British rock band who were proud of their roots and genuinely appreciative of the people who bought their records and went to their gigs. The audience recognised the band's sincerity, and Saxon gigs at this time just had such a great vibe. I instantly felt part of something special. It's a cliché I know, but it really did feel like I had become part of some giant, extended family.

Going to see Saxon was one of the few occasions in my school career when I did something (albeit inadvertently) that raised my profile and reputation with the school hard nuts. Word had somehow got around that Michael Anthony, one of the swotty kids from the top set, had been to see the loudest, heaviest, dirtiest, grimiest, heavy metal band on the planet (apart from Motörhead that is). I remember a kid called Mark – the most intelligent of the beef-cakes and aggro boys – approaching me as I lined up for the school bus. I knew of him, of course, but it was probably the first time he had spoken to me directly. Usually when he approached people outside his immediate group, it was, according to his reputation, because he wanted to fight them.

"Anthony, did you go to see Saxon?" he asked in an almost accusatory tone.

"Er . . . yeah."

"Woah! So you like heavy metal?"

"Er . . . yeah."

And off he ran, with a brief nod of respect to me and a big grin on his face. He seemed pleased that he'd been able to extract the required information from me. I was just glad that he'd got what he wanted without having to employ methods of torture.

There were to be plenty of other Saxon gigs in the 1980s, and to be fair to the band they *never* failed to deliver. But it's the earlier gigs that made more of an impression and have stayed with me. In October 1981, for example, they returned to Sophia Gardens on their *Denim and Leather* tour, with Tommy Vance lending his voice to the band's intro tape. Their performance combined the excitement of their quick ascent to the top of the New Wave of British Heavy Metal (NWOBHM) tree with an extra year's headlining experience. Singer Biff had become a master showman, demanding, and getting, the respect of the audience. "Is it loud enough for you?" he'd scream. "No", we'd all shout back. It brought a touch of pantomime humour to proceedings, but it was fun. They also had some great new live material. The addition of anthems such as 'Denim and Leather', and Saxon's celebration of the first ever Monsters of Rock Festival, 'And The Bands Played On', further enhanced the togetherness vibe that, as I've said, was such a strong feature of Saxon gigs in those days. I remember taking a moment or two to look around at the crowd during 'Denim and Leather', and seeing row after row of happy, smiling people linking arms or punching the air and singing along.

The magic of the 'Saxon experience' was reinforced in September 1982, when, along with school friends Gareth and John, I went to see Saxon at Bristol's Colston Hall. This was the first time I'd seen Saxon somewhere other than Cardiff, and, in fact, it was the first time I'd seen anyone outside my home town. We travelled with two other friends, Richard and Larry. Richard was the older brother of my friend Fog; Larry was Richard's mate. Richard had just learned to drive. He picked us all up in his old Hillman Imp and drove us to Cardiff Central where we left the car and took a train to Bristol. It's great to see bands in your home town, but there's something special too about travelling to see them. The effort you put in to get there seems to make the good gigs even more rewarding. This was *The Eagle Has Landed* tour. The band were promoting their new live album of the same name, a title that seemed to announce Saxon as a permanent top division rock band after years of hard work and incessant gigging. The band were possibly approaching their live peak – and could now deliver a set that expertly blended storming chart 'hits', heavier and more complex album tracks, and crowd-pleasing sing-alongs. They also debuted a new song – also called 'The Eagle Has Landed' – which to my ears sounded superb and augered well for the next studio album. It was wonderful to see that the crowd reaction was just as strong in Bristol as in Cardiff. I knew from reading *Sounds* and *Kerrang!* and listening to the *Friday Rock Show* that what I'd experienced at gigs wasn't a Welsh thing, or a Cardiff thing and that I was part of something much bigger. But here was the experiential proof. Music had the power to move people and bring them together across cities and, indeed, across nations.

That Bristol gig was also notable for some post-gig shenanigans that could have had disastrous consequences. Having just about made the last train home, and got back to Cardiff without incident, we picked up the car at the train station, and drove to what was then a piece of undeveloped land in Cardiff city centre at the top of Caroline Street and opposite the Wyndham Arcade. Getting chips from Caroline Street is part of the night-out ritual for many Cardiffians, and we were no exception. Richard, Larry and I headed off to the chip shop, leaving Gareth and John to mind the car. While in the queue for chips, we hatched a plan. I was to give Richard my red and white bobble hat to hide in his coat. We'd get back to the car looking worried and tell Gareth and John that a gang of Rastafarians had threatened us and pinched my bobble hat because they said it looked too much like one of their own. Richard and Larry would feign outrage, and decide to go back to confront our assailants and retrieve my 'lucky hat'. It was a ridiculous practical joke, lacking both feasibility and common sense, but Richard and Larry were determined to see it through, and I deferred to their greater age and wisdom. So we bought the chips, rushed back to the car, planted the chips on Gareth and John's laps, and hastily recounted the made-up story. Richard started the engine and moved the car to a more strategic 'getaway' point. He picked up his crooklock, and off he went with Larry to confront our imaginary adversaries. "It's a bit stupid," said Gareth, when they were gone, "they're just gonna get their heads kicked in. Or worse still, they're gonna lead them back here to us." And then we sat and waited, eating our chips, keeping an eye on the arcade opposite, and wondering how Richard and Larry were getting on. Or at least, Gareth and John were wondering how Richard and Larry were getting on. I was wondering what on earth they were doing and why they were taking so long. John finished his chips first and got out of the car to throw his wrapper away. Just then a police patrol car pulled up, presumably attracted by the strange position in which Richard had left the Imp.

"Oi Sonny," the policeman called to John, "if you want a piss, go in the lane."

"What?"

"I said if you want a piss, go in the lane."

"I don't want a piss, I'm throwing my chip wrapper away."

"I don't want any cheek from you boy. I've told you, if you want a piss go in the lane."

"Ok," said John, losing the will to explain.

The policeman came over, walked around the car a couple of times and looked thoughtful.

"So, what are you boys doing parked here then?" he asked.

"We've been to a concert," I said. "We're just waiting for our friends. They've gone to get more chips."

Unfortunately Richard and Larry chose exactly that moment to come haring back through the Wyndham Arcade at a speed more commonly associated with Olympic sprinters. One of them was triumphantly waving my red and white bobble hat around; the other manically brandishing the crooklock in menacing fashion. By the time they saw the policeman, it was too late. "Getting chips eh?" he said, eyeing us doubtfully and sensing some kind of victory. It took some time for the combined wit of Richard and Larry to talk us out of our predicament, but somehow they managed it. I'm not sure they'd find it quite so easy in this day and age. When Richard grew up he became a successful lawyer.

¡O¡ Heaven and Hell ¡O¡

The second band I saw, just a couple of months after that first Saxon gig, was Black Sabbath. It was 28 January 1981 and a rejuvenated Sabbath played Sophia Gardens as they neared the end of their massive *Heaven and Hell* world tour. Again I went with Helen and her friends, though a couple of school friends of mine, Gareth and Eamonn, were there, and I was able to meet up with some other people I knew, including a strange chap called Vincente.

I had actually been in junior school with Vincente, though I remember only two things about him from those days. First, the school operated a house system – rather like Hogwarts in the Harry Potter books. Vincente was in De La Salle House, which, by reputation was the most conventional and industrious of the houses, while I had been in the more sporty and robustly dependable St David's. Secondly, he had been my flag-bearing assistant when, as head boy, I was responsible for carrying the school flag on the annual Corpus Christi parade through the centre of Cardiff. Funny the things you remember about people – and how much you forget.

But, without doubt, Vincente had become a strange boy. It was rumoured, for example, that he kept a plastic bag and a leather glove down the side of his bed, bringing them out after hours to relieve his teenage frustration. The glove presumably just felt nice, while the bag collected the evidence and kept his bed sheets clean. It was also rumoured that when a female friend discovered the bag by accident and asked what it was, his response was to strike the bag so hard at the bottom that the contents were propelled straight into her face. I don't believe that their relationship blossomed into anything more mutually satisfying, but I haven't seen either of them for about 25 years now, so I could be wrong.

On the night in question, Vincente made an impression by asking Eamonn – the most experienced of our gig-going chums – half desperately and half ironically, if it was alright if he "headbanged with (his) mates"? "Sure," replied Eamonn coolly, "they're the ones over there in the denim jackets." And off went Vincente, with seemingly genuine gratitude, to search for a couple of needles in a great sea of needles. It was the last time I saw him that night. (One thing I have to thank Vincente for is turning me on to *Tokyo Tapes* by the Scorpions. Before he disappeared he happened to casually mention that *Tokyo Tapes* was a great live album. I'd heard very little by the Scorpions at the time, but for some reason the recommendation stuck in my mind. And boy was he right.)

That Helen and I ended up with tickets for this gig at all came as something of a surprise. Our initial efforts to get tickets had been unsuccessful and we were under the impression for a while that the gig was sold out. Then, somehow, one of Helen's friends came across some tickets in a small record shop in a part of Cardiff called Roath. I was so chuffed to be going. In the weeks leading up to the concert, I must have looked at my ticket every single day. It was number 410.

When the evening came, it was ice-cold and Bible-black, as though Mother Nature herself was aware of the band's reputation and had deserted us. On the way to the venue, I bought a cheap black and white Sabbath scarf (from a pirate merchandise seller) to tie around my wrist. 'THEY SOLD THEIR SOULS FOR ROCK N ROLL' said the lettering along the scarf in mock-gothic font. I thought it looked great. We got there as early as we could and started queuing. Since the Saxon gig I had acquired a denim jacket. It was a bit too long, as my mother sensibly always bought me clothes with 'growing space', but generally I felt much more appropriately attired. My 'lucky' bobble hat kept my ears warm. Then, disaster! As the queue started to move I realised that I couldn't find my ticket anywhere. Perhaps I dropped it when I bought the scarf. Perhaps I'd been pick-pocketed. Wherever it was, it wasn't about my person. The security men were patient with me.

"Take your time, son, check all your pockets," said one of them. I did, but to no avail.

"This one's a brave one," chipped in another, "he's not even crying!"

"Listen," I said, in desperation, "I've come with a group of girls. You've just let them in. I know my ticket number and they will have the numbers either side. And they can vouch for me."

The bouncers conferred. "OK," said the one who appeared to be in charge, "we'll go and find your friends and see what they've got to say."

In we went. When we found the girls they looked genuinely pleased and relieved to see me. Their instinctive responses clearly made a difference. They showed the chief bouncer their tickets and he seemed to be in no doubt that I was genuine. In a show of outstanding reasonableness, for which I'll be forever grateful, he let me in!

Not only was I lucky that the security staff were so reasonable, but, as it turned out, I was lucky that we'd arrived at the venue so early. As the hall filled up, it was soon obvious that not only was the crowd reaching full capacity but that there were still lots of people coming in. I became vaguely aware of a growing sense of unrest, with concerned looking bouncers rushing about the place as though reinforcements had been summoned. Then someone broke in through a skylight and dropped from the ceiling into the crowd below. I'd seen the same chap outside and had been struck by his distinctive appearance. Most notably he had what looked like some kind of dead animal tied to his belt. Several minutes later I saw him again, wriggling and kicking, struggling to free himself from the same group of bouncers who just minutes earlier had been so reasonable with me. It took four strong men to subdue him, and they had to carry him out of the building each holding a different limb (all still attached to his body, I hasten to add). The entourage was escorted by an anxious-looking supervisor on a walkie-talkie. This was the first time I'd experienced the depth of fanaticism that characterised hardcore Black Sabbath fans. I assumed that, like me, the now becalmed fan had lost his ticket or had it pinched. It was reported later though that an estimated 1,000 'extra' tickets were in circulation. Once the venue had reached (or perhaps surpassed) capacity, and it was clear that there was a problem, a decision was taken to close the doors. It was the only sensible thing that could have been done, but it meant that a substantial number of ticket holders were left outside. The anticipation and excitement of those unlucky enough to have been locked out turned to anger. The skylight intruder was one of those, and he wasn't the only one to break glass, as some people hurled bricks and stones through the cafeteria window. The trouble was only quelled when the band agreed to play a special set for those left outside and paid for tea and coffee to help keep everyone warm while they waited. I remember seeing a queue of cold, shivering and weary-looking people (including my friend Duncan and his Mum) as I left the gig after the 'first performance'.

Back inside the venue, with order restored, the gig itself proved to be a stunning experience. This time around I even enjoyed the support band – a northern group called AIIZ, who played a set of powerful yet quite immediate songs including a delightful romp called . . . er . . . 'The Romp' which invited and gained significant crowd participation. It turned out that they had a live album in the shops at the time called *The Witch of Berkeley*, which I later purchased as a deleted rarity from the marvellous Spillers Records ("Probably the oldest record shop in the world").

Then, with the lights dimmed and the crowd pumped up, Sabbath took to the stage. The next couple of hours surpassed my wildest expectations. Sabbath were simply superb. With Ronnie James Dio in full pomp, this was a band at its most theatrical and right at the top of its game. They mixed old (Ozzy-era) material and new tracks seamlessly, delivering a crisp and supremely exciting set with freshness and enthusiasm. The music press had reported animosity between new singer, the diminutive RJD, and old singer Ozzy Osbourne. Ozzy had claimed that Ronnie would need a bullet-proof vest if he got up on stage singing 'his' songs, and, indeed, it was reported that many hardcore fans had trouble accepting the former Rainbow front-man as one of their own. Ozzy fans would not have been palliated by Ronnie's retort that Ozzy "couldn't carry a tune in a suitcase". But there was no dissent evident that night at Sophia Gardens. My overriding memory of the concert is of the fervour of those present. I formed the distinct impression that the boy with the dead animal on his belt was not the only one who would have risked life and limb to get into the gig. This band clearly meant an awful lot to an awful lot of people. An impassioned Dio sang about kings and queens, blinding our eyes and stealing our dreams. No wildebeest in sight. Fists, peace signs and crosses punched the air rhythmically and *en masse*. Arms flailed, heads bobbed, and bodies jumped and surged in unison. This went beyond the good time togetherness of a Saxon gig. Something quite different was happening here.

I caught the eye of one of the crew, a gorgeous rock'n'roll dream who, I seem to recall, had an Australian accent (though that last bit could just be part of my fantasy). She took pity on my short and slight 13-year-old frame and pulled me up onto the mixing rig with her, giving me a fantastic if slightly uncomfortable vantage point for most of the show. With my scarf tied securely round my wrist, I joined in with the air punching. I also bought a great t-shirt that had a picture of the devil leaping across the world on the front, and a list of tour dates inside a cross on the back. It was size 'small' and came down almost to my knees, but I didn't care about that (and my mother would be pleased with the 'growing space'). For the whole of the gig, my identity was entirely merged with the band and the rest of the crowd. I was taken over completely by the experience. Musically there were a number of highlights, of which I still have clear memories. For example, the live performance brought home to me the power of a track from *Heaven and Hell* called 'Die Young', a song with a 'live for today' theme. I remember a great strobe lighting effect during the quieter passages and the crowd going absolutely wild when the song got heavy again. And the track 'Black Sabbath' itself was a revelation. Framed by giant gleaming crosses set diagonally on either side of the drum kit, Iommi's mighty riff sent dark thrills shooting through me. If Satan was indeed "coming round the bend", then Ronnie Dio was the puppet master, controlling his every move with bolts of electricity drawn from Iommi's guitar, his charge dancing to the rhythm of Butler's bass and the beat of Appice's drums. It was sheer magic – black or otherwise!

¡◉¡ *Diary of a Madman* ¡◉¡

In total I saw five concerts at Sophia Gardens in my first year of gigging. In addition to those gigs already mentioned, I saw Girlschool there in March 1981 on their *Hit and Run* tour, though I really only went because AIIZ again provided support and I'd enjoyed them so much at the Sabbath gig. I was given great encouragement after the gig by a South Wales Valleys rocker and his girlfriend who I met at the bus-stop on my way home. They were interested to know what gigs I'd been to and what I thought of the bands I'd seen. They were full of praise for my efforts to date, and gave me some tips about other bands they thought I might like. It was a lovely moment. I could never have imagined an 18 or 20 year old taking any interest in me six months earlier, and it added to my growing sense of belonging and the feeling that in finding rock music I'd discovered something very special. (I hoped too that one day I might have a pretty girlfriend like the kind girl at the bus-stop.)

Then, in late November 1981 it was my privilege to catch Ozzy Osbourne's *Diary of a Madman* tour with the late, great Randy Rhoads on guitar. It was rumoured that Ozzy, dressed down in denims and a beany hat, had wandered casually through the crowd while support band Girl strutted their stuff. I doubted this at the time, and still regard it as just one of the 1,001 unsubstantiated rumours about Ozzy Osbourne that did the rounds in the early and mid-1980s. I do have a strong memory, however, of pushing my way to the front of the stage on the right hand side and shoving my head inside one of the speaker bins – an act of absurdity that I regretted almost as I did it. The real significance of this gig, though I didn't realise it at the time, is that it was the only occasion I would ever get to see Randy Rhoads in the flesh. It wasn't just his performance on stage that made an impression on me that night. My friend Nigel and I were two of a significant number of fans who hung around the stage door after the gig hoping for a quick word or an autograph or two. On this occasion we were rewarded only with a brief glimpse of the band as they rushed out and piled into waiting vehicles. I don't remember how many vehicles there were, or who travelled with who, but I remember lots of pushing and jostling and a sudden surge from the waiting fans that pushed me right up against the window of Randy's car. Just a few millimetres of glass separated our faces. He looked at my own squashed face, smiled, nudged his travelling companion, and pointed at me. I guess my squashed face must have looked quite funny, but as the car drove off I felt ten foot tall. I loved his guitar playing – it was so soulful and atmospheric – and I never tired of championing his cause among my group of rock-loving friends. As a young 14 year old it was a real thrill to get so close to one of my favourite guitarists. However, just a few months later Randy was dead.

The sad news of Randy's death, from an utterly senseless private plane accident, was broken to UK rock fans by Tommy Vance, who played two tracks from Budgie's then current album *Nightflight* – 'Superstar' and 'I Turned to Stone' – in tribute. By all accounts Randy was a genuine and unassuming man who was more interested in improving his knowledge and ability as a guitar player than over-indulging in the hedonistic trappings of rock'n'roll success. 'Only the good die young' the saying goes, but in the context of rock and roll it is sobering to note that *even* the good die young. Randy's death seemed so unnecessary and so unfair, and those of us who had marvelled at his playing on *Blizzard of Ozz* and *Diary of a Madman* can only wonder at what might have been. Personally, for all his later commercial success, I don't think Ozzy has recorded anything of comparable creative note since.

For those of us who felt we had discovered a good thing, Randy's death was an unwanted reminder of the fragility of human life. Nothing necessarily exists and good things can stop existing at any time, whether we want them to or not. Rock musicians often show an acute awareness of the precariousness of their own existence, and that of their art, through songs that self-consciously, and with a degree of angst, overstate their case. *Diary of a Madman* itself contains an Osbourne/Rhoads/Daisley composition entitled, somewhat optimistically, 'You Can't Kill Rock and Roll'. One doesn't have to look too far to find other examples of songs that try to convince the listener that although, in the grand scheme of things, the odds are heavily stacked against it, *Rock Will Never Die.**

Beyond the actual mortality of those who create the music, the 'precariousness' of rock and roll is nowhere more apparent than in the nature of the gig itself. There is a striking difference between the 'lightness' of a gig, marked by its brief temporal duration, and its 'weight' in the lives of those who have been moved by it. For those aware of the contrast, it can be hard to let go of the experience and accept that the

---

* To quote the title of a Michael Schenker Group album.

gig is over. Anyone who has experienced that sense of total immersion in a gig is familiar with the feeling of emptiness that follows and the need to 'come down'. Imagine a gig where no one lets go of the moment and no one goes home. This is precisely what happened at another Ozzy Osbourne gig I attended – this time on 14 November 1983 on the *Bark at the Moon* tour.

With Cardiff omitted from the tour schedule, this was the second gig I attended at Bristol Colston Hall. My friend Ray and I booked tickets with the Concert Travel Club. I had used the Concert Travel Club to see Ozzy's spectacular show at Birmingham NEC on the *Speak of the Devil* tour and found the service to be excellent. The *Bark at the Moon* tour was a return to smaller venues, with Ozzy having a new album and a new guitarist, Jake E. Lee, to show off. We sat on the coach next to a guy called Mike, an amusing and friendly chap who had a big Randy Rhoads patch on his back and a slightly odd squinty eye. He turned out to be great company and spoke at length and with great enthusiasm about the entire Ozzy and Sabbath back catalogues.

It was a solid gig. Jake E. Lee was a good guitarist and no one could have any qualms about the quality of his performance. The new material went down pretty well, while a sufficient number of Ozzy staples were included to keep everyone happy. But what was significant about this event wasn't the main gig itself, but what happened at the end. People simply refused to leave! The band finished their set. The crowd bayed for more. The band returned. After one short encore ('Paranoid' of course) the band left the stage again. People immediately started clapping, shouting and chanting for more. But the band did not reappear. After a few minutes the house lights came on – usually a sure sign that 'that's all, folks!' But no one left. We must have stayed chanting and stamping and whistling for a good 20 minutes before Ozzy and the band were eventually forced back on stage in a half-undressed state. I couldn't believe that we'd done it. I'd never seen it happen before and I've never seen it happen since. It was an amazing thing to be part of, and again, it's ample illustration of how much these occasions matter to people. As an audience we were prepared to shout and scream for the best part of half an hour, just to hold on to the moment for a little while longer. And, as it turned out, it was just a little while longer. "Er, we haven't got anything else rehearsed," said a rather befuddled and semi-naked Ozzy, "so we're gonna do 'Paranoid' again."

¡O¡ *Bent Out of Shape* ¡O¡

The *Diary of a Madman* tour was not only the first and last time I'd get to see Randy Rhoads in the flesh, it was the last time I'd get to see anyone at all at Sophia Gardens. Black Sabbath were due to visit again on 13 January 1982 on their *Mob Rules* tour. Following their glorious gig on the previous tour and all the ticket shenanigans, this time I made sure that I got my ticket early and protected it with my life. I was playing in the snow in the front garden with my sister, then a toddler, when my father broke the bad news.

"Aren't you going to a concert at Sophia Gardens soon?"

"Yeah, Black Sabbath."

"Well, you're not now. It's been cancelled."

"Shut up, don't be stupid," I shouted, "how would you know?"

"It was just on the news," he said, with a sense of triumph.

My father disapproved of loud music, and men with long hair, and seemed to delight in adopting an obstructive, killjoy attitude whenever he could. That, at any rate, is how it felt to me as a 14 year old. The apparent smugness with which he delivered the news riled me. It was like he was saying "See, I told you these concerts aren't meant to happen." His report was accurate though. The roof of the Sophia Gardens Pavilion had been unable to cope with the weight of the heavy snow and had collapsed. "It must be some kind of curse," I thought, "clearly Sabbath and Sophia Gardens just don't get on."

The news, however, was worse than both of us realised. It turned out that the venue, which offered all sorts of events, including school holiday roller-skating and an annual circus, was beyond repair and had to be knocked down. Though gigs at Sophia Gardens are now a distant memory, the venue lives on in my concept of what a 'real' rock gig should be like. (The purpose-built auditorium erected by Marillion for the weekend in Port Zelande came very close to replicating aspects of the Sophia Gardens Pavilion – a big 'egalitarian' space, all on one level, with the stage sufficiently high to offer good views for everyone, but not too high to make the band seem remote.)

There were, of course, other venues in Cardiff. The Top Rank, for example, hosted Gillan and Marillion, the latter touring their debut album *Script for a Jester's Tear*, but the nature of the venue meant it had an over-18s policy. I don't doubt that the policy was applied fairly leniently for rock gigs, but as a particularly small 14 and 15 year old (I was a 'late developer') I struggled to pass as the age I was, let alone as an adult. In general, the demise of Sophia Gardens meant that Cardiff fell off a lot of tour schedules, and something of a gig-hiatus ensued.

In the meantime, the Council set about improving the situation by building the wonderful St David's Hall, a 'posh' concert hall with great acoustics, great views, and a multi-tiered auditorium that managed to preserve the warmth and 'intimacy' that so many concert halls of a similar size seem to lack. 'The Hall', as my friends and I affectionately called it, was officially opened by the Queen Mother in February 1983, though it was already in use before its official opening. I must confess to initial surprise that it was going to be used for rock gigs at all, but used for rock gigs it was. The first headline act I saw there was the Michael Schenker Group on the *Assault Attack* tour – a gig that was notable for the return to the ranks of original vocalist Gary Barden. Support was provided by Dutch rockers Vandenberg, who crammed all manner of rock clichés into an entertaining performance built on some extremely competent song writing (check out the exquisite 'Wait', for example) and the obvious talents of guitarist and main man Adrian Vandenberg. (Vandenberg, the man, may have gone on to bigger things with the 'hair metal' incarnation of Whitesnake, but personally I always felt it was a shame that he didn't manage to make it with his own band.)

Since then, the St David's Hall stage has been graced by many rock luminaries, including Deep Purple, Rainbow, Whitesnake, Metallica, Iron Maiden, Saxon, Dio, Thin Lizzy, Marillion, Gary Moore, UFO, Magnum, Queensrÿche and Rick Wakeman. Though Cardiff is better served in the current era, with a number of variously sized venues offering good gig opportunities, St David's Hall remains an important venue. In recent times I have been lucky enough to see Blackmore's Night, Gorky's Zygotic Mynci and modern day Thin Lizzy and Diamond Head line-ups perform there (as well as The Wiggles, the odd ballet, and several of my daughter's dancing shows). Other artists who have performed there include Jethro Tull, Foreigner, and Joe Satriani.

Back in 1982, the newly opened St David's Hall provided me and my friends with a new focus on Saturdays. Prior to the opening of 'The Hall', the regular Saturday trip to town generally involved a tour of the record shops (Spillers, Buffalo and Virgin at first, and then later the new HMV) to choose something to spend our meagre pocket money and hard-earned paper round pennies on, before we convened in Circles Restaurant in Howell's Department Store where we would examine our purchases in detail and talk about music. We had worked out that pots of tea in Circles came with additional jugs of hot water that could be refilled free of charge. This, effectively, gave us a base for the day – and on days where we had a lot to talk about we could make a pot of tea last for hours. Beyond that, we'd wander around town consuming pasties and big cream cakes at will, keeping an eye out for groups of attractive female rockers in the (usually vain) hope that they'd cast a glance in our direction. But, as I say, St David's Hall gave us a new focus, and we embarked on a mission to get to know the new building inside out, sensing that if we applied ourselves boldly, we would get our rewards on gig days.

St David's Hall itself has multiple levels, with a mix of escalators and stairs taking you up and down past restaurants, art exhibitions and a cafeteria. Being multi-tiered, the auditorium has numerous entry points. By chance we discovered early on that it was pretty easy to move between levels using 'unofficial' routes. This led to us making a concerted effort to explore further by brazenly walking through all unmarked doors and doors marked private just to see where they would take us. There were occasions when we were caught and sometimes this could lead to ejection. But we were not rowdy or unruly, and approached the matter rather strategically, which seemed to ensure that there were no consequences beyond ejection. We quickly acquired the knowledge we needed – namely how to sneak unnoticed into the auditorium for sound-checks and the like, and how to get into the stalls from higher up in the auditorium, if, for whatever reason we failed to acquire the tickets we wanted for a particular gig. We put this knowledge to use from time to time, but the opportunity to put it to really good use came with the announcement that Rainbow were to play a two-night stint there on 14 and 15 September 1983.

It was the excitement generated by the whole two-day period that made these gigs so special. Rock stars in the early 1980s didn't come much bigger than Ritchie Blackmore, the mysterious 'Man in Black' whose ground-breaking achievements with Deep Purple and then Rainbow in the 1970s, had been augmented by a recent string of chart hits that had won him, and his band, many new fans. Despite Rainbow's new commercial appeal, the man himself remained aloof and untouchable. I cannot begin to describe the thrill that some of us felt at the thought of being in the same general proximity as Ritchie, bassist Roger Glover and the rest of the band for that two-day period. Suddenly everything I loved and sensed about rock music seemed so real and nothing else seemed to matter. It felt like we were stepping out of our everyday lives into some kind of parallel rock universe.

Rainbow were touring on the back of their new *Bent Out of Shape* album. There was a general feeling that the album marked something of a return to form after the patchy *Difficult to Cure* and the follow-up *Straight Between the Eyes*. The latter was a more consistent album, but one which, for many, strayed too far into AOR territory. *Bent Out of Shape* seemed to get the balance just right. The opener 'Stranded', as well as 'Firedance' and 'Fool for the Night' were well-controlled yet meaty rockers. 'Street of Dreams', 'Can't Let You Go' and 'Desperate Heart' were top-notch slices of commercial hard rock that were performed with real feel. The album also featured two beautifully played instrumentals, 'Anybody There' and 'Snowman', both of which showcased Blackmore's mellower side to stunning effect. Blackmore sounded both masterful and relaxed. He had hit a groove, and in Joe Lynn Turner he had a singer who complemented his mood and tone perfectly. *Bent Out of Shape* may not be Rainbow's best album (it's let down by the inclusion of a couple of more run-of-the-mill rockers) but it does contain some of their best moments, and certainly there was enough here to suggest that gig-wise we were in for a treat.

On the day of the first gig, a group of us left school at lunchtime and headed straight to The Hall. With practised ease, we managed to sneak into the auditorium. We casually strolled up the aisle and sat down quietly just a few rows from the front. Up on the stage the roadies were working hard to build the set, which was already looking great. Small ripples of excitement shot through me. Just in front of us, another roadie sat twiddling with one of Blackmore's guitars. He nodded, said hello, and carried on with his job, trying to suppress a look of amusement. He'd seen it all before. We sat watching quietly, until after just a few minutes, Gareth's excitement got the better of him. He was the biggest Blackmore fan of us all.

"Ritchie!" he shouted at the top of his voice, "Ritchie, where are you?"

The guitar-tuning roadie looked at us again and laughed.

"You guys are gonna get your asses kicked," he said matter-of-factly in a soft American accent.

Two minutes later we were being escorted out by security men. Though the rest of us realised that the game was up as soon as Gareth had opened his mouth, Gareth himself was less inclined to leave and required more forceful eviction.

"Ritchie! Ritchie!" he continued to squeal as he was literally dragged out by his collar.

"What school do you guys go to?" asked the Head of Security as they finally got us all out. "Lady Mary," said Brendan with surprising pride and conviction.

"What did you tell him that for?" asked Gareth crossly. Brendan had come along for the ride; he wasn't even going to the gig.

"Well, how could I say anything else," he replied, unaware that he may have been overestimating the detective skills of our adversaries, "we're all wearing blazers with the school badge and name written on the front."

Despite this initial failure, the news that Rainbow would be holding a signing session in the HMV on Queen Street provided us with another chance, or so we thought, to meet Ritchie. We queued for ages in a state of heightened excitement, only to discover that Ritchie was not in attendance. However, Roger Glover, Joe Lynn Turner and David Rosenthal were, looking relaxed and happy as they chatted and signed autographs. I got them all to sign the front of my history file, asking them to sign "To Gary", which they all duly did. Gary was my history teacher. As well as being an excellent teacher and a fellow rock fan, he drummed for a local band called Vigilante, who we often went to see perform at venues like The Lion's Den (less exciting than the name sounds) and Bogey's Rock Club (*the* place for 1980s rockers to be seen).* Gary was friends with Steve Williams of Budgie, and used the drum kit previously owned by Williams that features on the back of Budgie's *Power Supply* album. He played the most amazing drum solos, which sometimes involved him leaving his stool mid-solo and drumming on whatever he could find around the stage. His headband and green satin shorts simply added to the entertainment value. We laughed, but we loved him for it. (Some friends and I once chanted his name right through a Pallas gig at Southampton University until the bass player stopped what he was doing, fixed on us intently and shouted "Who the fuck is Gary?")

---

* In terms of exposure, Vigilante probably reached their peak at around about this time, when Tommy Vance played a three-track demo on his BBC Radio 1 *Friday Rock Show*.

Anyway, for some reason I thought it would be amusing to get the various members of Rainbow to sign my history file in his honour. I still have that file now. "Hi Gary" wrote Roger Glover. And Joe Lynn Turner drew a little picture of a rainbow. I wondered if they'd have signed differently if they'd known that Gary was a history teacher in his late 30s rather than an impish 16 year old. Roger also signed my copy of Deep Purple's *Made in Japan* and my clear-vinyl limited edition of Rainbow's *Down to Earth* – instantly making them two of my most treasured possessions.

Though I queued with my friend Ray and others in conventional fashion, Gareth later recalled how some of our entourage, determined to get ahead of the competition, made their way down the litter-strewn alley behind the HMV in anticipation of greeting their idols when they arrived, as they surely would, at the back entrance to the shop. This was indeed the band's chosen entrance, though the subtlety of their 'back door' approach was somewhat undermined by the blazing headlights of their roaring BMW. Gareth, in particular, was delighted to be able to rub noses in such 'salubrious' surroundings with three-fifths of the band. With autographs duly requested and despatched, the band disappeared inside to prepare for the signing session proper, leaving Gareth and company babbling away like the over-excited schoolboys that, in fact, they were. Our punk friend Marv, who had no real interest in Rainbow, and, like Brendan before him, was simply along for the ride, was appalled at this overt display of hero-worship. Rooting through the alley's dirty giant bins, he emerged cheerfully with an empty condom packet. "To Rainbow love Marv", he wrote on it, and slipped it under the windscreen wiper of their flash car before fleeing the scene.

So what about the gigs themselves? Well, in keeping with the slick white stage set, Rainbow played impeccably and were classy and professional throughout. Blackmore directed the musicians like a magician, communicating his wishes with a series of subtle looks, nods and sleights of hand. I was impressed with Turner's 'live' voice and with the composure and contribution of new keyboard player Rosenthal. We had all heard stories of Blackmore storming off or refusing to play encores if he was unhappy with a gig or a crowd, but I'm pleased to report that no such moodiness was evident, and the band played encores both nights. Clearly the band themselves were happy with the shows, with recordings from the first night given a more general public airing. Commenting on the quality of Rainbow's live shows at the time, Blackmore's 'unofficial' biographer, Jerry Bloom, notes that: "Evidence of the band's tight performances was provided by the first of two nights at St David's Hall, Cardiff being recorded for US radio broadcast, with a couple of tracks released on the B-side to the 12-inch single of 'Can't Let You Go'.[4] Those tracks were 'Stranded' and 'All Night Long', and they were the first recordings I ever owned of tracks recorded at a gig at which I'd been present.

At the end of the second night's gig, three of us, Gareth, Pete and I, decided to hang around the backstage door for a while, intoxicated with the music but still a little disappointed that our attempts to outwit the St David's Hall security men and meet Ritchie Blackmore had come to nothing. Though I was resigned to failure and happy to go home, Gareth was contemplating one final effort. Meanwhile Pete was still smarting over the good fortune of his friend Mark. Like us, Mark had decided to go down to St David's Hall early on 'day one' to see what was going on. Unlike us, however, he decided to check out what was happening at the stage door and managed to get the gig of his life without really trying. Arriving by chance at around the same time as the local roadies, he was poking his nose around when he was mistaken for one of the hired hands, given a road crew pass and told to get to work. He worked hard for two days, but had quite an experience, and he got paid for it. We could see him at the side of the stage from our vantage point in the stalls – the lucky bastard. He even waved to us!

It was Gareth, however, who had the last laugh. We knew a kid in school whose father owned a hotel, and we knew from what he told us that there were only two or three out-of-town hotels where bands tended to stay. On finally returning home from the second gig, his hopes of meeting his idol apparently dashed, Gareth persuaded his brother Duncan, and Duncan's friend Quinny, to drive him to one of the hotels. With wonderful foresight, and considerable optimism, Gareth took with him not only his dog, Heidi, but his vinyl copy of *Green Bullfrog* – the legendary session album produced by Derek Lawrence. It had long been rumoured that Ritchie had played on the album, but for legal reasons the identity of the musicians remained hidden by cryptic pseudonyms and Blackmore had often denied involvement. At some point, however, Blackmore had told a guitar magazine: "That was me, Albert Lee and Jim Sullivan. Ian Paice and Roger Glover were on it and whoever else was around at the time . . ." and the record company had used the quote on the front cover of the 1980 American reissue (the version owned by Gareth).

As Gareth and co. loitered with intent near the hotel foyer, it soon became apparent, with the arrival of both Roger Glover and drummer Chuck

Burgi, that the choice of hotel was a good one. Gareth's decision to take the *Green Bullfrog* album with him quickly yielded fruit. While it's now well known that Blackmore *was* one of three notable guitarists involved in the project, it's also clear (from the sleeve notes to the 1991 Connoisseur CD release, for example) that Roger Glover had absolutely nothing to do with it. (Whether Blackmore was misremembering or citing Glover out of mischief is unknown.) Adamant that he had played no part in the *Green Bullfrog* sessions, Glover scrawled the following words across the front cover of Gareth's album: "I did not play on this album. Roger Glover".

It was Heidi, though, who really helped Gareth to strike gold. As her young masters made conversation with Glover and Burgi, she trotted non-chalantly into the hotel. Gareth saw his chance. "I have to find my dog," he told the doorman, "she'll only answer to me." It wasn't true, but it did the trick. He walked through the lobby and into the bar beyond, and there sat Ritchie Blackmore in post-gig reverie, stroking Heidi and chatting to the band's two female backing singers. Confronted with his idol, Gareth, in his own words, sort of shat himself. "Er hello Ritchie, can I have my dog back?" he managed to say, before nervously presenting Blackmore with his *Green Bullfrog* album, "Can you sign 'To Gareth'?" For the young man time stood still. Blackmore was notoriously moody. What would he do? Shout at him? Tell him to get out and leave him alone? Decline to sign and then ignore him? For Gareth there was so much at stake. A negative reaction from his hero would be crushing. But Blackmore did none of the above. Seemingly impressed that it was *Green Bullfrog* not *Machine Head* or *Down to Earth* or *Bent Out of Shape* that his young fan had proffered, he picked up a pen and started to sign, digging hard into the album sleeve and scraping into the card in an effort to get the ink flowing. There, alongside the words of bandmate Roger Glover, he wrote: "To Gareth, Ritchie Blackmore." The two shook hands and Gareth (with Heidi) ran away, desperate to cut and run while the going was still good and the memory was such a positive one.

ꞏ◉ꞏ *Damage Inc.* ꞏ◉ꞏ

Of course, you have to be a bit childish and a bit starstruck to indulge in the kind of antics I have described above, and, when St David's Hall first opened, my friends and I were both of these things. But these were simpler times, and, in my book, it's not unreasonable for children, even 15-year-old children to be 'a bit childish'. We were high-spirited and excitable, and our exertions were altogether healthier than some of the other things we could have been doing. Even so, it wasn't long before we came to feel ourselves a bit too 'mature' for such cat and mouse games – with our behaviour at the Rainbow gigs really driving the point home. Nevertheless, our early activities had led to the realisation that it was possible to sneak friends into gigs even if they didn't have tickets. In the early days of gigs at St David's Hall, ticket stubs were not removed until you entered the auditorium. This meant that if two people went in with their tickets, one could wait in the bar area while the other went back out with both tickets to bring a third person in. As people were free to move between bar and auditorium, a similar manoeuvre – with two people entering the auditorium and one of them bringing both tickets back out to the bar – was all that was required to get the third person in to the auditorium itself. As long as this was timed to coincide with the lights going down, a combination of the darkness, the fact that people tended to stand up, and the rush for the (admittedly limited) standing room at the front of the stalls made the 'ticketless' person virtually undetectable.

I must confess that even at the time I felt this was irresponsible and, in fact, I only remember using this trick twice. The first time was when we smuggled Pete in to see Thin Lizzy. He really wanted to go, but didn't have a ticket, and we were keen to give it a try, just to see if we could do it. It was March 1983. It was the *Thunder and Lightning* tour, Lizzy's last with Phil Lynott, and they opened with the storming 'Thunder and Lightning' itself. The sound, initially, was awful, and it took them two or three tracks to sort out the difficulties. We discussed this as we left the gig. "It was so bad I nearly got up and walked out in disgust," said Pete.

"But Pete, you were on a freebie," someone said, "you didn't even pay to get in."

"That just goes to show how bad it was," he grinned.

The second, and final, time I smuggled someone in was when I went to see Metallica on their *Master of Puppets* tour. It was 10 September 1986. Metallica had released the highly acclaimed *Master of Puppets* album earlier in the year and their tour had reached the UK. The quaintly named Anthrax provided support, and Metallica were joined by roadie John

Marshall who played rhythm guitar after singer and usual rhythm guitarist James Hetfield had broken his wrist in a skateboarding accident. I went to the gig with my anarcho-punk friend Marv, who himself promoted a lot of punk gigs and was very well connected with punk chums from across the UK. Metallica at the time were rather cutting edge. As the leading lights of the emerging 'thrash metal' movement they were a challenging band for your average British rock fan. They were faster and heavier and more aggressive than the NWOBHM bands who had themselves taken the heavier and more aggressive aspects of the big 1970s rock bands and pushed them to another level. Given their varied influences (including Deep Purple, the NWOBHM bands, Samhain and The Misfits), the themes of their songs, the rawness of their sound, and their presence on the independent Music For Nations record label, Metallica attracted a 'cross-over' audience of rockers and punks. A lot of the rockers were new-generation rockers, rather than the older fans of 1970s heavy rock, and tended to be at the younger, more energetic end of the gig-going spectrum. Metallica were one of the few bands that both Marv and I had some interest in.

I arranged to meet Marv outside the venue, and as I approached I noticed that he had someone with him I'd never seen before.

"Mike, this is Lee from Coventry. Can we get him in?"

I looked at Lee and nodded. He'd come all the way down just for the gig. How could I say no? "I s'pose so," I said, "we can give it a try anyway."

Lee smiled. And in we went.

"Marv, who's this Lee bloke?" I asked, as soon as I got the chance, "I don't really do this 'smuggling people in' thing anymore."

"Yeah, sorry about that. It was all very last minute. He promotes gigs like me. I told him we'd try to get him in. He's good as gold."

It turned out that he was, indeed, "as good as gold". Quiet chap, I thought, very inoffensive, no bother at all. The following year he joined Napalm Death, and two years after that he formed his own band – Cathedral. At some point Marv played me a Napalm Death album (*Scum*, I think). I couldn't imagine the polite bloke I'd met growling like that.

The gig itself turned out to be quite unforgettable, with the power and ferocity of the performance matched only by the infectious and unrestrained excitement of the crowd (with Marv and Lee leading the stage diving!). In his book *Justice For All: The Truth About Metallica*,

Joel McIver notes that the ten shows on the UK leg of the tour "were all chock-full of energy". McIver quotes Anthrax guitarist Scott Ian, who says: "the crowds were crazy and we really felt as if there was something happening." According to McIver: "Those who were there will recall [these shows] as the moment when the thrash metal wave revealed its true strength in Britain."[5]

Certainly nothing in my gig-going history could have prepared me for the intensity of the occasion. One local newspaper reported events thus:

HEAVY METAL FANS STORM STAGE

More than 30 young rock fans were thrown out of St David's Hall when trouble flared during a concert this week.

Seats were trampled on and security guards struggled with excited teenage fans during a mass rush onto the stage where cult heavy metal band Metallica were playing.

And leter (sic) *glasses were smashed and fans were being sick in the bar as security guards tried to calm the fans down.*

The fans, many as young as 14 and 15, were warned during the interval that if the stage was stormed againt (sic) *they would be thrown out.*

Dozens of teenagers ignored the warning and tried climbing onto the stage and were hauled off by extra security men draughted (sic) *into the main hall. More than 30 were thrown out during Wednesday night's concert.*

HEAVY

But general manager of St David's Hall, Mr Tony Woodcock, said the fans' behaviour did not mean an end to rock bands playing the venue.

"It was a pretty heavy night," he admitted. "But we feel it's very important to include bands like Metallica in our programme – we shouldn't have this sort of problem again."

He added that the amount of damage caused was still being assessed and that the promoters had accepted liability.

But he did not envisage similar problems with the imminent Motörhead and Iron Maiden concerts, he said.

"The crowd were very young and excitable and for some reason American groups tend to incite this sort of behaviour; the English bands like Motörhead and iron Maiden [sic] *tend to be more civilised."*

The management wer econsidering [sic] *the removal of the first five rows of seats in the hall and intended to deploy more security staff during rock concerts, he added.*

I was near the front of the stalls myself, and I recall very well the abundance of over-excitement that led to the newspaper report. Of all the gigs I've been to, there have only been a handful of occasions when I've seen a crowd in such a heightened state of arousal. Not that the band said or did anything to overtly encourage such excessive exuberance. The music and the power of the performance were sufficient and it really was something to behold. But there was no trouble as such. I don't believe that there was any intent whatsoever to cause damage – none that I witnessed anyway. The gig (and the crowd reaction) was a remarkable testament to the power of rock music. I was left in no doubt that Metallica were a band who were going places.

Tragically, while the band were clearly going places, Cardiff was one of the last stops for bass player Cliff Burton. The *Master of Puppets* tour was to be his last, with a freak tour bus accident in Sweden claiming his life just a couple of weeks later as the band made their way to Denmark for a gig in Copenhagen – another young talent who was taken too soon. Eerily, those of us who had purchased gig t-shirts were left with an item of clothing that showed a graveyard on the front, and a list of only partly completed tour dates on the back.

¡O¡ *Purpendicular* ¡O¡

When Deep Purple reformed in 1984 with the classic Blackmore–Gillan–Glover–Lord–Paice line-up, I was one of many who were extremely excited. Perhaps my expectations were unfairly high, but I have to confess that I was a little disappointed with the comeback album *Perfect Strangers*. There was nothing wrong with it, but, two tracks aside, 'Knocking at your Back Door' and 'Perfect Strangers' itself, it just didn't seem to measure up to the 1970s output. I decided against going to the Knebworth show in 1985, and thereafter deliberately avoided going to see Deep Purple live, disappointed at the predictable set lists, and slightly anxious that they'd under-perform and undermine the esteem in which I held them. I didn't want to see a band who were a shadow of their former selves, and

I heard nothing to convince me that anything other than this would be the case. I was not alone in thinking this way, as more and more people began voting with their feet and the band lost its way with both the music press and its record company. A legend was dying. I carried on buying the studio albums, however, and actually think that each album from that period offered something more than its predecessor. Others may disagree, but although it lacked a clear stand-out track, I felt that *The House of Blue Light* (1987) was a more consistent and coherent album than *Perfect Strangers*. *Slave and Masters* (1990), with Joe Lynn Turner replacing Ian Gillan on vocals, was a better album again, with stand-out tracks like 'King of Dreams' and 'Wicked Ways' suggesting that Purple were starting to find a place for themselves in the modern era. The problem with *Slaves and Masters*, though, was that it sounded more like a Rainbow album than a Deep Purple album, and with some members of the band dissatisfied with the musical direction, Blackmore for once was outvoted and Ian Gillan was invited back. Although recorded at a time of growing distance between Blackmore and the rest of the band, the next album, *The Battle Rages On* (1993) was perhaps the strongest of the three Blackmore/Gillan reunion albums, with the title track and 'Anya' providing the classics of the first, and tracks like 'Time to Kill', 'Ramshackle Man', 'A Twist in the Tail' and 'Nasty Piece of Work' the coherence and consistency of the second. The album also includes the wonderful but largely ignored 'Solitaire', one of the best songs from the entire reunion period. It was to be Blackmore's last studio album with the band.

With Blackmore gone, I suddenly felt more relaxed about going to see Deep Purple live. This wasn't the great Mark II line-up anymore, and, knowing that, my fear of watching a once great band undermine its legacy just seemed to fade away. Once Steve Morse signed up as a fully fledged member, Purple became a revitalised band with a new vibe and a new energy. My girlfriend of the time, Jo, convinced me to travel back to Cardiff from North-West Wales (where I was then living) to catch the band on their *Purpendicular* tour.

On the way down to the gig I picked up a copy of the new album, and against all expectations was blown away. To my mind *Purpendicular* was the first Purple album to *really* justify the reunion. That might seem a strange thing to say, given that Blackmore isn't on it, but for me *Purpendicular* has a joy and freshness about it that is conspicuously absent from some of the previous post-reunion albums. It sounds modern and alive, but at the same time it captures something of the looser and more experimental vibe of the early 1970s and of *Fireball*, possibly my favourite Purple album, in particular. Together, the opening four tracks, from 'Vavoom: Ted the Mechanic' to the immaculate 'Sometimes I Feel Like Screaming', are as good as *anything* Purple have *ever* recorded. 'Cascades: I'm Not Your Lover' keeps up the pace, and elsewhere the inclusion of tracks like 'The Aviator', 'Rosa's Cantina' and the more gentle 'A Touch Away' keeps things varied and interesting. At last Purple had freed themselves from the constraints of their glorious past, and having done that they could finally start living up to it.

And so, on 19 February 1996, I went to see Deep Purple for the first time, full of both anticipation and optimism. I had, of course, seen Glover before – with Rainbow. I had also seen Lord (Whitesnake) and Paice (Whitesnake and Gary Moore) play live. But this was the first time I had seen Gillan in the flesh, and it was the first time I'd seen this group of musicians perform together.

As it turned out, the gig was superb. As expected, the band drew heavily on its past, but this was no 'Purple by numbers' exercise, with their choice of tracks going far beyond the tired old set list they'd been lugging round for years. They opened, for example, with 'Fireball', and alongside tried and tested crowd pleasers like 'Black Night', 'Speed King' and 'Highway Star', they threw in 'Maybe I'm a Leo', 'Pictures of Home' (I think) and 'When a Blind Man Cries'. I had not expected to ever hear some of these tracks performed live; these were "now I can die happy" moments. The inclusion of 'Smoke on the Water' in the main set itself was a masterstroke, which left the running order and choice of encore unpredictable and helped maintain levels of crowd anticipation right to the end of the show. 'Smoke' also provided *the* moment of the gig, as Jon Lord used his solo spot to incorporate a rendition of 'Hen Wlad Fy Nhadau' ('Land of my Fathers'), the Welsh national anthem. It literally brought a tear to my eye as the audience picked up the tune and sang along. The bond between the new line-up and the audience was complete. Purple were back!

With Steve Morse on guitar, the whole band seemed relaxed and happy. Smiles and supportive gestures abounded. There was no hint in their performance of the kind of personal clashes and ego-problems that had reportedly plagued them for years. Indeed, the inclusion of no less than seven tracks from *Purpendicular* suggested that the band had plenty of confidence in both Morse and their new material. They were clearly enjoying themselves. Whatever others have said about the motives of the original reunion – and much has been written about that – this particular incarnation of the band were certainly not on a nostalgia trip or in it simply for the money. We were witnessing the creative rebirth of a rock giant.

¡◉¡ *"Robert the harp and the pricks"* ¡◉¡

In autumn 1994 an 'interesting career development opportunity' took me to North-West Wales, a stunning, peaceful and history-soaked part of the country. I lived there, first in a little village called Llanfairfechan, then in Bangor, then in the famously named Llanfairpwllgwyngyllgogerych-wyrndrobwllllantysiliogogogoch, then back in Bangor, until the summer of 2000. During my time in North Wales I became aware of a number of Welsh-language artists including Gorky's Zygotic Mynci, Super Furry Animals, Big Leaves, Topper and Catatonia. These were, after all, the days of 'Cool Cymru'! I was struck most, however, by two artists who seemed to me to be producing work of extraordinary and breathtaking beauty. The first was Siân James, a singer and harpist who both inter-preted traditional Welsh folk music and composed original material. I saw her play several times in Porthaethwy (Menai Bridge) with a backing band that included guitarist Tich Gwilym. When, in 2006, a rock guitar version of the Welsh national anthem was discovered on a 1970 demo tape by a band called the New Flames, there were those who thought that Jimi Hendrix might have been responsible. His version of the 'Star Span-gled Banner' is, of course, legendary, and he was known to have been friendly with New Flames bass player Viv Williams. Others, however, think it is far more likely to the work of Gwilym, who was well known in Wales for his rendition of the anthem.[*] His rock credentials also included work with Budgie's Burke Shelley in a group called the Superclarks. He certainly worked very well with Siân James, complementing and visibly complimenting her each time I saw them play together. My daughter's mother and I went to see Siân James while Alys was still in the womb. I remember her kicking very actively throughout the more uptempo songs from Siân's album 'Di-Gwsg' ('Sleepless'). Interestingly, after Alys had

---

[*] Unfortunately at the time the story was reported, January 2007, no one knew the whereabouts of Viv Williams. Tich Gwilym tragically died in a house fire in Cardiff in 2005.

been born the same songs played loudly would instantly calm her down. She would stop crying and stare in the direction of the speakers, listening intently, or so it seemed. It made nappy changing so much easier.

The other artists who made a great impression on me were Bob Delyn a'r Ebillion. The music of Bob Delyn a'r Ebillion is rooted in the Welsh folk tradition. Lyrically, too, inspiration comes from the traditional forms and imagery of Welsh life and Welsh poetry. The band is not a full-time professional outfit. It evolved from the street-busking experiences of some of the group members. They are more like a group of wandering minstrels bound by their love not only of music but of their land, its language and its culture. As singer, lyricist and harpist Twm Morys told writer Kate Crockett: "I don't see us ever splitting up. We are very good friends, like brothers really. It's more than just playing music."[6]

Twm himself is a very interesting character. Beyond the band, he is a published and respected poet – penning words that work both on the page and in performance. In the introduction to *The Bloodaxe Book of Modern Welsh Poetry: 20th Century Welsh-Language Poetry in Translation*, one of the editors, John Rowlands, notes the recent rise of performance poetry in Wales. He says: "Groups of itinerant poets (usually accompanied by musicians) have toured Wales and beyond to entertain a usually youngish audience in pubs or other popular venues. The most prominent of these troubadours is perhaps Twm Morys, who sings to his own harp accompaniment under the name of Bob Delyn (a pun on Bob Dylan, but of course 'telyn' in Welsh means a harp)."[7]

Earthy and unpretentious as he is, in Twm's hands the line between 'popular' lyrics and 'high-brow' poetry becomes very blurred. Indeed, versions of several lyrics from Bob Delyn songs appear in his poetry volume *Ofn fy Het* (*Fear of my Hat*): for example 'Y Teithiwr' ('The Traveller'), 'Y Clerwr Ola'' (The Last Minstrel') and 'Mil Harddarch Wyt' ('You Are a Thousand Times More Beautiful'). I've also seen the lyrics to 'Y Swn' ('The Sound') used in a poetry essay to demonstrate the strict rhyming patterns of the famous Welsh poetic form Cynghanedd.

As John Rowlands suggests, the name *Bob Delyn a'r Ebillion* itself gives you some idea of the playful linguistic tendencies and idiosyncratic world view of Twm Morys. 'Bob' could be from 'Pob' meaning 'all'. 'Delyn' is the mutated form of 'telyn', the Welsh word for harp. The word 'Ebillion' could mean 'drill bits', with 'Ebillion' being the plural of 'Ebill'. As well as being a great pun on the name Bob Dylan, I'd taken the name to mean something like 'All Harps and Drillbits'. When asked by Kate Crockett where the name came from, Twm Morys said: "I don't know, to tell you the truth, I don't remember! 'Ebill' means a lot of things – the peg which holds a harp string, a quarryman's chisel, and it can also mean a man's sexual organ . . . *Robert the Harp and the Pricks* is our name in English!"[8]

It is a measure of the man's outlook and integrity that Twm refused permission for translated versions of his poems to be included in the Bloodaxe Book, "adamantly regard[ing] translation as an aberration".[9] Thankfully, though, he has published some work in English, and to illustrate both the lyrical and sometimes mischievous feel of his work, I offer the following extracts from his poem 'The Unbearable Politeness of Being':

> *"Gee, who's busy on my buzzer?" – says she.*
> *I say: "It's me, the raunchy rancher."*
> *Door opens. This male stripper, – in base clef,*
> *says: "I'm Geoff, her chef and her chauffeur.*
> *Come in, We're having dinner . . ." – So I go,*
> *and I'm hero of some dumb horror . . .*
>
> *Chuck, her husband, much crisper – now he's food,*
> *and she lewd and nude as an adder,*
> *a terrific fat reefer – in one hand,*
> *the other hand, all tanned and tender,*
> *digging with a dagger, – holding high*
> *his eye like some sky on a skewer.*[10]

The content isn't typical of Bob Delyn songs. There *are* some quirky and playful songs, but at their best and most earnest Bob Delyn a'r Ebillion paint pictures of love and beauty, fragile things, joy and sadness, and a way of life that modern living often overlooks. We are not talking folk niceties here. Creatively, theirs is a world of hard-edged angst and artistic wonder. Musically, they are not prolific, with quality rather than quantity the order of the day. Those interested might want to check out *Sgwarnogod Bach Bob* (1990), *Gedon*, (1992), *Gwbade Bach Cochlyd* (1996), and *Dore* (2003) – all of which are produced by Gorwel Owen, who is also known for his production work with Super Furry Animals and Gorky's Zygotic Mynci.

This, then, is the band I went to see at Clwb y Felin in the North Wales village of Y Felinheli, halfway between Bangor and Caernarfon, sometime in the late 1990s. It was a small rugby club type venue. I was there early enough to watch the band arrive, set up and soundcheck. Guitarist Gorwel Roberts whet my appetite playing snippets of the Blue Öyster Cult classic 'Don't Fear the Reaper'.

This was home turf for the band, and slowly but surely the small venue filled up until it was packed to the rafters with an audience that was one of the most passionate of which I've ever been part. I'd guess there were around 300 people there, including TV presenters, local celebrities, and what seemed like half the cast of long-running Welsh soap opera *Pobl y Cwm* (*People of the Valley*). This was clearly an occasion to be savoured. The Welsh television channel S4C were filming, though mainly for a feature on support band the Strymdingars. The Strymdingars were not bad actually, turning in a decent enough cover of Lynyrd Skynyrd's 'Sweet Home Alabama', (with 'Alabama' changed to 'Felinheli' to please the North Walian audience), and playing a number of tracks from their debut album *Strymgynta'* (*First Strum*).

When Bob Delyn finally performed it was to an audience that was not only hot, sweaty and full of anticipation, but drunk on both the beer and the atmosphere. From start to finish I was struck by the quality of the music and the audience reaction. It's quite amazing that such a wonderful group can remain so obscure – though, of course, while music can transcend linguistic barriers, choosing to sing in Welsh obviously makes them a less attractive commercial entity to record companies and imposes significant limits on the size of their audience. One can only admire a band who, in full awareness of this, choose their own language and culture over the lure of the pound.

But what made this gig so memorable, and the reason I'm telling you about it now, was the performance of one song in particular and the effect it had on those present. The song concerned, 'Deuit Ta Bugale', is from the 1996 album *Gwbade Bach Cochlyd* (*Little Red Faces*) and is sung in Lly-daweg (Breton) – the native tongue of the band's female vocalist Nolwenn Korbel. I've no idea what the lyrics mean, though the title is translated as 'Come, Then, Children'. The rather cryptic sleeve note – "dance my sweet little things" – perhaps offers some sense of the song's intent.

With Twm crouched over his harp, a picture of concentration, the band, led by sax player Edwin Humphries, built an esoteric swirl that was beautifully conducted by Nolwenn's haunting vocals. Occasionally the musicians paused for the singer to deliver the chorus line (*Deuit 'ta bugale, deuit 'ta war an aod/Ha ni no plijadur plijadour plijadur*), which she did with striking nursery rhyme sweetness. Chorus over, the band picked up the theme with renewed vigour. With the track in full flow, a girl appeared on the stage, seemingly liberated from the heat and crush of the front row. She was followed by another, and then another. The first girl waved a small Welsh flag, but suddenly stopped and looked startled, like a rabbit caught in headlights. With knowing calm, Nolwenn took her hand, and led her dancing around the stage as the sound of the musicians grew and grew, and the music swirled and swirled until it was all-enveloping. The girl's friends followed as Nolwenn started to lead a kind of spiral dance of the sort more commonly associated with Pagan rituals. Others too spilt on to the stage and joined in. The impromptu formation weaved its way snake-like around the unflinching musicians. All were drawn to and lost in the music. The band had created a hypnotic Pied Piper-like effect and induced an utterly compelling trance-like state that felt timeless: a perfect moment that one would will again and again for all of eternity.

◉ *Robert Plant and Alison Krauss: Raising Sand* ◉

On 8 May 2008, my then-girlfriend (now wife) Chrissy and I went to see Robert Plant and Alison Krauss at Cardiff International Arena. Plant and Krauss were promoting their critically acclaimed album *Raising Sand* – an earthy collection of unique covers and interpretations of traditional songs. They were joined on tour by album producer T-Bone Burnett, a musical giant in his own right who had even played with Dylan on the Rolling Thunder Revue. Like the album, the gig was a wonderful mix of styles, spanning country, folk, blues and rock. It was an unbelievable show, full of delightful performances from top-notch musicians who treated each other, and the material, with a kind of reverence and respect that was simply awe-inspiring.

From a personal perspective, I was overjoyed with the inclusion of a few Zeppelin classics that I never thought I'd hear live. We were treated to a kind of high-volume slow swing version of 'Black Dog', an excellent version of 'Black Country Woman' (one of my favourite

tracks from *Physical Graffiti*), and a full-blooded version of 'The
Battle of Evermore'. Even if Led Zeppelin reformed for a full tour I
wouldn't have expected to hear this last song, with Sandy Denny's
vocals such an integral part of the original. It did occur to me briefly
that they might play it when, earlier in the show, the band segued into
the Fairport Convention classic 'Matty Groves', but I put the thought to
the back of my mind, telling myself not to get carried away. But play
it they did, with Alison Krauss turning in an immaculate performance.
The on-stage vibe, the power of the band, the superb lighting, and the
passion and delivery of both singers updated the song for the current
millennium without destroying any of the mystique of the original. It
was a performance that surpassed my wildest expectations. I could tell
that Chrissy too was getting excited. After 'Black Dog', she turned to me
in a highly flappable state, foregoing her usual grammatical precision to
exclaim: "That is the best thing I've ever heard ever!"

To draw too much attention to individual songs, however, would be to
miss the significance of this gig. These great performers gave it their all,
and, through their choice of material, they placed themselves in a great
musical tradition in which, ultimately, it is the music, not the careers,
status, wealth or persona of those presenting it, that matters. This was
music as it was meant to be – as living folk-art; as a vehicle to convey
experience and wisdom and joy and sadness; as a medium which is greater
and more enduring than the individuals who create within it.

The musicians clearly enjoyed themselves. Everything they did was
done well, and everything just seemed right. Perhaps more obviously than
at any other gig I have seen, the sheer joy of the music shone through
and transcended individual egos. Plant, a rock god, indeed *the* rock god
in some people's eyes, appeared frequently as humble backing singer, or
was visible at the side of the stage grooving along to the performances of
his fellow musicians. Throughout he remained modest and enthusiastic,
looking as excited and intoxicated by the fruits of the collaboration as
most of the audience.

¡O¡ *This One Sacred Hour* ¡O¡

I hope that in what I have presented above, I have managed to convey to
the reader something of the nature and value of the live gig experience. I

have, of course, left out many gigs that could, for one reason or another, have been included: the warmth of Marillion's Farewell to '83 tour gig at Birmingham Odeon; my first live Bob Dylan experience (which features elsewhere in this book); the 1985 Monsters of Rock Festival when, for the first time, I was part of a large crowd drawn from across the UK; Deep Purple's faultless performance at the revived Monsters of Rock festival in 2006; and Iron Maiden's triumphant 2008 Twickenham concert. But really, it doesn't matter who the band is or what the occasion is. If I've done my job well, you will recognise some of the experiences I have described in your own gig experiences. This, in itself, is testimony to the power of music to provide common and shared experiences which enrich our lives and bring us together in ways that our everyday jobs, politicians, and the promises of mass consumerism evidently can't.

While there are plenty of songs which in some way celebrate the live music experience, aspects of the special nature of the rock gig – as I have understood and felt it – are well captured by the band Magnum in their track 'Sacred Hour'. 'Sacred Hour' first appeared on 1982's *Chase the Dragon*, which, in the wake of the New Wave of British Heavy Metal, is probably the heaviest album in Magnum's back catalogue. Nevertheless, to call *Chase the Dragon* a 'heavy metal' album in the current era would be ludicrous. It has power and vocal passion, and its fair share of driving rhythms and lead breaks, but it's also choc-full of gorgeous melodies which are perfectly framed by Tony Clarkin's guitar and superbly embellished by the keyboard playing of Mark Stanway – the ultra cool 'flash rocking man' who was making his Magnum album recording debut.

'Sacred Hour' is a wonderful celebration of the rock gig, albeit from a performer's perspective. "We'd like to dedicate this song to everyone in the audience tonight," singer Bob Catley tells the crowd at the start of a live version included on the 2005 'expanded edition' of *Chase the Dragon*, "for this is the one sacred hour that we all spend together."

Thereafter, Stanway's layered synth/organ intro sets the tone, building an atmosphere of both splendour and reverence. The organ gives way to a gentler piano piece which re-iterates the theme and ushers in Catley:

> *All of my dreams that fell through*
> *And had tasted so sour*
> *Take second place in my mind*
> *For this one sacred hour*

Lyrically the singer strives to mesh co-existing feelings of excitement and vulnerability. Musically the whole band show their support, putting down a powerful marker before yielding again to Catley and Stanway:

Face through the clouds in the gods
Shine with awe and splendour
Rise up and roar they approve
Will they always remember

The vocal delivery, the awkward grammar and the lack of punctuation leave the reference to 'the gods' ambiguous. Is Catley simply referring to the faces of those at the back of the hall on the balcony? Or is this a nod to some unspecified feeling that what is taking place is so special that it must, somehow, be divinely ordained? Either way, the singer seeks and finds the approval of those present. Supported by some trademark Magnum backing vocals, he reports a moment of magic and tells us how much it means to him:

I hear the voice of the crowd
It will last forever
Locked in my heart
Kept away like a stolen treasure

The band crashes back in, this time for good – picking up the vibe and running with it as the track gathers momentum. And yet, at what should be the very moment of triumph, the singer introduces a sense of doubt that recurs three times before the song ends:

I can hear them calling
Hear the crowd applauding
If it's real I like the feeling
If I'm wrong who am I deceiving?

Stanway provides the bridge to the next verse, with prodded notes that betray a strong pomp rock influence. For about three seconds one could be forgiven for anticipating a segue into the operatic section of 'Bohemian Rhapsody'. Is this brief tip of the hat to the great Queen track part of the band's self-doubt? If so, it's quickly put to the back of the mind as Catley reassures himself, and us, that the experience he is recounting is recreated each time the band play:

Night after night
It repeats an exciting romance
Shared by us all
Though we met by a fleeting half chance

What were the chances of this happening? What fortune has brought these musicians and these music fans together at this time? And it happens again, and again, and again. Musically the pace grows to a gallop as the band use everything they know to drive the point home. They are the lords of this new church, and together we lose ourselves in the noise and the beauty of the moment. Knowing that for that short period of time everyone in the hall, including the band, is feeling the same, is a special experience indeed – and yet it's an experience that is so difficult to recreate in everyday life.

Caught
Trapped in time
No escape from this powerful dream world
Pleased though I am to be here
I am lost in the real world

The contrast drawn between the "dream world" of the gig and the "real world" is striking. We all knew that we were stepping outside our regular lives, but surely this experience *is* real and not part of some "dream world"? Yes, the experience is real, but in the context of our wider lives it appears fleeting and fragile. And hence the recurrent doubt. How can something so fleeting and fragile have so much meaning for so many people? And how can we capture and hold onto its magic so that it stays in our lives? In a sense it's the band's job to inhabit the gig-world and to do their best to recreate this experience "night after night". And yet, in a sense, their chosen vocation alienates them from the struggles the rest of us have – we only get to share in these moments occasionally.

And so there you have it – the joy, the wonder and the fragility of the live gig experience wrapped up in a five and a half minute nutshell. For the duration of the gig all else is forgotten. Nothing else matters as we lock into the music and feel a sense of togetherness with both band and the rest of the crowd. And yet the short-lived nature of the gig makes it difficult to hold on to its meaning and memory once it's over.

4

Truly, Madly, Deeply

There is, of course, more to rock music and rock fandom than the communal experience that is the live gig. A gig might sometimes be a special, almost spiritual experience. It might make you feel good. It might take you out of yourself and help you to forget your day-to-day worries for a while. But however good an experience it is, it is usually built on something that exists outside of itself – namely music that is composed and recorded away from the live setting. While gig goers come together to hear, enjoy and celebrate music in its most raw and powerful form, their love and understanding of the music usually starts elsewhere. Typically it starts in their bedroom, or living room, at friends' houses, youth clubs and rock clubs, or perhaps, these days, with a computer and an iPod. It starts with someone taking the time to listen to, and bond with, the recorded output of artists and bands they come to cherish. Indeed, for all I have said about the value and power of live music, I have never seen Led Zeppelin, the Doors, Aerosmith, the Scorpions, Kate Bush, Tori Amos, Geoff Mann or Twelfth Night performing in the flesh – and these are some of the artists and bands who, for one reason or another, mean most to me.

❤ *Made in Japan* ❤

So, how did it all begin for me? Well, my love of rock music developed slowly and unexpectedly – there was no 'history in the family' as they say

– not much of one, anyway – and it took a long time for the early seeds to grow and take root. It began, actually, with a group whose own family tree is, in the words of singer Ian Gillan, not so much a tree as a jungle. It began with Deep Purple.

The first time I heard the name Deep Purple was at my Nana Rees's house. Nana Rees is my maternal grandmother. My Mum's older sister, Aunty Kath, had divorced when she was still quite young, and she and her four children had moved in with my Nana and Grandad. My cousin Andrew is the oldest of Kath's children and is six years older than me. On one particular occasion, I remember Andrew and his friend Jeff shutting themselves away in my Nan's front room, making it clear that they were not to be disturbed. The sound of raucous music and frantic movement vibrated through the house soon after. Through a gap in the sliding doors that separated the front and back rooms, I was able to catch a glimpse of the action – Andrew and Jeff engaging in some weird kind of dance ritual. The dance involved a lot of jumping around and head shaking. Both young men moved with arms extended as though playing imaginary instruments, their lips gloriously and rather humorously pouted. That they'd attempted to ensure that their 'dancing' took place behind closed doors added a kind of mystique and made me even more curious. What forbidden fruits were these? Is this what all grown-up boys did?

I don't recall my age with any certainty, but I would guess that this was 1976 or 1977 and that I was nine or ten. I do recall, however, sneaking into the front room later on, when Andrew and Jeff had gone out, and, with almost trembling fingers, thumbing through Andrew's retrospectively rather modest record collection. Wings, 10cc, the Eagles, Focus, more Eagles . . . and then I came across it, in all its electrifying glory, the album Andrew and Jeff had been dancing to: Deep Purple, *Made in Japan*.

Largely gold with stylised black lettering, heavily laminated and smooth to the touch, it was a classy looking album. Single rectangular photos on both front and back cover showed the band performing live. On the front cover the band look so into it, so lost in their own music. The back cover gives an indication of how exciting Purple gigs must have been at that time, with no distance at all between the audience and the stage. Singer Ian Gillan dances around looking cool and clean cut, like a young rock and roll Richard Beckinsale (Godber from *Porridge* and father of Kate) – a strong image that made an instant impression on me.[*]

Inside the gatefold sleeve the 'Made in Japan' theme is developed, with red and orange artwork providing a simple representation of the land of the rising sun. Photos of the individual band members appear in the segments between the sun's rays, the colouring creating a kind of aura and imbuing the musicians with almost super-human qualities. On the left-hand side, guitarist Ritchie Blackmore, crouches almost god-like over Jon Lord's expression of pained ecstasy and Roger Glover's 'rock and roll cowboy'. On the right, we are treated to portraits of an absorbed Ian Paice and an intense, screaming Ian Gillan. Another band shot reinforces the physical closeness of band and audience giving a sense of 'chaotic intimacy'.

I read the track listing. For a young Neil Diamond fan, as I was at the time, it was astonishing: two records, four sides, and just seven – yes, seven – songs. How could this be? I didn't dare play it to find out (thinking instead I'd best put it back and get out of the room before Andrew returns.) But I guess I experienced the kind of thrill that young teenage boys feel when they first find themselves alone with a 'men's magazine' (or, without giving too many secrets away, a copy of their Mum's Kay's catalogue). I didn't' know it then, but I'd just had what was probably one of my most formative experiences.

I didn't think about *Made in Japan* again for some time. I finished primary school, a private Catholic school called De La Salle that was run by an order of brothers – and moved on to St Illtyd's, a comprehensive school run by the same order of brothers. Punk had hit the mainstream. My early memories of high school are of the Sex Pistols, Jilted John, Blondie and Ian Dury and the Blockheads. I also remember the smell of the local chip shop at lunchtime, football practice on the red-gra, Monday night gym club, learning about primary colours in art and learning about the difference between vertebrates and invertebrates in science. I remember a guy in my class called Paul who was the slowest but neatest writer I

---

[*] Until recently I had always assumed that the cover photos were taken at the gigs at which *Made in Japan* was recorded. However, according to Simon Robinson of the Deep Purple Appreciation Society, the front cover shot was taken at a special reopening gig for the Rainbow Theatre in London earlier that year, while the back cover shot was probably taken on Purple's September 1972 UK tour. I am very grateful to Simon for this information.

have ever seen, and I remember an obnoxious twerp with big ears called 'Flapper Evans' whose 'party piece' was to run up to people he thought he could beat-up (including me) and assault their testicles with a well-placed toe-poke. Despite performing well academically, I didn't really settle at St Illtyd's. It was two bus journeys to school, and two back again in the evening, and I hated the long days. I started to feign stomach aches and my mother, on the doctor's advice ("Good God, woman! You're asking this child to put in more hours each day than a fully grown man!"), set about moving me to a new school.

My new school, Lady Mary, was still about five miles and a slow bus journey away, but at least it was just one bus. What's more, I was back among friends I hadn't seen for six years or so from my first primary school – the rather grandly named Our Lady Queen of the Universe. (My mother moved me from there to De La Salle when the headmaster told her that I was disruptive and would be better off in a school for 'educationally sub-normal' children.) Those who remembered me greeted my arrival with some excitement. It felt like a sort of homecoming, and I enjoyed the brief celebrity status that being the new boy conferred on me.

In Form 2 (Year 8 in modern parlance) I became friends with a talented and dedicated swimmer with Commonwealth Games ambitions. With his olive skin, tight-knit curls and athletic figure, Eamonn was one of the more 'advanced' boys in our year. He stood out from the crowd, and revelled in his own self-image. His out-of-school life as a swimmer allowed him to mix with boys several years older than us, and gave him access to the knowledge we all craved about important things like the coolest music, the rudest jokes – and girls. He was older than his years, 12 going on 18, a would-be Greek God. And I was, well, just 12 and very, very small. But for a while, just a year or so, we were inseparable. It was Eamonn who really introduced me to rock music and the great rock tradition that had been temporarily obscured by the media attention that punk had demanded and received. He introduced me to Tommy Vance's *Friday Rock Show*, to the weekly rock newspaper *Sounds*, and to the record shop in Whitchurch Village where I bought my first Black Sabbath album. And he went to gigs too! I remember going to school the morning after Eamonn had been to see Rainbow on their *Down to Earth* tour. He'd made a point of getting in early and had ensconced himself in his chair (at the back of the class, of course) with a brightly coloured Rainbow scarf wrapped around his neck and a copy of the tour programme on his desk. He looked like the cat who'd got the cream, and talked about the night before as though he'd just had his first sexual experience. He was a huge Rainbow fan at the time.

"Rainbow is Ritchie Blackmore's band," he explained to me, when one of the singles from *Down to Earth* hit the charts. "You know, Mike, the guitarist from Deep Purple." Deep Purple? A little light went on.

"Er, yeah, my cousin likes them," I said, trying to sound both knowing and casual. I made a mental note to ask Andrew if I could borrow his album.

It took me ages to get around to approaching Andrew. If truth be told I was in awe of him a little, and I was terrified that he'd say no – which would have been a bit like him saying: "What? Lend it to you? You've got to be joking, you're just a kid." But in the end I plucked up the courage and he agreed to let me have it – though not before giving me instructions on how to look after it, and telling me in no uncertain terms what would happen to me if I gave it back to him damaged. And so it was. Three years or so after I'd first set eyes on it, *Made in Japan* was in my trembling hands again. I couldn't wait to play it. And once I started to play it, I just couldn't stop. I like to think that my grounding in what the internet tells me is 'early' and 'middle phase' Neil Diamond had taught me a thing or two about music. I could appreciate a melody and a good lyric, for example, and live versions of tracks like 'Crunchy Granola Suite' and 'Cherry Cherry', studio workouts like 'Lament in D Minor/Dance of the Sabres' and Diamond's excellent cover of Joni Mitchell's 'Free Man in Paris', had introduced me to the idea of instrumentation that works outside the constraints of your average three-minute pop song. More than that, being able to compare the exceptional *Hot August Night* (still one of my top three live albums) with studio versions of the same tracks made me aware that it's possible to change the pace of a song live, or embellish it in some other way, to great creative effect. But *Made in Japan*, this was something completely different – I simply didn't know that music like this existed. 'Highway Star', 'Child in Time', 'Smoke on the Water', 'The Mule', 'Strange Kind of Woman', 'Lazy', 'Space Truckin'. Night after night for about a fortnight, I rushed home from school dying to hear these songs again. There was only one record player in the house, and in fact only one living room in the house, but I'd lie on the floor next to the stereo for hours pushing my ears close enough to the speakers to drown out the sound of the television at the other end of the room, waiting for a chance to claim the space for myself and turn up the volume.

Even now, nearly 40 years after its release, *Made in Japan* positively crackles with energy and bristles with excitement. Whatever personal tensions might have been emerging within the band, however tired and in need of a break they were, *Made in Japan* showcases a band at the top of its game. There's power, there's subtlety, there's improvisation. The band is tight enough to keep every track together, but loose enough for the album to feel almost experimental in places, with every track providing opportunities for an extended workout. Every single one of the musicians makes a stunning individual contribution, but it's the interplay and group identity that reigns supreme. Recorded over three nights in Osaka (15/16) and Tokyo (17) in August 1972, the album captures thrilling performances from start to finish.

'Highway Star' gets the motor ticking over, its gentle organ intro giving sufficient encouragement for the bass and drums to slip us into gear. Blackmore arrives in style, and the band run through a frenetic version that accelerates away and leaves you gasping for breath. The soloing is fantastic. Lord and Blackmore run up and down the scales (electric) at breakneck pace, taking sharp bends effortlessly – speed kings both. "Oh my soul," moans Gillan between instrumental passages, as though the skill and dexterity of his colleagues is almost too much for him. It's a great way to start a show.

Lord's reverential organ then gently eases us into 'Child in Time' – a powerful piece built on a thoughtful lyric that Gillan sings superbly. In his autobiography, *Child in Time: The Life Story of the Singer from Deep Purple*, Gillan presents the lyric thus:

> *Sweet child*
> *In time you'll see the line*
> *The line that's drawn between*
> *Good and bad*
> *See the blind man*
> *Shooting at the World*
> *Bullets flying*
> *Taking toll*
> *If you've been bad*
> *And I bet you have*
> *And you've not been hit*
> *By flying lead*
> *You'd better close your eyes*

You'd better bow your head
Wait for the ricochet

In performance, however, there is an ambiguity in the way the first two lines are sung which echoes the title of the song and adds a touch of 'existential angst' to proceedings. "Sweet child in time," sings Gillan, "you'll see the line." The shift in presentation shows the child not as the recipient of patronising instruction, but as a traveller in time, a sweet, innocent and vulnerable young person at the start of a journey. The child also has a kind of innate, if undeveloped, wisdom. It is the *child* who comes to see "the line that's drawn between the good and the bad" and who watches "the blind *man* shooting at the world" (emphasis added). Indeed, the way I hear it, the vision of the child is *contrasted* with the 'blindness' of the adult whose "bullets" (real or metaphorical) cause harm to everyone who is unlucky enough to stray into the firing line.

The suggestion seems to be that while we all retain some of the innocence, purity and vision of the child, as adults we can easily lose sight of what is right and how we should live. As we struggle with life and become self-absorbed, we all fire metaphorical bullets. No one can claim innocence. No one is exempt. Nobody's perfect. And we all go wrong so often, we can hardly expect not to have to face the consequences of our actions at some point, even if, thus far, we've been lucky. If you've been bad, like the rest of us, and you haven't paid for your indiscretions yet, you'd better kneel and pray. And "wait for the ricochet."

That, at any rate, is what the song says to me – and the performance captured on *Made in Japan* takes the basic lyric and gives it an extraordinary metaphysical significance. Gillan, in particular, delivers a stunning performance that might just be the greatest rock vocal you're ever likely to hear – and I don't say that glibly. Having sung the verse beautifully, Gillan bares his soul, at first whimpering sadly like a lost child. But the 'oohs' quickly become 'ahs' and then 'arghs' and then full-blooded screams which get higher and increasingly gut-wrenching as the child's sadness becomes the adult's torment. A Paice-led bridge yields to Lord's Hammond organ as the band give the vocalist's torments full musical expression. In steps Blackmore, cool as you like, to drive the track into a long instrumental section which gets faster and faster and increasingly chaotic. On the surface all hell appears to be breaking loose. And yet, if you listen, you realise that Paice and Glover are always in control, and beneath the madness Jon Lord plays some unfeasibly cool, almost jazzy chords. But Blackmore is insistent. He cranks things up to 11 before the whole crazy cacophony grinds to a complete halt. After the briefest of pauses, Lord reintroduces the theme, and Gillan steps us for a vocal reprise. This time the bullets don't just euphemistically 'take toll': they "kill". As the song builds to its noisy climax, Gillan mutters away angrily like a man losing it in the confessional box or a man on the edge of insanity. I'd love to know what he is saying. His performance expresses perfectly, intentionally or otherwise, inner turmoil, and the personal struggle of the individual to be good, to be at peace with himself and to be at peace with the world around him. (It's not hard to see what attracted Tim Rice and Andrew Lloyd-Webber, and why Gillan was asked to sing the part of Jesus on the original cast recording of *Jesus Christ Superstar*.) But the lyric itself offers no easy way out and no resolution – as travellers in time we are thrown back on our own resources, our own experience, and our own sense of good and evil. No one can live our lives for us. We must make our own way. At the end the crowd sound stunned. Indeed, it audibly takes a few seconds for them to catch their breath before bursting into rapturous applause.

The reward for those regaining composure and flipping over the disc is a lively version of 'Smoke on the Water', with Gillan's introduction explaining the track's origins. This was before 'Smoke' had become the well-known and overplayed classic it is today, and the band play it like they mean it. Blackmore's meandering riff at the start of the track and his trade-off with Lord towards the end add a touch of improvisation, and Gillan sings the first line of the chorus half a beat later than on the *Machine Head* version. It's easy these days to forget just how good a track this is, but if you want to remind yourself, dig out this version and try to listen with fresh ears.

'The Mule' features another interesting lyric, and a lengthy Ian Paice drum solo. The single verse leads to a strange din that is reminiscent of the Doors at their most jarring – so much so, in fact, that the start of Paice's solo almost provides some relief. Everything louder than everything else indeed! Personally, I'm one of those who believe that drum solos are generally boring at gigs – give me an extra song (or two) any day. But as drum solos go, this one has got legs. It draws some infectious audience participation and holds interest throughout, before reintroducing the band (minus Ian Gillan) for a powerful but tense finale. There will be many who prefer the *Fireball* version – and, if push comes to shove, I might be one of them – but the live version works here.

With everyone having played themselves into form, Side Three contains two extremely strong all-round band performances. 'Strange Kind of Woman' is an excellent inclusion in the set, particularly as it was omitted from the UK version of the studio album *Fireball*. It is notable here for the extraordinary guitar/vocal interplay as Gillan and Blackmore trade licks. The singer imitates the guitarist so well at times that you have to really listen closely to work out who is who. And Gillan's trademark scream at the end of the track is simply breathtaking.

The high-tempo blues romp 'Lazy' has always been one of my favourite Purple tracks and is here introduced by Lord with a unusual and apparently random chord sequence that puts one in mind of the 1970s electronic game Simon. He teases the crowd with a snippet of 'Louie, Louie' before easing into the main riff. Blackmore noodles his way in and takes on the theme. Once the main riff is established, the band are off and running. The lengthy instrumental section at the start allows them to stretch out, before Gillan finally 'gets out of bed' just in time to deliver the lyric and contribute some fine harmonica embellishments. Some unexpected tomfoolery from Blackmore draws an enthusiastic crowd response, before the band milk some old blues clichés to bring the track to a rousing conclusion.

The main set is brought to an end by a lengthy version of 'Space Truckin'', which takes up the whole of Side Four. Whereas the studio version would have wrapped up at around the five-minute mark, Paice's galloping drums drive us into an extended interpretation that I can only describe as 'progressive space rock'. For those who like this sort of thing, the improvised feel of the music creates a sense of excitement that is simply a joy. Nine and a half minutes in, Lord grinds out a snippet from Holst's *The Planets* (from Jupiter: the Bringer of Jollity), while Blackmore is back in at around 13 minutes for a quiet solo that references his work in the underrated and sadly neglected 'Fools' from the *Fireball* album. Purple were to push the boundaries of the track even further on later tours, but weighing in at around 19 minutes, the *Made in Japan* version provides plenty of scope for experimentation, and allows the band to bring proceedings to a suitably frazzled end.

The 1998 CD remaster of *Made in Japan* includes a bonus disc of encores. 'Black Night' apart, the encores are a little ragged in comparison with the tracks on the original release, but their inclusion does, at least, give the album a more balanced and rounded feel – recreating the experience, as the best live albums do, of a complete gig. Taken as a whole, the performance captures a sense of excitement, spontaneity and 'danger' even, that only the very best bands can generate.

Despite later replacing Gillan and Glover with David Coverdale and Glenn Hughes, Purple maintained the style and quality of their live performances throughout Blackmore's 1970s tenure. That this is so is evident from the companion *Made in Europe* album, recorded during Blackmore's last European tour with the band, and the Purple Records release *Live in Paris 1975: La Dernière Séance*, which captures Blackmore's very last show in its entirety. Just listen, for example, to the start of *Made in Europe*. As Blackmore's 'preparatory noodling' subsides, David Coverdale calmly announces "rock'n'roll", and the mighty riff of 'Burn' explodes through your speakers. It never fails to send shivers down my spine.

☺ *Purple and Zeppelin* ☺

"Who's the greatest heavy rock band ever?" my friend Harvey once asked me. I thought for a while and, not without reservation, answered "Deep Purple".

"Nah. It's Led Zeppelin," Harvey grinned back, "people who say Deep Purple always have to think about it first. Zeppelin fans know that it's Zeppelin. Purple were always a bit too arty for my liking, but Zeppelin just get you. Man, no one plays the blues like Led Zeppelin."

I think Harvey had a point or two. I recognise, for example, the power of Led Zeppelin and the *sensual* pull of the band. I recognise too that while Zeppelin are a very direct and hard-hitting band, Purple have a more varied and arty approach that *does* give pause for thought. When you answer "Led Zeppelin" to Harvey's question you are shooting from the hip. When you answer "Deep Purple" you must first draw the disparate elements together, with the cerebral exercise required inevitably introducing a hint of hesitation. It should be said that Led Zeppelin were always very good at creating a mystique around themselves that has been preserved over the years by the clever management and marketing of their image and their back catalogue. It's not that the history of Deep Purple is without incident or intrigue – think, for example, of the sad and senseless path travelled by the late Tommy Bolin – but it is surely true that Purple's reputation was built on music alone and was not augmented by the dark and demonic associations and tales of general decadence that seemed to follow Led Zeppelin around. I am not suggesting that Led Zeppelin lacked substance in any way, but they certainly knew how to package and present themselves to maximise their impact. By simply letting their music do the talking, Purple failed to capitalise on the kind of image and product management that would have made it easier for them to preserve their own status and reputation. How often I've wished that the band had been able to prevent the release of all of those pointless post-reunion compilations, and how often I've wished that I could remove 'Smoke on the Water' or 'Black Night' from all those crappy rock compilation albums you find in the supermarket bargain-bins.

Of course, Deep Purple have sometimes been their own worst enemies. While Zeppelin maintained the same line-up throughout their entire recording career, in-fighting and seemingly frequent changes in personnel have not helped Purple's cause. Having said that, as far as Purple line-up changes go, the reality is somewhat different to the perception. In over 40 years of their recording history, only 13 musicians have appeared on Deep Purple studio albums. Of these, five have appeared on 11 or more of the 18 studio albums Deep Purple had released at the time of writing, with the other eight musicians making appearances on just four albums or less. Ian Paice has appeared on all 18, Jon Lord on 16, Blackmore on 13, Glover on 12 and Gillan on 11. Of the remainder Steve Morse's tenure now stretches well beyond a decade (and four albums), while Don Airey's inclusion has ensured continuing stability and was negotiated with Jon Lord's blessing. (Indeed, could anyone else possibly have replaced Jon Lord?) Tommy Bolin's involvement was for one album only, an aberration that bucked the pattern in the 1960s and 1970s of Purple sometimes changing singer and bass player but maintaining the Blackmore, Lord and Paice triumvirate. Similarly, Joe Lynn Turner's one album contribution provides the only example in the entire Purple back catalogue where one of the Evans–Simper, Coverdale–Hughes, Gillan–Glover partnerships was broken. In short, contrary to the 'musical chairs' perception, there has always been a sufficiently stable core of musicians and a strong enough evolutionary thread to preserve both the integrity and identity of the band. Nevertheless, as I said above, changes have not always helped – with the consolidation and growth of the Morse years showing clearly the value of stability (in both band line-up and personal relationships).

Now, I don't want to get drawn into a divisive Purple versus Zeppelin debate. To my mind they are both great bands who should be treasured and respected by us all. I do, however, want to say a little more about Deep Purple because it seems to me that while Zeppelin's position in rock history is assured, and even Black Sabbath's flailing reputation has been restored, Purple do not get the credit and recognition they deserve.

Most people, for example, will recall that Kula Shaker's version of 'Hush' brought that song to a wide audience in the 1990s. It is not unusual, in fact, to hear 'Hush' sampled these days for TV commercials, with the Mk I Purple version featuring on the most recent adverts that I've seen. But how many people realise that they are listening to Deep Purple? And how many people realise that it was Deep Purple who first brought this Joe South song to a worldwide audience of hungry rock fans?

It almost goes without saying that the impact of the Mk II line-up on the early 1970s rock scene was immense. The bludgeoning power of *In Rock* (1970), the experimentation of *Fireball* (1971) and the classy rock perfection of *Machine Head* (1972), rightly established Purple as one of the greats. If they'd recorded nothing else after, these three albums alone would represent a phenomenal achievement, and a legacy of which the band could be justifiably proud. When you add the bold *Concerto for Group and Orchestra* (1970), the astonishing *Made in Japan* (1972) and the often (unfairly) overlooked *Who Do We Think We Are* (1973) to that list, you can't help but feel a sense of awe. But how many modern day music fans realise just how popular Deep Purple were? Indeed, the exertions of the Mk II line-up made Purple the biggest-selling album band in the United States in 1973, with the band outselling even Led Zeppelin and the Rolling Stones.

I know of no other 'mainstream' rock band (with the possible exception of Queen) that has blended rock with such a range of musical styles with such stunning creative success. Check out the back catalogue and you'll see, for example, the strength of the classical influences from the very start. Listen to 'Anthem' from *The Book of Taliesyn* (1969) or the forgotten gem 'April' from the third album *Deep Purple* (1969), both of which pre-date the *Concerto for Group and Orchestra* and the *Gemini Suite* (the latter of which was performed by Purple in September 1970). Though Purple moved away from such overt classical–rock fusion, Lord and Blackmore's knowledge of classical music often informed both their soloing and the interplay between them, as evident, for example, on the title track of *Burn* (1974) and the 1984 reunion album *Perfect Strangers*. Jon Lord's interest in classical music is also much in evidence on his solo releases, from the more immediate and accessible *Sarabande* (1976) and 'Bach onto this' (from 1982's *Before I Forget*) to the fully fledged classical exertions of later albums like *Pictured Within* (1998), *Beyond the Notes* (2004), the *Durham Concerto* (2007), *The Boom of the Tingling Strings* (2008) and *To Notice Such Things* (2010). Outside of Purple, Blackmore's own classical interests found expression in some of his Rainbow-era musings, including 'Difficult to Cure' and 'Anybody There'. A guitar player I met once told me that a lot of the time Blackmore's playing is based around arpeggios. "That's not uncommon, is it?" I asked. I lacked technical understanding but had read about the then-current fashion for 'Bach 'n' Roll', and the playing of people like Yngwie Malmsteen. "No, it's not uncommon," he replied, "but the thing about Blackmore is that you don't realise they are arpeggios or what he's really playing until you try to learn the songs."

Those who know Deep Purple only through greatest hits collections might easily fail to recognise the strong blues influence on Purple's output. In the sleeve notes to the reissue of *The Green Bullfrog Sessions*, producer Derek Lawrence says: "nobody knows or understands just how good a Blues player Ritchie really is."[1] Well, there's plenty of evidence in Purple's back catalogue. From the early mayhem of 'Wring that Neck' (from *The Book of Taliesyn*), to *Machine Head*'s 'Lazy', to 'Place in Line' (from *Who Do We Think We Are*), to the rich blues rock of *Burn* and 'Mistreated' in particular, the blues feature heavily in Purple's history, spanning all line-ups. Blackmore even incorporated a piece called 'Blues' into some of the Mk III performances, later recording it on the Rainbow *On Stage* album.

People often credit David Coverdale and Glenn Hughes with bringing a strong funk and soul influence to Deep Purple, and indeed these influences *are* evident on *Burn* (to some extent) and on *Stormbringer* (1974) in particular. Purple are arguably at their most soulful on tracks like 'Holy Man', and at their most funky on tracks like 'Hold On' and 'You Can't Do It Right'. (Tommy Bolin also plays some pretty funky stuff on the *Come Taste the Band* album – check out the wonderful 'Gettin' Tighter' for example.) Journalists at *Classic Rock* magazine have adopted the moniker that the KLF coined for Glenn Hughes during their 1992 collaboration and call him 'the Voice of Rock'. In our house, though, we call him 'the voice of Stevie Wonder' – which I guess gives you some indication of the contribution he made to Deep Purple! But I have to say that if Ian Gillan wasn't a soul singer exactly, he could certainly be soulful when he wanted. Check out the exquisite 'When a Blind Man Cries' or the quieter sections of 'Child in Time' that I've described above. The new approach brought by Coverdale and Hughes was undoubtedly a departure, but it wasn't *quite* as radical a change as is sometimes supposed. There is no doubt, for example, that Hughes gave the funk element more explicit expression and developed it further, but in truth it was there all along, barely disguised in MK II tracks like 'No One Came' and 'Never Before'. Indeed, it seems to me no accident that Hughes and Coverdale were recruited. Like good chefs who know their herbs, Purple created a new flavour simply by changing the *balance* of their ingredients. Blackmore, Lord and Paice clearly knew which way they wanted the band to go – even if Blackmore did later come to feel that he had lost control a little. (And Lord and Paice certainly seemed happy to give expression to funk and R'n'B influences in their post-Purple collaboration with Tony Ashton.)

Beyond Purple most of the band's musicians have taken creative turns that are further testimony to the talent and musicality of this unique band. Ian Gillan went on to dabble in jazz-rock fusion with IGB (the Ian Gillan Band), before shortening the name and the length of the songs and unleashing the madcap and colourful Gillan on the world. Blackmore, of course, went on to further critical and commercial acclaim with Rainbow, and, post-reunion-split, has reinvented himself as some kind of renaissance-folk-inspired minstrel with Blackmore's Night. And David Coverdale produced a couple of fine solo albums before first Lord and then Paice joined him alongside bassist Neil Murray and guitarists Bernie Marsden and Mickey Moody in the early heavy rhythm and blues version of Whitesnake.

It's well worth reminding ourselves just how popular Purple and the 'splinter bands' were around the time of the New Wave of British Heavy Metal, and of the esteem in which they were held by some of the bands who emerged around that time or soon after. Saxon, for example, name-check Purple on 'Play it Loud' from the *Denim and Leather* album, while Iron Maiden and Metallica (Metallica's Lars Ulrich anyway) made no secret of their admiration for Purple's achievements. Even now it is not unusual for contemporary musicians to acknowledge their debt. In the credits to their excellent 2005 album *Second Life Syndrome*, for example, Michal Lapaj of Polish prog-metal band Riverside gives "a big bow to Jon Lord for all my keyboard playing".

And, of course, it's not over yet. Purple are still out there and doing it, releasing the occasional album, undertaking world tours and playing to decent sized crowds everywhere. They even headlined the re-launched Monsters of Rock Festival at the Milton Keynes Bowl in 2006. If I have a criticism at all it is that they *still* appear to rely too heavily on *Machine Head* for much of the live set, choosing to ignore some superb material from more recent albums like *Purpendicular* and *Rapture of the Deep*.

For me it is the breadth of the music and the willingness to experiment across styles and genres that makes Deep Purple (its musicians and its splinter groups) so special. On that note, if I had to pick one Purple-related album from within the 'family jungle' to illustrate this breadth, that album might well be Roger Glover's soundtrack to Alan Aldridge's beautifully illustrated children's book *The Butterfly Ball and the Grasshopper's Feast*. Not so much because it's the best – though it is a great listen – but simply because it's choc-full of surprises from start to finish. Listen to Glenn Hughes' wonderfully soulful and uplifting vocal on 'Get Ready', or Coverdale's richly crooned warning on 'Behind the Smile' ("Behind the smile the stranger lies/Beware of what is in his eyes"), or the quality of bass player Glover's songwriting and composition across an astonishing range of musical styles. A supporting cast of guest musicians make this a real treat – and who could resist the thought of Ronnie James Dio playing and singing the part of a frog on the otherworldly 'Sitting in a Dream' and the Beatles-like 'Love is All'.

☺ Who do we think we are? ☺

Having discovered such wonderful music, realising that there were others who felt the same as me was one of the most important moments of my school career. Slowly a loose cluster of friends emerged, bound together by a love of rock music. This shared interest instantly gave us something in common that seemed to override and render insignificant the differences between us. It wasn't a tight-knit group – we all had other friends and interests – but our shared musical taste provided a sense of identity, belonging and security.

I say 'shared musical taste', though in reality this oversimplifies and understates matters to some degree. What we had was an overlapping, criss-crossing family-resemblance-type pattern of musical taste. Deep Purple, and the Deep Purple splinter groups, offered a relatively common thread within this web of preferences, but there was variety, and this variety was important. Our individual preferences became personal statements and gave us all separate identities within the group. What we undoubtedly shared was the same *kind* of interest in rock music, and this had a significant bearing on the form that at least some aspects of our social lives took. Listening to, talking about and sharing music was a real joy. The overlap in our taste gave us common ground. The differences in our taste gave us things to talk about and enabled us to help shape each other's 'musical identity'. We spent a lot of time hanging around record shops, going to each other's houses to listen to music, planning trips to gigs, swapping albums, and sharing the latest news.

My earliest 'rock buddy' was Eamonn, the swimmer, though it wasn't long before he drifted off (breast stroke, I think) and went his own way. His big band was Rainbow, though he was also the first to introduce me to Led Zeppelin, UFO, Sammy Hagar, Foreigner, Styx and Dire Straits.

From the age of 13 I was quite good friends with Gareth, aka 'Peach'. Gareth was great fun, and our friendship peaked during our O-Level years (when we were roughly aged 14–16) when we sat next to each other in English and had an ongoing hair-growing competition. Unfortunately we were separated by our Form 5 (Year 11) English teacher (it still riles me), who felt that our preference for a more 'interactive' style of learning was too disruptive for others. You will have gathered from earlier references that Gareth was a huge Deep Purple and Ritchie Blackmore fan. He was also a big fan of Queen, as were his whole family, though he showed a clear preference for their rockier material. It was said that when Queen released their disco-funk influenced *Hot Space* album, the whole household went into mourning – though I distinctly recall Gareth's mother counselling and encouraging him to try to appreciate the band's openness to exploring different musical directions. Gareth was, in fact, a very musical chap. He played the piano and liked to dabble a bit with other instruments. He had two brothers and a sister and his Mum was always very welcoming. There always seemed to be lots going on at Gareth's house.

Another friend, who I strongly associate with Gareth, was an extremely jolly and genuine chap called John. His good heart and openness to others often left him vulnerable to a bit of leg-pulling, but he was also great fun. John was a big Deep Purple, Whitesnake and Iron Maiden fan. He once broke his ankle on a school skiing trip, and we managed to get Iron Maiden to sign his plaster cast. (He is the same John who was 'caught' throwing his chip wrapper away after the Saxon gig in Bristol.)

Other good friends at the time included Ray and Pete. Pete had a very straightforward interest in Deep Purple and the splinter bands (Rainbow, Gillan and Whitesnake), while Ray had rather more idiosyncratic tastes. He was more into Rainbow than Purple, and liked an interesting spread of artists including Tank, Meatloaf, Nazareth, Dio, Elton John, Kansas, Jethro Tull, Pallas and Marillion. I saw my first Marillion gig with Ray – at Birmingham Odeon on the Farewell to '83 tour.

Ray and I became very good friends, particularly after he'd left school, and at that stage we hooked up with Fog. Fog had been part of the scene in the early days, but left our school early during Form 3 (Year 9). He re-emerged a couple of years later and we became pretty tight. His taste was perhaps the most contemporary and varied of us all, with a strong focus on bands like Iron Maiden, Motörhead, Budgie, Judas Priest, Thin Lizzy, IQ and Twelfth Night. He later went on to develop an interest in the 'indie' and 'psycho-billy' scene, with bands like The Damned, King Kurt, Demented Are Go, and the Psychedelic Furs featuring among his favourites.

At its extremities Fog's taste may well have had points of contact with Marv's. Marv, who I've also mentioned in earlier sections, was an 'anarcho-punk' whose taste was uncompromising and generally (Metallica, Kate Bush and Twelfth Night aside) far removed from my own. But he knew a lot about the rock scene and always had something interesting to say about it. As with Ray and Fog, Marv and I became very good friends towards the end of our school days and maintained the friendship well into our adult years.

The picture of the early group would not be complete without reference to Richard and Duncan, older brothers of Fog and Gareth respectively. Richard, actually, became quite a good friend for a while. I went to several notable gigs with him, including Saxon in Bristol, Ozzy Osbourne in Birmingham, and Marillion in Southampton (when he put me up in his university digs). Richard had extremely broad taste which, in addition to rock music, took in jazz, blues and reggae. Duncan I knew a bit less well, though I always found him friendly and knowledgeable. I remember him turning up late and unexpectedly for a Michael Schenker Group gig. Gareth had decided he had too much revision to do to come – but he gave Duncan his ticket, and a message to pass on to me. Over the din of the support band, Duncan stepped closer and shouted in my ear: "Gareth says 'Diphtheria'." It was an odd message – in fact to this day I still don't know what he meant. The memory always puts me in mind of a *Just William* story I read as a young boy, when, having misunderstood a discussion he overheard, young William Brown attempted to convince his teacher that the reason he failed to turn up for school was that he had been suffering from leprosy. I could imagine Gareth doing that.

As for my own tastes, like Gareth, John and Pete, I was keen to the point of obsession on Deep Purple, Rainbow, and the other Purple splinter groups. I soon discovered Black Sabbath, and of all the NWOBHM bands I was most fond of Saxon. I was also much taken with the first Michael Schenker Group album, and, as I listened more, I became a big fan of Michael Schenker himself. I found myself strongly attracted to his image. Indeed, from the tousled 'little boy lost' staring out from the cover of UFO's *Obsession*, to the spikey haired figure crouched over his trademark Flying V circa *One Night at Budokan*, to my mind there are few more iconic heavy rock guitarists. And he certainly has the 'tales of rock'n'roll' to prove it. How much more rock 'n' roll can you get than cutting off your famous blond locks and leaving them behind as you disappear without a trace? And how many guitarists can say that they have turned down opportunities to join both Aerosmith and the Rolling Stones? In terms of his playing, his most gorgeous and fluid melodies are truly sublime. At his best he is simply dazzling. He stirs the soul and takes you as close to the Platonic Form of beauty as a heavy rock guitarist possibly can. In lesser hands, the so-called 'Baroque and Roll' of the 1980s sounded contrived to the point of being tacky. In Schenker's hands even cameos such as 'Bijou Pleasurette' (from the first MSG album) are more 'priceless treasure' than 'minor pleasure'. And who can forget the moment he cuts loose on the live (*Strangers in the Night*) version of the UFO classic 'Love to Love'? This outpouring of pure emotion against a backdrop of melancholic order remains, for me, one of heavy rock's finest moments. Gareth was somewhat perturbed by the increasing prominence I gave to Michael Schenker, but I stick by my assessment of the aesthetic appeal of his playing and urge anyone unfamiliar with his work to explore further.

Through this small network of friends I was able to build my knowledge of rock music and the 'rock heritage' we had acquired. Rock music became interwoven with almost every part of my life and became increasingly important to me. There were times when it did seem that my enthusiasm was pushing me just a little too far. During my days as a promising young cricketer,* for example, I remember making my way to the crease to try to bat for 20 overs with Rainbow's 'Long Live Rock 'n' Roll' whirling around my head. Even at the age of 18, I remember going into an A-level exam with Marillion's *Misplaced Childhood* album hindering my ability to concentrate. These days I would be described as a bit of an 'anorak' for the form that my early interest in rock music took. I developed a habit of trying to systematically listen to all the albums I owned once every month, giving each song marks out of 10 and ranking albums in order of preference. I also started keeping a list of gigs I'd been to, listing not just the names of the bands, but the band line-up, the support band, and the names of the friends I went with. I maintained this particular practice between November 1980 and February 1984. I know this because I discovered the list in a box of stuff that my father recently retrieved from his attic.

For the most part I was able to integrate music with my other interests (mainly sport related) and my school work. Music was almost always a help and never *really* got in the way of anything. Neither, at this time, did I limit my friendships to those who shared my taste in music. As I noted above, we all had friends and interests beyond our little group. Eddie is a good example of this.

◉ The Man in the White Coat ◉

Eddie was a funny guy – always joking, always fidgeting, always 'chops-ing'. It was Eddie who told me that "every house has its porno mags", setting me off on a fruitless search of my Dad's bedroom for the magazines that 'belonged' to our house. He was also the only person I knew who seemed to have no trouble admitting that he had measured the length of his penis with a ruler. His apparent comfort with such frank admissions

---

* For most of my early and mid-teens I attended 'Glamorgan Colts' nets and was coached by Tom Cartwright, a distinguished first class bowler who, in his prime, had represented England.

perhaps gives you some idea of the type of character he was. In school, he was well known as the class joker. I was not in his maths class, but one incident simply demands to be reported 'for the record'. He was always flirting, or at least trying to flirt, with the (relatively) young teacher who had developed a reputation – probably entirely undeserved – for 'getting off with' sixth-form boys. For Eddie, and others, this was a turn-on, and, to his mind, it made her fair game.

"Has anyone got a ruler?" she asked one day.

"Hey miss, you can borrow my 12 inches," shouted Eddie, turning around and grinning at the rest of the class.

"Eddie, you've got a mouth like the Mersey Tunnel," said the teacher, exasperated.

"Yes miss, and we all know what you've got like the Mersey Tunnel."

Not for the first time in his school career, Eddie's speed of thought and sense of appropriateness were out of sync. Those present say that even before he'd finished his sentence he knew he'd gone too far.

Eddie lived near Gareth, and although he wasn't into rock music, he was good friends with most of the people I knew who were. Gareth and the other kids from the area often enjoyed making a nuisance of themselves on the nearby private golf-course. They'd hide in the bushes until the golfers had sent their balls down the fairway and then nip out and nick the balls, giving the angry but helpless golfers a wave as they ran off. Eddie, for all of his daytime bravado and success in avoiding 'the tractor man' (the course maintenance man who fought a noble but losing battle against the wit and will of the troublesome teenagers) always refused to mess around on the golf-course at night. He had heard that there had been a gruesome and unsolved murder at some point in the past, and the story, whether true or not, had really freaked him out. Gareth and others were constantly encouraging him to try to overcome his reluctance and Eddie was slowly coming around to the idea. One summer's evening when I happened to be staying at Gareth's house, Gareth and I made a particular effort to convince Eddie that he ought to confront his irrational fear. "Come with us tonight," we said, "we'll go when it's dusk so it won't even be fully dark." Somehow the persuasion worked. I guess Eddie didn't want to be known as a coward. And perhaps my presence – as I wasn't one of the usual crowd – made some difference. And so, as the sun went down, and night started to descend, the three of us set off down the road heading for the golf-course. We walked through the entrance, past a small outhouse and some trees and bushes, and were just about to step out onto the course itself when Gareth suddenly stopped dead.

"Mike, did you hear that?" he said, pulling my arm.

"No, I didn't hear anything."

"There is it again. Listen."

The bushes behind us started to rustle, first quietly, then louder. As we turned towards the source of the sound and stared into the gathering darkness, we could just about make out a moving shape. Within seconds we were confronted with a terrifying sight as a lumbering madman emerged and lurched towards us. We could now see that he was wearing a long white, blood-stained butcher's coat and brandishing a large meat cleaver. His head was covered with a brown paper bag with holes cut out for eyes. It was Eddie's worst nightmare!

"Shit!" we cried. "Run for it!"

But Eddie was already gone. He was off like a shot, haring onto the course and across the fairway for all he was worth. No one was timing his run, but I swear that if they had been a few world records would have been under threat. Gareth and I tried to keep up with him, but Eddie was way ahead and didn't look back once. In the end Gareth and I were laughing so much we had to give up running. The man in the white coat was our friend John. The coat and meat cleaver came from Gareth's brother Duncan who 'borrowed' them from the local butcher's shop where he had a part-time job. It was Duncan too who was making the rustling noises and who pushed John out at the right moment. The peep-holes in the brown paper bag turned out to be pretty useless – apparently John couldn't see anything and had no idea whether he was even pointing in the right direction.

Gareth and I walked back to his house. John and Duncan were already there. There was no sign of Eddie. Despite his haste and fleetness of foot he got back about 20 minutes after us. I have visions of him just keeping on running, Forest Gump style, until his fear subsided and his anxiety levels returned to normal. In keeping with the culture of the house, Gareth and Duncan decided to write a song about it. I felt honoured to be part of the burst of musical creativity that produced 'The Man in the White Coat'. I helped with the lyrics, of course, but as I couldn't, and still can't, play a musical instrument with any proficiency I was allocated the drums – and spent a joyful hour tapping away on the back of one of the old acoustic

guitars that was lying around. Gareth complimented my drumming actually, which was a nice confidence boost after the disastrous guitar lesson
he had given me some time earlier: "I'm not being funny Mike," he had
said, as I butchered the riff to 'Smoke on the Water' for the umpteenth
time, "but you know you said you were a quick learner . . ."

☺ It's all in the jeans (and t-shirt) ☺

I liked the simplicity of the rocker's attire – jeans, t-shirt, trainers and
denim or leather jacket. This was a practical and all-purpose everyday
look. It was easily and cheaply available, and it provided a marked
contrast to the effort required by more fashionable looks. It was an
unpretentious way of dressing that made it easy for anyone to gain
acceptability. In this sense it was a great leveller, making personal
substance more important than appearance at a time when, for many
of my peers, image was everything. Of course, the rock 'uniform' was
still, in its way, an image, but it was one with which I was comfortable. I
imagined that my appearance said: "I like heavy rock. I don't like discos
and I don't like dressing up to impress people. What you see is what you
get." In the early 1980s, British rockers, at least, tended to be a pretty
grounded bunch – and that suited me just fine.

Band and gig t-shirts were a common feature of the 'rock look'.
Not only did they provide interesting talking points, but, whether you
were from Cardiff or Carlisle, Birmingham or Bangor, Swansea or
the Shetland Isles, they were a convenient and fairly reliable way of
identifying potential friends. One of the most significant friendships I
formed in this way was with a girl called Siwan, a Welsh speaker from
Caernarfon. Along with my school chum Brendan, and a girl in our
school year called Sarah, I had been selected to represent the school
at an all-Wales sixth-form conference entitled: '1984: Appearance or
Reality'. The event ran for the best part of a week in Coleg Harlech
in Gwynedd, North Wales. Sixth formers from schools across Wales
attended what was, quite genuinely, a 'meeting of minds'. The organisers
had put together a very stimulating lecture and seminar programme
based around the themes of George Orwell's great novel *1984*. We were
invited to compare our perceptions of our own society with the grim
and soul-destroying totalitarian society depicted by Orwell. As is the

norm at these kinds of events, the best talking and thinking was done outside of formal lectures – in the local pub and in study bedrooms, when, in self-selected groups of new friends, we raged into the night. I remember animated exchanges with an Indian lad called Chanchal from Ammanford, a spiritualist called Barclay from the South Wales Valleys (who later got a job with Barclays Bank), and a likeable comic called Max. But most of all, I remember Siwan.

Siwan had, in fact, picked me out on our first night there having spotted my heavy rock t-shirt. She put the word around that she was looking for the boy in the Saxon top. When we met we talked first about music, and then about where we were from, and then about all sorts of social and philosophical issues. We agreed to stay in touch after the conference. We sent each other music tapes, and she sent me a single earring, the matching one of which she claimed was owned by Fish, then lead singer with Marillion. We continued to write to each other for the next two and a half years, by which time she was training to be a nurse, and had taken a number of lifestyle decisions that were rather too conventionally decadent for my liking. Her musical taste also underwent a speedy transformation when she got a new boyfriend who introduced her to a band called Spear of Destiny. I imagine that by then I had become rather too intense a writing partner for her. In fact, I imagine that my letters would have been rather too intense for almost anyone! I still have all her letters in a box in my attic, which is a good indication of how important her friendship was to me for a while. Bizarrely, I also have a copy of some extracts from the last letter I ever sent her. I hadn't intended it to be the last letter, but it contained material sufficiently weighty for me to feel the need to 'preserve' some of it in an old notebook. In it, I spoke of a forthcoming new start for me at Swansea University following a frustrating couple of years and a disappointing one-term spell at Southampton University. I set out my hopes for Swansea and commented on the natural beauty of the area. I hoped that I'd find the course, the people and the city more to my liking than Southampton and concluded: "If all else fails, at least I can talk to the sea." I didn't mean this in any dark way. I meant only that a second university disappointment might undermine my feelings of kinship with others and result in a relatively hermitic lifestyle in which I'd take more pleasure in nature than people. Moody teenagers tend to be melodramatic like that. In fact, I was initially rather pleased with the 'poetic' way in which I'd made the point. However, having sent the letter, it did play on my mind that she might have thought I was contemplating walking into the sea 'to end it all'. I somehow sensed that the heaviness of the letter and the weight of responsibility I'd placed on her to respond might have been too much for her. She didn't reply. I didn't chase a reply. And I never had any direct contact with her again.

I did have some indirect contact with her though. During my first year at Swansea – which in the event went very well – I became acquainted with a bloke called Dave who shared accommodation with two good friends of mine – a guitar-playing geologist called John (Johnny 'Cardboard') and a flame-haired (for 'flame' read 'orange') marine biologist and drummer called Joe. While enjoying an end of year pint with the gang at a pub called The Inn on the Lake, Dave happened to mention that he had got a summer job as a porter in Ysbyty Gwynedd, the main NHS hospital in North-West Wales (the hospital, in fact, where my daughter Alys would be born some years later). Although I hadn't heard from Siwan for nine months or so, I recalled that this was where she was doing her nursing course. As Dave was from Wrexham in North-East Wales and didn't know anyone in Gwynedd, I gave him Siwan's address and suggested that he look her up and give her my regards. This, I reasoned, would be a gentle way of showing her that I was fine and all was well. And so we all went away for the summer, reconvening at The Inn on the Lake three months later to compare notes on our holiday adventures. As it turned out, Dave had given Siwan more than just my regards.

"Oh, Mike, I looked that girl Siwan up. She'd moved address but I tracked her down."

"Oh yeah? How is she?"

"Yeah, OK. She's alright, isn't she? I slept with her but she told me not to tell you."

Of course I only have his word for it that that's what happened, but at the time I felt like I'd just watched a spoilt child trample lilies underfoot.

"Cheers, Dave."

☻ Men of Harlech ☻

My week in Harlech was significant for two other reasons. First, let me tell you about the strangest and possibly scariest experience I have ever had. Harlech is a small, pretty remote town on the north-west coast of

Wales. It is dominated by an imposing and foreboding castle built in the late thirteenth century by English monarch King Edward I to keep a watchful eye over Snowdonia. Harlech also has a wonderful beach, which I particularly recommend at sunrise on a clear spring morning. From almost anywhere in the town you can look across the bay towards Criccieth and the Lleyn Peninsula. It really is an area of outstanding beauty. Harlech is also known through the work of the Fifth Baron of Harlech, David Ormsby-Gore, who established and gave his name to Harlech Television (HTV), the regional TV station well known to those who live in Wales and South-West England. Apart from that, Harlech is perhaps best known for its college – a place that gives working class and disadvantaged students a second chance to pick up the formal qualification they need to get them to university. Many Coleg Harlech students go on to study at one of the Welsh universities, with Swansea and Bangor being popular choices. Given their backgrounds, Harlech students have a reputation for free thinking, experimentation and radicalism. (Almost without exception, the Harlech students I met when I was at university were what one might call 'characters'.)

There could then be no better location, intellectually or spiritually, for the Orwellian-inspired course. There is so little to do, in modern entertainment terms, that one is thrown back on one's own resources and encouraged both to think and to appreciate the thoughts of others. One has the sense of being somewhere special. Not so much a step 'back in time' as a step 'out of time' to a place where minds are unshackled and unfettered and anything can be thought. The sense of perspective this provides allows one to view the present from afar, like climbing the castle and surveying the bay with a telescope. The week in Harlech was quite unlike anything the city-dwellers among us had experienced before, though the thought of spending two years in the place might just explain the more outrageous behaviour of some of Harlech's 'stir-crazy' mature students.

Almost from the time I arrived, strange things started happening to me. I was sure I kept hearing people calling my name. Someone would whisper "Michael, Michael" in my ear. I'd turn around but there was no one there. It started to bother me, but I assumed it was the wind playing tricks or that I'd just misheard sounds that were part of general group chatter. Sometimes it happened in the college buildings; sometimes it happened outside. Sometimes it happened when I was with others;

sometimes it happened when I was alone. Once or twice I asked others if they had called me, but I didn't tell anyone that I seemed to be hearing voices. In fact, I didn't think of it in that way – I just assumed that I was mistaken. Although it sounds too silly to mention, I also started to experience occasional nervous feelings in the pit of my stomach – the kind of feelings you get when your father deliberately drives too fast over a hill when you're young.

On the last night of the course, I had arranged for Siwan to call for me and Brendan on her way to the last night party. She was late. We waited. Ten minutes passed . . . then another ten . . . then another ten. She eventually turned up over half an hour late.

"I'm really sorry," she said, "but I went to my room earlier and found my room-mate Glenda in a terrible state. She was sat quivering in the corner like a nervous wreck. It's taken me this long to calm her down."

Brendan and I were suitably sympathetic. "What was wrong with her?" I asked.

"Well," said Siwan, "it's really strange. She got into the lift to go up to our floor and she says that as soon as the doors shut she was attacked by voices."

"Attacked by voices? What sort of voices? What did they say?"

"That's the strange thing," she said. "They just kept saying 'Michael' over and over again."

I felt a sudden bolt of panic. I must have looked like I'd seen – or at least heard – a ghost.

Harlech was also significant for the impact it had on the growing friendship I shared with Brendan. We had known each other – or at least, been aware of each other – since the first year of high school. As each year resulted in the more narrowly defined 'streaming' of pupils according to ability, and as O-levels and A-levels gave us more choice in the subjects we studied, so our school careers slowly converged. Brendan was a wordsmith, an intellectual, and a man of tricks and gadgets. We were both outsiders of sorts, and, finding common ground, we struck up a friendship that has survived to this day. But although the friendship had been slowly growing, it was that week in Harlech – the room sharing, the all-night chats, the new and interesting people we met together – that really cemented our friendship. Music, of course, played a part. I had already started sharing some of my more accessible musical taste with Brendan. A band that had captured my imagination at the time was the Fish-fronted incarnation of Marillion (hence the later ear-ring gift from Siwan), and with Fish's self-professed love of language and poetic yearnings very much to the fore, I was sure Brendan would like them. Marillion had recently released their second album, *Fugazi*, which came with lyrics. Brendan was a top English literature student – and I was keen to get his take on the poetic value (or otherwise) of Fish's words. I remember us reading them together at the back of a Cardiff University Law Department lecture theatre before a demonstration 'moot' for sixth formers thinking of studying law. "I don't know," he said thoughtfully, "they're interesting enough, but I'm not sure they'd pass as *poetry*." As time went by I suppose we were half amused and half dazzled by Fish's 'way with words'. The giant Scotsman certainly had his lines, but he tended towards the verbose, and liked to mix his metaphors as freely as his reputation suggested he liked to mix his drinks – that is, in large quantities, with immense pride and with no sense of shame whatsoever. Marillion's debut album, *Script for a Jester's Tear* (1983), had had a profound effect on me. It was perfect for angst-ridden teenagers and would-be denizens of bedsit land. The follow-up, *Fugazi* (1984), was written more quickly and takes the angst up-market. The bedsit has become a hotel room, and both the production and the album cover are a bit more glossy. For me, *Fugazi* has less of an edge and is a less successful album for that reason. Even so, the band retained a sense of drama throughout and there's plenty for the early-period Marillion fan to get their teeth into. *Fugazi* is Fish at his best – or worst, depending which way you look at it. His later replacement in the band, Steve Hogarth, has, at various times, sung tracks from the Fish-era, but he has never sung anything from *Fugazi*, always claiming that the lyrics on the album are too personal to Fish and that he "can't feel them". The lyrics *are* 'difficult to feel', but not necessarily because they are too personal. Layers of over-clever wordplay and congested imagery often make it hard to see (and feel) the point. To be sure, there are plenty of strong images and striking phrases, but they tend to trip over each other as they jostle for attention, and, in the context of the full lyric, they are almost invariably over-dressed for the occasion.

Despite these reservations about *Fugazi*, I do think that Fish's poetic intent is to be applauded, as is his desire to write intelligent and emotionally literate lyrics. As I said above, he does have his lines, and I still think now that the debut *Script for a Jester's Tear* contains some of his best work. In fact, it's probably some of the more quirky songs from the early days, like 'Garden Party' and 'Charting the Single', that, lyrically, better stand the test of time – perhaps because they are tongue in cheek and enable the writer to go at his subject a little less earnestly. It's also worth noting that *Clutching at Straws* (1987), Fish's final album with Marillion, is considerably less wordy than some of its predecessors.

Unfortunately, however, some of Fish's work suggests that his rock star lifestyle fuelled a form of self-indulgence that drew him further into himself and pulled him away from some of the more accessible themes of the debut album. For Marillion as a band, Fish's character and his poetic leanings were probably both a blessing and a curse. It is probably true that his unique style and immense presence gave the band a strong enough identity to survive and outgrow the early 'Genesis-clone' jibes. It's probably also true that this same style and presence gave the band the 1980s baggage that even today, in media terms, they struggle to leave behind. As I said, at the time Brendan and I were half-amused and half-dazzled. I was definitely more dazzled than Brendan; Brendan was probably more amused than me.

By far the greatest fun we had with Fish's words was trying to decipher the lyrics of Marillion B-sides. In particular we had amusing disagreements about some of the lyrics in 'Cinderella Search', the B-side of 'Assassing'. The singer bemoans his failure to find his Cinderella, despite the fact that he "always used the clean sheets" (as, indeed, all gentlemen should). Or was it "the cue sheets" he always used – in which case one can understand a perceptive female companion becoming suspicious. Similarly, at the end of the song did he welcome us "back to the sawdust" to crawl on our bellies like the evil snakes we are, or "back to the circus" to rejoin the rest of the clowns?

We also marvelled at the epic 'Grendel', the B-side of the 12-inch version of the band's debut single 'Market Square Heroes'. At almost 18 minutes long, it's a glorious slice of 'neo-prog' built on the Beowulf legend. As it gathers in pace, it romps towards a fearsome and bloody finale aided and abetted by a time-signature that even I can tell is borrowed from the Genesis classic 'Supper's Ready'.

There were tracks too where the actor and dramatist in Fish seemed to find it hard to resist the odd well-placed spoken line. Brendan and I argued at length about the wording of a line in 'Chelsea Monday' (from *Script for a Jester's Tear*) that is allegedly delivered by bass player Pete Trewavas.

The would-be princess has taken her own life to secure her 15 minutes of fame, but was she "only a dreamer", "only a dream" or "only dreaming"? Similarly, Brendan was quite taken with a strange line from *Fugazi*'s 'Incubus', a song about using 'private' footage of one's sex life to taunt or wreak revenge on an ex-partner. (Nice.) "An irritating speck of dust that came from absolutely nowhere," Brendan would periodically announce in his best Shakespearian voice. Fish's early work would prove to have a limited shelf-life for us both, but he sure as hell kept us entertained for a while, 'dodgy poetry' and all.

◉ Adventures in a yellow Renault 12 ◉

I don't mind telling you again that as I entered my mid to late teenage years, I became quite an intense young man. While the level of intensity I displayed would have been quite off-putting for some people, for those who shared my more 'intellectual' interests and 'social concerns', it provided the basis for a different kind of friendship. I know that not everyone wants to sit around contemplating the lessons that could be drawn from the Russian Revolution, or wondering how Hitler could come to power in an 'advanced' and 'civilised' nation like Germany, or wondering whether Keynesian or Monetarist economics offered the best hope for the future, or pondering the likely outcome of the Cold War and the escalation of the nuclear arms race, but Brendan was happy to chew the fat *and* pick over the bones of such discussions. Intense we could be, but such intensity requires an outlet, and, in this respect too Brendan was a good friend and great fun.

I was amused to discover recently that it's not just angst-ridden teenagers who need this sort of outlet. Hard-working young musicians need it too. There is a curious part of Ritchie Blackmore's character, for example, that comes through strongly in Jerry Bloom's unauthorised biography – and that's his tendency to indulge in pranks of a certain nature. Bloom quotes roadie Ian Hansford who describes Blackmore's antics with a catapult and some gooseberries around the time Deep Purple were rehearsing material for the seminal *In Rock* album at the Hanwell Community Centre. Hansford recalls:

> I can remember him hitting this girl, who was laden with carrier bags, right in her back. She dropped her carrier bags, turned round and slapped

some old man thinking he'd hit her in the back. A bit further down the road, there was a woman inside a ladies hairdresser's having her hair done. The hairdresser was inside the shop with her back to the door which was open. Ritchie hit her right in the middle of the neck! I remember him hitting three skinheads once as we were going to Fulham and he hit this skinhead on the ear. These skinheads turned around to confront who was behind them by which time we had gone past. Also we were going down two consecutive Fridays either to Bristol or Bath and I think we were going through Marlborough and this window cleaner was up his ladder and the band let fire three in one go. The following Friday the same bloke was further down the road at another house and they did him again.[2]

Bloom also describes how, in his early years with Purple, Roger Glover was often the "hapless victim" of Blackmore and Gillan's "mischievous mayhem". Blackmore himself is quoted as saying: "We actually tied Roger up in a Marshall case and we left him on the Severn Bridge. He was the bass player – you had to do that to bass players. We went back for him later, and he was wriggling, trying to get out. We could see this wriggling Marshall thing! It's Roger Glover!"[3] "On other occasions," says Bloom, "Glover would be stripped naked and kicked out of the car, left to fend for himself while getting to the hotel."[4]

Bloom's book lists a long history of pranks, which were often played on new band members and often involved supposedly supernatural happenings and attempts to scare people. Glenn Hughes, Don Airey and Joe Lynn Turner were all victims, with one-time Rainbow keyboard player Tony Carey on the receiving end of some particularly vindictive behaviour. Speaking of his own treatment, when Blackmore tapped up his room to freak him out with weird noises in the middle of the night, Glenn Hughes notes: "That's Blackmore. He's 60 now and I believe he carries a water pistol to this day."[5]

As for the behaviour of me and my friends, most of our pranks were made possible by Brendan and his yellow Renault 12. The old yellow Renault 12 – which was, in fact, his parent's second car – was not exactly in tip-top condition. It had no second gear, no right indicator, and proudly displayed a picture of the then Pontiff, Pope John Paul II, in the back window. In many ways – certainly in his dress sense and the ambition he harboured at the time to be a lawyer – Brendan was as straight-laced and conventional as they come. To those who knew him, however, he had a surprisingly eccentric turn and a love of the bizarre.

At the time he didn't drink, and he therefore tended to drive us around. It was often said that it was impossible to tell from his behaviour whether he drank or not. He took his driving test against his instructor's advice – and passed. That's typical of the man. He's a maverick, but he's smart – and is very adept at pulling things out of the bag. It was Brendan's eccentricity that somehow led to us driving around a pitch and putt golf course on my eighteenth birthday. Brendan was also the master of the "Black Oak Road death trip". He drove the entire length of the long and winding road on the wrong side until he pulled up outside our friend Fog's house with a triumphant and cheery "There you go, lads". We sat in stunned silence, until someone meekly piped up: "I don't believe he did that."

Our version of the gooseberries was 'chipping' – in other words, driving past people who were walking along minding their own business and throwing a handful of chips at them. One night we used some small apples we found in a pub car park, executing an 'attack' on a couple of skinheads in the manner described by Ian Hansford above. And for antics involving driving off and leaving people, our victim of choice was a chap called Keatsy (first name Stephen) – an old school chum and a massive U2 fan.

Keatsy, Brendan and I were mates for while, but although Brendan and I enjoyed Keatsy's company and he, I assume, enjoyed ours, Keatsy held some outrageous right-wing views (surprising for a U2 fan) that sometimes marked him out as the butt of our jokes and made us feel that we *ought* to try to teach him a lesson. If we drove to a pub for instance, we'd leave when he was in the toilet, or we'd find some other way of making sure that we got to the car first. As Keatsy reached for the door Brendan would drive off, and just as he caught us up, Brendan would drive off again. Of course, if Keatsy had just stayed still and not played along there would have been no fun in it, and we'd soon have stopped. But he never learned, and he spent many a night chasing us around pub car parks.

When he did manage to get in the car, he could be something of a liability. He liked to abuse joggers, despite being one himself. His favourite line, which he'd shout out the window with gleeful enthusiasm, was: "Hey Grandad, get in the bushes and have a wank". The absurdity of this amused us. Isn't that the worst heckle you've ever heard in your life? Try saying it as you pass a jogger at 30mph. Actually, don't bother trying. Take it from me, it's a completely useless heckle – there's no way you can get it all out in time. And even if you could get it all out in time, well, it kind of speaks for itself really. Brendan and I would giggle uncontrollably at Keatsy's heckling incompetence – and, of course, our laughter only served to encourage him. We also found it funny that he was prepared to engage in such ridiculous behaviour just yards from his family home. He lived near a lake that was popular with joggers, but the thought of them recognising him and seeing the car stop outside his house just seconds after he'd abused them never seemed to deter him in the slightest.

Keatsy was, as the reference to jogging might suggest, something of a fitness freak. He was obsessed with hygiene too – or, at least, he was very harsh on those whose personal hygiene didn't measure up to his own professed high standards. He claimed that he got up before the rest of his family as part of a regimented exercise and hygiene routine. "I always get up first," he said, "I pull back the curtains and take some deep breaths, then I do my press-ups, then I do my sit-ups, and then I shower and dress before the others get up for breakfast." You tend to take it on trust that friends are telling the truth about these things. After all, why would anyone lie? We only put his account to the test twice – and then, not wittingly. On the first occasion he fell asleep while we were watching a late night film at his house. There were some marker pens on the table nearby, so we decided to write some swear words on his face. When he woke up it said 'twat' on his forehead, 'knob' on his left cheek and 'prick' on his right. He went to bed that night without washing. He got up without exercising or showering, and he went down to the breakfast table where the rest of his family, including his young sister, had already congregated. He called us "a pair of bastards" the next time he saw us. We thought it was his own fault for lying about his routine.

The second occasion was inspired by the night he showed us a short story he had written about the Four Horsemen of the Apocalypse. He had a literary interest in the supernatural and fancied himself as a bit of a Dennis Wheatley. We knew that he was staying up late one night to watch *The Exorcist* and attempted to unnerve him by constructing what we took to be a representation of a 'black altar' in his back garden. We returned to his house after hours, sneaked up the lane and through the gate, and made up inverted crosses and a pentagram out of a load of bamboo sticks that were lying around. Once again, he failed to get up before his family, so when he pulled back the curtains to do his deep breathing, morning had already well and truly broken and his Mum was already on the case. "I think the local kids have been in the garden again," she said. "Do you know anything about this, Stephen?"

◉ *The Eleventh Hour* ◉

My 'ghost' experience in Harlech, and the general themes and discussions of my week there, triggered in me a kind of mini-existential crisis. I won't deny that the 'ghost' experience unnerved me, and, indeed, I started wearing a cross around my neck and going to church again for a short while. In the meantime, concerned at the reduced level of effort I appeared to be putting into my studies, my sixth-form tutor suggested that I go and visit a friend of his who was a priest. It wasn't that he thought I needed religious counselling – though the priest was very reassuring when I told him about my Harlech experience – but he knew that the priest was a skilled counsellor and thought he might be helpful. In fact the priest listened attentively and let me talk about a wide range of things that were on my mind. I particularly remember discussing anxieties about the nuclear arms race, and I referred to the lyrics of a song from Magnum's second album (*Magnum II*) called 'Firebird'. The priest was interested in hearing more about this 'protest song'. I had not, until this point, thought of it as a 'protest song' at all. This was a term I associated with the 1960s, student rallies and concerted political agitation. It was a term that somehow seemed to devalue the music – as though the music was there only to serve the needs of protest and had no value in its own right. And yet, over time, I became more inclined to think that taking time out to listen to songs that were critical of the establishment or the status quo in some way was not only 'educational' but could itself be an act of protest or defiance. This seemed to add a dimension to the way I listened to music. It became much clearer to me that listening to music could itself be mind shaping and character building in ways which had implications for one's future actions and choices.

Magnum were a band I hooked into in a very personal and introspective way, with their album *The Eleventh Hour* making a particularly strong impression on me. Originally released in May 1983, *The Eleventh Hour* proved to be their last album for Jet Records and, despite reaching number 38 in the UK album charts, it was something of a commercial disappointment. Sandwiched as it is between the success of both its predecessor, *Chase the Dragon* (1982), and its eventual successor, the masterful *On a Storyteller's Night* (1985), it is neither the best known nor the most critically acclaimed Magnum album. Nevertheless it spoke to me, and it remains a highly valued part of my music collection. While many, including guitarist, songwriter and album producer Tony Clarkin came to feel that the production had not brought the best out of the material, I was not alone in judging it to be an album of substance. Mark Putterford of *Kerrang!*, for example, gave it four and a half stars out of five, describing it as "an album crammed with intricate ideas and sophistication." He even *praised* Clarkin's production for giving the album "a rough kind of edge" that preserved its "British feel".[6]

For me, everything about the album worked well. One has to remember what was happening at the time of its release. By now 1980s materialism reigned supreme. For those of a less materialistic disposition, and those with a conscience, this was a worrying and almost apocalyptic period. The Cold War produced real tensions, the CND movement was a visible force, and the threat of nuclear war seemed very real. *The Eleventh Hour* captures the mood of the times. It is a coherent and consistent album, with both the title and the Rodney Matthews cover art reflecting and reinforcing the lyrical themes.

The cover art was not only aesthetically appealing, but utterly compelling. It features a masked lizard disguised as a kindly old man trying to entice a multi-ethnic group of wide-eyed and innocent children across a thin ravine that appears to be the only thing separating good from evil. A dollar sign embellished with a serpent on the back of the lizard's throne appears to be a dead give-away, but the children seem both unaware and vulnerable. The malevolent-looking potions and syringe around the throne suggest that the lizard has a few nasty tricks up his sleeve.

The industrial wasteland which provides a backdrop to the lizard's trickery and seduction suggests that many others have been tempted to cross the divide. Futuristic-looking fighter planes and shark-like missiles suggest war and turmoil. The children, the young and precious souls, would appear to be our last hope. It is the eleventh hour, and it is up to the children, the last generation, to reject the advances of the lizard, and pull us back from the brink. The dominant colours, violent shades of purple, and fiery orange, are both beautiful and sad, emerging, as they do, from ugly chimneys on the war-ravaged horizon that are stifling and polluting planet earth. In the sleeve notes to the 2005 expanded edition, Clarkin says: "I still love Rodney's drawing of black and white children playing together, with a city in flames and various power stations in the background, and war planes flying overhead. It was very powerful imagery."[7]

Indeed it was, and it represented the album's themes perfectly. I read an interview once in which Clarkin confessed that lyric writing did not come naturally to him but was something he had to work at. On the evidence of *The Eleventh Hour*, it was well worth him putting in the effort. Though there is occasionally awkwardness in his phrasing, the lyrics are full of acute observations and noble sentiment. They are focused enough to be biting and contemporary, but 'open' enough to require engagement and interpretation.

'The Prize' kicks the album off in fine style, warning that we are travelling a road that will bring about our demise "with the prize hardly won". It is left to the listener to decide what the prize is and what can be done about it. "The race is on."

'Breakdown' has a kind of squashed 'olde-worlde' feel to it, and imparts a grim but sympathetic wisdom that speaks to thoughtful and troubled teenagers ("protected by some, taken granted by all") everywhere:

> *You won't beat the pack, that's no revelation*
> *Come snapping their jaws right on your heels*
> *Making your way through all this confusion*
> *The harder you try, the less it reveals*
>
> *I know what happens the moment you turn out your light*
> *I know what happens it happens to me every night*
> *You start to breakdown*

As the song gathers momentum, singer Bob Catley's performance oozes empathy and compassion. Clarkin's solo runs into 'The Great Disaster', darting between the speakers before prompting Catley to unleash an angry diatribe which warns of the ill-intent of those who fool us with their "skilful disguises" and "shining appearance" as they drive us towards the "final blunder". One might think that hope resides in the younger generation (after all, why issue a warning if there is no chance of anyone heeding it), but on this occasion the lyric seems to embrace the outcome against which it is warning with a sense of depressing inevitability:

Innocent faces look up in the classroom
Soon, their time will come

'Vicious Companions' provides further cautionary words as Clarkin continues to build his critique ("See the hungry cry for the children/Watch the greedy call for more"), while 'So Far Away' is a more straightforward war song, echoing the themes of previous efforts like 'Solider of the Line' (from *Chase the Dragon*) and 'All of my Life' (from *Magnum II*). "I'm definitely an anti-war person," Clarkin told Dave Ling in the sleeve notes to the expanded edition of *Chase the Dragon*. "Not what you'd call a pacifist; I just hate the foolishness of it all."[8]

'Hit and Run' and 'One Night of Passion' appear to be departures from the theme. The former is a song about 'buying romance', while the latter deals with personal turmoil and regret following a one-night stand. Both are about loneliness, with the need for love and affection leading someone to behave in ways of which they are not particularly proud.

'One Night of Passion' does, however, strike a positive note that is maintained throughout the rest of the album:

Someone
Somewhere
Is taking note how you care
Hold on

'The Word', while recognising the difficulties and challenges we all face, also offers positive advice:

Life is a precious thing
So don't use it up
Start living it day by day

Despite the anxiety of most of the album's lyrics, and the sense of possible, if not impending, disaster, it was lines like this that for me made *The Eleventh Hour* an album of hope. It is, after all, the *eleventh* hour, not the *twelfth* hour, not midnight and not even two minutes to midnight. That means that there *is* time for change, and, of course, recognising problems is often the first step to their resolution. From this starting point, I derived many positive messages from the album: 'be yourself', 'don't give up', 'keep thinking', 'maintain a sense of realism – you will take knocks', 'it's ok to make mistakes', 'you're not alone'. The way I've always heard the album's final two tracks bears out this optimistic interpretation. On 'Young and Precious Souls', for example, against the backdrop of music that swirls and gallops like the triumphant theme tune to an all-action superhero cartoon, and the realisation that we've been "bought and sold", Clarkin finally issues an explicit battlecry:

> *Come all you young and precious souls*
> *Your legacy waits, come on take a hold*

Similarly, I always derived comfort from the album's closing track, the calmer and beautifully crafted 'Road to Paradise'. I once put this track on the end of a compilation tape I made for a friend of mine – and he spent years thinking it was David Bowie! But it's not Bowie it's Magnum, and while the lyric reminds us that the road to paradise is fraught with perils and wrong turnings, it also allows Clarkin to remind us that we're all in this together ("We're all spinning on a roundabout") and to leave us with a powerful message:

> *I don't need to fight just to prove that I'm right*
> *I don't want the world upside down*
> *I don't need to fight just to prove that I'm right*
> *I just need the world spinning round*

The Eleventh Hour is an album of focused good intent that is vastly underrated both musically and lyrically. Despite bad associations with the period of turmoil and uncertainty that followed its release, it seems that even Tony Clarkin himself is now ready to reappraise it. As he told writer Dave Ling: "Maybe it is an album that deserves more attention than it's received."[9]

My love of rock music had become an important part of both my social life and my 'inner life', providing a kind of belonging and sense of identity through the friendships I'd formed, but also helping me to ask important questions and think about how I might go about trying to answer them. While rock music has never stopped being fun for me, and I have always enjoyed a wide range of bands, over time I certainly became drawn to bands who 'had something to say', bands who took a more thoughtful and artistic approach to their craft and who presented ideas and observations that stimulated my own attempts to form political and philosophical views. It is not unusual for young people to start reflecting seriously on social and political issues in their teenage years, and it is not unusual for contemporary rock music to act as some kind of midwife or companion to these thoughts. In many ways music both fuelled the intensity I have referred to above and provided some relief from it.

5

God and the Devil

Whatever I might say about the essence of rock and roll and the meaning that rock music has had in *my* life, for as long as rock music has endured there have been people who have regarded it not just as a corrupting influence but as the work of the devil. Of course, it is true that the history of rock music is littered with examples of poor behaviour. However, it is one thing to claim that trashing hotel rooms, taking drugs and sleeping with groupies sets a bad example; it's quite another to claim that such behaviour is inspired by the devil who is using rock stars and their music to steal people's souls. Yet this is precisely the claim that some Christians, mostly those of a fundamentalist persuasion, have made as they have campaigned to warn people off rock music in general and heavy rock music in particular.

Given the volume, force and aggression of a lot of rock music, it is natural, I suppose, for those who recognise the power but who cannot embrace it to be intimidated by it or to fear it. This fear has been exploited with joyful and careless abandon by attention-seeking rock bands who like to shock. The easiest way to do this is to combine the most threatening features of the music with lyrical themes that play on people's deepest anxieties.

There has been a kind of rolling and progressive dynamic at work here for practically the entire period of time that I have been interested in rock music. It works like this. Christian critics notice aspects of certain rock musicians' lifestyles and artistic output and express concern that the musicians are, through their influence, corrupting young people or undermining Christian values. Musicians respond by resorting to irony or attempting to shock. The critics take this as further evidence of godlessness and become more vocal and definite in their opposition. Musicians get more angry and frustrated and *do* start to actively oppose Christianity – or, at least, the forms of Christianity that are actively critical of them. Again, this induces a harsher response from the critics who themselves become increasingly angry, organised and militant. As mutual resentment and anger build, opposition on both sides comes to take on more violent, aggressive and sinister forms. I am, of course, simplifying matters. Not all bands fit this mould, not all Christians fit this mould, and the progression is not always linear or chronological. But one can, without question, plot a course through rock history that illustrates these developments well.

From the rock perspective (and notice I'm already talking as though there are two distinct and necessarily opposed camps here) one sees this dynamic in its mildest form when frustrated bands find ways to poke fun at or further antagonise their critics. "You're a bad and unholy influence," scream worried parents and the Christian Right. "Yeah, alright then, if you say so," reply the bands. One gets a sense of this, for example, from the title of the Rolling Stones album *Their Satanic Majesties Request* (1967) and the track 'Sympathy for the Devil' from *Beggars Banquet* (1968). One might also note the backward message that Iron Maiden placed on their *Piece of Mind* (1983) album after the controversy surrounding the previous album, *The Number of the Beast* (1982), led to fundamentalist American Christians encouraging teenagers to rid themselves of evil by casting their Maiden albums into the flames. The backwards recording in fact captures intoxicated drummer Nicko McBrain impersonating Ugandan dictator Idi Amin and telling anyone who could be bothered to go to the trouble of playing the message backwards: "Don't meddle wid t'ings yo don't understand."[1]

From the Christian perspective one sees the dynamic at work in rumours that particular rock bands have had a more direct and sinister association with evil through participation in all manner of supposed black magic and occult practices, or through active involvement with known opponents of Christianity such as Anton LaVey and his Church of Satan. (Is that really LaVey lurking on the balcony on the cover of the Eagles' *Hotel California*?) Such rumours almost always turn out to be untrue, or at best to have been twisted, sensationalised and blown out of all proportion, but once they are placed in the public imagination it is almost impossible to eradicate them from common (mis)perception. If such associations do lead some young people astray, it is often the fault of the rumour mongers, not the bands themselves.

That's not to say that there has always been smoke without fire. Record companies and publicists have often spread rumours and promoted controversial images for commercial gain. It wasn't the Christians, for example, who put around rumours that Black Sabbath bassist Geezer Butler had "successfully raised a demon in a churchyard"[2] or that Sabbath once flew to Germany with five return tickets and one single. The returns were said to be for the band and their manager, the single for "the sacrifice victim – the one that they would bring along to dispose of during the set."[3]

It's also true that many rock musicians *have* shown some interest in the occult. It's just that the kind of the interest they have shown is consistent with the kind of widespread interest in such matters that cuts across class, social background, profession and nation and is by no means specific to rock and roll. How many of us, for example, have taken part in pub discussions and extended late night chats about what is or what might be? Why are we here? What happens when we die? Is there a God? Is there life after death? Is there a spirit world? Can spirits be contacted? Can the future be foretold? Whatever one's religious (or irreligious) leanings, and whatever one's approach to analysing these questions, they are questions that most people grapple with in some way at some time. Many, many people, not just rock stars, have explored some of these questions and expressed their curiosity by dabbling with Ouija Boards or going to fortune tellers or having Tarot readings. In and of themselves these things have little to do with Satanism and black magic, but fundamentalist Christians do tend to lump all things to do with the 'paranormal' in together, fearing them as tools that Satan uses to taunt us, trick us and possess us.

Much has been said and rumoured about guitarist Ritchie Blackmore's interest in the spirit world, and, though he wouldn't have written the lyrics himself, his back catalogue includes the Rainbow track 'Tarot Woman', from *Rising* (1976), and the Deep Purple track 'Fortune Teller', from *Slaves and Masters* (1990). However, comments made by former Rainbow and Ozzy Osbourne bassist Bob Daisley, quoted by unauthorised Blackmore biographer Jerry Bloom, put the nature of Blackmore's interest into some kind of perspective. Daisley says: "I was always quite interested in séances; occultism, I don't mean anything negative or dark and neither was Ritchie. He didn't like that. He didn't like people who wore crosses upside down or anything satanic. He was interested in spirituality and occultism but only in a positive light."[4]

Much has been said too about former Rainbow and Black Sabbath frontman Ronnie James Dio, he of the horned devil hand sign and the controversial *Holy Diver* album cover, whose Sabbath output includes the tracks 'Voodoo' and 'The Sign of the Southern Cross' from 1981's *Mob Rules* album. But according to Bloom, Dio's own *active* interest in "spiritualism" ended at the Chateau d'Herouville near Paris in late 1977, when Rainbow were recording their *Long Live Rock 'n' Roll* album. Dio reports participating in a séance at the Chateau, and the effect it had on him. He says: "Most séances will swear at you or use bad grammar, but this one said, 'I am Baal, I create chaos. You will never leave here, don't even try.' We tried again later and the spirit asked, 'Where's Blackmore? Oh never mind, here he comes.' The door opened and in walked Ritchie! Even he turned ashen . . . I thought this was the last séance for me, as soon as it began, 'I am Baal, I create chaos' I was fucking out of the room."[5]

For those inclined to believe in these things, such stories might be a source of concern. But they do also cast a certain light on the *kind* of interest that these musicians have or had in the occult. Perhaps Mr Dio was not the devil incarnate after all.

One can perhaps understand the Christian view that participation in such practices is dangerous (to quote Nicko McBrain again: "don't meddle wid t'ings yo don't understand"), but it's much harder to understand the extreme response that leads to moral panic, the mass burning of records, and the association of certain performers with the Anti-Christ. The Christian paranoia which developed through the 1980s, in the United States of America in particular, was fuelled by controversy around 'backmasking'. The idea seemed to be that rock musicians were recording backwards messages of satanic intent and hiding these messages in their album tracks. While the messages could only be revealed if the tracks were played backwards, the message would be conveyed subliminally to all those listening to the music in the normal way. To parents up and down the country the message seemed to be: "Satan's after your children, folks, and he's using subliminal messages to do it."

The irony seems to be that Christian wrath was largely focused, at least in the higher profile cases and media portrayals, on a number of mainstream rock bands such as Queen, ELO, Pink Floyd, Iron Maiden, Judas Priest and Styx, who *clearly* had little interest in Satan as a theistic entity or a metaphysical reality and certainly had no explicit interest in doing his bidding. Both Ozzy Osbourne and Judas Priest have endured court cases in the United States after young fans committed suicide. Though the cases highlighted the tragedies of the deaths, to British rock fans it was simply inconceivable that either artist would use messages of any sort – forward/backwards, explicit/subliminal – to encourage fans to take their own lives. Indeed, both Priest vocalist Rob Halford and Ozzy Osbourne have since commented on the commercial absurdity of attempting to diminish one's fan base in this way. In Ozzy Osbourne's case, a sober listen to the lyrics of the 'offending' song make it quite clear that 'Suicide Solution' is, in fact, a warning of the dangers of alcohol abuse.

Osbourne became such a target for the Christian Right that he has, on occasion, expressed concern for his personal safety. "The clergy is in a more dangerously powerful position than you or I will ever be," he told one interviewer. "Because if a cardinal gets on the pulpit and tells his congregation that I, Ozzy Osbourne, am the reason for all the badness in the world, then you're gonna get some nutcase want to wipe me out ... I've had threats to my life. Part of the reason I run around so much on stage is because somebody told me that a moving target is harder to hit."[6]

For those of us removed from the excesses of America, the ire levelled at the more mainstream bands by the Christians simply seemed to reinforce an impression of Christianity as a sombre, austere, prohibitive, killjoy type of religion. To many a rock fan it simply felt like the power and passion of heavy rock was itself was being branded as evil – something to be feared and rejected – irrespective of the lyrical or artistic intent of the many and varied bands who wrote, recorded and performed it. Something apparently missed by the critics was that their wholesale and misinformed condemnation of heavy rock and heavy metal had more power than the music itself to drive young people to the 'dark side' and find evil there. The surest way to get teenagers to buy heavy metal albums is to tell them that they are dangerous and that they should keep away from them. (How often do bans on music videos help push the songs higher up the charts?) The Christian Right might have been better advised to either ignore Ozzy Osbourne or engage with him in a more constructive and thoughtful manner. But they didn't. They let their fear and fanaticism get the better of them – and did themselves no favours.

Music has, in fact, had an association with the devil that extends back centuries – long before the dawn of rock music. One is reminded of the period described so wonderfully by Umberto Eco in *The Name of the Rose*, when the Church seemed to embody a theological approach that regarded all forms of physical pleasure as potentially sinful and favoured a lifestyle that attempted to free the soul from earthly desire. It's also worth noting the infamous *diabolus in musica* ('the devil in music') – the musical interval or 'tritone' that produces a sound so dissonant that it was thought to express evil. Classical composers either avoided the interval altogether, or used it with conscious artistic intent in a very tightly controlled manner. On the whole, however, Christians *have* clearly embraced music. Even the Catholic Church has long recognised the positive power of music, its value as a form of creative expression, and its place in attempts to give 'Glory to God'. Pope Gregory I – who reigned between AD 590 and 604 and who gave his name to Gregorian chanting – is credited with asking "Why should the devil have all the good songs?"[7] Whether these are his words or not, the sanction and impetus he gave to this form of musical worship speaks for itself. And of course, the use of music in the Latin mass, traditional hymns and, now, more modern forms of music, are familiar and common features of Catholic practice. Evangelical Christians too see music as central to their worship, favouring more upbeat and intoxicating music over traditional hymns and more solemn and reverential forms of musical expression. Gospel music, which is closely linked with blues and soul, is often recognised as a genre in its own right and is well known for its celebratory and uplifting qualities. With regards to rock music, there are, it must be said, a variety of Christian perspectives. Not all Christians take the fundamentalist line. There are, indeed, Christian rock and metal bands, of which Stryper are perhaps the best known. There are plenty of Christians of all denominations who see the value and potential of rock music for worship.

There is, then, no necessary connection between music and evil or rock music and the devil. From this perspective the wholesale condemnation of rock music and heavy metal by US fundamentalists looks silly and excessive and, quite simply, turned people off. Nevertheless, there *was* extremity bubbling away beneath the surface. In focusing on more mainstream acts, the Christians didn't so much take their eye off the ball, as follow the wrong one.

By far the most sinister developments were the emergence of death metal and black metal as distinct extreme metal sub-genres. The former always seemed to me unpleasant; its mucky, gory themes offering violent entertainment at best. It all smacked of an unhealthy obsession with body fluids, a craving for attention and a love of sensationalism. By way of contrast, exponents of black metal held an uncompromising and hostile anti-Christian line that would increasingly lead to real violence.

The black metal movement grew out of the over-the-top devilish bravado of New Wave of British Heavy Metal stalwarts Venom, the theatrical anti-Christian posturing of King Diamond, and the extreme shock tactics of American thrash metal giants Slayer, whose aggressive intent was a source of inspiration for many of those who took the Satanic imagery more seriously than, in reality, Slayer did themselves. The emergence of a recognisable black metal scene in Norway in the early 1990s was accompanied by a programme of direct action that led to a series of murders, suicides and prison terms, and a substantial number of church desecrations and arsons over a number of years. The violence wasn't always outwardly directed either, but sometimes turned inwards. Mayhem vocalist Dead, for example, committed suicide in 1991. He was found by band-mate Euronymous, who was later himself murdered by Varg Vikernes of the band Burzum. It is also reported that despite some overlap in themes and musical styles there was significant conflict between the Norwegian and Finnish scenes and between the Norwegian black metal and Swedish death metal scenes. One can't help feeling that, despite the notoriety it brought the movement, the violence could only have been undermining and self-defeating. Amid the madness, those who felt most committed to the cause did make some effort at piecing together and formalising a set of doctrines and values that provided some sort of ideological underpinning for the genre. This perhaps found its most advanced expression in the cosmic 'Chaosophy' of Jon Nödtveidt of Swedish blackened death metal band (yes, I know) Dissection. Nödtveidt was co-founder of the Misanthropic Luciferian Order (MLO), and was able to spend seven years working up the detail of his thought after being convicted for his part in the murder of a gay man in Gothenberg. Just two years after his release he committed suicide, allegedly dying alongside a copy of the 'Satanic grimoire', *Liber Azerate*, written by the MLO 'Magister Templi' Frater Nemidial.

Let me put my own cards on the table. I was brought up as a Catholic and, as such, taught to believe in the reality of both God and the Devil. But the Catholicism that I knew was about the life of Jesus. It was about making moral decisions for oneself and trying to live a good life, as God, the creator and loving father, intended. We were taught that the Devil wished us to live differently and that his common *modus operandi* was to find clever ways to tempt us into living as *he* wished, but the everyday significance of Satan was played down to such an extent that he really didn't feature in my thoughts or my life at all. Catholicism for me was a positive faith. It was about forming a personal relationship with God and trying to be a good person. One prayed to God for guidance, and one also prayed to the Virgin Mary when intercession and a healthy dose of female intuition were required. I didn't find Catholicism to be the heavy-handed guilt-laden faith that media portrayals and 'received wisdom' assume it to be. There was no hellfire and damnation in my Catholic upbringing – not at home, not in school and not in church. We all know that the Church had been assertive and done some terrible things in the past, but the Catholicism that I knew had become a *relatively* tolerant faith – certainly in the way it was taught to me. Of course Catholics generally believe that their faith is the one true faith. But in the modern world it's a religion that can co-exist and can find points of contact with other faiths and denominations.

In my late teens I stopped going to church and came to regard myself as a 'lapsed Catholic'. I didn't stop trying to live a good life, but I lost the ability to commit to some of the metaphysical beliefs – of an independent creator, of the Holy Trinity, of the transubstantiation, for example – that underlie the faith. I wouldn't call myself an atheist – I continue to believe that 'spirituality' and the ability to see the wonder in things is important – but neither can I call myself a believer. My upbringing has left me open to seeing the good things in Christianity (and other religions) – in both a practical and a moral sense. Artistically too, I have been left predisposed to recognising the power of great art to show us something of the wonder and beauty of the world, the potential of man, and the kind of humility we should show when confronted with expressions of 'the divine'. My upbringing has also left me vulnerable to being spooked by talk of devils and demons. My peers and I, for example, were all familiar with 'the Exorcist fortnight' – the period of time it took all but the hardiest of Catholic teenagers in the 1970s and early 1980s to recover from their first viewing of the famous movie.

In the light of this 'confession', you may well wonder what I think of many of those I have mentioned above. Well, I always thought Venom were just silly. I think of Slayer and most death metal bands as I think of slasher-movies – as gratuitous, distasteful and unnecessary. Black metal I generally regard as musically awful, philosophically weak, and, so the evidence suggests, something of an unhealthy obsession for some of those involved. (Not that I'd campaign to have it banned or encourage people to publicly burn their albums.) The Christian metal band Stryper I always found rather sickly and unconvincing. As for the Christian fundamentalists, they always seemed to me to be way off the mark – and the best argument for LaVey-style Satanism I've ever heard.

☉ Stairway to Hell? ☉

As far as my own experiences of God and the Devil in rock music are concerned, there are two bands or artists in particular – Black Sabbath and Geoff Mann – that I would like to discuss in more detail. But first, let me tell you about an experience I had with Led Zeppelin.

All 1970s and 1980s rock fans had heard the stories about Led Zeppelin: Jimmy Page was a magician; Jimmy Page was obsessed with Aleister Crowley; various members of the band had sold their souls to the Devil; and Robert Plant had come up with the lyrics to 'Stairway to Heaven' while under the influence of someone or something at a séance. One day, soon after I first went to university, my friend Harvey told a group of us, over a pint or two of ESB in one of the college bars, that devilish messages could be heard in 'Stairway to Heaven' if the song was played backwards. I regarded this as doubtful at best. There were too many good things in the music for it to be evil, and anyway, what sort of idiot would sit and listen to records backwards for goodness sake. It seemed a hopelessly inefficient way of communicating with people – whether it was the work of the devil or not. Even if I wanted to trawl for backwards messages, my own record player, and I assume most other modern record players, could only play forwards, and I lacked the technical know-how to do anything about it. Harvey, however, did have the know-how, and a cheap old record player to boot. There was, we all agreed, something enthralling about the power and imagery of Led Zeppelin, so we decided, as young men do, to explore further. We congregated in Harvey's room and recorded the track onto a blank cassette. Harvey had heard that the backwards messages were hidden in the verse about bustles and hedgerows, so he tried to identify, isolate and then reverse the relevant portion of tape by cutting it with a scissors and reattaching it with some kind of glue or tape. When this proved to be ineffective, he somehow managed to disengage the drive of his record player so that he could manually rotate the turntable backwards. Surprisingly, to me at least, 'Plan B' worked. We all grabbed a pen and piece of paper and sat listening, ready to write down anything we heard. As Harvey attempted to maintain a constant speed, Robert Plant's voice crooned and crowed and whimpered and wavered unevenly. On the first play there was a mixture of raised eyebrows and blank looks around the room. After a couple of goes we stopped to compare notes. Though we had not all picked out the same words, there was remarkable convergence and general agreement that we *could* make out words that, despite being interspersed with mumbling from which nothing could be gleaned, made up the following sentence:

> *Lord of all creation*
> *My sweet Satan*
> *Yours is the path that makes me sad*

In general the exercise generated amusement more than fear, but for me the experience was a bit shocking – at least at first. What were we to make of what, between us, we thought we had heard? Did we really hear those words? If so, were they put there deliberately? Again, if so, were they put there by the band or by the devil himself? Were the band aware of the 'message'? What was its purpose? And what about that claim that Plant had written the lyrics while 'under the influence' in a séance?

Well, in his book *When the Levee Breaks: The Making of Led Zeppelin IV*, Andy Fyfe shows that despite reports from Plant and Page of an intense creative burst during the initial writing of the lyrics at Headley Grange, the lyrics changed significantly as the band jammed and rehearsed its way to something approximating to a full version of the song. In fact, according to Fyfe, "the first complete run-through . . . has only two verses, and most of the lyric was changed by the time the band came to the final version."[8] Furthermore, when the band left Headley Grange *en route* for Island Studios, the lyrics still lacked "any mention of bustles or hedgerows"[9]. It seems then that the very verse in which my friends and I thought we heard a backwards message was not even included in the original run through and was finalised sometime between the initial writing and rehearsal sessions and the full re-recording that took place a week or so later. There seems to be no indication either that the energy of Plant's original creative burst was connected to a séance in any way. Once again, it seems that a whole myth has grown up around just a grain or two of truth.

With regards to the 'message' itself, I think it's worth noting again that the lines I have reported above were pieced together from fragments jotted down by around half a dozen people, all of whom were 'primed' for the occasion. We sat down full of anticipation in the knowledge that we were *trying* to hear a backwards and slightly 'Satanic' or occult-influenced message. Would I have heard the same thing without the prior discussion and priming, if, say, someone had just taken me aside and played it to me without telling me what it was? There is no way of knowing. (One can't hear something for the first time twice.) But I doubt it.

As noted earlier, Christian claims that the devil and his charges have used 'backmasking' techniques to subliminally transmit messages with evil intent have not been uncommon. It's the *subliminal* aspect of the claim that makes the discussion particularly tricky, and perhaps, ultimately, it is a matter for experimental psychology to investigate whether it is possible for backmasked messages to subliminally influence attitudes and behaviour when a record is played and heard the normal way – i.e. forwards. I know of no scientific evidence that shows that it is possible, while there does seem to be a growing body of work, from which Vokey and Read's *American Psychologist* paper is perhaps the most widely quoted example, that has failed to find any evidence of effectiveness.[10] At a purely personal level, I have always regarded claims of intent to influence people in this way as ludicrous. When reversed and revealed, the 'messages' often seem grammatically awkward – little more than barely audible snippets of sentences that don't usually make much sense or say very much at all. As far as Led Zeppelin are concerned, despite my initial shock at what I thought I probably heard, I don't believe for a moment that the band was using backmasked messages to subliminally influence, corrupt or draw their listeners to Satan. Indeed, while noting Page's 'occult interests' (he *was*, of course, enormously interested in Crowley), Andy Fyfe also notes "Plant's down-to-earth hippie ideals" and describes the words of 'Stairway to Heaven' as "a yearning lyric of longing and questing".[11] Plant himself has expressed his sadness at the rumours and controversy surrounding the song, stating that it was written "with every best intention".[12] There are those who might argue that the band themselves were innocent and unwitting victims who were simply used by the Devil without their knowledge, as he seeks ever more cunning ways to corrupt the minds and souls of the young. To those who think like that, there is nothing one can say – as nothing will count as evidence either for or against their dogma. My experience with 'Stairway to Heaven' has neither stopped me listening to Led Zeppelin nor enjoying their music. And I don't believe that being a Led Zeppelin fan has had any adverse effect on my mind, my soul, my general character or my ability to be a reasonably decent human being.

⊙ We Sold Our Soul for Rock 'n' Roll ⊙

I remember quite vividly the moment I first became aware of Black Sabbath. I must have been eight or nine, and my parents had taken me and my sister to Bessemer Road Market in Cardiff. This was, at the time, a common Sunday afternoon event. The market was thriving, and there was many a bargain to be had as men with loud voices and fat-looking money bags offered huge discounts on items you couldn't (or wouldn't) buy in the shops. As my parents listened to a man who promised to chuck in not one, not two but three free something-or-others if they bought his latest offering, I was drawn to a picture of four strange looking men on a t-shirt displayed on a nearby stall. They had long hair, they wore dark clothes, and they wore crosses around their necks of the sort you normally only saw in Church. I felt an instant sense of danger – a disturbing thrill. Then my mother pulled me away, and the moment passed.

As far as I recall, I first knowingly *heard* Black Sabbath when my next door neighbour Helen played me the single 'Neon Knights'. This was the summer of 1980. I had just turned 13 and the New Wave of British Heavy Metal was kicking into gear. I was aware that the single came from their new album and I was also vaguely aware that they were widely revered as one of the giants of the heavy metal genre. Not long after this, I went to visit my school friend Eamonn and he took me to his local record shop in Whitchurch Village. There I bought the album *Heaven and Hell*. I liked the look of the sleeve. The front cover featured three angels who sat playing cards and smoking. The back cover featured a superb sketch of the band looking truly grand, swathed in masses of glorious hair and variously resembling, or so it seemed to me, travelling troubadours, members of the French aristocracy and American country gentlemen. At the same time I bought the 'new' Black Sabbath single *Paranoid*. On inspection, as I travelled home, I noticed that although the album did indeed contain 'Neon Knights', it didn't have 'Paranoid' on it. What's more, on checking the song-writing credits of both the single and album, I noticed that someone called Osbourne had apparently replaced Ronnie James Dio. I assumed it was this way around as the single was newer than the album. I got home and played the single straight away. What was going on? It was alright, but it sounded like they'd stepped back in time. Compared to *Heaven and Hell* even the sleeve was dull, and the sound was somehow oppressive, distant and doomy.

I think it was later that week watching *Top of the Pops* that I realised that Osbourne was the original singer and that 'Paranoid' was a much earlier song that had been re-released.[*] I felt such a sense of relief – the version of the band that I liked was intact and, indeed, I was soon to discover, on a world tour that would bring them to Cardiff at the end of the year. In the meantime, I slowly came to appreciate both 'Paranoid' and the B-side 'Snowblind'. I still thought that the sound seemed a little dated, but decided that I would explore 'early' Black Sabbath further as soon as the opportunity presented itself.

That opportunity came when I stumbled across the compilation album *We Sold Our Soul for Rock 'n' Roll* in the Castle Street branch of Virgin Records. At just £3.49 it was almost affordable from one week's pocket money alone. I remember too that I bought *Lovedrive* by the Scorpions the same day. I rushed home in a state of great excitement and couldn't wait to play them. I took to *Lovedrive* instantly. It was just the kind of thing I liked – not too far removed from Purple and Rainbow, some furious yet melodic guitar playing and some lovely sounding ballads. And was that a reggae influence I spotted? With a guest lead guitarist who shared my first name (Michael Schenker, brother of rhythm guitarist Rudolf) and a woman's breast on the back cover, what more could a young 'metal head' want? And then I played Side One of the Sabbath album.

My first disappointment was realising that this wasn't a double-live album – a format I found very exciting at the time after my experience

---

[*] *Heaven and Hell* was released in April 1980. 'Neon Knights' was released in July 1980 and reached number 22 in the UK singles chart. 'Paranoid' was re-released in the summer of 1980, reaching number 14 in the UK singles chart.

with *Made in Japan* – but a two-LP studio compilation. But that minor disappointment was nothing compared to what was to follow. I remember being overwhelmed by both the intensity of the music and the images invoked by the lyrics. Satan, war, wickedness, lost love, death, destruction, graves, drugs, revolution, mental illness, Satan again. I persevered and got through all four sides but it was like a bad dream. What had I bought? I was feeling thoroughly miserable, I had a pounding headache, and the image inside the gatefold sleeve was so disturbing that I didn't even know if I wanted to have it in the house. It was a picture of a pale, drawn looking woman lying in a coffin in clothing that was both seductive and off-putting. She looked dead, but her eyes were open, or at least half-open. And she held a gleaming silver cross.

The songs themselves were lifted from the first six Sabbath albums – from the debut *Black Sabbath*, released in February 1970, to the 1975 album *Sabotage*. All feature the classic, and original, Sabbath line-up of Tony Iommi (guitar), Geezer Butler (bass), Bill Ward (drums) and Ozzy Osbourne (vocals). I'm not in general a fan of compilation albums, but there's no denying that this collection had a strong coherence, maintaining an incredibly consistent sound and vibe from start to finish.

The album kicks off appropriately enough with 'Black Sabbath' itself, heavy rain and the tolling of a church bell setting an ominous scene. The band crash in, with Iommi's dark and towering riff oozing menace. His use of the tritone – the so-called 'devil's interval' – is stunning. This is the riff that inspired and defined a whole approach to heavy music, and it's not difficult to see why. The riff gives way to a brooding bass guitar, which, in a moment of eerie calm, ushers in a troubled singer. Ozzy's initially imposing tone quickly gives way to fear and desperation. Satan, it seems, has arrived on earth to spread mayhem and destruction and has singled him out for special attention. The vocal delivery paints a far more vivid picture than the lyrics do on their own, and between them the vocal performance *and* Iommi's riff give the song a terrifying power. As Satan delights in the chaos he has invoked, the frightened singer flees, crying to God for help. The pace of the music quickens to a doom-laden gallop. The singer runs, Satan pursues, panic spreads. The singer runs faster. Satan hounds him down. What torture and torment await? "No, no, please no!" wails Ozzy, feeding our imaginations. Is this the end for him? Is this, indeed, the end for us all? With superb timing the band bring the pandemonium to an abrupt halt. The silence implies the triumph of evil.

In comparison, 'The Wizard' is relatively light and breezy, with some rather nifty harmonica producing a kind of dark country sound. Despite its 'magical' theme, it's actually a very positive lyric, with the wizard vanquishing evil power and leaving people feeling fine.

Side One closes with 'Warning' – an extended blues-rock romp ('prog blues' anyone?) that is blessed with some cool, jazzy drumming from Bill. It was recorded as a live jam, possibly in one take, and, in fact, the whole band are on form. Geezer's bass line bobs along ominously, Tony Iommi mixes savage amusement with ice-cool licks at will, and Ozzy's delivery shows the kind of vulnerability and longing that were recurring features of his performances throughout his Sabbath years. It's a love song, of sorts, but it's a love song with a twist. The first verse sets the scene, with Ozzy noting the natural portents (thunderclouds, a shivering sea and a moaning wind) that should have alerted him to the fact that his relationship was doomed from the start. The anxiety dream of the second verse, in which the singer sees his lover with another man, provides a further sign of what's to come, before the third verse brings the singer face to face with the sadness of the inevitable break-up. The musicians give perfect expression to the feelings of their angst-ridden colleague. There's stunning bass/lead guitar interplay and even a brief neo-classical interlude from Iommi before he kicks back into a dark chord which is the cue for the whole band to pick up the mood and drive Ozzy through a reprise of the third verse. Although it's rough around the edges, 'Warning' provides not just a link with the musicians' blues-rock past (with Mythology, the Polka Tulk Blues Band, and Earth), but a clear demonstration of a sense of song composition and drama that even today sets Sabbath apart from the multitude of bands they have influenced. Somewhat ironically, the songwriting credit for 'Warning' goes to legendary rock drummer Aynsley Dunbar and colleagues (Dmochowski, Hickling and Moreshead on my remastered CD version). I must confess that I've never heard the original and have no idea how radically different Sabbath's interpretation is. Nevertheless, both lyrically and musically it presents itself to the retrospective listener as typical Sabbath fare. For me there's a magic here that captures perfectly what early Black Sabbath were about.

Side Two opens with 'Paranoid', the big-hitting single from the album of the same name that I had somewhat unwittingly purchased with *Heaven and Hell*. Famously written by Iommi during his lunch break, it is possibly the best known of all Sabbath tracks. Its quick-fire staccato riff quickly bores its way into your skull without even asking nicely first, while a restless and lovelorn Ozzy draws a connection between his inability to find happiness and his mental health.

Next up is the weighty 'War Pigs', which might itself have been the title track of the band's second album had they been left to their own devices and the record company not got so nervous. This was, after all, the time of the Vietnam War. It's a strikingly ambitious composition, so ambitious, in fact, that Bill Ward has taken great delight in drawing attention to the "waltz-time" drumming at the start.[13] The spacey opening section invokes a kind of 'air raid' anticipation, before a sparse attacking riff creates the space for Ozzy to snarl and shriek his way through the first verse, in which army generals feed "the war machine" and spread "death and hatred to mankind".

The funky middle section of the song allows the singer to expand on his theme. The 'evil' of the generals' actions is linked to the remote decision making of politicians, who "treat people just like pawns in chess". The politicians remain safe at home while the poor are sent off to fight and die in wars that mean little to them but satisfy the vanity and ideology of their masters. The disastrous consequences are set out in a striking final verse:

> *Now in darkness, world stops turning*
> *Ashes where the bodies' burning*
> *No more war pigs have the power*
> *Hand of God has struck the hour*
> *Day of judgement, God is calling*
> *On their knees the war pigs crawling*
> *Begging mercy for their sins*
> *Satan, laughing, spreads his wings*
> *Oh Lord yeah!*

Lyrically the song has come in for some criticism, even appearing in a list of 'worst ever lyrics'. Presumably the criticism stems from the first two lines of the first verse, in which the word "masses" is rhymed with, er, "masses". Personally I think the criticism is unfair. The lyric as a whole is a fine effort, and even the rogue lines themselves work better in context than one might expect. Early Sabbath lyrics are not the poetic endeavours of Oxbridge english literature graduates. They are rock lyrics written by working class boys from industrial Birmingham. As such they are best appreciated not in isolation but in their natural home – embedded in the music. (The written word can attempt to whet your appetite, but it is *always* better to go back to the musical source to hear the lyrics as they were intended to be heard.) Though Geezer Butler's lyrics, like Tony Iommi's songwriting, did become more sophisticated over time, Sabbath's music often gives Geezer's words a weight and depth they cannot support alone – and that is particularly the case here.

The appearance of Satan in the lyric is striking. But it is important that one listens to the lyrics properly. Although Satan is delighting in war and the sins of those who have caused it, these are the very things the song is railing *against*. Despite late repentance, the war pigs are judged by God and considered beyond redemption: they have literally gone to the Devil. If you want a comparison, think of 'Masters of War', Bob Dylan's vitriolic rant against those profiteers who manufacture weapons and make their living from the death and misery of others. Dylan reminds the perpetrators of evil that forgiveness cannot be bought and that such is the magnitude of their crimes that even Jesus would find it hard to forgive them. Like 'Masters of War', 'War Pigs' is a powerful and hard-hitting piece, which, sadly, remains as relevant and biting today as it was when it was written.

Before you've had time to draw breath, Ozzy's deep roboticised warble announces the arrival of 'Iron Man', and suddenly you're in the throes of some bizarre science-fiction parable as 'Iron Man' somehow returns from the grave to wreak vengeance on those who had wronged him in life. With Ozzy's vocal melody following Iommi's heavy, doomy riff exactly, the song almost feels like a dark nursery rhyme – though it's probably more like 'comic book metal', and these days I can't help but imagine a figure in medieval knight armour clinking around haplessly.

If anything, Side Two then gets even *gloomier* as its yields its last offering: 'Wicked World'. Originally the B-side of Sabbath's first single – a cover of the relatively snappy Wiegand-penned track 'Evil Woman' – its inclusion here would have pleased those who missed out on the early release. Opening with a perky little blues riff, 'Wicked World' soon degenerates into a grim downer of a track. "The world today is such a wicked place," announces Ozzy, and things sort of go downhill from there. It's one of Sabbath's most bleak lyrics: drudgery, unhappiness, disease, war, fatherless children, politicians pushing people around. It's all here, condensed into four and a half minutes of abject misery.

Side Three kicks off with the relatively lightweight 'Tomorrow's Dream'. Lyrically, it's about leaving an empty relationship behind. It's not as doom laden or sparse sounding as some of the earlier tracks, but neither is it punchy enough musically to lift the gloom. 'Tomorrow's Dream' is the first track on the collection pulled from *Volume 4*, and I have to say that *Volume 4* is not an album I took to easily. In fact I didn't take to it at all until the summer of 2006 when I bought the remastered version on CD. I have somehow always associated it with the smell of damp trainers and oppressive school corridors on wet winter days. The first copy I bought was a second-hand copy from a student at Southampton University who liked to 'recycle' his albums when he got bored with them and use the proceeds to buy new ones. It didn't help much that the sleeve was slightly tatty and the vinyl slightly scratched. It all reinforced my view of *Volume 4* as a bit of a grubby album. In the context of *We Sold Our Soul* the temporary passage from gloom to grubbiness gave some sort of relief – but it's not what you'd call pleasant.

'Fairies Wear Boots', from *Paranoid*, is a grimy, acid-tinged tale, rumoured to have been written as an act of revenge after the band had been attacked by a gang of skinheads, while 'Changes' (the second track from *Volume 4*) is a downbeat ballad with some nice piano touches, showing that even on a collection as bleak and uncompromising as this one, Sabbath had a mellow side. For those who know this song only through the Kelly and Ozzy Osbourne duet that charted well in the wake of *The Osbournes* TV show, all I can say is check out the original.

Two tracks from the *Master of Reality* album, 'Sweet Leaf' and 'Children of the Grave', close Side Three in fine style. 'Sweet Leaf' is, of course, the Sabs' paean to marijuana. It begins with deep coughing which, allegedly, captures one of the band members taking a hit from a bong. The mighty riff, one of Iommi's most powerful, has stood the test of time and still sounds great today. 'Children of the Grave' offers another reflection on the mess that the powers that be are making of the world and the responsibility that is falling on the younger generation to do something about it. An outro featuring the repeated whispering of the song title and the eerie sound of guitar notes wavering in and out of pitch give a supernatural twist to proceedings and add to the track's apocalyptic feel.

Side Four hits you when you're down with 'Sabbath Bloody Sabbath' charging from the speakers and demanding your submission. This is the title track of Sabbath's fifth album, and, if you hang on in there through the pulverising opening, it becomes clear that by now there was a definite craft to their songwriting – their competence and comfort as musicians allowing them to employ 'light' and 'shade' techniques to ever greater effect. In fact there are few better examples of this than 'Sabbath Bloody Sabbath', despite the fact that both musically and lyrically it's one of their most angry songs. It oozes desperation and resentment. The singer has been manipulated and used. He feels the "gates of life" are closed to him. He has sought answers for this sorry state of affairs, but has received none. He craves some form of escapism (notably at "the hands of doom") and he vents his anger on those he feels are responsible for the miserable nature of his existence. This is a real outsider's anthem. Only the mellow jazziness of the 'chorus' of the first part of the song offers any thought or hope of what might have been, but even then the mood of the music is quickly undermined by the lyric, suggesting isolation, manipulation and resentment.

The rumbling riffola of the second part of the track sees the singer running full pelt into oblivion, forsaken by all, including God – though one does get the sense that the singer has accepted his fate and has even come to revel in it. 'Sabbath Bloody Sabbath' is a tale of frustration, alienation and unfulfilled potential that speaks not just to working class kids who see no future for themselves outside of factory jobs and poverty, but to anyone who has ever felt trapped, manipulated or abused.

The inclusion of 'Am I Going Insane (Radio)' is, in some ways, unfortunate, as it's probably the weakest track on the otherwise excellent *Sabotage* album. Although it was probably the only track on *Sabotage* with radio potential, it's worth noting that the 'radio' of the title does not serve notice of intended commercial activity, but, rather, utilises Birmingham humour and rhyming slang to give some additional indication of the song's subject matter. Radio = Radio Rental = mental; Radio Rental being the name of a popular UK company from whom people used to hire standard household electrical equipment. The song ends with some unnerving and incessant giggling which gives way to the anguished cries of some clearly tortured soul. The cries lead into a truncated version (an 'edit' if you will) of 'Laguna Sunrise', an instrumental from *Volume 4*. In its proper place, 'Laguna Sunrise' is a lovely piece of music. Following as it does the strait-jacketed moans of the poor insane wretch at the end of the previous track, it comes on like a sick joke. Is this deliberate misrepresentation or clever track ordering? I don't know. But whatever the intention, personally I found the juxtaposition of the two disturbing.

'Laguna Sunrise' yields to 'Snowblind', another track from *Volume 4* and another drug song. Its quirky riff creates a strange sense of displaced time which helps convey the lyrical theme quite effectively. The lyric itself contains the kind of unresolved ambiguity that reinforces the 'blindness' of the title. 'Snowblind', I have always assumed, refers to the state of intoxication that the singer craves, though conceivably it may also refer to the singer's 'blindness' to everything else, including the harm he may be doing to himself. Through the conscious blurring of the seasons, coldness and ice are associated not just with winter and death but with happiness, sunshine and flowers. In his sleeve notes to *Volume 4*, Hugh Gilmour says that: "Snowblind captured the hollow emptiness suffered by the use and abuse of something that was undoubtedly a huge contributing factor to making life on the road both bearable and unbearable . . . the bleak world of cocaine addiction."[14] There is little clear evidence here though that the band were ready to identify with the "bleak world of addiction" to which Gilmour refers. Indeed, there is a fast and furious change of pace midway through the song that sees the singer in defiant mood, extolling the virtues of his drug use and the sense of belonging it creates. It is true, however, that this mood of defiance disappears as quickly as it comes, lasting, it seems, only as long as the latest high, and contributing further, intentionally or otherwise, to the ambiguity of the imagery.

We Sold Our Soul's closing track, 'N.I.B.', takes us back to the first album, and ends, where we began, with Satan taking centre stage. An attention-grabbing bass intro from Geezer presages one of Iommi's most catchy riffs and one of the band's most dynamic performances. Again it looks like a love song, as the suitor, initially anonymous, offers the subject of his advances all manner of apparently unobtainable treasures ("the sun, the moon, the stars"). It's only when he seems to have ensnared his victim that the suitor reveals his identity:

> *Look into my eyes, you will see who I am*
> *My name is Lucifer, please take my hand*

Iommi is in electrifying form throughout, capitalising on the drama of the revelation by dragging the band first through a reprise of some of the earlier verses and then off into oblivion with a mournfully furious double-tracked solo.

And so, after a roller coaster of a journey which at times threatened to fade to black, a careful piece of track ordering brings us back to where we started. In both 'N.I.B.' and 'Black Sabbath', it appears that the devil has designs on a human subject and seeks to capture the poor unwitting soul.

Should we be afraid? Should parents up and down the land be concerned? Are Sabbath siding with Satan? No, not at all. Both 'Black Sabbath' and 'N.I.B.' hit my ears like cautionary tales, and this is particularly true of 'N.I.B.' After all, don't Christians believe that the Devil tries to tempt us using all his cunning and guile? Doesn't Satan come in disguise? ("Sometimes," as Bob Dylan tells us on his *Infidels* album, "Satan comes as a man of peace.") And shouldn't we learn to recognise him so we can resist him at all costs?

In an interview with journalist Mick Wall, carried in *Classic Rock* magazine, lyricist Geezer Butler explained that 'N.I.B.' was actually "about Satan falling in love, a complete send-up of . . . the black magic thing. I couldn't think of what to call it, and at that time, we used to call Bill Ward 'Nib', because of his beard – it was pointed like a pen nib. So I thought, well, let's call it after Bill and call it 'Nib'. To make it a bit more interesting I'll put full-stops in it – hence N.I.B."[15] So much then for the rumour that 'N.I.B.' stood for 'Nativity in Black'! (Though for anyone who's listened to the lyrics properly, the term 'Nativity in Black' has no relevance to any of the words and is, quite frankly, a preposterous suggestion.)

Nevertheless, despite such insight, from the horse's mouth as it were, I did find *We Sold Our Soul* scary, and continued to find it scary for a good few months. The dark themes, the references to Satan, and the doomy and sometimes chilling music would have been unsettling for many a sensitive young Catholic soul. I *was* drawn to the music, and I did like it. The problem was that I found playing it on my own in my bedroom to be an unnerving experience. In fact, I had to take the album to youth club to get used to it. There I was able to crank up the volume and listen to it in company in a 'safe' environment. It was not unusual to find me hogging the record player and thrashing around with my pool cue playing imaginary guitar in-between shots. Over time repeated plays led to increasing familiarity and with it desensitisation. By the time I went to see Sabbath live in January 1981 (admittedly now with Ronnie James Dio at the helm) they had been well and truly assimilated into my emotional and psychological make-up.

Given the way I felt on first hearing the album, was this self-administered desensitisation process really a good idea? If the album scared me that much, wasn't I simply playing on my own psychological vulnerabilities and putting myself in harm's way? Well, with the advantage of hindsight, I can confidently say that it most certainly *was* a good idea. Despite the band's image, proper consideration of the lyrics showed me that they were on my side, not trying to steal my soul. It became quite clear to me that their image was just that – and, in fact, it gave them a powerful way of getting their message across. Indeed, all my subsequent reading – of rock magazines and books about Black Sabbath – has simply reinforced the view I formed quite early on that there was nothing here to fear. It did take me a while to get used to the music – but I'm so glad I put in the effort.

That it did take me a while was, it seems, no accident. As Ozzy Osbourne told rock journalist Geoff Barton:

> We were originally called Earth. We used to go to rehearse in this community centre in Six Ways, Aston. Across the road there was a movie theatre. There was this horror film on, and either Tony or Geezer, I can't remember exactly who, said: 'Isn't it weird that people like to pay money to see scary films? Why don't we start writing scary music?' That's how it happened.[16]

With the band hitting on this 'Hammer Horror' approach to heavy blues-rock, and looking for a new name, they settled on 'Black Sabbath' after a song Geezer had written. The title was inspired by the Mario Bava/Boris Karloff film of the same name,* and the music by Butler's bass rendition of 'Mars' from Gustav Holst's *Planets Suite*.[17] With the track already an integral part of their live set, and fitting their new approach well, it seemed a logical choice.

The name was certainly different, and immediately set Black Sabbath apart from the crowd. Nevertheless, the band could surely not have imagined what they were about to unleash. The actions of the record company didn't help, with the debut album's artwork featuring not only a creepy, grainy photo of a pale young woman dressed in black (taken at Mapledurham Mill in Oxfordshire near Reading), but an inverted cross inside the original gatefold sleeve and a rather grim verse that seemed to cast the cover photo and some of the album's lyrics in a dark light. The band have always maintained that this was entirely the record company's doing,

---

* See David Tangye and Graham Wright, *How Black Was Our Sabbath: An Unauthorised View From The Crew* (Pan Books, 2005), p.26. For more information on the film *Black Sabbath*, see *DVD Delirium: The International Guide to Weird and Wonderful Films on DVD* (FAB Press, 2006), pp.78–9

and that they hadn't even seen the sleeve before the album's release. But, before they knew it, they were saddled with a satanic image, and attracting the unwelcome attention of Christian groups and occultists alike.

Despite Tony Iommi's insistence that "we just picked the name because we like it,"[18] the die had been cast. Strange people started turning up at Sabbath gigs, and sometimes the band received rather strange invitations. In their excellent book *How Black Was Our Sabbath: An Unauthorised View From The Crew*, former roadies David Tangye and Graham Wright comment on one particularly notable incident that explains the band's subsequent liking for crosses. They write:

> On one occasion Sabbath declined an offer by a Satanic organisation to play at Stonehenge in Wiltshire, and were then informed they were being cursed. Alex Sanders, the 'Chief Witch' in England at the time, warned the band that these people were serious, advised them to wear crosses around their necks and reassured them that he would put a protective spell around them.[19]

The band would later be plagued in America by extremists on both sides of the metaphysical divide, but despite the rumours and media stories, Tangye and Wright insist that the "closest brush with real black magic would have been Geezer Butler reading Dennis Wheatley horror stories in bed."[20]

What then are we to make of the references to Satan in their work? We have already heard Geezer's explanation of 'N.I.B.' We have also seen how the notion of Satan is used in 'War Pigs', and it should also be noted that 'Black Sabbath' itself is a descriptive work that makes no pro-Satan (if I can put it that way) remarks or observations at all. (Indeed, when in 'Black Sabbath' the going gets tough, Ozzy calls on God for help.) How many other Sabbath songs actually mention Satan? Do you know? Well, there aren't many. By my reckoning, of the 58 tracks with lyrics recorded by the original Sabbath line-up, only six refer explicitly to either "Satan" or "the devil" or "Lucifer" by name (though there are other songs that mention "hell" or "evil" or, in one case, "Lord of this world, evil possessor"*), three of which we have already discussed. *None* of the references to Satan in these six songs can be called positive. 'Into the Void', from *Master of Reality* (1971), for example, features

---

* 'Lord of This World' from the *Master of Reality* album (1971).

an environmentally aware science fiction lyric based on the idea of man escaping to a new world "where love is there to stay" and leaving the polluted and damaged earth "to Satan and his slaves". 'The Writ', from *Sabotage* (1975), is reputedly a song about dodgy managers and business associates who rip bands off and force them through expensive and lengthy legal proceedings before they'll give them their fair share of royalties accruing from their creative endeavours. "Are you Satan, are you man?" sings Ozzy as he tries to understand the kind of person who could behave like that. Finally, as the singer is chewed up and spat out by *Technical Ecstasy*'s 'Gypsy' (1976), the seductress is referred to as "the devil in drag".

By way of contrast, it is worth noting that there are in fact *more* songs which contain explicit references to God (or 'Christ' or 'Jesus') in Sabbath lyrics than there are songs which refer explicitly to Satan. There are at least ten in fact. We've already seen above the way that God features in 'War Pigs', sitting in judgement over those who have caused misery by planning and prosecuting wars, and I've also noted Ozzy's plea to God in 'Black Sabbath'. Some of the other references to God are no less interesting. 'Megalomania', for example, (from *Sabotage*, 1975) bemoans the apparent absence of a "sympathising God", while 'You Won't Change Me' (from *Technical Ecstasy*, 1976) features a depressed-sounding singer who desperately hopes that there is a God and that God will help him. 'Swinging the Chain' (from *Never Say Die!* 1978) simply notes "Oh God, what a terrible, terrible state we're in", while 'Spiral Architect' (from *Sabbath Bloody Sabbath*, 1973) features a "Child of God sitting in the sun giving peace of mind". 'Sabbath Bloody Sabbath' (from the album of the same name) features a quite bizarre piece of epistemology ("God knows like your dognose"?!), while 'Thrill of it All' (from *Sabotage*, 1975) has Ozzy wondering whether the state of the world causes even Jesus to lose faith in mankind. But the biggest surprise is perhaps 'After Forever' (from *Master of Reality*, 1971), which is chock-full of *positive* references to God and Christ. It is true that the track 'Under the Sun' (from *Volume 4*, 1972) contains less than complimentary references to "Jesus freak[s]" and "preacher[s]", but it is not so much an anti-Christian song as a plea to be left alone – and it's equally dismissive of "black magician[s]".

I was fascinated to discover that Geezer Butler, the man responsible for most of the early Sabbath lyrics, was, like me, brought up a Catholic. In an interview with Dave Thompson of *The Rocket* in 1994, he said:

I was brought up an incredibly strict Catholic, and believed in hell and the devil. But though I'd been taught about God and Jesus, no one ever went into what the devil was all about, so when I was 16 or 17, I went about trying to find out. And because I wrote most of Black Sabbath's lyrics, some of that ended up in the songs . . . but it was never advocating Satanism. It was warning against evil.[21]

These comments of Geezer's are consistent with those made by Bill Ward in an interview he gave to *Disc and Music Echo* way back in May 1970. He said: "We don't do black magic but we play some doomy numbers. Our songs are more likely to be about dreams and things like that. We do a couple of numbers about black magic but they are really warnings about the dangers of it – they are anti-black magic songs."[22] In other interviews Geezer himself has reminded journalists of the wide range of topics covered by Sabbath's lyrics and complained about the extent to which early Sabbath were misunderstood: "Sabbath even did a blatantly pro-God, Christian hymn type of song," he told *Metal Sludge*, ". . . and people still took it the wrong way. They thought we were taking the piss out of it!"[23]

Black Sabbath's music does live on the dark side – and its motifs, musical and lyrical, are powerful and designed to unsettle. Yet what people often fail to realise is that much of their output is about confronting and overcoming evil and injustice. I'm not sure to what extent the band would agree with this interpretation – I'm not sure how self-consciously they approached their art – but there is ample evidence throughout their work. They make you confront evil and injustice in various forms, they make you feel its presence and its power and its impact on people's lives. They let you see it in the world around you and then, usually, they offer you some hope of avoiding or transcending it. In this they share more with the techniques of some evangelical Christians than both they themselves and their godly detractors probably realise. I saw the technique at work almost every day as a student, when Christians and Socialist Workers alike employed it enthusiastically in their attempts to win converts. Day after day they would preach on college steps. (I'm sure it is still a common occurrence.) With the best of intentions the Christians try to convince you that you're a sinner, and once they've destroyed your self-esteem and feelings of self-worth they offer you salvation. The Socialist Workers try to convince you of society's inexorable drive to self-destruction and then try to convince you that they offer the only way of avoiding it. Black

Sabbath, without preaching and without a supporting ideology, show you that the world can be a scary and depressing place – and then offer you a kind of salvation through music.

At times in my more intense and troubled teenage years, the apparent bleakness of aspects of their vision also offered a kind of affirmation, a validation or endorsement of what I saw around me. I didn't always like what I saw and while parents and teachers told me I was being stupid, and many of my peers were more interested in fashion, nightclubs and discos, Black Sabbath provided some reassurance that I *was* seeing things correctly. The world could be a mad place, driven by unrestrained greed, self-interest and desire. Things might be alright for some, but they were bad for others. And things would get worse unless we did something about it.

There was also a real sense in which the music functioned as a kind of therapy. This was recognised by Geezer himself in an interview with Mike Saunders of *Circular* just before the release of *Volume 4*. He says: "People feel evil things, but nobody ever sings about what's frightening and evil. I mean the world is a right fucking shambles. Anyway, everybody has sung about all the good things . . . we try to relieve all the tension in the people who listen to us. To get everything out of their bodies – all the evil and everything."[24]

Certainly Black Sabbath tapped into my own Catholic psyche. Catholicism taught me that God and the devil were metaphysical realities. Sabbath, at least in *some* of their very early work, presented God and the Devil as metaphysical realities. Catholicism taught me that I should follow the example of Jesus, rejecting Satan and his ways. Sabbath showed me that Satan, or at least 'evil', was alive around me – in war, in the deceit of politicians, in the twisted desires of the power hungry, and in some technological 'advances', and that it *ought* to be rejected. Sabbath showed me too that life isn't always fair or just. Themes that recur throughout their 1970s albums include unhappiness; frustration with a life that's been mapped out for one; resentment at a failing education system; frustration with dead end jobs and lack of opportunity; the suppression of individuality; the confusion and dissatisfaction of youth; and the uses and abuses of state power. Here were four working class boys from industrial Birmingham who knew about poverty and adversity and who found the sound and imagery they needed to convey their experience and bring it alive. *Of course* their vision was bleak and doom-laden. As Ozzy Osbourne told biographer Mick Wall:

Everyone else was into Flower Power, singing drippy little songs like
'Love Grows Where My Rosemary Goes' and 'Flowers in the Rain'.
And it really made me angry and sick. It was all right for rich hippies
living in California to sing about things like that, but what did we, living
in Birmingham without two pennies to rub together have to do with
any of that? The music we developed after changing our name to Black
Sabbath was loud and it was furious because that's exactly the way we
felt at the time.[25]

That's not to say that Black Sabbath are all anger and ferocity – either
musically or lyrically. Even within the context of *We Sold Our Soul for
Rock 'n' Roll*, one can find positive lyrics. I have already mentioned that
'The Wizard' is a song about vanquishing evil, while, despite his own
sorry state, the 'narrator' in 'Paranoid' is still able to encourage others
to be happy. Also worthy of reference is 'Children of the Grave', which
urges the younger generation to "show the world that love is still alive".
But *We Sold Our Soul for Rock 'n' Roll* is a particularly doomy collection.
It may contain many of Sabbath's best known tracks, but if one looks
beyond it, one realises that it is not really fully representative of the
eight albums they recorded with Ozzy Osbourne. From *Sabbath Bloody
Sabbath* on their music became more experimental, less doomy, more
varied and more ambitious. Certainly for me it has a very 'progressive'
feel. Lyrically too, the mood gradually lifts, becoming brighter, more
positive and more 'poetic'. Look, for example, at a sample of the rich
imagery one finds on the sadly underrated *Technical Ecstasy* and *Never
Say Die!* albums – there are references to "pretty silly ladies", "fatalistic
ships", "summer love", "silent emptiness", "ghostly shadows", "sisters
of sadness", a "sleepy city", "a distant dreamer", "the queen of dance",
"widows weeping", "babies sleeping", "poets yearning" and "lovers
learning". Given its subject matter, even 'Johnny Blade', a track about a
disillusioned and disenfranchised street fighter, is beautifully expressed.
Johnny is said to be "a spider" whose "web is the city at night". He's
"a victim of modern frustration", "society's own child" for whom "life
has no meaning". As with 'War Pigs', Sabbath managed to conjure a
track whose relevance to modern life has, if anything, grown rather than
diminished over time.

But what of the hope and *salvation* I've said they offer? It runs through
their work like the wording on a stick of (Brighton) rock, and it's not difficult
to illustrate. 'A National Acrobat' (from *Sabbath Bloody Sabbath*), for

example, carries the message: "Just remember love is life and hate is living death". On 'Spiral Architect', from the same album, the singer notes that "Laughter kissing love is showing me the way". 'Symptom of the Universe', from *Sabotage*, is another track which, despite its dirty, bludgeoning riff, is full of wonderful sentiment that is captured well in the final stanza:

> *Woman, child of love's creation*
> *Come and step inside my dreams*
> *In your eyes I see no sadness*
> *You are all that loving means*
> *Take my hand and we'll go riding*
> *Through the sunshine from above*
> *We'll find happiness together*
> *In the summer skies of love*

And salvation does not come through love alone. 'Hard Road' (from *Never Say Die!*), for example, offers the useful advice "Forget all your sorrows, don't live in the past", while 'Never Say Die' (the track) not only contains a strong 'don't give up' message, but, in a line reminiscent of 'Children of the Grave', again places faith in the next generation: "Children get together, you can save us all."

As for the excesses of so-called 'black metal', it should be very clear by now that bands of this ilk who claim to have been influenced in some way by Black Sabbath can, in reality, have very little in common with them. Such bands seem to me to be like the school bully who spoils the game by picking up the ball and bursting it or running away with it. Commenting on the spate of church desecrations I referred to earlier, Geezer Butler once said: "I think it's sad that those bands in Norway are trying to get publicity by burning down churches. Music shouldn't ever preach hatred or intolerance, there's already enough of that in the world."[26]

☉ *Singing psalms and smiling* ☉

We Sold Our Soul for Rock 'n' Roll aside, very few albums have had the kind of unsettling impact on me that I described earlier in this chapter. Ozzy Osbourne's *Diary of a Madman* produced a mild version of the same effect, released as it was in a pre-MTV and pre-*Osbournes* era when rumours of the Double-O's extra-curricular activities were rife and it was possible for talented publicists and PR men to get 'the kids' and their anxious parents to believe anything. But, perhaps strangely, the only album that has really come close is the solo vinyl debut by Christian artist (and later Church of England vicar) Geoff Mann.

The album concerned is Mann's 1984 offering *I May Sing Grace*. I had encountered Geoff Mann on record previously, as lead singer with 1980s progressive rock band Twelfth Night. Mann recorded two vinyl albums with the band – the simultaneously complex and elemental *Fact and Fiction* (December 1982), and the live album *Live and Let Live* (1984). I also managed to get hold of the earlier cassette album *Smiling at Grief* (January 1982) – which featured early versions of tracks that would later appear on *Fact and Fiction* alongside instrumental material from the pre-Mann stage of the band's evolution, and additional tracks that, for whatever reason, didn't see the light of day on more significant releases. (It's notable, though, that opener 'East of Eden' was released as a 7" single and performed by the band on the BBC television programme *David Essex's Showcase*.)

I will turn my attention to *I May Sing Grace* shortly, but it's worth lingering for a while on Mann's work with Twelfth Night as this demonstrates very clearly his character, his passion, his way with words, his strong sense of social justice and his acute awareness of the absurdity – madness, even – of many of the economic and political principles and practices which shaped western society in the early 1980s. On *Fact and Fiction*, for example, Mann variously rails against wanton and rampant consumerism, "excess profit", the nuclear arms race, suppression of the individual, the pressures of social conformity, and "selfish desires" that "simply lead to pain"

Fact and Fiction opens with 'We Are Sane', a grand, three-part epic about the use of technology for the purpose of social control and "the enforcement of order". The main character, Mary, is engaged in an apparently hopeless struggle to preserve her sense of self in the face of a humdrum daily office routine and a fearsome onslaught on her individuality by bureaucrats, technocrats, advertisers and profiteers.

> *She stares out of the window*
> *Her will is still in bed*
> *She has no memory of herself*
> *For care has drained her head*
> *The poster on the billboard says she should paint her lips*
> *Like the smiles on the TV people.*

As Mary struggles, State technicians work "to build a component" for people to carry around "at all times", so the powers that be can "keep track of their actions, their interests, their morals, their time-out". In words reminiscent of Orwell's *1984*, plans are hatched to pipe through "musak to maim" the thoughts of the general population and, just in case people manage to break through "their limited truth", messages of fear "to contain them". The band used to do a live introduction which went something like: "Twenty years from now we'll all carry around little boxes. We'll be permanently plugged into them, and we'll walk around trying to convince each other that really we are sane." It all sounds rather prophetic now, and 'We Are Sane' is possibly the only rock song I know that justifies (or perhaps explains) my near phobia of mobile phones. For Mary herself, the new device is hardly needed. She has already been ground down and had the stuffing knocked out of her:

> *This woman's place is in a home*
> *Society has judged*
> *She does not fit official standards*
> *And they cannot be budged*
> *There's something in her eyes that says*
> *The struggle's gone too deep.*

Fact and Fiction's second track, 'Human Being', continues the theme, though this time it's not modern technology that stifles human potential but the cycles of history. 'This City' paints a vivid picture of scenes from inner-city life, while the title track focuses minds on the "power blocks" of the Cold War, the deceptions of politicians and the false promises of the money-god. 'Creepshow' takes some recognisable stereotypes in the form of Amanda (who "must love her Daddy's banker") and "Cyril-has-or-might-have-been" (who "must fill his lust"), and makes of them a circus freakshow that is held up to us as a mirror. Lyrically, social critique and political protest are the order of the day. Musically, the musicianship is superb and the playing emotive. The inclusion of two optimistically titled instrumentals, 'World Without End' and 'The Poet Sniffs a Flower', gives the album a more rounded feel.

Of course, from hippy idealism to the vitriol and violence of the anarcho-punk movement, it is not unusual to find protest in rock music. Indeed, as I argued in an earlier chapter, opposing conventional wisdom and social norms is one of the ways in which rock music sets itself against the establishment and challenges the status quo. But while protest may not be uncommon, it is the particular form that it takes in the hands of Geoff Mann that marks him out as unique. This uniqueness lies partly in the quality of his words, and partly in the balance he achieves between piercing critique and hope for the future. He was a multi-talented individual who was as competent an artist, writer and performer as he was a lyricist. It is something of an irony that, initially at least, there were those who regarded his singing as one of his lesser talents. For example, in describing *Fact and Fiction* as "an unfulfilled masterpiece", *Kerrang!* scribe Malcolm Dome urged the band to get rid of their "disastrous vocalist". Those 'in the know' knew better. By the time Dome's *Kerrang!* kolleague (sic) Derek Oliver came to review Mann's early solo albums, he was drawing vocal comparisons with David Bowie, Iggy Pop and Jim Morrison, describing Mann as "an electric warrior of the finest order". Hardly "disastrous" in either aesthetic or commercial terms![27] I suppose the truth of the matter is that, whatever Geoff Mann's merits as a vocalist, for those who relate to his work – as with Dylan perhaps – the *technical* qualities of his voice hardly seem to matter. What matters most is that he had a vision and was able to present it. Geoff Mann *was* a critic – but he was never *just* a critic. He wrote from a position of personal strength and depth, offering positive messages that counterbalance his often cutting and perceptive social and political comment. Ultimately, he offered a fresh and thought-provoking vision of what human relationships and human life could be like. Here was a man who wanted to help people catch a glimpse of what they might be, and what it might mean to be fully human. Here was a man who wanted to show us where joy and love reside, and he did that partly by trying to show us where it was lacking and where it was needed. His personal struggle to practice what he preached is evident throughout a body of work that is infused with both sincerity and humility.

'Love Song', *Fact and Fiction*'s closing track, is an excellent example of this, illustrating as it does the positive energy, vision and belief that lies behind all of Mann's work. Twelfth Night, of course, took their name from the title of the Shakespeare play in which the lovelorn Duke Orsino tells his musicians, "If music be the food of love, play on." 'Love Song' was thus an apt anthem for the band, and was used to close not only *Fact and Fiction* but many of their gigs. The chorus is inspiring:

Don't hold back
Don't think that hope is pointless
Love is a, love is a, love is a, love is
An open door
Don't believe that life is closed against us
Love is a, love is a, love is a, love is
An open door

Also significant, as a portent of the future, is the reference to "the carpenter" in the closing lines of the song:

If it seems that your hoping heart
Has led you into pain
Take a tip from the carpenter
Forgive and love again
And again

Mann, as noted above, was a Christian and, as such, was driven by imperatives that went beyond what he felt he was able to achieve with Twelfth Night. His desire to do God's will and to use his music as a medium to express his faith doubtless influenced his decision to leave the band. Highlights from his final gigs with Twelfth Night – at London's Marquee Club on the 4 and 5 November 1983 – were captured on the *Live and Let Live* album. This featured not only staples from *Fact and Fiction*, but a new instrumental called 'The End of the Endless Majority', the anti-war epic 'Sequences', and the excellent set opener 'The Ceiling Speaks'. Lyrically, 'The Ceiling Speaks' is another track which gives a very strong indication of the direction in which Mann was going. It appears to be a love song, and in a way it is, though as with 'Love Song' itself, the twist in the tale comes with a late reference to Jesus. "And Christ, I love you," shouts Mann, which might well be taken to be an expression of the depth of his feelings for a loved one, much in the way that someone might say, "God, you look beautiful tonight". Except that once one realises that Mann is a Christian, it is clear that he is singing about his relationship with God. The fact that this is not revealed until the last line, and even then in a form modelled on a common blasphemy, allows the song to mean different things to different people.

If truth be told, it was through the *Live and Let Live* album that I discovered Twelfth Night, by which time Mann had moved on and started a solo career. Nevertheless, his contribution to Twelfth Night made a huge impression on me, and on many others. And so it was with great anticipation that I purchased his first solo vinyl release, *I May Sing Grace*. I have to say that on first play, *Grace* was probably the most disappointing album I had ever bought in my life. Like *We Sold Our Soul for Rock 'n' Roll*, it was an album that I initially found very difficult to play because of the unpleasant effect it created. I don't think I was alone in responding in this way. Indeed, while happily advertising the availability of Geoff's first solo album, the (at the time) cassette-only release *Chants Would Be a Fine Thing*, the Twelfth Night newsletter, *Night Moves*, warned fans of the idiosyncratic nature of Geoff's work: "Please note that Geoff's tape is highly individualistic and does not sound like Twelfth Night," ran the editor's note, "– so don't expect *Fact and Fiction Part II*."[28]

I May Sing Grace is such a low-budget affair that it almost sounds unfinished. At times it's not so much rough around the edges as just rough. It has an abrasive, almost grainy and grating quality that contrasts markedly with both the musicianship and sophisticated arrangements of Twelfth Night and the increasingly slick production used by some of the heavy rock bands I was listening to at the time. In fact, the album has a kind of 'black folk' feel to it – spacey and slightly depressing. The tracks themselves are more overtly Christian than Mann's Twelfth Night material, and are referenced by Biblical verses which presumably mark out passages which either inspired the songs or which Mann felt would make useful 'further reading' for anyone inclined to follow his newly created tributary back to its source. As I say, at first I struggled to get comfortable with the music and to come to terms with it. In fact it took about a year for the album to hit . . . but when it did: BANG! It came on like a revelation. Or like the instant release of tension following a very bad headache. Or like a Eureka moment. Actually, I remember the moment very well. I *was* in the bath. I was revising for exams and feeling extremely anxious as I struggled to prepare for an A-level economics paper. I needed a break. As I ran the water, I rifled through my record collection and settled on the rather lonely-looking and underplayed Geoff Mann album. I cranked up the volume, laid back and tried to relax. It was like clicking a switch. Suddenly the album made sense. I could feel the words *and* the music, and for the first time they seemed to work together. All at once I was comfortable with the tone and feel of the music. As for the necessarily low production values – cost almost certainly had something to do with it – they simply stopped bothering me. As with Black Sabbath, the internalisation and integration of sounds that initially had the power to create such visceral disturbance was both a form of submission and a kind of transcendence. And it felt good! The experience provided a sense of perspective and some much needed personal reassurance. It was a timely reminder of what is really important in life and what, in the grand scheme of things, matters less. It put my anxiety in context and brought me sufficient peace to unblock my overstuffed mind.

Lyrically, *I May Sing Grace* covers a great deal of ground. Some tracks deal with themes that are familiar to Twelfth Night fans, particularly where Mann notes the madness of travelling a road that seems to lead only to misery. In 'For More Than a Day', for example, Mann catalogues a whole litany of superficial and misguided attitudes, sad situations, and damaging and destructive practices. He observes "refugees" wandering aimlessly, "eyeless idols" staring blankly, "big machines . . . left to rot and rust", "innocence hanged", "lack of care", "needless death", and "bunkered big men who know their power drill". Modern consumerism does not escape Mann's critique:

> *Department stores sell shiny sores to stick upon your skin*
> *Design their special goods to fall apart when you're not in*

"Doesn't it sound crazy to you?" he sings in pained plea.

Elsewhere he provides a clear focus on things that he believes have more value. One of the album's key themes is fulfilment and self-realisation through love, and in 'I Wouldn't Lie to You' Mann presents the essence of his message in bold and forthright terms:

> *Together is right for us humans*
> *Love is the glue of our bonds*
> *Without it all things fail to renew*

Again the message is inspiring, though it should be noted immediately that for Geoff Mann the forms of love and self-realisation about which he is singing cannot be separated from his faith. The verse I have quoted continues:

> *In Christ we can find our humanity*
> *Without missing anything out*
> *I wouldn't lie to you*

Though faith need have nothing to do with it, it is from this perspective that album opener 'Piccadilly Square' urges us to look beyond appearances and reach out to the tramp whose personality lies buried beneath old newspapers. Who knows what circumstances conspired to put the tramp in this predicament? But by the grace of God, one might reflect, there go I.

To focus on 'love' in the way that Geoff Mann does is to focus on relationships and the possibilities that they bring. In the following passage, from 'My Soul', Mann takes a familiar model of love – the idea of a couple joining together in marriage ('til death do us part') – and uses it to cast light on the way he feels about his relationship with God:

> *Eternal life awaits us*
> *There will be no divorcing*
> *The bride from her beloved*
> *The love between them coursing*
> *My soul*

Though Mann clearly wears his faith on his sleeve, to his eternal credit he is not afraid to criticise organised religion (including Christianity) where he sees it going wrong. The best example is perhaps 'For God's Sake', in which he finds it hard to disguise his contempt for those who abuse their faith by using it to justify sinful acts against others.

> *Both sides in war for blessings pray*
> *Scatter refugees from fields of play*
> *Financial farmers planting bombs*
> *Crops of death to prove a pointless point*
> *Catholic killers rant and rage*
> *Provo Marxmen come of age*
> *Troubled conscience turning page*
> *Dredging obscure scripture*
> *That might justify more murder*
> *For God's sake*

Regardless of one's religious (or non-religious) persuasion, there is much of general value in Mann's work that really does demand a wider audience. This is true not just because of his social and political comment, not just because of his own criticisms of certain types of 'religious' practice, and not even because of the positive vision of Christianity he presents. Much of what he says in the context of his relationship with

God has relevance to human relationships in general. Love often requires selflessness and a willingness to sacrifice something of oneself for the good of the loved one and the overall relationship. Striking the right balance to ensure that both partners are fulfilled and the relationship is a truly happy one is not easy, but Mann's lyrics often encourage useful reflection on these matters. Look, for example, at the following verse from 'I Wouldn't Lie to You':

> You ask a question
> Which is "Why is loving so hard?"
> Shouldn't it be easy to do?
> Well it is very easy to take love
> And fatal to pay with indifference
> Which is what so many lovers go through

This is one example of many, and I would urge anyone who has found any part of the foregoing discussion interesting to explore further. For anyone who does want to explore, it is worth noting that while the original (vinyl) version of *I May Sing Grace* is now very difficult to find, it is possible to get both this and *Psalm Enchanted Evening*, the album that followed it, on the *In One Era* CD. The matter is explained by Andy Labrow in his *In One Era* sleeve notes:

> In 1990 Geoff had the idea to release a CD compilation of *I May Sing Grace* and *Psalm Enchanted Evening*, his (vinyl only) solo albums from 1984 and 1985, with the new title of *In One Era . . .*, omitting a track off each album so it would fit on a single CD. The original albums, recorded on very low budgets, were Geoff's second and third after leaving Twelfth Night. They formed a sort of musical training ground, developing his style of wobbly guitar, the desire to compose and a calling to express his Christian faith through music. A deal was struck but unfortunately the album never appeared, although one track, 'For God's Sake', did appear in May 1991 on a (ACM Journal) magazine sampler CD. Several months after Geoff's death in 1993, a chance phone call to myself from Malcolm Parker, a long time Geoff Mann fan, led to him offering Jane Mann (Geoff's widow) a new deal to release the album on his record label using Geoff's ideas and specifications. Explaining the album title in a letter in 1990 Geoff wrote . . . *'In One Era, a pun of course. I don't know if you use the phrase 'In one ear and out the other'. It refers to a statement that no-one listens to!'*

I'd like to say that it's available from all good record shops, but I know that it probably isn't. For the most part it has indeed become a statement that no one listens to!* As for the omitted tracks, while 'For More Than a Day' (from *I May Sing Grace*) is one of my favourites, the track omitted from *Psalm Enchanted Evening*, 'Peacemeal', is, for me, the weakest track on the album and the one I would have omitted myself. Its omission thankfully allows the album closer 'Flowers' to be retained.

I may stand alone here, but for me 'Flowers' is a real gem – a little known and sadly neglected masterpiece. It's not only the best track from these two albums, it's one of the strongest tracks Mann ever wrote or contributed to. It encapsulates an almost Buddhistic attitude to the beauty that can be found in the simple things around us ("Flowers, oh consider how they grow"), things we come to take for granted because of their familiarity and availability or just because we're too busy to stop and take notice. Consistent with Mann's earlier work, he draws a contrast between the natural beauty of flowers ("growing outward from God's thought") and the ugly 'functionalism' of many of the artefacts, structures and processes that mankind creates – in this case our buildings ("Towers, pulsing pictures to your screens"), TV entertainment (the "moron machines" of Twelfth Night's 'Creepshow'), and the use we make of our time (the "hours" which "capture people in their snares" and hang over "the starving" like an executioner's axe). The last of the song's three verses captures the optimism of Mann's faith but also its challenging nature:

> *Jesus, Jesus Christ has died for you*
> *The card is marked RSVP*
> *Jesus, see Him nailed upon the wall*
> *Don't waste your time hoping he won't come down*
> *Jesus isn't wasted in the heart*
> *Jesus lives in humble souls*
> *Jesus doesn't need your patronisation*
> *Love is the word He bleeds from hands*
> *Into your open heart*
> *Transfusing and clean*
> *And He loves flowers*

---

* At the time of writing, however, it was still available from Malcolm Parker at GFT (Cyclops Records) – and for an extremely reasonable price.

As the verse nears its end, Mann really goes for it, hollering out the word 'love' in such an incredibly impassioned way that his voice breaks, a soulful electric guitar skilfully picking up the pieces and bringing a sense of order and beauty back to proceedings. Again the closest comparison I can think of is a Dylan song, 'Precious Angel' from the *Slow Train Coming* album, where, like Mann, Dylan is content to let his voice reach for the ideal and audibly fail – a clear acknowledgement of his own imperfections and limitations in the face of something greater. 'Flowers' is a truly unique track delivered in such a personal and heartfelt way that it's impossible not to feel the sincerity and hope of the artist. Listen to it in the dark, either cranked up loudly or in headphones. Let it wash over you.

There are many who are critical of the herd-mentality and hypocrisy of Christianity, and the criticisms are often justified, but in Mann's work we are presented with a living, breathing, experiential and overwhelmingly positive vision of Christianity. We may not be able to embrace it fully or throw ourselves into it, but it is impossible not to recognise and respect it.

And respect is precisely what Mann commanded among his peers. As noted above, he died young, two months before his thirty seventh birthday in fact. He left behind a wife and three children, and, by all accounts, a huge void in the lives of those who knew him. His life and music are celebrated on the album *Mannerisms*, a more than ample indication of the esteem in which he was held. The album features some of the most popular progressive rock bands of the last 30 years – including Pallas, IQ, Pendragon and Twelfth Night, along with other bands and musicians Geoff had played with – all offering different interpretations of Geoff's songs. Such tributes are usually reserved for luminaries such as Bob Dylan or The Beatles.

At the time Geoff Mann was diagnosed with cancer Twelfth Night were preparing *Live and Let Live* for an expanded reissue on CD. At Geoff's insistence work was hastened so that he might see it in its final form. In the event, he passed away before its completion – though, fittingly, the band dedicated the album to him. In his sleeve notes to the album, Twelfth Night drummer Brian Devoil speaks glowingly of his friend and former band-mate:

> Geoff developed a great rapport with his audience who were entertained, challenged but never patronised by him, and who respected him for what he was, a man of the highest integrity. His sense of humour and quick-

wittedness are well known, likewise his distaste for the pretentious, the uncaring corporation, the pressure to conform to somebody else's norm. He always believed in giving everything. Geoff had such a positive effect on everyone who knew him, he was almost universally loved, and his passing is not only a sad loss to us, his close friends and family, but to his congregation, fans all over the world, and society as a whole.[29]

When *Kerrang!* announced his death, they referred to his contribution to the 'Rock and Satanism' debate in which, under the watchful eye of journalists Jon Hotten and Mörat, Geoff went head to head with self-professed 'satanist' Glen Benton of the American death metal band Deicide. "Throughout their discussion", says the magazine, "Geoff's calm and articulate manner continually embarrassed a deliberately provocative Benton."

Shortly before his death, *Record Collector* magazine reviewed his *Second Chants* album and called Geoff Mann "the Daevid Allen of the pulpit"!* It's an amusing and somehow touching description, which, even for someone like me who knows Geoff Mann only through his work, seems to convey something of the spirit one senses on his records. But what was Geoff Mann really all about? How did he conceive of his own efforts? Let me quote to you from a letter written by Geoff to my friend Marv at a point fairly early on in his solo career. He writes:

> I am involved in writing, painting and, of course, music. I've made 3 LPs since leaving Twelfth Night (and a cassette album), which have sought to examine my relationships with the world, my faith, and the implications of spirituality as a Christian in response to the existential joys and dilemmas of being human. These involve both the inner, personal struggles, such as the paradox between knowledge of goodness of truth and living it, and also wider social struggles. These are, for instance: 'How do we seek peace in a world of violence?' 'How do we achieve justice where every move we make is potentially damaging to someone?' and other such questions.
>
> Of course, I don't sit down with a list of questions and try to write a song for each which wraps the whole thing up, such a thing is not possible. But these are the questions we live with, and illumination, albeit very painful sometimes, does come and can be shared between each other in songs and so on. My work goes through different stages, depending on my main concern at a given time. Sometimes it is more inward looking and personal, sometimes outward looking."

---

* Daevid Allen of Gong fame.

The letter ends with Geoff Mann's characteristic sign-off: "I wish you God's peace."

○ Heaven or hell? ○

For artists so apparently diverse in musical style, image and reputation, at times there is a remarkable convergence of lyrical themes in the work of Black Sabbath and Geoff Mann. Take a few moments to read through and consider the following pairs of lyrics.

	Lyric 1	Lyric 2
1.	Look at the wheat in the field Look at the beauty revealed Look at the power of the sun celestial burning Look at the girls and the boys Look at the children with their toys Look at the planets in their spaces each one turning This is the beauty of Creation	Of all the things I value most of all I look upon my earth and feel the warmth And know that it is good
2.	Could it be you're afraid of what your friends might say If they knew you believe in God above They should realise before they criticise That God is the only way to love	Some may say it's all unreal That's not the way I feel My heartbeat dance and play Nothing more to say
3.	We talk about freedom As if it was all just a matter of law We talk about peace while we polish our guns Don't we	Since he passed the motion They're building in the ocean And he's saying all men should be free What a combination Peace and radiation And he's saying free men should fight for me
4.	All that I have has come from you Yet I became a thief To make and keep one part myself In darkness I would cuddle death And value it as life A fool's gold glory was my wealth	Won't you help me Mr.Jesus Won't you tell me if you can When you see this world we live in Do you still believe in Man? If my songs become my freedom And my freedom turns to gold I'll ask the final question If the answer could be sold

5.	Have you ever thought about your soul – can it be saved? Or perhaps you think that when you're dead you just stay in your grave Is God just a thought within your head or is he part of you? Is Christ just a name that you read in a book when you were at school?	All of the mindless cruelty With which we form our world Can be wiped out by God's great love He will forgive and set you free If you will die in Him Believe and you will see His dove
6.	The flags we weave Only deceive We must believe We must believe in love	Your world was made for you By someone above But you choose evil ways Instead of love
7.	Give it all and ask for no return And very soon you'll see And you'll begin to learn	And when I asked Why I did not have all the love I needed I got my answer I got my answer Because I did not give away All that I had
8.	The food of love became the greed of our time And now we're living on the profits of crime	It seems that paradise has been well locked and barred To all the issue of Adam It seems that children must pay for their parents crimes Until they wish they'd never had them

In the extracts tabled above there are passages from both artists dealing with a range of issues including creation, belief in God, politicians talking peace as they plan for war, illusory wealth, valuing the wrong things in life, the afterlife, the power of God, the choice between good and evil, the value of selflessness, and unconditional love. Be honest with yourself, is it obvious to you which lyrics are written by the Christian artist and which are written by the 'heavy metal' band with the satanic image? Obviously if you're already a fan of either artist, the test will be easier. But at the very least, I hope the lyrics set out above demonstrate some unexpected similarities. For anyone still not sure about who wrote what, here are the answers for you:

	Lyric 1	Lyric 2
1.	Geoff Mann: 'Creation' (Genesis 1:31; John 1:1-5) from *Psalm Enchanted Evening*	Black Sabbath: 'Spiral Architect' from *Sabbath Bloody Sabbath*
2.	Black Sabbath: 'After Forever' from *Master of Reality*	Twelfth Night: 'The Ceiling Speaks' from *Live and Let Live*
3.	Geoff Mann: 'Kingdom Come' (Matthew 6:33 & John 10:9) from *I May Sing Grace*	Black Sabbath: 'All Moving Parts Stand Still' from *Technical Ecstasy*
4.	Geoff Mann: 'Afterwards' (Luke 15: 4-7; John 3: 1-3), from *I May Sing Grace*	Black Sabbath: 'Thrill Of It All' from *Sabotage*
5.	Black Sabbath: 'After Forever' from *Master of Reality*	Geoff Mann: 'Afterwards' (Luke 15: 4-7; John 3: 1-3) from *I May Sing Grace*
6.	Twelfth Night: 'Sequences' from Live and Let Live	Black Sabbath: 'Lord of This World' from *Master of Reality*
7.	Black Sabbath: 'It's Alright' from *Technical Ecstasy*	Geoff Mann: 'Slow One' (Mark 10:15 & 10: 17-31) from *I May Sing Grace*
8.	Black Sabbath: 'Hole in the Sky' from *Sabotage*	Twelfth Night: 'East of Eden' from *Smiling at Grief*

And so, what does my experience of Black Sabbath and Geoff Mann say about my own experience of God and the Devil in rock music? Well, while one can't escape the metaphysical trappings of early Black Sabbath, or the personal faith that so inspired and influenced Geoff Mann, I don't think I can say with any certainty that I've *really* encountered God or the devil through the work of either.

Black Sabbath probably brought me as close as I'd like to get to experiencing the reality of evil through music. There's a grimness and nastiness about some of the extreme metal bands who cite Sabbath as an influence, but my general feeling is that it's better to keep away from that sort of music, whether or not you're worried about its association with the devil! A full and proper listen to Black Sabbath makes it hard to reach anything other than the Christian conclusion that *if* the devil exists, he's a force to be avoided. The truth of the matter is that the doom-laden sound and metaphysical imagery of the early Black Sabbath albums is driven not by an interest in propagating evil, but by experience, energy and anger that is rooted in the frustrations and constraints of the industrial working class world from which their music allowed them to escape. Leaving aside early references to 'God' and 'Satan', their lyrical themes are sufficiently broad to reach out to people in a much more general way. Anyone who has ever felt trapped, inhibited or let down, either by a loved one or by society in general, could potentially find plenty of solace and support in the music of the original Black Sabbath line-up. Indeed, that's probably why the music has endured and retained a broad appeal.

As for Geoff Mann, his work almost certainly brought me as close as I'm likely to get to experiencing God through music, and did a considerably better job of it than most of the music I heard in church as a child. I believe that his work can provide considerable comfort and spiritual sustenance to people irrespective of their religious views. It is music I've returned to time and again for the calmness, humility and optimism of its vision.

Black Sabbath and Geoff Mann both had a considerable effect on my thinking and development, and I continue to listen to both to this day. Both have helped me to understand more about the world around me, and to develop a stronger sense of self. At a personal level, I remain outside Catholicism and Christianity, sceptical of the existence of spirits and demons, but concerned about the influence of more extreme forms of both organised religion and occult practice. But despite such scepticism, I recognise the importance of faith to others, and I like to think that I have remained aware of the profound importance of spirituality in human life. Reflecting on the world around us, learning to see wonder and beauty in it, learning to distinguish between things that matter and things that don't, deciding what kind of world we want to live in, learning more about ourselves, learning to love, recognising injustice when we see it, recognising when action is required – these are all important aspects of what it is to be fully human. In my own little supra-humanistic world, I'm happy to take whatever help and insight I can from any artist who tries to provide it. Black Sabbath and Geoff Mann have plenty to offer in that respect. I commend them both to you.

6

Hippy, Heavy, Horny, Happy

Denim and Leather

Whatever your view – if you have one – of the heavy rock band Saxon, there is no denying that for those of us who discovered rock music at around the time of the New Wave of British Heavy Metal (NWOBHM), the lyrics of 'Denim and Leather' capture something of the spirit of the age:

> *Where were you in '79 when the dam began to burst*
> *Did you check us out down at your local show*
> *Were you wearing denim, wearing leather, did you run down to the front*
> *Did you queue for your tickets through the ice and snow*
>
> *Did you read the music papers from the back to the front*
> *Did you find out where to see your favourite band*
> *Did you listen to the radio every Friday night*
> *Did you hang around your local record store*
>
> *Denim and Leather brought us all together*
> *It was you who set the spirit free*

For me these words caught something very real and very special. It wasn't *just* that they accurately described some of the things I did (that is, read *Sounds* and *Kerrang!*, listen to *The Friday Rock Show*, get anxious about gig tickets, hang around record shops). At that time rock music, more than anything else in my life, made me feel truly alive, and the friendships and sense of belonging that accompanied these activities enriched my life beyond expectation. In the words of the song, "denim and leather brought us all together", and for me, this 'coming together' to appreciate the creative endeavours of those whose music spoke to us and for us, was a new and powerful experience. As I've already said, live performances often had a particular place and power in this respect.

Saxon knew that, as hard-working and good at their craft as they were, they were only up on the stage because of the people who bought their records and went to see them play. "It was you who put us here today," sang Biff, with sincerity and gratitude. "It was you who filled the concert hall." Sadly, the days of bands paying their dues and earning their success by building a following on the road seem to be part of an 'old school' concept of what rock music is and what it stands for. Some of the appreciation and mutual respect between band and audience that so often accompanied this way of 'making it' seems to have gone now. Popular bands these days usually have the string-pulling power of major labels to thank, and clever PR people who know how to market 'product'. Which isn't to say that there aren't hard-working bands or that popular bands on major labels aren't any good – it's just that the dynamic between band, fan and label seems to have changed. Back in the NWOBHM days, there seemed to be values inherent in rock music that offered an improvement on mainstream youth culture and provided pointers to a 'better way of being'. I really believed that. The whole culture around heavy rock music at the time seemed to offer possibilities that didn't rely on ego and self-aggrandisement or competition with others. That's how *I* felt, anyway, and that's how I remember things. Rock music *seemed* to offer a way of life that made everyone a winner.

❂ *Southampton* ❂

In 1985, at the age of 18, I went to Southampton University to study politics and international relations. Despite having become a very intense and rather introspective teenager, I left home for university with very high hopes. My choice of A-level subjects (modern history, economics and a curious part-politics, part-law subject called British constitution) and my musical tastes had reinforced my natural tendencies and I had become a historically aware social critic of sorts – or at least, that's how I liked to think of myself. I saw rock music as a living medium which had the potential to offer new insight, new hope and real alternatives, and I saw my academic studies as a means of unveiling similar insights and alternatives from other sources. I thought that university would be full of people like me. People, that is, who agreed that the world was in a mess and who wanted to do something about it. I suppose lots of idealistic teenagers have similar thoughts and hopes. In the event, Southampton University was not what I expected. It didn't seem to be full of people like me at all. It seemed to be full of the kind of people I had disliked at school – except that students at Southampton University had more money. The local youths from the nearby Flowers Estate obviously shared my misgivings, though while I prepared to do battle with words, they had settled on a programme of more direct action.

I was placed in a hall of residence called Montefiore House in a part of Southampton called Swaythling. With two other halls nearby – Connaught and Stoneham – the area boasted a not inconsiderable student population. The main University campus lay about a mile away in the 'pleasant' Highfield part of the City. Within days of term starting, news spread of a stabbing on the main walking route to the campus, and other reports emerged of violence between locals and students. Some students claimed that they had been shot at with airguns, and a number of us experienced verbal abuse and threatening behaviour. The Student Union issued safety advice and proposed alternative walking routes, especially after dark. And yet, despite abhorring the behaviour of the locals and getting thoroughly depressed by the whole ludicrous situation, I couldn't help feeling that the locals had a point. One student I met, for example, owned a Porsche and liked to drive around the Flowers Estate to show off his wealth and taunt the youngsters hanging around on street corners. Other students thought nothing of getting drunk and defacing street signs, stealing traffic cones or generally making nuisances of themselves. Many local people felt understandably aggrieved at the large influx of 'bright young things' who seemed to have little respect for the local community and who seemed to them to do little more than piss away their grants (we still had them then) or parental allowances, and flaunt their privileged status. Yes, the local people had a point – unfortunately some of them chose to express it very badly. Poor behaviour all round, then, was the order of the day. These things did nothing to help my general state of mind, or to help me feel that I belonged.

My initial bad impression was compounded by some early social experiences. Very soon after arriving in Southampton, I was invited to a party by Richard – he of the post-Saxon gig crook-lock incident, with whom I had attended some of my earliest gigs. Richard was now a law student in the third and final year of his degree. "Bring your new mates along," he said, and so I did. As we got ourselves drinks and looked to mingle, we noticed a curious thinning out of people. Ten minutes later, as I went in search of a lavatory, it was obvious that a lot of people had chosen to congregate on the overcrowded stairs. "Have you seen all the fucking hippies here?" I heard one young man say, "I fucking hate hippies." A nice welcome, I thought.

Something similar happened when a group of us decided to try the local brew at a popular student pub on the main Portswood Road. We found an empty table, and within minutes noticed that the people either side of us had also moved on. It was inexplicable. Yes, most of us had long or longish hair, and we looked different to most because we wore jeans and denim or leather jackets, but that wasn't unusual – not where I came from anyway. We were not loud, or rude, or aggressive or insulting. And yet people tended to turn their backs on us, or give us a very wide berth. These experiences were an eye-opener, and a good indication of the extent to which 'image' mattered to many students in Southampton in 1985.

⊛ Silkie and the cheese ⊛

Things at Southampton weren't all bad. My best mate from school, Brendan, also managed to get a place there, to read law. As luck would have it, Brendan also ended up in Montefiore House – or Monte, as we came to call it. Monte was a strange place. It consisted of a mix of rather exposed and worn looking blocks of student rooms, along with newer more modern blocks of self-catering flats. Brendan, a vegetarian, secured a place in a self-catering flat, which gave him more control over his diet. He shared the flat with several other first-year students. There was Ed from Aylesbury – home of Marillion – who liked to wax lyrical about the market square that inspired the title of the band's first single. Ed was a mathematician with an off-the-wall style of humour that lay somewhere between *Monty Python* and *The Young Ones*. His mother had proclaimed him a "comic genius" and, in his own inimitable laid-back manner, he pursued the twin aims of trying to get a degree while seeking a suitable publisher/broadcaster for his 'groundbreaking' comedy. Brendan and Ed became great friends. There were other characters in the flat, however, whose friendships with Brendan proved shorter-lived. There was a normal and well-adjusted guy called Razi. There was Mick Interesting, who I thought was OK, but whose nickname – of which he remained blissfully unaware – tells you all you need to know about his relationship with Brendan and Ed. There was Junkie James, an introverted, ever so softly spoken and painfully shy maths student who found social interaction difficult, but who found solace in cannabis and sometimes other substances of a less than legal nature. There was also a very friendly chap called Dwayne who bought himself a car when he couldn't find a girlfriend, and then left Southampton for one of the old polytechnics where he felt his abilities would stand out more. And then there was Trevor, a happy-go-lucky kind of guy from the Isle of Man who spoke often about his joy at having left "the island" and of the opportunities his arrival on "the mainland" opened up for him.

The flat that this strange assortment of young men shared was modern, comfortable, clean and well-equipped. In contrast, I had a room in one of the old blocks. My accommodation came with breakfast and evening meals included in the price, though we had to walk to the nearby Connaught Hall for our food. The block I lived in consisted of several identical floors with shared bathroom, lavatory and kitchen facilities which were basic at best. Given the accommodation's open nature, those of us who lived on the ground floor occasionally found ourselves sharing the bathroom and shower facilities with local tramps. And although everyone on each floor had a key for the kitchen door, security was quite lax. Often food or drink placed in the shared fridge seemed to disappear. This was infuriating, especially for those like my friend Rob who had Type-1(insulin-dependent) diabetes, and who, more than I realised at the time, needed access to particular foods at particular times to help keep his blood-sugar levels within manageable limits. Matters came to a head for me on an occasion when I'd made a particular effort to walk to the local shop to purchase a lump of cheese with the intention of making cheese toasties later that evening. On returning to the fridge to collect it just a couple of hours later, I found that it had been opened and almost half of it had already been eaten. Worse, across the top of the label, someone had written their name in biro – "SILKIE". I was incensed. I mashed up the remainder of the cheese, stuck a few used matches and other bits of rubbish in the mess, and alongside the name SILKIE added, in my own fair hand, "IS A WANKER!" I 'knew' it was my cheese because I remembered the weight and price of the pack. Only on my next visit to the shop did I realise that a lot of the packets of cheese carried the same weight and price. SILKIE turned out to be the hall warden, who bore more than a passing resemblance to Geoffrey from the children's TV programme *Rainbow*. While someone *had* stolen my cheese, it is unlikely to have been poor old SILKIE who probably just bought his own. It still amuses me now to think of the bewilderment on the innocent SILKIE's face when he went to the fridge to get his cheese only to find it all mashed up and the label carrying some unwarranted personal abuse. (On the other hand, it might have been him – the wanker.)

❁ *Harvey* ❁

Anyhow, as I say, Southampton wasn't all bad. As well as Brendan and Ed, there were other good people around who quickly became friends. Rob, for example, lived in the room next door. He was a huge Rush and AC/DC fan. In stature and appearance he resembled 'new' AC/DC vocalist Brian Johnson, right down to the hairstyle and ubiquitous flat cap. We called him 'AC/DC Rob'. Further down the corridor was the ever-so-friendly and extremely sensible Will – a mulleted Lancastrian from Bolton who insisted on calling Brendan 'Brent'. I also liked a Cornish chap from Redruth called Tony, who lived across the road in Connaught. We often referred to him as 'Connaught Tony' to distinguish him from another Tony – a more unusual chap with a strong prog-rock fixation and a wine-lover's interest in real ale. (Monte Bar, incidentally, claimed to have the biggest – and cheapest – selection of real ale in the whole of Wessex – wherever that is.) There were others, too . . . but most of all there was Harvey – or 'H', as he liked to be called.

Harvey was the real deal. Neil from *The Young Ones* meets rock god meets secular Jesus. In his own mind, I think, he was half-hippy half-biker. In him the late 1960s met the 1980s and produced one of the nicest, most open, most genuine human beings it's ever been my privilege to meet. He also had the most astonishingly comprehensive record collection – in rock terms at least – that I had ever seen, and a knowledge of rock history to match. His vinyl collection spanned almost an entire wall of his student room, and he knew at a glance if anything had been removed or put back in the wrong place. There was seemingly no artist or band worth knowing about that he didn't know about, but what impressed me most was his ability to appreciate almost anything. There weren't many bands we discussed about whom he didn't have something positive to say. He was equally at home discussing Gong and Slayer, and often provided insights that were typically idiosyncratic. I remember, for example, him once trying to convince me of the merits of Slayer's *Reign in Blood*.

"H," I said, as I examined the artwork and accompanying album information, "this album is only 28 minutes long. What a rip off!"

"It's only so short," he replied, without so much as a hint of irony, "because they play the songs so fast."

If Karma is a metaphysical reality and the measure of a man's wealth, then Harvey was undoubtedly a very wealthy man. He was an environmental scientist, deeply concerned for the planet and the plight of man. Despite his healthy scepticism towards big business, his dislike of all things 'trendy' and his disgust with the prevailing 'loadsamoney' mentality of our peers, I don't recall ever seeing him treat anyone with anything but respect. He looked for the good in people, just as he looked for the good in bands. And he trusted everyone. In fact, the trust he showed in people bordered on naïvety and expressed itself in a worrying reluctance to take personal security seriously. He was out of the habit, for example, of locking the door of his student accommodation. A group of us, concerned at the carelessness of his extreme 'let and let live' attitude, decided that for his own good it was high time we taught him a lesson. As we all sat in Monte Bar one evening, enjoying a quiet pint, a couple of us nipped back to Harvey's unlocked room and removed the entire Led Zeppelin section from his vinyl collection. Led Zeppelin were his favourite band. "Whenever I don't know what to play, I put on Zeppelin," he once told me, "and they never let me down." His collection was so large that the removal of the Led Zeppelin section hardly made a dent in it. But, sure enough, on his return from the bar, it took him just a few seconds to realise all was not well. "Fucking hell, where's my Led Zep albums?" he shouted. The purpose of the exercise was to show him a possible result of his carelessness, not to cause him distress, so we returned the albums immediately and came clean. To our surprise, the exercise failed to have the desired effect. Harvey reasoned that the chances of a *real* thief stumbling across his unlocked room were not significant enough to merit the extra effort involved in turning the key in the lock. He also told me once that anyone who thought they needed his possessions more than he did should probably have them anyway. This reminded me of my own non-materialistic puritanical phase when I concluded that the only possessions I should keep were the ones that were essential to my health and happiness. Thankfully this left me free to retain most of my record collection with a clear conscience, but it did result in me giving away around 20 albums (including AC/DC's *Highway to Hell*, the *Phenomena* project featuring Glenn Hughes, and *Drama* by Yes) which I now wish I'd kept.

We still felt that Harvey should be made to see the error of his ways, with the failure of the first 'theft' simply spurring us on to greater efforts. The shock of each episode elicited the same initial, instinctive response. "Fucking hell, where's my lid?" he said, on discovering the disappearance of his motorbike helmet. However, once the initial shock had worn off, each 'theft' had precisely the same effect on Harvey's behaviour – which is to say, no effect at all. After just a few attempts we gave up. However, I heard that later on in the year Harvey returned to his room one night to find that someone had stolen his door.

❁ *Acid freaks from Tennyson* ❁

One night we were invited to a party in Tennyson Road at the "humble abode" of a hippy-type bloke who called himself 'Apollo Moon Unit' (but whose real name was Freddy). He was not someone I knew well, but I had seen him around. He was a mathematics student of sorts, though I understood from others that his studies were suffering from a mixture of excessive drug taking and a relationship with an older woman who, as everyone liked to add, "had children". I later heard from an unverified source that he dropped out of college with an expensive cocaine habit and a spiralling debt.

Anyhow, on the night concerned, word got around our extended group that there was a party at Freddy's house. Harvey and one or two others decided to go along early to assist, if I remember correctly, with the baking of some 'special' cookies. Those of us who were less enthusiastic decided to go later. Harvey had got wind of the fact that there would be LSD in circulation.

I was aware of the 'mind-expanding' claims made for LSD and its active ingredients – by Aldous Huxley, for example, whose book *The Doors of Perception* made quite an impression on me. (I was an avid Huxley reader at one time and was much taken with his short novel *The Genius and the Goddess*.) I was also aware of widespread use of LSD in artistic and rock circles, particularly in the 1960s. However, despite some high profile endorsements, LSD always struck me as an unpredictable and dangerous drug that had the potential to drag down and psychologically terrorise a random sample of those who chose to try it. Brendan's flatmate, Mick Interesting, told stories of someone he knew who had had a bad trip and was still having flashbacks several years on. I was to hear of, and meet, other LSD casualties later. At Swansea University, for example, I met a Jim Morrison lookalike called Vic who told me earnestly that he had "been to hell" on acid. "No, really," he insisted, recognising that I took him to be speaking figuratively, "it actually took me to hell." He told me of his guilt at having once sold an acid tab to an "LSD-virgin" whose first experience with the drug "left her permanently traumatised". I also met a mature student called Steve who had a dribbling problem and displayed some strange facial twitches. I was told that he had taken a lot of drugs in his youth and that acid had done for him too. Closer to home, my punk friend Marv described an occasion when he misjudged the strength of an acid tab and was still tripping hours later while he did his family duty and connected his younger brother to his dialysis machine. This, he said, had been the scariest experience of his life. As I say, LSD has always struck me as a dangerous and unpredictable substance – not something I either wanted or needed. In so far as I thought there was any value in Huxley's experiments, I was far more interested in the potential of the human mind and the human will to approximate to such states naturally. Otherwise, it seemed to me, it was simply an artificial and unsustainable con – good for a bit of escapism if you're lucky, but of limited usefulness.

Harvey himself did see the merits of LSD, but he was typically knowledgeable and considered on the subject and approached the drug cautiously and with respect. "You should only take acid," he told me, "if you're a stable kind of person. And even then, you should only take it if you're happy and relaxed and with people you trust. It'll enhance whatever mood you're in. If you're insecure and moody, it'll make you worse. It can make you paranoid."

As laid back as he was, Harvey was absolutely firm in his conviction that drug taking should always be a personal and informed choice and that no one should ever be put under any pressure to take drugs. I remember his outrage and immediate intervention when he chanced upon an ill-conceived plot to spike someone's drink "for a laugh". He was also the man we turned to when Connaught Tony's homemade cookies gave him heart palpitations and induced a panic attack. And again, when Brendan's flatmate Junkie James confided in one of us that he had been reading up and had decided to experiment with heroin, it was Harvey who successfully talked him out of the idea – to the immense relief of everyone who knew James and had any kind of sympathy for him.

And so, back to the party in Tennyson Road. I turned up with Brendan, Will and AC/DC Rob at around 8pm. We were greeted in the hall by a happy and welcoming Freddy. "Which one d'ya want man?" he asked, showing us his hands. One hand contained acid tabs; the other, tablets that would apparently counteract any stomach cramps that the acid might induce. We declined his kind offer and instead decided to wander around to get our bearings and get a drink. As I walked towards the back of the house, I noticed a bonfire raging in the back garden. "They're burning televisions," someone said, just as I saw two lads stagger towards the bonfire with a television set and drop it on the top. We headed to the front room – Freddy's room – which would have been the lounge had the property been a family home. I spotted Harvey sitting on a mattress looking intensely interested in nothing in particular but grinning broadly like a Cheshire Cat. Next to Harvey was Tony – not Connaught Tony but real-ale-and-King-Crimson-loving Tony who sat 'digging' the music in his own peculiar anti-rhythmic way. Like me, Tony had little interest in drugs. What's more, despite his passion for ale, he never got drunk. Tony was stone cold sober – though you'd never have known that from watching him dance.

I tried to engage Harvey in conversation, but soon realised it was a lost cause. I concentrated instead on our surroundings. The wall at the far end of the room was covered in a gigantic Pink Floyd poster featuring artwork from *The Wall*. Party guests lined the wall like spiders, feeling their way around the poster, exploring every detail of the characters. One lost soul was trying to climb into the mouth of the biggest character, clawing at the wall frantically and with increasing frustration as the two-dimensional poster held firm against the three-dimensional hallucination. Then, without warning, someone accidentally smashed the coloured bulb in a lamp in the corner, changing the colour and ambience of the whole room and triggering panic among a small group of acid users. Most vividly, I remember someone lying on his back in the middle of the room kicking his legs and throwing out his arms in true dying fly fashion. "Fucking hell, Freddy!" he squealed again and again, in a mixture of terror and excitement. To give Freddy his due he was in attendance almost immediately and after several torrid minutes, which must have seemed like an eternity to the victim himself, managed to calm him down.

Brendan and I conferred. It clearly wasn't going to be our kind of party at all. We decided to do the usual thing and head off to St Mary's in search of some alternative fun. St Mary's was Southampton's red light district. The surplus of affordable rented accommodation ensured an interesting and culturally diverse mix of low-income families, ethnic minority groups, prostitutes and students. The size of the student population was such that, on any given weekend, it was a fair bet that thirsty, horny or lonely students would be able to find an open front door and a student party. I remember one occasion when Harvey led the march to St Mary's convinced that there was a party for us in the notorious Derby Road. He had the address written down. Sadly for him, he'd either been given, or had written down, the wrong house number. Thinking we had reached our destination, he raced ahead of the rest of us and rang the doorbell. We caught up with him just in time to see a scantily clad lady open the door, look him up and down and say: "It's ten pound with a rubber, love." His face was a picture.

"I don't need to pay for it," he kept telling us, as we continued searching for the right house in fits of uncontrollable giggles.

On the night of Freddy's party, Brendan and I had no such trouble. I don't recall the address, or whose party it was, but I have strong memories of playing air guitar to the entire original studio version of Lynyrd Skynyrd's *Freebird*. (I seemed to acquire a large UFO patch at some point in the process, which was too big for my back but made an excellent beer mat.) Some time after this, I was queuing for the lavatory when I noticed a drunken beefcake trying to push his way into the toilet ahead of a very pretty, if rather conventional-looking, girl who'd been waiting for her turn patiently. Made courageous by the cans of alcohol I'd consumed, and outraged by the 'injustice' of the situation, I dashed forward and applied sufficient pressure to knock the drunken oaf off course, ensuring that he fell away from the door. He picked himself up, a little shaken, and to my immense relief, retreated like a wounded animal. The girl smiled at me and took her turn. I was rather pleased when, on her re-emergence from the bathroom, she approached me with another beautiful smile and, as though exercising psychic foresight, said, "Remember 'Freebird'." I took this to mean that she had seen me playing air guitar and liked what she saw. My act of chivalry had clearly added to the good impression I'd made. This was her coded way of telling me that she was single and interested in me. She didn't linger for conversation, however, and I didn't pursue her. I took the "remember" to mean "we'll talk some other time, not now" and I was happy enough with that. (I never saw her again – despite secretly hoping for weeks afterwards that my 'freebird' was just around every corner.)

Brendan and I conferred again on the landing. As we did so, a large wicker laundry basket opened behind us, and, jack-in-a-box-like, out popped Paul – a 'speed-freak' acquaintance of ours who went by the name 'Hot Knife'. He too had been at Freddy's party, though he had indulged rather more significantly than we had. "Shit man," he said, freeing himself of linen, adjusting his cowboy hat and doing his best to fix on us intently, "it's the acid freaks from Tennyson."

✹ *Haunting the Chapel* ✹

The 'acid freaks' story makes me smile these days. At the time, however, I was starting to feel a growing sense of distance between myself and some of my new friends, and that was exactly the kind of evening that contributed to the way I was feeling. The drug-taking was part of it. While some used drugs moderately and with caution, others seemed to regard getting wasted or stoned as their very *raison d'être*. Although drug-taking has a long-established tradition in rock circles, the 'waster mentality' was not part of my own experience of rock music in the first half of the 1980s. This growing sense of distance was really brought home to me during another notable evening which contained a bizarre mix of the cerebral and the downright silly.

A group of us sat around in Connaught Tony's room, drinking, talking and listening to music. I don't recall how it came about, but a guy called

Nick put forward the view that morality is an illusion, that everything is relative, and that all human bonding and social behaviour is simply "tribal". Our own bonding as a group of rock fans, he claimed, was just another example of the tribal nature of human existence, an existence marked by competition, opposition, and struggle. What we call 'moral values', 'good' and 'evil', 'right' and 'wrong', said Nick, are merely social constructs created within groups or tribes to bind them together and to help them survive and assert themselves over other groups. For us as individuals it's simply a case of choosing which side we are on. Once we have chosen our side, it's us against them: it's a case of dog-eat-dog and survival of the fittest.

In contrast, the view I held at the time went something like this: i) human beings are essentially similar; ii) being together and caring for one another is a better way for human beings to live; iii) such a perspective embodies values that are in some way 'universal', transcending time, place and social grouping; and iv) some of these values can be found in aspects of rock culture and could help make the world a better place, if only people would embrace them.

Nick and I were clearly poles apart, and that was fine – I was used to people disagreeing with me. I felt the full force of his views and regarded them as a challenge, but, intellectually, his 'relativism' didn't initially worry me. What did worry me, as the discussion unfolded, was the agreement Nick's views garnered among my friends, and the implications this had for how, as friends and rock fans, we understood and related to each other. For Nick, rock fans chose rock music as a way of creating an identity that was different from, and necessarily in conflict with, other groups of people. For me, however, rock music was not something I liked because I was different to others, it was something I liked because of what I shared and had in common with others. Rock fans exhibited a shared response to something good – something that transcended occupation, background and national identity; something that could bring pleasure to an ever-growing number of people. I didn't think of my status as a rock fan as a tribal matter at all, not least because rock music and rock fandom were national and international phenomena that clearly extended beyond regional groupings and affiliations. For me, being a rock fan wasn't about joining one tribe and rejecting others. It wasn't about choosing sides – it was about finding meaning that could extend to anyone and everyone. I really believed that what I had experienced through rock music held this sort of general significance.

It had been an uncharacteristically intense discussion – but it wasn't long before the conversation turned once more to music, with Connaught Tony introducing us to the dubious delights of Slayer's *Haunting the Chapel* EP. At the time, thrash metal was still in its infancy and was something of an underground movement in the UK. By any known standards Slayer were a challenging listen, musically and lyrically. Their speed and power guaranteed some form of reaction, disbelief and incredulity being the most common among the rock fans that I knew. It was rather like heaping intensity on intensity. Last orders at Monte Bar beckoned. Someone suggested it would be good fun to leave the EP blasting away on full volume while we were out. And so it was that we locked Tony's door from the inside and, great escape fashion, wriggled out through his bedroom window and legged it – leaving his neighbours to 'enjoy' 15 minutes or so of loud, brash and some would say offensive thrash metal. The silliness provided some welcome relief. Once happily ensconced in Monte Bar, the tension of the foregoing discussion was forgotten, and the mood of the group returned to something like normal.

While the silliness of the evening soon passed, the conversation stayed with me. For the first time I realised that I could not assume that those who looked like me, dressed like me, bought the same records and went to the same gigs as me, *were* like me in their basic outlook and attitudes. Although not all of my friends were rock fans, or dressed like rock fans, musical taste had played a huge-role in my friend selection, particularly at university, and was absolutely central to my sense of identity. But now, with several of our group declaring themselves to be advocates of some form of 'tribalism', 'relativism' or 'Social Darwinism', I was discovering that at least as far as new friends were concerned, I could take little for granted. I started to feel quite a strong sense of distance and alienation, not only from the general student population – which is something I felt almost from the time I arrived at university – but from my own group of friends as well. Where was the widespread interest in politics and social change that I had expected? Where was the drive to create a better world and a better way of life for people? It suddenly seemed conspicuously absent among most of my immediate peers. The image-led nature of student life, the excessive wealth and complacency I had seen – everything suddenly seemed so artificial. Even the undoubted intelligence that had won people places at the University in the first place – ostensibly to engage in study that would further human knowledge and understanding – suddenly seemed fake or at best passionless and purely 'cognitive'. I am, of course, generalising, and recognise that my own mindset and relative immaturity played a key part in shaping my perception. But at the time, I dug myself into a bit of an intellectual hole. The more I dwelt on the matter, the more I came to feel a profound sense of dissatisfaction and dislocation. I rejected Nick's hypotheses utterly, and yet didn't my own experience at Southampton seem to support his tribal and relative interpretation of life? Though again I am generalising, I had found that elements of Southampton's student fraternity could be unwelcoming and unfriendly towards those who looked different or dressed differently. As far as the rock fraternity was concerned, I had started to lose my bearings a bit and was no longer sure about what I did and didn't share with my new friends beyond taste in music. The more I reflected on what 'tribal' might mean, the more I realised that we probably didn't even have enough in common to call ourselves a 'tribe'. Whatever shared musical taste is, and whatever role it plays in social bonding and group identity, on its own it's not enough to support even a 'tribal' way of life, let alone a 'world view'. I recalled the values that had impressed me so much when I started going to rock gigs and buying rock albums: the sense of community; the sense of there being a history and tradition which demanded respect; the generosity of spirit fans exhibited towards each other; the desire to listen to and share music with others; the value attached to the creative and aesthetic qualities of the music; the idea that the music was more important than money; the focus on originality; the strong work-ethic that accompanied success; the bond that emerged between band and audience; the down-to-earth dress code; and the lack of overt interest in image and fashion. These things were found in abundance around the rock scene in the early 1980s, but I now realised that they were not a fixed, essential and immutable part of it. (My mistake, of course, was to think that certain values *necessarily* accompanied the music and that sharing musical taste *necessarily* meant that people shared other values – but I was too young and naïve to see, or to want to see, my error at the time.) As would soon be clear from the way rock music began to break out into an ever-increasing number of genres and sub-genres, the music itself was morally neutral, though it could be used to support or endorse any number of outlooks, moral codes and ways of life. The Southampton group was starting to look like no more than a superficial grouping of disgruntled teenagers who happened to share a dress code and broadly similar musical taste. We were more like a gang than a tribe. Is this how those people in the pub who moved away from us saw us – as some dirty-looking gang to be feared? I had been shaken. My mind was a mess. My world had become fragmented. And I was starting to feel homesick, resentful and bitter.

As this mini-crisis hit, I started thinking more generally about my course. In fact, I was now able to admit that I didn't really like my course much either. I was there to read politics and international relations. As it turned out, this necessitated choosing a number of other first year courses which I didn't really want to study. The course did give me my first taste of philosophy (a subject I enjoyed) and sociology (a subject I didn't enjoy but regarded as 'significant') but none of the other courses seemed to have the weight or bite or relevance I was looking for. Most distressing of all was the realisation that I had to take a compulsory statistics course ('Quantitative Methods D', in fact) which seemed to me at the time to have absolutely no relevance to anything I had come to university to study. When, later in the term, I realised that I had no desire or motivation to apply myself to 'quantitative methods' and that further modules were compulsory right through my degree, I gave serious thought to the possibility of changing either my subject or university. My personal tutor, a thoroughly reasonable chap called Fletcher, tried to be helpful. After talking things through he concluded that "they don't teach what you're looking for anywhere". I decided that I had to leave.

✹ Hippy, Heavy, Horny, Happy? ✹

Although there was much I disliked about my life in Southampton, there were things I knew I would miss. As much as I had come to feel something of an outsider, I had found a small number of good friends who tended to share my views about university, if not my emerging political and philo-sophical opinions. I felt that by leaving I was letting these people down. One such person was Harvey. Harvey had not been present at the 'tribal-ism' discussion and remained unsullied by its after-effects. He had invited me to go to stay with him for a weekend at the end of term, an invitation that I had accepted with some enthusiasm. As we packed up our stuff and headed off to his mother's house in Sendmarsh, a rural idyll not far from Guildford, I wondered how on earth I was going to tell him that I was leav-ing. The truth was that I needed time to let my decision sink in and work out myself what was really going on in my head. After several abortive attempts to 'spit it out', I did my best to put my decision and all my anxieties around it to the back of my mind. Harvey had told me a lot about his home life and his friends. I was determined to have a good few days with him, knowing that I'd be seeing considerably less of him in the future.

Well before the end of term, and well in advance of my decision to leave, we had already done the first year student thing and exchanged home addresses. In the name column of my address book, Harvey had written the phrase which I will forever associate with him:

H [ippy, eavy, orny, appy]

And here we were weeks later, sitting in his local pub consuming a devilish brew called ESB and reflecting on our recent experiences. How did we measure up to the 4Hs?

Were we 'Hippy'? Yes, we were a bit, at least in aspects of our outlook and our hair length. Updated hippies for the 1980s perhaps, but Harvey's interest in environmental science, his general love of life, and our shared aspiration towards a 'live and let live' type philosophy, gave me no doubt that had it been 1967 (the year of my birth incidentally) we'd have been wearing kaftans and marching for peace.

Were we 'Heavy'? Yes, we were definitely heavy, especially if the adjective was supposed to describe our taste in music, our leather jackets and our occasional moods of gloom and doom when university life got the better of us.

Were we 'Horny'? Yes, we were undeniably horny, but frustrated with it. Southampton University had failed to deliver on the woman front. The people I knew were more interested in getting plastered than getting laid and, though I always kept a keen eye out, Southampton University did not seem to specialise at all in the kind of woman I was looking for. (Though to be fair, I don't think I was exactly the kind of bloke that most female students at Southampton were looking for either.)

And were we 'Happy'? No, not very. And that got me down, and it got H down even more, because while I was a fairly self-contained and thoughtful type, H had an extremely sociable and sunny disposition and was 'used' to being happy.

"What on earth are you two moaning about?" said Harvey's father as he joined us in the pub and listened to us talking about our first term as students. "Cheer up for goodness sake. You're home for Christmas. You're privileged enough to have places at university. You've got no responsibilities. You've got your whole lives ahead of you. You can do anything you like. The world is your oyster."

It was a welcome pep-talk, sincerely intended, from a man who appeared to have grabbed hold of life with both hands and who knew how to live. He tried to show us that night, too, though I feasted too quickly and made myself sick. I've always been a lightweight in that respect. "Someone make sure that drunken Welshman's alright," I heard him say, just before I crashed out on his bathroom floor. I was so drunk, even the girls who were with us were happy to use the lavatory while I lay prostrate at their feet. That's one way to make an impression I suppose.

As it turned out, it was an excellent weekend, which, once I'd recovered from the Friday night drinking, gave me an extraordinary feeling of well-being and freedom. I spent the weekend riding pillion on the back of one of H's friends' motorbikes – another Nick, who turned out to be rather gung-ho and a bit of a risk-taker. Overtaking BMWs and Mercedes on the A3 was both an exhilarating and a frightening experience for me, particularly as the helmet I was given didn't fit properly. While I quickly became accustomed to, and enjoyed, the power and acceleration of Nick's bike, when the proposed Sunday trip to biker-haven Box Hill proved too difficult to co-ordinate, I was simultaneously disappointed and relieved.

The weekend also allowed us to take in a Magnum gig at the Hammersmith Odeon – my first and thus far only visit to the legendary venue. Magnum were touring in support of their *On a Storyteller's Night* album and, with a surprise *Top of the Pops* single to boot, were doing an extremely good job of it. Harvey and I, along with AC/DC Rob and some other college friends, had caught the band's Portsmouth gig a few weeks earlier, but seeing them at the Hammy O, supported by the excellent IQ, was one of the high points of my gigging history. Doing it with Harvey and his mates, and meeting up with Rob and a couple of girls he'd brought along, made it even better.

It troubled me that I went through the entire weekend without telling H my news, and soon afterwards I wrote to him to try to explain my decision. By then I had made preliminary enquiries with other universities, and reported that I hoped to have another stab at it at Swansea University the following academic year. My plan was to study a different kind of politics course which drew on a more philosophical approach to politics through Ancient Greek political life and thought. Most notably, the new course I had chosen lacked a compulsory statistics component (though I did end up taking a formal logic module). Harvey took the news much better than I'd expected. In fact, he was extremely supportive, which made me feel even more guilty about having kept him in the dark for so long. He wrote: "It's a pity you had to leave but I'm sure it's the right decision and it didn't surprise me much to find out that you'd left. I know exactly how you feel." He was sceptical, however, about my chances of having more luck elsewhere. "Don't let it get you down," the cheery old bugger wrote, "but I don't think you'll find it much different in Swansea." His own solution was to go back to Sendmarsh far more frequently to spend as much time as he possibly could with a new girlfriend. When he wrote again mid-way through the spring term, it was with the news that AC/DC Rob had also decided to leave. "Things haven't been going too well for him lately," wrote Harvey. "Basically if something could've gone wrong it did. Plus he had pretty similar reasons for not wanting to stay as you did (especially QMD). He's applied to Exeter, Bristol and SWANSEA to do a course in geography. Who knows, you might meet up with him next year." Who knows indeed?

Though the distance and divergence in our lives made it difficult, we did make some effort to keep in touch, with plans to get together tending to revolve around the annual *Monsters of Rock* festival at Castle Donington. Harvey was particularly enthusiastic about getting a big crew together at Donington 1986 for a bill that featured Ozzy Osbourne, the Scorpions, Def Leppard, Motörhead, Warlock and comedy act Bad News. He raised the possibility six months before the event itself, telling me: "Hopefully I'll see you soon, but if I don't, make sure you stay in touch cos I want to make sure we get together for Donington. That means your mates, my mates, Steve's mates, Tony's mates, all together as one crowd. We'll make it a good one." Whatever personal confusion and fragmentation I was experiencing, the spirit of NWOBHM was alive and well in Harvey's heart. God bless him! He kept me posted as his plans for camping and partying developed, but by the time the event came around a combination of voluntary work commitments and a distinct lack of finance prevented me from going.

I did, however, go the following year, for a bill that contained a bizarre but largely enjoyable mix of hair rock and thrash metal. Bon Jovi headlined over Dio, with Metallica and Anthrax providing the guts at the heart of the event, and WASP and Cinderella doing their best to inject a bit of early excitement. With Harvey's plans rather less well-formed than the previous year, I booked onto an organised coach trip with my friend Marv and his mate, Steve Riddle (who, no word of a lie, had a brother called James). Harvey and I agreed that the only way we'd manage to get together would be to try to get to an agreed meeting point on the festival site at a pre-arranged time. "Directly after Cinderella have pissed off, I'll head for the BOGS (whether I need to go or not)," wrote Harvey, "and hopefully we'll bump into each other. How about meeting on the path to the bogs at exactly the other side of the race track?" And he provided me with a hand drawn map which was striking for its simplicity.

Incredibly, given what was reputedly a crowd of 80,000 people, we DID manage to meet up at the appointed time "on the path to the bogs at exactly the other side of the race track". After much smiling and handshaking we worked out what to do next.

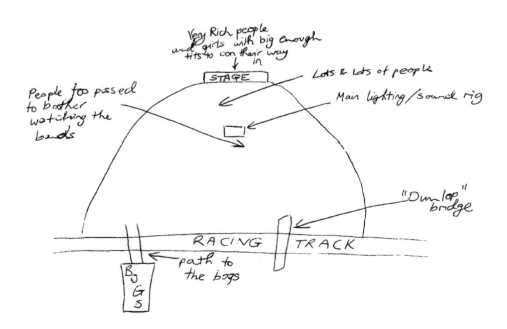

"There's a group of us sitting next to the people with that big Confederate flag over there," said H, pointing into the distance. I could see the giant flag to the right of the stage, about 100 feet from the front. "Come on back with me now," he said, "and bring your booze."

"We haven't got any," I replied, "it's my round and I'm just about to buy some." I gestured towards the queues at the nearby bars.

"Well you go and buy some now before the next band comes on," he said, "and I'll see you back at the flag in about 15 minutes." And off he trotted.

In the event, it took me longer to buy the drinks than anticipated. Meanwhile, Marv and Steve, who I'd left having a quiet smoke, had wandered off somewhere in fits of giggles, leaving me with six pints of freshly purchased beer. "Ah well, there's still H and his mates," I reasoned, "and Marv and Steve know where to meet us." I looked across the crowd towards the flag – and to my horror saw that it was now right down the front near the middle of the stage. It was bopping up and down and being waved about with some vigour, with thousands of people between where the flag was now and where it was when Harvey first pointed it out in its state of rest. I tried hard, but couldn't find Harvey and his mates. All I could do was drink the beer and enjoy the music. (Life's a bitch, eh?) More by luck than design, I did manage to find Marv and Steve again, just before Bon Jovi came on. Having sobered up to watch Anthrax and Metallica they had since had another smoke. They were still wandering around giggling, seemingly oblivious to the passing of time.

And that was the last time I saw Harvey in the flesh. I heard he was going off to South America on some environmental expedition, and after that things just sort of drifted – as old college friendships sometimes do. Shame.

✵ *SMF (Southampton Metal Fanzine)* ✵

Harvey wasn't the only person I missed from Southampton. There was Brendan (of course), and Ed, and, for a while at least, AC/DC Rob, and I did what I could to stay in touch. Much of my contact initially focused on efforts to establish a Southampton University Rock Society. Work to create the Society (Rock Soc) had begun back in the autumn term, with Rob, Ed and I (as putative secretary, treasurer and president respectively) submitting the required documentation to the relevant Student Union committee. The truth of the matter was that I was driving this harder than anyone else, and despite considerable early enthusiasm (an initial meeting had drawn a whole bar full of people), once I'd gone there was no one who wanted to join Rob and Ed in making sure that things happened. Harvey's own position was not atypical: "There is total apathy surrounding the Rock Soc," he told me, "'Oh, Mike's left, you'll have to organise everything now H'! I'm willing to do my part, but I'm not willing to take on a position of responsibility. The fact that I spend as much time in Guildford as possible now means that I would not have the time to do anything but support events. I'll talk to the others, but we still need a few people willing/able to really commit themselves to it."

It wasn't, however, apathy or lack of commitment that finally killed our plans, but the Union itself who, surprisingly, rejected our request to have the Society formally recognised. The Union secretary wrote to us to inform us of the decision. (I wasn't there to receive my letter, but Ed sent it on rather belatedly.)

> With reference to the Constitution you submitted to set up a Southampton University Rock Society, the Internal Affairs Committee Meeting of Monday 20th January decided not to accept this Society as a new Club within the Union. The reason being that if (sic) was felt that the aims stated in your Constitution duplicated the aims and activities of an already functioning Society, i.e. Rocktrips. This decision was ratified by the Administrative Committee Meeting of Thursday 23rd January.

None of us knew anyone involved in the Rock Trips Society, and there was little sign of them being active, but there was nothing we could do. The letter signalled, in Ed's words, "the Rock Society's final demise".

Of course, given my departure, it shouldn't have mattered to me much, except that I'd hoped to cut my teeth as a writer on the planned Rock Soc publication *Southampton Metal Fanzine* (or, with a tip of the hat to Twisted Sister, *SMF*). Now back in South Wales, and still looking for gainful employment, I had some time on my hands, and put a great deal of effort into generating content for a proposed first edition. I had, for example, produced three album reviews: Aerosmith *Done with Mirrors*; Malice *In the Beginning*; and Stevie Nicks *Rock a Little* – which I gave seven, eight and nine out of ten respectively. I had reported on Marillion's two-night stint at St David's Hall, Cardiff on their *Misplaced Childhood* tour, and I had interviewed Carl Sentance from Welsh rockers Persian Risk. Risk are perhaps now best remembered for providing the mighty Motörhead with guitarist Phil Campbell. At the time, however, they were championed by *Kerrang!* and appeared to be on the verge of some kind of breakthrough. I had spotted Carl at the bar of my local pub, and to my delight he invited me to his house to speak at greater length. Quite a coup, I thought! In addition, I wrote a feature on Magnum, with the band providing signatures and messages of support to accompany the piece. I also did a postal interview with former Twelfth Night vocalist Geoff Mann. With the Society's demise, sadly none of the material saw the light of day.

❀ *Korea* ❀

In addition to maintaining contact from afar, I did return to Southampton for the occasional weekend. I went back in March to catch Pallas on *The Wedge* tour, for example, and in May I went to stay with Brendan and Ed for 'the birthday weekend'. As it happens the three of us have birthdays on consecutive days, and in 1986 these birthdays fell a Friday, Saturday and Sunday. Free from the pressures of forthcoming exams, I was able to spend the weekend sitting in the sun, visiting people and relaxing with a pint or two. Somehow it turned into a weekend of relative-excess, fuelled by birthday celebrations and the Spinal Tap-like antics of a band called Korea.

In preparation for my arrival, Brendan had kept an eye out for things to do. The Friday night, Ed's birthday, involved the usual 'drink and chat' type activities as we visited bars that for me were now 'old haunts'. On the Saturday night, my birthday, Brendan had spotted that The Glitter Band were playing at nearby Connaught Hall. It sounded like fun – so off we went, in a high-spirited mood, keen to see what the evening would bring. The Glitter Band themselves were quite entertaining, providing a pleasant musical distraction as we sat laughing, chatting and enjoying each other's company. There should have been a support band, but for some reason they didn't appear. After a proficient set, the Glitter Band encored with the Led Zeppelin classic 'Rock and Roll' for which I felt compelled to make my way to the front of the stage to shake my head a little. Suddenly I was aware that I was flanked by flowing hair on both sides. Instinctively I linked arms with my co-revellers, and by the end I realised I was headbanging with a bunch of modern-day glam rockers. They turned out to be the support band – Korea. They *had* turned up at the venue after all, but sadly their equipment had not. Apparently it was in the back of a broken-down transit van somewhere on the M3. They were mightily impressed with my solo headbanging exploits, though, and invited me, Brendan and Ed backstage with them "to party".

"Hmmm, this might turn out to be quite a birthday treat," I thought, until the band realised that the beer in their dressing room was in very short supply and that unless more beer was forthcoming they would only be able to offer us orange juice. Brendan and I managed to convince the event organisers that we were the band's manager and tour manager respectively, and while we weren't able to procure any more beer, we did manage to send out for kebab and chips for everyone. The fact that Korea hadn't played meant that there was little chance of any immediate female or 'groupie' attention, and it soon became clear that if they wanted any 'action', they would have to venture beyond the backstage area. There followed a rather tedious traipse around the student halls as we desperately sought a party to entertain our glamorous guests. The hunt for parties, booze and women who met the band's rock 'n' roll expectations wasn't really a success, and so well into the early hours we wished the band all the best for the future and retreated to Brendan and Ed's flat armed with numerous copies of signed posters they had insisted on foisting on us. I remember that the keyboard player, Paul, was less interested in finding a party than the rest of the band, and seemed much happier sitting and chatting with the three of us about his life as a musician and his plans for the future. The quiet of the flat provided an ideal opportunity for a further catch-up with Brendan. We spent hours talking that weekend, reflecting on our own hopes for the future, and listening to Kate Bush. As for Korea, I never did hear any of their music.

✳ *Swansea* ✳

Harvey turned out to be right about AC/DC Rob. He did turn up in Swansea, and in a manner that really set the tone. The entire first year arts and social sciences intake were crammed into the College refectory to hear the College Principal address the new students. As the Principal stood up to speak, the students stopped talking and sat down. At that precise moment, I was distracted as a familiar and ramshackle figure shuffled into the room. As I recognised him I instinctively rose to my feet and almost involuntarily exclaimed, "Jesus Christ! Rob! What the hell are you doing here?"

"Ssssssshhhhhh" came the combined response from the room, as all eyes fell disapprovingly on the pair of us.

Harvey might have been right about Rob, but he was wrong about Swansea. It *was* better than Southampton. Much better. It's difficult to say why. Perhaps it was the course, which I took to instantly. The location certainly helped. Swansea University is situated right opposite Swansea Bay and is just a short distance away from the Mumbles (home of Catherine Zeta Jones) and the beautiful Gower Peninsula. The mix and friendliness of the people suited me better too, and there seemed to be much less of a focus on wealth and image. There was a discernible cultural difference between South Wales, with its socialist values and traditions, and the more hard-nosed capitalist ethos that was dominant in the south of England. I am sure the fact that I was a year older (and wiser) also made a difference, both to my expectations and to my ability to cope.

Rock music was, of course, still an important part of my identity, and though I enjoyed mixing with a broader range of people I still gravitated towards fellow rock fans to some extent. There was already a thriving Rock Society in Swansea, and I also got to know some hardcore rock fans who lived near me in the campus halls of residence. There was Danny, for example, a happy-go-lucky Scandinavian chap who managed to get himself a 'DJ' slot on the University radio station. He would often let me sit in on his shows on a Saturday evening, or let me rifle through the station's record collection and suggest tracks. He was a nice guy. He was fun to be with, and a great drinking partner, but as time went by, he seemed to become increasingly unfocused and rather lost. He reminded me, in fact, of the way I was in Southampton. I had no contact with him after our first year, and have no idea what became of him. There was also Paula, who was a teenage rocker's dream. She had an astonishingly sexy, smouldering look, but a bit of a 'life is elsewhere' attitude. She had a boyfriend back home – an older man, a biker, who, I was told, was "in trouble with the law". Then there was Tertia, a very genuine, unspoilt and pretty girl from a small rural town on the English side of the Welsh Marches. She had some great friends from home – down-to-earth rocker types who visited once or twice while we lived in halls, and whom I enjoyed meeting very much.

It was good to have friends who had a similar interest in rock music. From what I remember, Paula and Tertia got on really well. Danny and I got on well too, until he started drifting off, but I have to say that we didn't really bond as a group. It wasn't unusual for me to go for a drink in the college bar with Danny or Tertia or Paula, but I think it's fair to say that we all made better friends elsewhere. For my own part, I made some good friends on my course, and made some particularly good friends in the hall of residence where I stayed in my first year. There was John, a geologist from Seaford near Brighton, whose mum lived in a house that had originally been built for Mr. Woolworth. There was Joe, a marine biologist (and future vicar) who knew John already from sixth-form college days. The first thing Joe ever said to me was: "Hi, I'm Joe, I'm a Christian." To which I replied: "Hi, I'm Mike. I'm a lapsed Catholic." And there was 'Fat Matt', an insightful and charismatic psychologist with whom I shared a growing interest in (writing) poetry. These were the three with whom I formed the closest bonds, but there was others too – Steve, Mark, Paul, Chris, Fraser, Phil and Dom – and together we formed a well-rounded and supportive group of chums.

As it happened, some of my new friends shared my musical taste and some didn't. But that didn't matter. In what was clearly a healthy shift in attitude for me, shared musical taste ceased to be a prerequisite for new friendships. And for the most part, even the new friends who did share (or at least appreciate) my musical taste did so without buying into the whole heavy rock image. Despite his love of dance music, his pink clothes and his trendy haircut, for example, Matt had a surprising liking for bands like Kiss, Rose Tattoo and Twisted Sister. "I've never really stopped liking rock music," he told me once, "I just stopped listening to it." Apart from me, only John and Fraser dressed in a way that gave any indication that they might be heavy rock fans, and that meant that once again I was singled out for the way I looked – though this time in a good way. I quickly became known as 'the hippy' (every group of students should have one), which gave me a nickname and a place in the group that I quite liked.

Though the group identity was not built on musical taste, there was still a sufficient number of rock fans, and sufficient tolerance of each others' tastes, to ensure that music still featured heavily. John was a guitarist and shared much of my musical taste. Joe was a drummer, and though he was more obviously into jazz and more quirky, indie and punk flavoured music (like the Violent Femmes) he wasn't averse to a bit of rock. John and Joe formed a band called Four Minute Warning who mixed original compositions with covers by artists like the Rolling Stones and Jimi Hendrix. In fact, they were half decent, giving a good account of themselves in a College 'Battle of the Bands' competition which was won by a young group called the Manic Street Preachers. It was also a good period for crossover albums. Bon Jovi's *Slippery When Wet*, for example, appealed to almost everyone in the group, and Magnum's *Vigilante* became something of a soundtrack to our summer term.

In my second year, my girlfriend of the time, Jo, introduced me to Struan, an active and adventurous guy whose hobbies included scuba diving, rugby and collecting empty Newcastle Brown bottles for his 'sole-destroying' homebrew. He had a keen interest in politics and green issues and we hit it off immediately. His home address at the time featured a house called Hogdigging Cottage in a place called Dirty Corner, and that somehow seemed appropriate. Soon after we met he moved into a flat with me, John and Joe and a rather eccentric friend of ours, Phil, who we called 'Philthy Animal'. Struan proved to be something of a kindred spirit – both musically and intellectually. He was determined to live his life in as unfettered a way as possible and used to sign-off all his letters with the phrase "No hassles!" After graduating he moved to Africa to run an ostrich farm. That tells you a lot about the kind of man he was.

I continued to take some interest in the Swansea University Rock Society, attending events and going on the occasional organised trip, the most notable of which was a Queensrÿche gig at Newport Centre. If you wanted to see top bands then travelling was essential, though despite being off the main tour circuit, Swansea did host the occasional interesting gig. Anarcho-punk band Chumbawamba played the Student Union, for example, sometime after the release of their *Never Mind the Ballots* album. As we waited for the band to come on stage, a rumour went round that the singer, Danbert Nobacon, had been arrested earlier that day for shoplifting and might not even appear. A visiting American philosophy student I knew called Jim was incredulous that a band with such a strong anti-state message was allowed to propagate its views so openly (an odd view for him to hold, I thought, given that America is supposedly 'the land of the free'). "If the government wanted to," he told me, "it could use the gig to wipe out all the anarchists within a 50 mile radius." It was probably true that if the government wanted to then it could have, but the government probably didn't see Chumbawamba and the two Swansea University Anarchist Society members as much of a combined threat – especially as the Anarchist Society members always seemed more interested in skateboarding than 'smashing the state'.

Another group who came to Swansea were biker band Dumpy's Rusty Nuts. They were great fun, and once more brought Harvey to mind. Back in Southampton Harvey had introduced me to their *Somewhere in England* album. He was a big fan, and I'll always associate Dumpy's standards such as 'Box Hill or Bust' with Harvey and his mates. (I bought the later album *Somewhere Else in England*, but it wasn't nearly as good.) In my third year, AC/DC Rob moved in with us, and I was delighted when he easily hit it off with John, Joe, my girlfriend Jo, and the rest of our housemates. It somehow seemed fitting that he was back on the scene. We've kept in touch ever since.

✸ *The solution to the problem of life . . .* ✸

While my expectations of rock music and fellow rock fans were shattered by my initial experiences at university, I emerged from my confusion by realising that it was my own narrow thinking that had got me into such a mess. The developments and changes I have described above did not diminish my love of rock music or afford it any less important a place in my life, but they did enable me to start to integrate it into my life in a more balanced way. I started playing football again, for example, and threw myself into my studies, switching once and for all away from politics to philosophy. Philosophy gave me a natural way of exploring the questions about human nature and moral relativism that were increasingly occupying my mind. It felt like the discipline I'd been seeking all along, and I dived into my new-found philosophical quest with enthusiasm and openness – and with Plato's Socrates as my guide.

Studying philosophy in Swansea also meant that it wasn't long before I was introduced to the work of Ludwig Wittgenstein. The department was a Wittgensteinian stronghold which claimed a direct line of descent from the great philosopher himself. Wittgenstein had written some of his most famous material in Swansea when visiting his former pupil Rush Rhees. When Wittgenstein died, Rhees became one of his literary executors.

Rhees taught a philosopher called Peter Winch, who in turn taught our Head of Department, D.Z. Phillips. Wittgenstein was not an easy writer to study, but his work is marked by an aphoristic style that could bring even the driest of philosophical discussions to life. I was particularly taken with some comments he made towards the end of his first book (the only one published in his lifetime) *Tractatus Logico-Philosophicus*. Wittgenstein writes:

> The solution of the problem of life is seen in the vanishing of the problem. (Is this not the reason why those who have found after a long period of doubt that the sense of life became clear to them have then been unable to say what constituted that sense?) (*Tractatus Logico-Philosophicus*, Proposition 6.521)[1]

How well those comments chimed with my own experience as, slowly, "the sense of life" returned to me, and some of the personal problems connected to the fragmentation I experienced vanished. Such problems can be very real, but they are often problems that are at least partly to do with the way you live: they do not have answers that are *purely* intellectual like a maths problem or a logical puzzle.

As if in sympathy with the personal upheaval I was trying to overcome, my time in Swansea coincided with a period when the heavy rock scene itself began to noticeably fragment. Hair metal ('American glam metal' as my friends and I called it at the time) and thrash metal (and its derivatives) came into vogue alongside the more traditional heavy metal and hard rock music that I preferred. The new genres brought with them clear differences in outlook. Hair metal tended to be party music, and was often accompanied by an extreme hedonism and that 'waster mentality' that was completely alien to me. Thrash metal was full of anger and aggression. This was fine when the energy was channelled positively and directed at the right targets, but more often than not, the music went with lyrics and imagery which were violent and venomous. Both genres were predominantly American – at least initially – and a strong 'Fuck you!' attitude tended to prevail in both. Though I liked particular bands and albums, and though there was variety of both music and outlook among the bands within each genre – compare Bon Jovi with Motley Crüe, for example, or the quirkiness of Anthrax with the intensity of Metallica and the violence and hostility of Slayer – I couldn't really embrace the overriding ethos of either new movement. These emerging factions brought home the point once more. There is a great variety in rock music, both in terms of the music itself and in what it means to the people who listen to it. Heavy rock, hard rock, heavy metal – call it what you will – probably never has been one thing with one neat set of musical and social values. There never was a party or a manifesto you signed up to. There always was room for individual difference and choice.

Of course, through all of this fragmentation and change the power of rock music to inspire, move and influence remained undiminished, and my own love of rock music remained undiminished. At the end of it all, I was still a bit 'hippy'. I was still 'heavy' too, though the moods of gloom and doom were less frequent. I was still 'horny' for sure – what young man isn't – but I was certainly less frustrated than I had been. And with more realistic expectations of rock music and of life in general, and with a more sensible attitude towards others, I was much closer to being happy.

7

Morrison Hotel

A Matter of Life and Death

I gathered myself, took a deep breath and approached my hero. His immense presence filled the room, and when he spoke he commanded (if not demanded) the attention of all. It was my turn. "Can I ask you a question that will probably shatter all my illusions?" I asked. He eyed me cautiously, temporarily disarmed by my approach.

"Er . . . yeah, what is it?" he replied, clearly unsure what he was letting himself in for. I held up a fish-shaped earring, the blue and green marble body and silver casing sparkling intermittently as it caught the light.

I gathered myself again, and rather feebly hit him with the 'big' question: "Did you used to have the other one of these?"

I was talking to Fish, then lead singer of progressive rock band Marillion, perhaps the most successful of the bands at the forefront of the prog revival of the early 1980s. I had just been to see them filming at the HTV studios in Bath for a regional youth programme called *Side Step*. My friend Brendan's dad worked for HTV and had picked us up a couple of tickets. I had managed to get a couple more from the Marillion fan club – The Web – and offered them to friends Gareth and Mitch who joined us on the 75 minute drive from Cardiff. The band played several tracks for the programme and, once the TV crew had what they wanted, continued playing for half an hour or so for the sake of the audience. There were probably about 70 or 80 of us, all effectively hand-picked from within the fan base, and we were thrilled when Fish announced that, despite rumours (or, at least, worries) that the band were on the verge of selling out to popular fads and the lure of the singles market, their next album would be a concept album featuring only two tracks – Side One and Side Two. It sounded like a throwback to the grand progressive rock ventures of the 1970s and it was exactly what those present wanted to hear. That album turned out to be *Misplaced Childhood* – the album which allowed Marillion to scale commercial heights hitherto unimaginable for a 1980s progressive rock band. It's funny how things turn out.

Knowing that those present were fan club members, the band seemed only too happy to come out after the show to chat and sign autographs. It was the chance I'd been waiting for. The earring had been given to me by an old friend, Siwan.* Siwan claimed to have followed Fish into a shop on Bangor High Street the day Marillion played Bangor University (in Gwynedd, North Wales) on an early tour. She said she had seen him buying something and, soon after he left the shop, noticed a box beneath the glass counter with just one earring in it. "Where's the other one?" she asked the sales assistant (in Welsh, as Welsh is her first language).

"It was bought by the gentleman who was in here a little while ago," she was told. Of course, realising what a coup this would be, she immediately snapped up the other one for herself. In due course she sent it to me as a gift. And now here I was, swinging it in front of Fish in a TV studio in the south of England. He took it in his hand, turned it over once or twice and examined it carefully. I was aware of a small crowd forming around us and people pushing in to get a closer look. I was trembling with excitement and anticipation.

"Well," he said finally, "it looks very much like one that I used to own, but I've got loads of them and I tend to lose them on tour."

"Thanks," I smiled, and nodded at him, instantly at ease and content. "Can I have your autograph?"

As Fish took my ticket from me and signed the back I felt relief: "Yes!" I congratulated myself, "he said he *might* have owned the other one."

Quite why I thought this was such a triumph eludes me now. In fact, it wasn't long before I started to feel pretty stupid about the whole conversation. Of all the things I could have asked him! A question that would "shatter all my illusions"? And so what if he did have the other

---

* The same Siwan who features in Chapter 4, 'Truly, Madly, Deeply'.

earring? Did I think it brought me closer to him in some way or gave us some kind of special connection? How creepy! I had got an awful lot of pleasure and sustenance from his lyrics, but really, to carry a fish earring around with me, what was that all about? Hell, I didn't even have my ears pierced! I'm cringing as I write, even though I know that I was a young boy then and shouldn't be too hard on myself. The earring does still have sentimental value for me – not because my early 1980s prog rock idol, Fish, *might*, at one time, have owned one like it, but because Siwan gave it to me. I still have it today . . . in a box . . . somewhere.

It is not unusual for people to get tongue-tied or to say stupid things around those they most admire. Without having to think too hard I can give you other examples from my own experience (and I'm sure you'll be able to think of some from yours). In 2006, my cousins Chris, Jon, William and I went to see Iron Maiden on their *A Matter of Life and Death* tour. We had bought our gig tickets, but also had backstage passes that Steve Harris had left for us via an association with a good friend of Jon's. We sat around in one of the bars, just up some stairs from Maiden's dressing room, discussing what we'd say if at some point in the evening we came face to face with the great man himself.

"We should thank him for the passes for a start," someone said.

"Yeah, and we could talk to him about football," said someone else. It's well known that he is a huge West Ham United supporter, and West Ham had signed not one but two central defenders from our own team, Cardiff City. As we finished our drinks and shuffled back down the stairs on our way to the auditorium, a fire-exit door rattled, and in walked Steve Harris. He stood just a yard away and stared at us. To a man we froze, our bravado and good ideas apparently left back in the bar.

"Alright," I finally managed to mumble, half nodding my head in salute.

"Alright," he replied, his eyes already darting off in a different direction and his body soon following. So there I was, starstruck and tongue-tied aged 39. And yet, despite experiencing a number of these mildly deflating situations, I still feel a ripple or two of excitement whenever I am presented with an opportunity to meet or converse with a rock musician I admire. I remember, for example, the thrill I felt when after e-mailing 'new' Marillion vocalist Steve 'h' Hogarth to compliment him on a TV appearance that had turned me back on to the band, I received a brief personal reply. Why should a short e-mail from a relative stranger be the cause of so much excitement? Full marks to Steve Hogarth for replying, but the truth of the matter is that I don't know him from Adam; and he doesn't know me either.

Curiously, I've never really had the same trouble with sports stars. Perhaps it's because I've always been around them. For most of my childhood my mother worked for Glamorgan County Cricket Club, and I often found myself in the presence of top class cricketers. Similarly, my father had grown up in Pontcanna, Cardiff, and was good mates with a number of Cardiff City footballers with whom he stayed in touch over the years. I also worked as a Welsh Rugby Union steward, and often saw big-name players around the National Stadium before and after internationals. Certainly familiarity can take some of the novelty and excitement out of such situations. I think it's more than this, though. I think it's at least partly because sport, though it's always had some place in my life, just means less to me. For me, rock and roll is the promised land. Brief contact with musicians I admire is the closest I'm ever likely to get to touching this glorious 'Otherworld' or really feeling a part of it. Sport is far more mainstream, far more conformist. It's not that there aren't sportsmen I admire and respect – it's just that for me sport lacks the profundity and emotional pull of rock music. What's more, I don't have such high expectations of sports stars. I'm always pleased if I get to meet them, but I don't really find myself wanting to talk to them about anything in particular. I understand what they do and its significance, but there's no mystery, no edge, no danger. There is less at stake, less risk of disappointment, and I find it easier to take them as I find them. With musicians I often feel as though I do *want* to say more even though, more often than not, I don't know *what* to say.

⦿ Beyond praise and echoes ⦿

I have long been fascinated by the relationship between rock stars and their fans. Whether we are talking about screaming girls unable to contain themselves in the presence of their idols, autograph-hunting anoraks, groupies looking for notches on their bedposts or angst-ridden teenagers hanging on their heroes' every word, the patterns and forms of relationship are instantly recognisable and well-established.

As fans we come to know musicians primarily through their recorded output, their live performances and the things they say about their music in interviews. We have their art, and yet for many of us this is not enough. Because their music stirs something in us, and because in some way we connect with it, we often think we know *them*, have some kind of bond with them, or have some other kind of purchase on their souls. We are thrilled to have contact with them and to be brought so close to the source of the creative talent that means so much to us. It doesn't occur to us that there is only so much contact and personality to go around. Sometimes we are so keen to show them that we know them, understand them and are somehow like them, that we completely fail to relate to them in a normal manner. It's a complaint that Dylan makes in his great disillusionment hymn 'Idiot Wind':

> *People see me all the time*
> *and they just can't remember how to act*
> *Their minds are full of big ideas*
> *images and distorted facts*

Sometimes we just forget that most of the time our heroes inhabit the same space and do the same things as the rest of us. My wife Chrissy and I went to see Marillion at Bristol Colston Hall on their *Somewhere Else* tour (2007). We arrived mid-afternoon, and as we walked down Lodge Street with our friend Ed on our way to check out the venue, we noticed Steve Hogarth walking up the hill towards us.

"Hello," he said, no doubt spotting our Marillion t-shirts.

"Oh, hello, h," replied Chrissy, in joyful surprise, "I didn't expect to see you here."

He looked at her, half amused and half puzzled. He was, after all, one fifth of the reason we were there. "Well I do live in the real world," he said, and off he went to check out the shops and cafés and enjoy the afternoon sun.

While the way fans respond to so-called 'stars' can clearly present challenges to the artists, the relationship between artists and their fans also holds risks for the state of mind, the self-image and even the personal development of the enthralled fan. While I've not had many particularly great meetings with musicians I admire, I've not really had any particularly disappointing ones either. Others have not been so lucky. My friend Ian's big hero is Mike Scott of The Waterboys. Having been a fan for years, Ian was finally at an event where he had the chance to meet him. Ian wanted to say something "good" to his idol, something that would make it clear to him that he wasn't just another fawning fan. (The last thing in the world you want when you are 40 years old is to meet one of your heroes and have them think you haven't progressed beyond the teenage sycophant stage.) Nothing obvious came to mind, however, and as Ian walked closer he still had no idea what he was going to say. In the end, as he shook his hero's hand, he said: "I hear you've got a big drug problem in Glasgow." ("I didn't plan to say it," Ian told me later, "the words just came out." He was mortified.) Now, Ian has got a very strong North-West Wales accent, an accent which, to the uninitiated, appears to be infused with more than a touch of Scouse.

His hero looked pissed off. As he pulled his hand away and moved on quickly, he said: "It's no worse than the one you've got in Liverpool."

"But I'm not from Liverpool," Ian shouted after him, "I'm Welsh." And that is the only contact he has ever had with his ultimate musical idol.

They do say "never meet your idols", and, if you have any choice in the matter, that can sometimes be sensible advice. There is a story, well known among Aerosmith fans, about an American policeman picking a collapsed junkie out of the gutter only to find himself arresting his boyhood hero – Steven Tyler. By his own admission, Tyler was at a point in his life where he had hit rock bottom – much like the distressed cop's new image of his fallen idol.

And even rocks stars can be starstruck. In their biography of Doors' vocalist Jim Morrison, *No One Here Gets Out Alive*, Jerry Hopkins and Danny Sugerman describe Morrison's first meeting with "one of his high school heroes" – the beat generation poet Michael McClure. Though the two later became friends, according to Hopkins and Sugerman, "the meeting was a disappointment to them both. Michael McClure hadn't read any of Jim's poetry and Jim's shyness caused him to get impossibly drunk."[1]

Noting the dangers here, some rock stars have, indeed, chosen not to meet those they most admire. Despite being greatly influenced by Cream bass player Jack Bruce, Black Sabbath bassist Geezer Butler told writer Joel McIver: "I don't want to meet him – everyone that I've ever met that I worshipped has been a disappointment, so I want to keep him as my hero. I wouldn't know what to say to him!"[2] Geezer's bandmate Ozzy Osbourne has reported adopting a similar policy:

If I have people I've admired from a distance and have the occasion to meet them, I've been very disappointed. I've had this picture in my mind, and when I meet them, it's never right. I'm a big Beatles fan; I was on the Concorde with Paul and Linda McCartney. I could have met them but I didn't because I didn't want to shatter my fantasy.[3]

All good psychologists will tell you that praise can positively reinforce behaviour when we have worked hard and done good deeds. What's more, the way others respond to us is clearly an enormous contributor not just to the way we behave but to our sense of self-worth. Anyone who has ever created anything will know that while the praise of others does not necessarily validate or invalidate your creation, it usually makes you feel good about yourself and what you've done. Praise, then, is an important and appropriate response to creativity. However, one sometimes reads of rock stars whose egos are so fragile that they require constant attention and praise to keep functioning and to hold themselves together. Conversely, one sometimes meets rock fans who are so insistently and overwhelmingly gushing in their praise of their idols that one suspects an unhealthy obsession and a loss of perspective. Excessive praise from those who simply want to endear themselves to another person is not a good or a healthy return for an artist. The philosopher Friedrich Nietzsche knew this, and captured the point in a typically concise aphorism:

The voice of disappointment: "I listened for an echo and heard only praise . . ."[4]

Every teacher wants to see their influence on a promising pupil, every artist the impact of their work on their fans – but does moving beyond praise really mean simply *echoing* what our teachers and heroes do? I once saw a TV programme in which a young Marilyn Manson fan went to extraordinary lengths to look like his idol. Despite hours of meticulous preparation and attention to the smallest point of detail, when brought face to face with Manson, the young fan claimed that he was not copying the rock star but simply being himself. It seemed an absurd and transparently false claim to make – after all, wasn't it clear for all to see that the pupil was simply aping the master? Maybe, but the truth of the matter is that at that stage of his life, being himself probably did mean copying someone else. That, perhaps, brings us to the crux of the matter. It is all very well living in the space created for us by our idols when we are teenagers, but the point, surely, is to transcend our influences and come to stand on our own two feet. When attraction and respect becomes something more like hero-worship, we are in danger of stunting our personal development and emotional growth. The trick is to assimilate and move beyond what we've learned from others, not to reinvent ourselves in their image or live in their shadow.

¡○ *The Lizard King* ○¡

Despite his death almost 40 years ago, Jim Morrison's iconic status remains compelling for each new generation of rock fans. He may be dead and buried but he lives on in rock history, his legacy lying in wait for those unsuspecting innocents who will, as sure as night follows day, become entranced by the sensual pull and wanton destructiveness of his words, looks and reputation. Part of Jim Morrison's talent and appeal lay, I think, in his appreciation of the power of symbols – be they linguistic, aural or visual – to move, excite and disturb. He played with the elements (earth, air, fire, water), the cycle of life (birth, sex, death), the imagery of the four seasons and promises of love and knowledge in ways that continue to draw people in, irrespective of whether or not they were around at the time.

While Morrison clearly knew a thing or two about tapping into our 'common psyche' (for want of a better term), author Doug Sundling has commented on the tendency of Doors fans to worship a somewhat idealised notion of who Jim Morrison was and what he stood for. Sundling writes:

> I have never viewed Jim Morrison as a demigod, as a 20th Century Dionysus, or the Doors as a greater-than-life entity. From my 16th birthday onward, I have looked to the Doors as fellow artistic spirits who had successfully forged a path to express a creative vision we share. Consequently, I haven't had the problem I see of so many Doors fanatics: when the worshippers leave their adolescent view of life, the god becomes all too human. Having now outlived Morrison, I understand what Jim's – and the Doors' – artistic vision can't portray: the wisdom that comes with having lived into your thirties, into mid-life, into old age. That perspective of life never came to Morrison, for like a fiery and intense burst of brilliance, like so many artistic spirits who choose not to burn the candle at both ends but with a blowtorch in the middle, Jim, though very gifted, paid a dear price for being a jerk.[5]

For my own part, I sensed very quickly that there was something of enduring value in the Doors' music (or "artistic vision"), but was, with some self-awareness, more prone to hero-worship than Sundling. If I had for a while been in awe of Fish, it was purely a cerebral attraction. Fish wrote words that helped me to reflect on things that were important in my life, but he did tend to wallow in self-pity and inhabit a rather insular world of bedsit squalor and 'Hotel Hobbies'. Morrison's influence had a strong sensual dimension and engaged the whole body. It was a manifesto for personal change and *action*. I put away my *Script for a Jester's Tear* and checked into *Morrison Hotel*.

As far as I remember, my first taste of the Doors came when I caught a late night documentary about them on TV. I saw it by chance, and have no idea what it was called, but it focused on Morrison's awareness of the rock gig as a vehicle for moving, motivating and inspiring large numbers of people. This chimed with my own experience. I was too young (and born in the wrong country) to have had a reasonable chance of seeing the Doors play live, but here I was, well over a decade after Jim Morrison's death, transfixed by his brooding, groin-thrusting power and the control he seemed to have over his audience as he taunted and toyed with them, whipping up a storm of excitement, anticipation and fury. His image still seemed fresh and relevant, but I needed to hear more to know what I thought of the music.

Around the same time, I found myself in a temporary job working for the local Council. I happened to share an office with a bloke called Keith who had been a keen music fan in the late 1960s and early 1970s. He had acquired a record collection of which he was justifiably proud, but I got the impression that his family and work commitments now left him with little time for music, and I think he was pleased to have found a kindred spirit. He gave me a log book to look at, in which he kept an alphabetical list of all his albums. "Tell me if there's anything you fancy hearing," he told me, "and I'll bring it in for you." I had a good look through and, not wanting to push my luck (at least not at first), I asked to borrow just two – *Electric Ladyland* by the Jimi Hendrix Experience, and *13*, a Doors compilation album released in November 1970 when the band were still a going concern. On the strength of *13* I bought the first Doors album, and although I found it interesting, I was just a little disappointed with the heavy psychedelic vibe and a production that made it sound very much of its time. My interest in the Doors might well have stopped there had not my friend Harvey lent me his *Absolutely Live* tape at a later point in time. The live set gave me some more overt and fresher sounding blues-rock reference points that helped me relate to the music and made me anxious to hear more of the studio material. I was also drawn to 'The Celebration of the Lizard', a lengthy piece built around a shifting, evocative and partly spoken lyric. Suitably impressed, I purchased and avidly devoured all the albums recorded by the Doors with Jim Morrison, including the posthumous poetry album *An American Prayer*. I was sufficiently gripped to want to know even more, and read Jerry Hopkins and Danny Sugerman's excellent biography *No One Here Gets Out Alive*, as well as Frank Lisciandro's *An Hour for Magic*, and Morrison's own poetry volumes *The Lords* and *The New Creatures*. The timing couldn't have been better, or worse, depending on your point of view. I had just dropped out of university. I was a confused mass of contradictions and frayed ends. I felt strongly that rock music had let me down. I was experiencing a sense of fragmentation and knew that I needed to re-evaluate my personal and moral bearings. I was on the verge of a period of exploration and re-assessment of who I was, where I was going and what I wanted out of life. In short, I was ripe for the plucking.

I may not have been around to see the Doors perform live, but it was soon apparent that I was just as vulnerable to their influence as many of those who *had* been around at the time. Sex, death, desire, fear, chaos, disorder, alienation, transcendence, riots, rock theatre, poetic drama – these are just a few examples of words and phrases that attach themselves to the Doors' music and suck you in like a moth to a flame. Words and images swirl around Doors songs like Ray Manzarek's organ – stirring, awakening, arousing something in us . . . something we know not what. "Think of us as erotic politicians," Morrison told one journalist[6], while another, Gene Youngblood of the *Los Angeles Free Press*, described their music as "the music of outrage", claiming that it possessed "a beauty that terrifies".[7] James Douglas Morrison, self-appointed poet, shaman and Lizard King, strides god-like over the music, calling us all to the dance.

I liked the irony of Morrison's 'Lizard King' persona, and its implicit critique of society's tendency to perceive visionaries, eccentrics, non-conformists and well-meaning social critics as a threat. With perfect awareness Morrison embraced the power of the imagery, using it not only to confirm his own 'outsider' status but to draw people to him on his own terms. Nietzsche, it seems to me, taunted the literary and philosophical world in a similar fashion. Back in my own little world, I noted that Cardiff punk band Icons of Filth adopted their moniker with the same sense of irony – though, of course, they lacked the musical charm to appeal to anyone beyond a very small anarcho-punk hardcore.

I identified strongly with the notion of being an outsider. In his Foreword to *No One Here Gets Out Alive*, Danny Sugerman writes:

> . . . identifying with Jim meant that you were an outsider who *preferred* to look in. Rock and roll has always attracted a lot of misfits with identity problems, but Morrison took being an outsider one step further. He said, in effect, 'That's okay, we *like* it here. It hurts and it's hell, but it's also a helluva lot more *real* than the trip I see *you* on'.[8]

This seemed to me to provide some validation of the "trip" I had chosen for myself, and I started to wish that I had just a fraction of Morrison's ability to influence people. "Oh to be able to shock and affect, to shine and influence, to cause to reflect," I wrote in my newly acquired notebook, and my thoughts turned towards the purchase of a pair of attention-grabbing black leather trousers. I even got as far as dragging a friend out shopping with me. "You're only thinking of buying those so you can be like that singer you're always talking about," he said. Of course he was right, and I realised I was just being silly. Praise and echoes, eh? In truth, I lacked both the confidence and physical presence to have pulled it off anyway.

At a more introspective level, I was much taken with the idea that I shared with Jim Morrison something of the lot of the misunderstood and tortured artist. Again in his foreword to *No One Here Gets Out Alive*, Danny Sugerman notes Morrison's kinship to those "wounded, gifted artists who felt life too intensely to bear living it."[9] It was a compelling and romantic notion, and I came to see my growing intensity as part of a creative impulse that could be harnessed in the service of artistic expression. I was already reading Huxley and Orwell, but I now started reading Nietzsche and Kerouac too. I started to take my reading far more seriously and acquired a new thirst for knowledge. I felt driven by some kind of unspecified 'higher purpose'. I started to keep a notebook (referred to above), jotting down thoughts and quotes and sometimes just lists of words that I liked. And, almost inevitably I suppose, I started trying to write poetry. There are no doubt thousands like me who, during angst-ridden teenage years, reel off reams and reams of heartfelt, 'important', and very bad poetry. We are spurred on by the likes of Jim Morrison, Morrissey, Joni Mitchell and Fish. I suspect that Jim Morrison in particular has a lot to answer for!

Though one reads mixed reviews of Jim Morrison's ability as a poet, poetry clearly mattered a great deal to him. The desire for recognition as a poet was an important part of his personal identity. In reading about Jim Morrison, one often comes across the following extract written by one of Morrison's poetic heroes, Arthur Rimbaud:

A poet makes himself a *seer* by a long, prodigious, and rational *disordering* of *all the senses*. Every form of love, of suffering, of madness; he searches himself, he consumes all the poisons in him, and keeps only their quintessences. This is unspeakable torture during which he needs all his faith and superhuman strength, and during which he becomes the great patient, the great criminal, the great accursed – and the great learned one! – among men. For he arrives at the *unknown*! Because he has cultivated his own soul – which was rich to begin with – more than any other man! He reaches the unknown; and even if, crazed, he ends up by losing the understanding of his visions, at least he has seen them! Let him die charging through those unutterable, unnameable things: other horrible workers will come; they will begin from the horizons where he has succumbed.[10]

The active quest to reach for "the unknown" and the desire to express one's newfound and hard-won knowledge in poetic or lyrical form is consistent with a notion that is evident in the Doors' early music – the notion of 'breaking through'. In the Elektra biography that accompanied the release of the first album (January 1967), Morrison said: "I like ideas about the breaking away or overthrowing of established order – I am interested in anything about revolt, disaster, chaos, especially in activity that seems to have no meaning."[11] In a *Newsweek* interview in October 1967 Morrison said: "Right now, I'm more interested in the dark side of life . . . But in our music it appears to me that we're seeking, striving, trying to break through to some cleaner, freer realm."[12]

The idea of breaking through the social and conceptual constraints that have been imposed by one's upbringing impressed me, as did the idea of opening oneself up to new experiences in the name of knowledge. Even "activity that *seems* to have no meaning" (my emphasis) might, after all, turn out to be significant. I had found a new quest. What I was supposed to be breaking through to, and how I was supposed to do it, I did not yet know – but immersion in the work of Jim Morrison seemed a good place to start, and he offered plenty of pointers to other literary and artistic sources.

Being thrown back on my own resources in this way was a move away from social and political optimism and a feeling of kinship with my fellow man, towards a more individualistic and self-absorbed way of being that primarily sought *self*-knowledge, *self*-understanding and *personal* coherence. This kind of self-exploration required a serious assault on the upbringing and moral values that had made me who I was. It instantly put me into an antagonistic relationship with those I loved and who loved me. It felt dangerous. It felt like dancing on the edge. At times it was intoxicating. At other times it was very uncomfortable. I felt like the ground was giving way under my feet. For a few short months Jim Morrison was my guide. But while he may have liked the experience, I did not. I sought not disorder and madness but sanity and stability, order beneath the chaos. I wanted, and needed, to pull back from the edge. Above all, what I needed was to discover things that would strengthen my resolve, take me back to my fellow man and make me a better human being.

Nevertheless, this new quest did require me to put myself out there, and that is what I tried to do. The drug and booze fuelled parties I went to, the outrageous antics and desperate promiscuity I observed, may have lacked the ideological imperative of the 1960s, but they did signal a significant shift in what I was prepared to do and tolerate 'for my art'. Explaining his approach to life, Morrison is quoted as having said: "Let's just say I was testing the bounds of reality. I was curious to see what would happen."[13] I had no intention of pushing at "the bounds of reality" too hard, in case I fell through them and didn't come back, but I was certainly curious to see what happened when other people pushed. I developed an almost anthropological approach to my social life. I became, for a while, a kind of voyeur of decadence, a social observer, a spy in the underworld – not so much testing the boundaries myself, but watching others do it and noting what happened when they did.

ꙮ *Strange Days* ꙮ

In his book *People Are Strange: The Ultimate Guide to the Doors*,[14] Doug Sundling does an excellent job of placing the Doors in their time, providing extensive information about popular Amercian culture (in the form of TV schedules and lists of popular songs, albums, films and books)

at the time of each of the Doors' album releases. In contrast I discovered
and listened to the Doors *out of time*.

In the Rock and Roll Hall of Fame Induction Booklet 1993, long-time
Doors producer Paul A. Rothchild says:

> The Doors were never part of any movement. Indeed, during an era of
> very high fliers, their visionary trajectory sought an orbit positioned well
> outside of the rock norm. Their journey was driven by a unique group
> vision and a determination to push the envelope of poetry, spirituality,
> intellect and psycho-sexual exploration in popular music as far as
> possible.[15]

The breadth and ambition of such a quest goes some way to explaining
why, with some concessions to the passing of time, the Doors still seemed
relevant to me in the mid-1980s and why they still have relevance and value
today. I made no particular effort to 'think myself back' to the 1960s, but,
quite simply, I was *struck* by the relevance of most of the music in a way
that made it impossible to ignore. Much of the material on the *Strange Days*
album, for example, is a case in point. The album was released in October
1967, but it seemed to describe fairly accurately the youth culture all around
me in 1986 and the way I felt about it. *Strange Days* is full of lost and lonely
people trying metaphorical masks on for size, desperately seeking someone
or something to give them the help, reassurance and validation that they
need. It describes a world of alienated and confused people drenched in
decadence and night-time sin, trying to convince themselves and others that
they are happy, but conspiring only to produce an extraordinary shallowness
that screams 'THIS IS NOT REAL' at those of us who are not taken in. It
also seems to describe well the futility of our chemical fixations and our lust
for 'groundless' sex, where brief moments of gratification might provide
us with temporary solace but ultimately leave us feeling empty, alone,
unwanted and unsure of ourselves. Doesn't it sound familiar?

In his sleeve notes to the 2006 reissue of *Strange Days* for the *Perception*
box set, Barney Hoskyns, author and co-founder of the online library *Rock's
Backpages*, notes that despite being recorded at the height of the Summer
of Love, *Strange Days* showed that there was "a darker truth to chemical
escapism"[16]. "With its radical cover," writes Hoskyns, ("the band replaced
by a small troupe of Fellini-esque freak show performers") "*Strange Days*
remains a masterpiece of post-psychedelic pop, beat poetics and deceptively
solicitous love songs. Arguably it is the Doors' greatest album."[17]

The Doors' greatest album it arguably is, but like much of the Doors' music, *Strange Days* is, as I've suggested above, far more than a landmark rock album or an historical curiosity. It's of its time, but not *just* of its time. It has a relevance that has endured for over 40 years and shows no sign of abating. What's more, in lengthy album closer 'When the Music's Over', it contains a statement of portentous anxiety that has hung over popular music ever since like a looming apocalyptic thunderstorm. 'When the Music's Over' reminds us of the unique power of music to drive change and inspire hope – but it is also a clear warning that we cannot take the music for granted. *Strange Days* will continue to be a relevant album for as long as there is music and young people who put their faith in it. But there is nothing to say that the music will continue. Even endurance must have an end – and the Doors' music will cease to have relevance, will cease to endure, when *all* the music is over.

'When the Music's Over' has always been one of my favourite Doors songs. It's one of Morrison's best lyrics – a claim borne out by the number of lines which have been used as titles of later books, compilations or live albums (*A Feast of Friends*; *Alive, She Cried*; *Dance on Fire*). The vocal highlights include an apparently pained and impassioned call for the world to be delivered to the younger generation, and a frenzied plea to Jesus for salvation – half mocking perhaps, but certainly desperate. For many of us, music keeps a flame burning, and we follow its guiding light, allowing ourselves to be lured by the promise of a better life, someday, somewhere, somehow. Morrison's plea expresses the desperation we might feel when even the last saving grace – the music which seemed to offer us so much hope – is itself in danger of coming to an end.

But will the music *really* end? How can this be? As noted above, Morrison was singing during the Summer of Love, and we've had over 40 years of music since. At the time music was everywhere, and youth culture was marked by a real sense of optimism that the world could change and that young people could drive this change. So what were the Doors trying to tell us? Interviewed for Jim Ladd's *Inner View* radio special (1976), Doors guitarist Robby Krieger said:

> We were never really protagonists of the flower movement; in fact we were the complete opposite . . . love and peace and everything's great – that was only half of the side of the coin. We were providing a glimpse of the other side as well.[18]

The 1960s were indeed strange days, and writer Doug Sundling is not alone in drawing our attention to "the Jekyll and Hyde nature of the times".[19] It is true that rebellion was possible and that social gains were made. But it is also true that such gains were often accompanied by struggle and violence, that key social and political figures were assassinated, that war continued to break out all over the world, and that the Cold War cast long shadows with man's ability to create ever more destructive bombs making global obliteration a real possibility. Meanwhile, the 'no rules', 'anything goes' spirit that accompanied social and moral liberation often seemed to contain the seeds of its own destruction. It was like setting hungry children free in a sweet shop and telling them they could eat anything, as long as they didn't make themselves sick. Awareness of the ambiguities of their age, a refusal to be taken in by only part of the picture ("half of the side of the coin," to quote Robby Krieger again), is one of the things that gives the Doors a relevance that transcends their cultural milieu. One sees this well expressed in the song 'Five to One' from the *Waiting for the Sun* album (July 1968). On the face of it, it's a celebration of the growing strength and power of the younger generation. For that reason it is often taken to be a political song. It features on the same album as the hard-hitting war song 'Unknown Soldier', and appears, at first sight, to be more of the same. However, as Hopkins and Sugerman note, a careful reading of 'Five to One's' third verse makes it clear that Morrison is having a dig at the hippy generation. "Listened to in its entirety," they say, "the song seems to be a parody of all the naïve revolutionary rhetoric heard on the streets and read in the underground press in the late sixties."[20]

With influences on the Doors' music stretching back into Greek art and mythology, they present the ambiguities of the age as immutable and even tragic aspects of the human condition. Much of Morrison's work seems to deal with impermanence and suggests that even, and perhaps especially, good and beautiful things are fragile, fleeting and transitory. We cannot or should not take anything for granted. Joy and beauty and happiness are not easy to find or hold onto. Music can help us to see them and to come together in fruitful and positive ways, but again you can't *assume* that even the music will continue. It will end when those who create it create it no more, and when new generations fail to produce new musicians and artists and spokespeople. It will end when creative energies are overwhelmed by the darker, more selfish forces working against them. Or it will end when the motivating, rabble-rousing, life-changing power of rock music is hijacked by music industry entrepreneurs and used to feed the corporate mindset, generating wealth for the few rather than personal, social and political awareness. How close are we to the end of music? Are we closer or further away now than we were when the Doors sang their song? I'll leave it to you to decide.

The Night Life

I

A crazed night
The Model
The Angel
Rocking the bar
Set them up
Knock them down
Play it again Sam
This is the night life

Beyond the summer rain
Beyond the day's disdain
Where an old lady tuts
To make the bus come quicker
Gone is the dead day
This is the night life

At the place of the theft
Video starists roost
Screaming and screeching
Up above the former gigging Maiden
We wanted to rock the foundations
Phone numbers passed on backs of tickets
Drunken and confused bearings
Enough to base a feeling on?
This is the night life?

II

Cute or newt?
Yes please

Shoot, shoot, shoot
I've done my time
Now wrap me in an ego boost

Alternative club
Still knocking them back
You've hours to double your number

Walking resurrection of a younger teenage dream
But I was sorry to be author
Of the fake and pointed laughter
That I realised after
Hid a poor transvestite scream

Among old friends and words aside
I remembered my "quiet ride"
"Where have you been?"
"Well, without making a scene
I had to go because you cried.
And if this is your night life
Can you blame me if I'd rather hide?"

III

There's something so unreal
About the hustling midnight deals
And the fighting men
The hunts, the tricks, the treats
There's something so unreal
About the hustling midnight deals
And the bustle
Of the hustling midnight streets

There's something so not there
About the things that glow with dare
Beneath the sparkle
Of the vibrant neon glare
There's something so not with it
This thing isn't of the spirit
It's the desperate joy
Of night life's hopeful stare

IV

Is this really the sum of the life
That you hide from the sight
Of our natural light?
And try as you may
You will not convince me
I'm wrong when I say
That there's something about it
That cannot be right

Temporary occupant
Spirited visit
Now I'll retire from the call
That belongs to your night

◉ The Doors' artistic vision ◉

In *People Are Strange: The Ultimate Guide to the Doors*, Doug Sundling describes what he calls "The Doors' artistic vision", illustrating its various elements through an analysis not only of the Doors' songs, but of the major social, economic and political events of the time. He attempts to show that the elements of the Doors' artistic vision were a source of enduring inspiration and bring a form of coherence to the body of work that is made up of the six original Doors studio albums. Sundling notes some of the difficulties the band faced in maintaining their inspiration and their standards under the weight of fame and commercial pressures, but he argues that after an inevitable transitional phase the artistic vision was given more mature expression on the later albums as the Doors metamorphosed into shamanic bluesmen. This view sees the first two albums as explicit and full-on statements of what the Doors were about. The third and fourth albums are seen as transitional as the band ran out of old songs and had to learn to write new material in the studio. Album five is said to continue the transition, with the band caught between "their old psychedelic, poetically ambiguous selves" and "all-out bluesmen",[21] while album six pushes the Doors as close as they would get to "mature blues".

What, then, are the elements of the artistic vision that Sundling has divined? At its heart, the vision consists of the following notions:

- Our socialisation is full of repression and constraint, and more often than not causes us to become detached from our true selves and our happiness.
- To 'find ourselves' and be truly happy, we must transcend convention and our inherited thoughts and values. (The process of transcendence is often represented lyrically as some form of symbolic death.)
- To transcend our limited horizons, we must journey into the unknown, opening ourselves up to new perceptions, and being ready to explore our experiences and emotions fully.
- This journey can be scary and painful as we leave our traditional comforts and compensations behind.
- Moments of sanctuary we experience on this journey, usually through love of some sort, are fleeting.
- The goal is to achieve some kind of breakthrough leading to metaphorical rebirth and self-realisation.

In keeping with the interpretation provided above, it is Sundling's view that all of these elements are clearly in view on the first two albums. The debut album, *The Doors*, is described by Sundling as: "a series of songs which oscillate between pursuing the need both for the sanctuary of love and for the freedom to explore the unknown."[22] Against a background of psychedelic sounds and 1960s indulgence, these conflicting needs create a tension which is well illustrated, for example, in 'The Crystal Ship', in which a youthful, vigorous and confident Morrison asserts that he'd rather take off to experience life's thrills than stay with his lover. The title of the song suggests that Morrison's chosen lifestyle finely balances beauty, exploration and fragility. The album is bookended by opener 'Break On Through (To the Other Side)' – a bold statement of general purpose and intent – and the bizarre mix of eastern-tinged psychedelia, personal searching and Greek mythology that is album closer 'The End'. In a 1969 interview Morrison told Jerry Hopkins that he didn't know what he was trying to express in 'The End'. It apparently started out as a love song, a goodbye to an old girlfriend, though, according to Robby Krieger, Morrison added more and more "weird stuff" to it every time the band developed the song.[23] Most notably, 'The End' features a famous Oedipal section in which the son returns to the family home to kill the father and have sex with the mother. The 2006 reissue is even more shocking, with Morrison lapsing into a clearly audible 30-second incantation that is heavily reliant on the F-word. For all of its shock value, within the context of the artistic vision the passage can be interpreted as representing the son freeing himself from the constraints of family life, transcending instilled concepts and values and leaving the father and mother behind. Producer Paul Rothchild saw it as signifying the death of "alien concepts" and "the beginning of personal concepts".[24] Despite it clocking in at over 11½ minutes, the band recorded 'The End' in just two takes, with producer Rothchild and engineer Bruce Botnick splicing together the first half of the first take and the second half of the second. In his sleeve notes to the 2006 reissue, Ben Fong-Torres quotes Rothchild's recollection that six minutes into one of the takes he turned to Botnick and said: " 'Do you understand what's happening here? This is one of the most important moments in recorded rock 'n' roll.'" "When they were done," says Rothchild, "I had goosebumps from head to foot. It was magic."[25]

According to Doug Sundling, much of the material on the first three Doors albums was drawn from the band's so-called "acid fertility" period when they were closest to the source of their vision and had time to work up songs in clubs. However, while the band had sufficient material ready for both their debut and the *Strange Days* album, the material didn't quite stretch far enough to ensure that *Waiting for the Sun* maintained standards. Once the pressures of fame and recording contracts hit, they had less time to write and develop new songs and had to learn to write material in the studio in-between hectic touring schedules. What's more, their "meteoric success" created "the inevitable conflict . . . of maintaining contact with the creative and social forces upon which the artist draws."[26] "How," asks Sundling, "could millionaire musicians like the Doors sing about the hypocrisy of a plastic materialistic society detached from the roots of life?"[27] As a result, the third and fourth albums, *Waiting for the Sun* and *The Soft Parade* (July 1969) are, in Sundling's opinion, "not as strong conceptually as the first two".[28] He is particularly critical of *The Soft Parade*, describing it as "a compilation of musical clichés and rip-offs"[29] which provides "at best a fuzzy sketch of the Doors' artistic vision."[30]

While rock journalist (and Morrison's soon-to-be Wiccan wife) Patricia Kennely wrote: "If T.S. Eliot had been a rock group he would have been the Doors and done *The Soft Parade*,"[31] and engineer Bruce Botnick describes the album as "a noble effort . . . in their fight through the fog of ignorance and fear",[32] *The Soft Parade* was not generally well received by the critics. The album was released just a few months after the infamous Miami show on 1 March 1969, a debacle which led to allegations that Morrison had exposed himself to the audience. Partly frustrated by his perception of what the audience wanted from him, and partly inspired by the *Living Theatre* show he had attended just a short time before, Morrison delivered a riotous and incendiary performance that brought him a good deal of unwanted legal and media attention and led to a widespread ban on Doors gigs across the United States. Morrison was subsequently charged with a range of offences for his conduct that night: lewd and lascivious behaviour, indecent exposure, open profanity, and drunkenness. He was eventually acquitted of the first and fourth of these, but found guilty of indecent exposure and profanity.* In media terms the Doors' bubble had burst. Doug Sundling notes that: "The consensus opinion was that during this period Morrison was basically a disinterested, drunken asshole."[33] Writing in 2006, David Fricke referred to "Morrison's runaway drinking and wild-animal reactions to celebrity," and described *The Soft Parade* as "a protracted studio creation".[34] Back in the day, journalist Lester Bangs proclaimed that the Doors' "artistic stock had hit an all-time low".[35]

Discovering a band retrospectively means that one doesn't have the same kind of personal stake in their output and development, and doesn't have the same kind of problem adjusting to 'unexpected' change as those who were around at the time. One has the whole body of work to discover away from cultural trappings and media reaction to each individual album. I understand why some people were disappointed that the Doors moved away from the blueprint of the first two albums, but musicians can't survive simply by producing copies of their earlier work. (In fact, if I have a criticism of the *Strange Days* album, it's that it follows too closely the format and structure of the debut.) Even if the change of styles was in a sense 'enforced' – as the band ran out of early material and had to learn to write in a different kind of way and under new pressures – it shows progression and adaptability and, with the benefit of hindsight, makes the Doors a more interesting band. I love the variety across the Doors' albums

---

* Morrison received a posthumous pardon from the Governor of Florida in December 2010.

and would think less of them if they hadn't experimented with their sound. Removed from the context of fan and media expectation, there is much to enjoy on both *Waiting for the Sun* and *The Soft Parade*. (Indeed, it's worth noting that *Waiting for the Sun* features not only Morrison's lyrical claim to be the omnipotent Lizard King – in 'Not to Touch the Earth' – but the lyrics of the epic poem 'The Celebration of the Lizard' on its inner sleeve.)

Despite Doug Sundling's criticism of both albums, he *does* see in them evidence not just of transition but maturation. Of the divergence of *Waiting for the Sun* from the first two albums, Sundling writes, "The Doors were realising they would have to live with the swirling whirlwind of the times. The passionate and frustrated urgencies to find love or freedom became muted to tones of being patient, of experiencing the pain and joy of living without fighting life."[36] Of *The Soft Parade* he notes that although it is framed on "a pattern quite consistent with the previous albums", "a more mellowed tone" has emerged. "[The Doors'] artistic vision is revealing that they are coming to terms with their own individual vulnerability, and are more at peace with it, now both susceptible and ready for *love*."[37]

In Sundling's view, the next album, *Morrison Hotel* (February 1970), continues this evolution as the band "seem more grounded in the realities of life" and more content to "let it roll".[38] According to Sundling, as the Doors edge uneasily towards "mature blues", *Morrison Hotel* "expresses the ascension into what the blues often embraces – the fulfilment of love", with Morrison apparently "willing to be a spy rather than a conquering Lizard King."[39]

By the time the band recorded *L.A. Woman* (April 1971), Sundling believes that a clear transformation had been effected. They may not have learned how to pack the "strong emotional punch" of "true blues,"[40] but they certainly seemed comfortable in their new skin. Of *L.A. Woman* Sundling writes: "those weren't the blues spun from the souls of slaves adrift in a strange land with no roots save the humanity of their own people. The blues with which the Doors rendered their artistic vision came from the souls of struggling artistic spirits adrift in their own culture and land."[41] Sundling notes that while remaining "emotionally provocative", "the lyrics seem to be more like a free-association outburst of poetic images" which leaves room for the listener to "interpret them differently every time you hear them."[42] He takes this as a sign of maturity, and finds in the work many 'traditional' Morrison motifs.

There is some corroborating evidence of the kind of 'creative calmness' that one might expect to accompany this alleged maturation. For example, Bruce Botnick, who produced *L.A. Woman* with the band after Paul Rothchild decided to stand down, has commented on the positive vibe around the album. "Everybody was full of creativity and joy," he writes. "Jim was all over the place with ideas, inspired" and wore "the biggest smile you can imagine."[43] Ben Fong-Torres further notes that: "Given freer reins, Morrison became more responsible."[44] There is other evidence, however, including evidence in the lyrics themselves, not of maturity and fulfilment, but of sadness, weariness and decay. Without wishing to detract from the creativity of the band or the quality and significance of the music, it's the latter picture, perhaps, that provides a more realistic interpretation of where Jim Morrison ended up.

Morrison Hotel

Does Sundling present *too* unified a view of the Doors albums? Was there really such a smooth evolution towards the "fulfilment of love" and "mature blues"? I have no doubt that Sundling is right to draw attention to the consistency of some of the later lyrics with *aspects* of what he sets out as the Doors' artistic vision, but to what extent do these elements remain sufficiently intact for us to speak of *one* enduring vision? Indeed, can we even be sure that the band shared, and continued to share, each other's perceptions and ideas? It is interesting to note that while Jim Morrison contributed the bulk of the songs to the early albums, songwriting credits on the first three albums are attributed to the Doors as a group. Morrison did not insist on separate songwriting credits until the fourth album, *The Soft Parade*. The reason for his insistence seems to have had nothing to do with either money or ego, but everything to do with artistic integrity. While Robby Krieger had contributed songs to every album, his input on *The Soft Parade* was more significant. Krieger is given sole credit for 'Tell All the People', 'Touch Me', 'Wishful Sinful', and 'Runnin' Blue', while he co-wrote 'Do It' with Morrison. The titles of the first two alone give some indication of Morrison's unease at singing these songs without people knowing they had been written by Robby. Morrison had emerged as a reluctant leader, a man already wearying of the constant attention of his fawning public.

The last thing he wanted to do was give the impression that he was enjoying his public persona or seeking to enhance it by encouraging the wrong kind of people to follow him in the wrong kind of way. What's more, Morrison told Jerry Hopkins in a *Rolling Stone* interview that he and Robby Krieger had "very different visions of reality",[45] making one wonder whether, by the time of *The Soft Parade*, it was still possible to speak of "*the Doors'* artistic vision" at all.

To be sure, Sundling advances an interesting hypothesis and is at his most enlightening when demonstrating the continuity of some of the themes in Morrison and the Doors' work. However, where Sundling sees a "shamanic bluesman" towards the end of Morrison's days, I see weariness, personal struggle and less grand ambition (more shambolic than shamanic). Where Sundling sees evolution and maturity, I see a falling away from the original vision and impulse. (Not that this is any more or less valid a shift than the one Sundling describes.) The original vision set out by Sundling has, as its end point, a breakthrough to self-realisation. Within this quest, Sundling describes very well the ongoing tension between the dual need for sanctuary and exploration. This tension is, indeed, a recurring theme across all of the Doors' albums. However, by the time of *Morrison Hotel*, and perhaps even before then, this noble quest seems to have become a much more basic struggle between the need for love and desire. To illustrate the point, let's take a closer look at *Morrison Hotel* itself.

While Bruce Botnick regards *Morrison Hotel* as "a transitional period for the band",[46] and many critics of the time remained lukewarm, others feel differently. David Fricke, for example, has described it as "one of rock's great resurrection records, a striking fight for life by a band under attack but uncompromised."[47] "After the hell and orchestras of 1969," he writes, "the Doors were a rock 'n' roll band again."[48] Biographers Hopkins and Sugerman are no less enthusiastic, noting that *Morrison Hotel* was "Lyrically . . . Jim's best work in years," with the rest of the band "providing their strongest support yet."[49]

Musically, *Morrison Hotel* is a clean, crisp blues-rock album, uncluttered by both the horns and orchestration of *The Soft Parade* and the psychedelia of the early albums. Perhaps the more direct adoption of the blues-rock idiom reflects the band's need to clutch at roots of some kind, and in this sense *Morrison Hotel* provides an oasis of relative calm in troubled Doors' waters. 'Roadhouse Blues' kicks off the album in fine rocking style, with Morrison urging his driver to stay in control, at least until they get to the roadhouse. On the surface it's a simple upbeat blues romp, but pay attention to Morrison's references to his morning drinking (in a line that Alice Cooper later claimed he 'inspired'), the uncertainty of the future and death. Morrison is in no doubt that his city needs saving, and quickly. It's a much darker track than we often realise.

'Waiting for the Sun' follows, with Morrison using Biblical imagery, the language of freedom and the language of the seasons to suggest that the time is ripe for some kind of rebirth or breakthrough. However, as Morrison metaphorically waits for the sun, it's never made clear who or what the sun is, nor indeed why Morrison *needs* to wait for it. While the time might be ripe for some kind of breakthrough, Morrison, it seems, cannot get there or get us there alone. This is a theme that recurs throughout the album. Morrison often appears needy, vulnerable, waiting, let down and confused, sometimes, as here, lamenting the strangeness of his life and hinting at false dawns, dashed hopes and ongoing unfulfilled yearning.

'You Make Me Real' continues the theme of dependency, with Morrison recognising that he needs his lover to feel real in what appears to be a straight-forward, punchy love song. Sundling's view – that the artistic vision matures – depends on the recognition and acceptance of vulnerability, a readiness for love, and the further equating of love with freedom, fulfilment and self-realisation, and here Morrison does seem to come close. There are, though, carnal overtones in the lyric – however poetically expressed – and such a strong sense of neediness that one has to wonder: is this really pure love or simply a hint that what Morrison actually needs is to submerge himself in sensuality and physical pleasure as just another means of consolation and escape?

The bizarrely titled 'Peace Frog' – the blood song, as I think of it – seems to mix reflections on a flailing and failing society with Morrison's memories of a formative early childhood experience in which he witnessed a particularly gruesome-sounding road accident. And yet there is also the appearance of a mysterious female character who seems to offer the singer some hope of escape from the rising blood-levels, and some means of coping with the ghosts of his past. 'Peace Frog' segues beautifully into 'Blue Sunday' which continues the theme of finding consolation, or even salvation, in the arms of one's true love. Perhaps *this* is really as close as Morrison comes to the "fulfilment of love". Again, though, it is noteworthy that it is the girl who tells Morrison that he is her one and only, and it is the girl who waits for his return – not the other way around. Though he clearly appreciates her love, regarding her as *his* girl, and thinking the world of her, we are left unsure whether he really reciprocates in kind. Would he *really* wait for her and give up his ways for her? Even Morrison's most tenderly crooned love song is so reminiscent of 'The Crystal Ship'.

Musically, 'Ship of Fools', is an amusing carnivalesque swirl. Lyrically, it is again possible to recognise Morrison's growing disillusionment with a failing youth culture and the dream gone bad. Even the alternative scene, which seemed to offer an escape from the smog, turns out to a 'Ship of Fools' – a kind of Pleasure Island for hippies – and Morrison's wryly expressed hope for the future seems tinged with more than just a hint of sardonic wit. Perhaps mankind *is* dying out, and all we really have left is our foolishness and whatever temporary solace we can find.

'Land Ho!' starts with the wanderlust of an old sailor who attempts to transmit his good natured frustration to his grandson. The grandson quickly sets off on a journey of adventure alright, but it's a journey through the seas of a decadent and seedy underworld. The young 'sailor' returns to safe ground – the woman who loves him – from time to time, but he knows that it won't be long before his wanderlust gets the better of him again. Occasionally he spies land and promises some night-time loving – but he makes no promises beyond the night.

'The Spy' is another wonderfully crooned lyric which comes all dressed up in dreamy guitar licks and a cool, knowing rhythm. I related to this song straight away, and recall my own observations of the pleasure, desperation and sadness of fellow revellers. In Morrison's hands, however, one can't help feeling that there's something vaguely sinister or creepy about the lyric, as though it's a prelude to action of some impure kind and that he has every intention of using the knowledge he has acquired for his own twisted ends.

If 'The Spy' is a 'gathering lyric' which doesn't give much away, 'Queen of the Highway' could, in contrast, be one of Morrison's most overtly self-referring songs, and one in which he both recognises his unsuitability for domesticated family life and tries it on for size. It's telling, I think, that while the woman in the lyric modifies her behaviour to fit the demands of married life, there is no indication that Morrison himself becomes 'a good boy'. Indeed, at the point of discussing raising children together, Morrison's weary allusion to the circle of life is more reminiscent of Camus' *Myth of Sisyphus* than a man who has just pledged "Til *death* do us part" with all that that entails. There is, all the same, temporary happiness, with Morrison's expressed hope that things can continue for just a short time longer reminding us that in his world such things are always temporary.

'Indian Summer', the first song ever recorded by the Doors, is a gentle piece which appears to be a profession of love, but which, nevertheless, again finds the singer torn between love and desire. The person to whom he is singing may well be his favourite lover, but the lyric seems to acknowledge that she is one of many, suggesting that once again fidelity may be too much for his partner to expect.

The closing track, 'Maggie M'Gill, is a stark tale of a mystery woman who, apparently short of options, likes to let it roll in ways that are left to our imagination. But is it more than this? Is this also part confession? Is this Morrison describing the legacy he would leave a child of his own – the offspring of a drunk, left with nothing to do but join the ships of fools where people blindly indulge in their pleasures of choice? Is this, indeed, a description of the cycle of unfulfilled and unfulfilling pleasure-seeking that had come to characterise Morrison's own life and that he had come to see all around him? Certainly such an interpretation fits with the themes of the album. But there's more. Morrison stakes his claim to be a bluesman (of sorts), finding in his observations truths that stretch back across ages and generations. His lyrics are comments on the human condition, and he seems reconciled to these 'truths', accepting that the cycle will keep rolling on. But, contra Sundling, there is no suggestion of fulfilment here. *Morrison Hotel* has no happy ending.

As I have tried to show with this brief overview, *Morrison Hotel* cannot represent acknowledgement of "the fulfilment of love". It consistently shows Morrison pulling away or refusing to commit himself to love, however important a role his lover plays in offering him solace, sanctuary and consolation. On the early albums, where the tension between the need for sanctuary and the need for exploration emerged, love provided temporary solace and nourishment as our hero went out in search of some greater truth. By now, however, Morrison appears to have lost faith in the counter-culture and become weary of his own quest: *Morrison Hotel* begins and ends with songs of beer and promiscuity. As Morrison grows weary his need for "the sanctuary of love" is expressed more openly and mournfully, but despite acknowledging his vulnerability and need for love, his wanderlust won't go away. All too often he takes what by now must have been the easy option, and gives in to his baser instincts and harder-to-break habits. It is this aspect of his struggle that makes it possible to recast the tension between 'the need for sanctuary' and 'exploration' as a struggle between 'the need for love' and 'desire'. There is little here about 'breaking through' and little of the mind-expanding pyschedelia of the early albums. But in writing about less, Morrison perhaps shows us more of himself and more of what we share with him – the personal tussle between the security of love and the rage of desire is something that we all struggle with to some extent. In focusing lyrically on such a common struggle and drawing musically on a more straightforward blues-rock tradition, the Doors perhaps made the most timeless and universally accessible of all their albums.

Something similar could be said of the final album, *L.A.Woman*. This time, however, the lyrics sometimes take a more menacing turn. 'Been Down So Long', for example, explores the tension that can exist between emotional and sexual fulfilment. The singer feels as though he is imprisoned, and seeks someone, anyone, who can set him free. While he appears to be hoping for the kind of personal contact that will liberate him, his frustration with its absence seems to lead him to a form of sexual desire that is at once aggressive and vengeful.

'Cars Hiss By My Window' explores the same conflict, as the laid back blues groove and the almost idyllic description of a beach and its waves at night contrasts markedly with the coldness and remoteness of the girl at his side. The sad surrender to the escape of sexual desire is dangerous but seemingly addictive – a strange kind of love.

The album's title track, 'L.A.Woman', is without question one of the greatest tracks the band recorded, but in this context its fine lyrics lend weight to the idea that, despite remaining curiously drawn to the nightlife and culture around him, Morrison was growing weary of it and was disillusioned with where it was taking us. Like 'Strange Days' before it, 'L.A.Woman' is full of unfulfilled, lost and lonely people. Add underworld sleaze and motel murder to the mix and you have a heady brew. Only the thought of Mr Mojo risin' can temporarily change the mood (from sad to gladness perhaps), Mr. Mojo risin' being an anagram of Jim Morrison and the name that Morrison famously claimed he would use to contact the Doors' office after he had escaped to Africa. (Album opener 'The Changeling' also hints at escape and thoughts of leaving town.)

'Hyacinth House' provides yet another statement of weariness and paranoia, while also exhibiting, it seems to me, some remarkably frank and lucid self-analysis. A close reading of the lyric makes it hard to resist the conclusion that Morrison is expressing sorrow for having wrecked both his health and his good looks. Once again he acknowledges his vulnerability and loneliness, clearly stating his need for a new kind of relationship with someone who understands and sympathises with his plight without making demands on him. One can't help wondering what on earth has happened to the confidence and power of the Lizard King. It is not without justification that writer Dylan Jones has described *L.A. Woman* as "a sad synthesis of exhaustion and regret.[50]

What, then, is Jim Morrison telling us on these later albums? My reading is that Morrison seems to have concluded that temporary solace is all there is. Such is the tragedy of human existence. This is not the shift that Sundling detects or requires to establish his thesis, but is, in marked contrast, a deep and thoroughgoing pessimism. We are 'Riders on the Storm', thrown into this senseless world and left to fend as best we can. Sometimes, for a while at least, love, or sex masquerading as love, can make it bearable.

In the context of my characterisation of the original artistic vision described by Sundling,* it is only the last of the six bullets that is missing. There is no inconsistency between the first five bullets and anything you find on *Morrison Hotel* or *L.A. Woman*. In this respect, Sundling is right to stress continuity. However, it is the final bullet – the idea that it is possible to achieve some form of breakthrough or self-realisation – that gave the original vision its drive and power, and it is precisely this element that is *missing* from Morrison's later work. Without it, the goal and direction are lost. Morrison does not, as far as I can see, replace the final bullet with any kind of positive alternative. Having lost faith, he simply throws himself headlong into moments of sanctuary and consolation: an intellectual pessimist; a practical nihilist.

So, if it's not the case that Jim Morrison came to equate self-realisation with finding fulfilment through love, what *has* happened to the quest to 'Break On Through (To The Other Side)' that was announced so boldly at the start of the Doors' debut album? Perhaps Morrison simply gave it his best shot and failed. Perhaps he came to realise that conceptual

---

* See above p.224.

renewal (the shift from inherited to personal concepts) is both a more complicated and a less radical notion than he'd originally thought. Perhaps, in the spirit of the age, the notion of 'breaking on through' itself grew stale and became a kind of lifeless, 'inherited' concept – over-dramatised, over-romanticised and too closely connected to the fashionable need to flout convention through the reckless pursuit of pleasure. Or perhaps he just became too disillusioned, sick and weary to worry about it much. Certainly, the positive aspects of the Doors' initial vision seem far more evident in the understated stability of Morrison's bandmates, who, in so far as they indulged in the vices of the time, did so in a more controlled and reasoned manner and saw the value of activities such as transcendental meditation alongside other 'solutions' offered by the age.*

What of the notion of 'breaking on through' itself? It's certainly a powerful and inspiring slogan, but as an *idea* it can appear rather nebulous. To what are we trying to break through? To 'freedom'? OK, but what does that mean in real terms? Freeing oneself *from* constraints, *from* one's past, *from* the values and expectations of one's parents is fine as far as it goes, but where does it leave us? If one wishes to connect the notion of 'breaking on through' with the idea of 'transcendence', one must also consider what 'transcendence' means. It doesn't just mean leaving things behind. It means aspiring to and reaching something higher and better – in some sense going and growing *beyond*. But what are we aspiring to, and what are we reaching for? I'm not sure you'll find a clear answer in the work of Jim Morrison.

It is true that there can be many constraints on our thinking and behaviour, and that such constraints can stifle creativity and lead to an absence of joy and pleasure. But it is also true that too much pleasure can lead to a lack of thought, a lack of substance and a lack of desire for personal growth. Jim Morrison was clearly aware of our need to free

---

* Indeed, speaking on a Planet Rock radio special (*My Planet Rocks*, broadcast on 13 July 2008) Robby Kreiger noted that he met Ray Manzarek and John Densmore at a transcendental meditation meeting with the Maharishi. There is also a story, cited by Hopkins and Sugerman and Sundling (See Hopkins and Sugerman, *No One Here Gets Out Alive*, p.92, and Sundling, *People Are Strange: The Ultimate Guide to the Doors*, p.165) that while Jim Morrison rejected transcendental meditation for himself, he attended a meeting in the early days of the Doors so that he could look into the Maharishi's eyes to see if he was happy. He concluded that he was.

ourselves from things which stifle creativity, knowledge, self-expression and growth, but he ventured too far into the pleasure dome, diluting his original drive and vision until he had simply replaced the old gods with new demons – demons from which he couldn't escape. We are left with a body of work that hints at a grand and noble venture, but that ultimately expresses a personal struggle that is human, all too human. For Jim Morrison it was a struggle that led not to a "cleaner, freer realm" but to the Père La Chaise cemetery in Paris.

ꙮ Ecce Homo? ꙮ

More than most, the Doors were overtly aware of the power and significance of the rock gig. In April 1969, for example, they recorded material for PBS television which included not only live performances of tracks from their forthcoming release (*The Soft Parade*) alongside some of their older songs, but an interview with Richard Goldstein of the *Village Voice*. At one point Goldstein asks the band what fans expect from the Doors. Robby Krieger replies that in America the fans seem to come to the gigs for some kind of religious experience.[51] Elsewhere in the same film, Morrison is seen engaging in discussion with a 'Minister-at-Large' from the Evangelical Reformed Church. The pair briefly discuss the possibilities provided by rock gigs for communication and communion with people on a large scale, with Morrison suggesting (perhaps jokingly so) that the kind of experience that the Doors provoke and inspire is akin to a form of secular religion.[52]

If part of Jim Morrison and the Doors' initial aim was to use rock music to bring large numbers of people together, it's ironic that I discovered and turned to them precisely at the point where I felt that rock music had let me down and I needed a period of 'gathering in' and introspection. What was I expecting from them? Was I looking for something to validate my early gig experiences? Was I looking for a band who could restore my faith in rock music? Or was it just that I too needed to find a new friend – someone who I felt understood, someone who could help me explore and understand myself better? The answer, probably, is that I was looking for all of these things, and the Doors offered windows of perception on them all. I have no doubt that part of their initial aim was to use rock music to communicate in a positive way with their audience. However, I also have no doubt that

Morrison's understanding of what he was doing, and his expectations of what was possible, changed quite radically as the Doors' career progressed.

There is, perhaps, a tension between what might still be regarded as the real purpose of much of the Doors' work – to encourage self-awareness and self-realisation – and the use of a medium which can potentially employ techniques of 'crowd psychology' to whip large numbers of people up into a riotous frenzy. There is a fine line between raising awareness on a mass scale and engaging in some form of mass manipulation, and it's not always easy to see when that line is bring crossed. In the case of the Doors, Morrison clearly started to believe they were failing to raise awareness, with most of the audience just not getting it, and the band's reputation now preceding them at every turn. Their sensational performances seemed to Morrison to have succeeded only in generating a sheep-like mentality among the majority of gig-goers, who came more interested in scandal and titillation than enlightenment and celebration or, indeed, music. It was his growing frustration with this state of affairs that led him to reassess the nature of the rock gig and what could be achieved through it. As he told one interviewer some time after the Miami gig:[*]

> It used to seem possible to generate a movement – people rising up and joining together in a mass protest – refusing to be represented any longer . . . The love-street times are dead. Sure, it's possible for there to be a transcendence – but not on a mass level, not a universal rebellion. Now it has to take place on an individual level – every man for himself, as they say.[53]

Commenting on the Miami gig itself, Morrison provided the following 'explanation' of events to Salli Stevenson of *Circus* magazine:

> I guess what it boiled down to was that I told the audience that they were a bunch of fucking idiots to be members of an audience. What were they there for anyway? The basic message was realise that you're not really here to listen to a bunch of songs by some good musicians. You're here for something else. Why not admit it and do something about it?[54]

There is a view that Morrison's treatment at the hands of the law and his vilification in the press in the aftermath of the Miami performance made him a wiser, more introspective and more thoughtful man, at least

---

[*] 1 March 1969. See above p.226.

for a while. He was wounded, as well as hounded, and it's tempting to think that the Miami experience was pivotal in shaping his attitude towards his audience and his career. The truth, however, is that the frustration, contempt and boredom that boiled over that fateful night had long been brewing. Hopkins and Sugerman, for example, report that Morrison's "boredom with rock stardom" was evident over a year before Miami, as the growing "sex-idol hype", and "mindless, misguided approval" detracted from Manzarek and Morrison's original conception of the Doors as "an intelligent, volatile fusion of theatre, poetry and well-executed, exploratory music."[55] According to Hopkins and Sugerman, even before the release of the third album, *Waiting For The Sun*, Morrison had become "blatantly contemptuous" of his audience, spitting at them or "getting so drunk that the performances often suffered".[56]

With respect for his audience all but gone, Morrison himself knowingly crossed the line, coming to see the audience as an object for his personal manipulation. He knew he could create a sense of danger, uncertainty and chaos, and he admitted to trying to provoke riots from time to time. But even this shift in attitude, and the onstage experimentation that followed, seemed to bring him little satisfaction. While viewing footage for the *Feast of Friends* documentary that he'd commissioned friends Paul Ferrara, Frank Lisciandro and Babe Hill to make, Morrison realised that once he'd triggered forces that led to riotous behaviour in crowds he had little or no control over them. "The first time I saw the film I was rather taken aback," he said. "I suddenly realised in a way that I was just a puppet of a lot of forces I only vaguely understood."[57]

It is sometimes said that Jim Morrison was a reluctant leader – a man who didn't want followers but who, given his looks, charisma and chosen profession, inevitably attracted them. The problem wasn't that he had fans and admirers – after all, we all need people who believe in us, and it was the fans who supported and sustained his lifestyle – but rather that he acquired *en masse* the wrong kind of fans: people who branded him, packaged him up and followed him for what were, to his mind, all the wrong reasons. Once Morrison had created a public persona he lost control of it. His audience came with expectations and made demands on him. He could wind them up and give them a good time – but only if he played his part as their dancing monkey. In many ways Miami was the culmination of Morrison's growing frustrations, and after Miami he struggled on feeling increasingly trapped and disillusioned.

When, in March 1971, Morrison took off for Paris with his long-time girlfriend Pamela, it was to escape the constraints of his rock star life. As writer Salli Stevenson told Jerry Hopkins and Danny Sugerman: "He thought it was a place where he could be himself and not have people hounding him and making a circus out of his life."[58] While in Paris he told one of his new Parisian friends Yvonne Fuka: "I'm so sick of everything. People keep thinking of me as a rock and roll star and I don't want anything to do with it. I can't stand it anymore. I'd be so glad if people didn't recognise me . . . who do they think Jim Morrison is anyway?"[59] What Morrison wanted most of all was to be taken seriously as a poet. Viewed retrospectively, his sabbatical in Paris was a last desperate attempt to leave the madness of stardom behind, regain some sense of self and give himself a fighting chance of achieving that ambition.

Jim Morrison was doubtless an extremely complex character, and even through the music and stories alone I, like many thousands of others, felt what biographers Hopkins and Sugerman call "the force of Jim's personality".[60] But, re-reading *No One Here Gets Out Alive* while preparing to draft this chapter, I found Morrison a far less appealing and compelling character than I did when I first read the book in early 1986. His constant testing of friends, his strangeness and unpredictability with people, the co-existence of cruelty and tenderness, the occasional violent tendencies, the alcohol-fuelled aggression – none of this makes him the kind of person most of us would want around. In this connection it is perhaps worth noting writer Dylan Jones' assessment of Morrison as "pop genius but amateur human being."*

---

* Dylan Jones, *Jim Morrison Dark Star* (Bloomsbury, 1991), p.65. Elsewhere in his book, Jones delivers a scathing assessment of Morrison's character: "Morrison was the sexiest bookworm to ever pick up a microphone, he was an inspired lyricist and one of the most celebrated pop icons of the Sixties. But Morrison was also a wilfully enigmatic, pretentious loudmouth, a self-proclaimed poet who wore the convenient mask of the drunk. He was the impotent alcoholic, the scarred idol. He was the King of Corn, the consummate showman, the petulant clown. He was too clever for his own good, and often too stupid to care." (p.181) Jones believes that had Morrison lived, "he would undoubtedly have undone all he had achieved during the last five years of his life; as it is, he remains, along with James Dean and Jimi Hendrix, one of youth culture's most revered heroes, a hero dead before his time. A hero who got out just in time," (p.10) got out, that is, "before he was found out." (p.183). Jones's assessment is apparently sanctioned by Patricia Kennely who told him: "No one has ever gotten it as right as this before."

Perhaps, in part at least, Morrison's behavioural excesses can be
explained – though not excused – by the need to cope with the pressures
of fame. Perhaps these *were* his ways of dealing with an often-reported
deep-rooted shyness. And perhaps Morrison's much-vaunted intelligence
contributed to the frustration and boredom that he came to feel. But
nevertheless, the detachment and contempt for others that show themselves
in Hopkins and Sugerman's descriptions reveal not just a flawed character
but a disturbed, unsettled and unhappy man. How I managed to overlook
all this the first time I read *No One Here Gets Out Alive* heaven only
knows. That I did shows, perhaps, the power of images, symbols and
music to overwhelm not just the senses but the intellect. It is a testament
to the magnetic appeal of sensuality and danger in music, and perhaps it
shows the overriding force of other, more obviously appealing aspects of
Jim Morrison's character and public persona: the rebellious and timeless
rock star look, the rich, crooning voice, the promise of knowledge that
goes beyond what our parents and teachers and politicians think they
know, the prospect that it *is* possible to 'Break on Through' to something
better. Like others, I suppose I saw what I wanted to see in him – and was
taken in completely by the power of his art.

That's not to concede that Morrison was, in his personal life, a
complete monster. The PBS video referred to above contains some great
footage and often shows a softer, smiling Jim Morrison engaging in a
relaxed manner with friends and fans. What's more, those who knew him
best, including Danny Sugerman, are full of counterbalancing tales of
intelligence, insight, compassion, generosity, and striking good manners.
Speaking on *My Planet Rocks*, a Planet Rock radio special,* guitarist
Robby Krieger, the youngest of the Doors, noted that: "You could meet
him and five minutes later feel that he was your best friend." Krieger
further notes that although Morrison didn't rush around the stage like a
madman, that feeling of closeness somehow seemed to transmit to the
audience. Krieger himself developed a kind of big brother/little brother
relationship with Jim. He was "the most amazing guy I ever met," says
Krieger, "the most influential person in my life . . . and it's too bad he's
not here anymore."

Read again those famous Rimbaud lines that I quoted near the start
of the chapter. In this context, what are we to make of the life of James

---

* The same broadcast (13 July 2008) referred to above – see footnote on p.235.

Douglas Morrison? He certainly engaged in a "long, prodigious . . . *disordering* of *all the senses*" but how "rational" his quest remained is open to doubt. Did he reach "the unknown"? Did his search leave him "crazed"? Did he lose "the understanding of his visions"? Whatever the answer to these questions, the tragedy perhaps is that Morrison did not die, as Rimbaud might have hoped, "charging through those unutterable, unnameable things". He died, in the words of T.S. Eliot, "not with a bang but a whimper",* and by then, creatively speaking, he wasn't doing much charging through anything.

The platform given to popular rock singers enables them to say and do things that the rest of us couldn't, even if we wanted to. And let's be in no doubt – Jim Morrison did use that platform to say and do some pretty extraordinary things. He left behind a solid body of work, with the six albums recorded with the Doors at its heart, and it's a body of work that's been enormously influential. Morrison's personal flaws and descent from rock god to disillusioned alcoholic – about which my information is, of course, second and third hand – do not negate the value and relevance of his art, even if they did bring him to a rather unfortunate and premature end. There are many positive things in the work of Jim Morrison and the Doors. Ultimately it doesn't matter that there was no happy ending and no smooth evolution to a maturely expressed vision of self-fulfilment. What matters is that we appreciate the power of the work, and learn from both its positive and negative aspects. Unfortunately, while most of us can choose to check in and out of *Morrison Hotel* any time we like, the manner in which Morrison checked out ensured that he would stay there forever. For Jim, at least, *Morrison Hotel* became 'Hotel California'.

Twilight of the Idols

If Jim Morrison is a good example of how fame and the pressures of celebrity can help destroy someone, his biographer and protégé Danny Sugerman is a good, if somewhat extreme, example of what can go wrong when someone becomes so influenced and entranced that they fail to move out of their hero's shadow. Sugerman's story is superbly rendered in his gripping autobiography *Wonderland Avenue*.

---

* The closing line of Eliot's poem 'The Hollow Men'.

My original reading of *Wonderland Avenue* took place on holiday with friends in mid-Wales. In fact, the book belonged to a friend who had bought it that very day in a second hand book shop in Hay-on-Wye ('Town of Books'). I picked it up and started to browse and ended up reading it for the next two days solid. I found it morbidly compelling and utterly depressing. I became very bad holiday company but I just couldn't put it down. Some passages were so striking and, in some cases, harrowing, that I was able to reference them in conversation years later, even though I didn't actually re-read the book for another 18 years.

Wild child Sugerman was introduced to the Doors at the age of 12 by a young college student, Evan Parker, who earned himself some pocket money as a baseball umpire in the Little League in which Sugerman played for one of the teams sponsored by his father. After an initial altercation, Sugerman and Parker became friends. Parker also earned some money as a roadie for up-and-coming local band the Doors, and offered to take Sugerman to a concert as a reward for hitting a home run and winning a crucial baseball match for his team. The effect of the concert on Sugerman, a troubled adolescent, was nothing short of transformational: "I couldn't talk about anything else for days afterwards. Nothing had ever affected me so much. I had to know – where else did this happen? Did other people react the same way? Were all the bands around this great? . . . It was as if I had been asleep for twelve years and suddenly been slapped awake."[61] After seeing the Doors in concert, Sugerman tells us, "something inside me opened up to the larger, greater possibilities before me as a teenager . . . Simply witnessing Morrison in concert opened me up to my own potential."[62]

Going to the concert with Evan Parker allowed Sugerman not just to experience the band live but to meet them in the flesh. When Parker became a concert promoter and the Doors opened offices in West Hollywood, Sugerman was like a dog with a bone. He started hanging around the Doors' office, even in preference to attending school, and when manager Bill Siddons came to feel that his frequent presence was getting in the way, Morrison stepped in and saved the day by giving him a paid job managing fan mail.

Sugerman's divorced parents did not approve of his love of rock 'n' roll, nor of his acquaintance with the Doors, and yet he continued to seek his father's approval. He even arranged an ill-fated dinner with his dad and Jim at which he told his father: "Rock 'n' roll isn't just a hobby. It's so much more than that . . . it's more like it's the only thing that means anything to me."[63] Morrison's presence at the meeting, which Sugerman hoped would provide his father with some reassurance, proved nothing less than disastrous. As a "sloshed" Morrison ordered yet more drinks, and expressed surprise at the underage Sugerman's mealtime abstinence, Sugerman's father asked him if he always drank so much. "No," answered Morrison, "sometimes I drink more."[64]

Despite the impression that the Doors' *music* made on Sugerman, it is striking that as the book progresses, it becomes less and less about music and more and more about drugs. Sugerman's descent into drug addiction is shocking, and it was a path he chose despite Morrison's explicit attempts to warn him off both speed and cocaine. If Morrison did indeed open Sugerman up to his own potential, it was potential that, after Morrison's death, he spent most of his time neglecting and destroying. The depths to which he sank are such that at times, in relative terms, Sugerman almost makes his hero look like an angel. As in Morrison's case, the pain, escapism and death that feature strongly in the later stages of the book contrast markedly with the attempts to 'Break on Through' that characterise Sugerman's early experiences with both drugs and music. Sugerman's life at that point is well summed up by the striking blurb on the back cover: "By the age of twenty-one he had an idyllic home, a beautiful girlfriend, the best car in the world, two types of hepatitis, a diseased heart, a $500 a-day heroin habit and only a week to live."

Sugerman, of course, survived well beyond a week, renewing a career in rock and roll and, most notably, becoming a successful writer. But this outcome was far from certain. Even before his doctor's ultimatum he was aware that his lifestyle was unsustainable. Using alcohol and other drugs to disorder one's senses is arguably fine, until the substances became the dominant partner. At this point it stops being Dionysian revelry and becomes an illness. "I wasn't doing the drugs anymore," Sugerman tells us, "the drugs were doing me . . . I was paying a horrible price for something I no longer wanted, but something I *needed*."[65] The problem, he says, is that as hard and painful as the addiction had become, it always seemed less painful to keep taking the drugs than to do away with them. It was only after the warning of imminent death, and a second period of hospitalisation, this time sectioned in a mental institution, that Sugerman decided that he wanted to live. "I want to go home," he told his psychiatrist, "I want to go back to work. I want my family back, I want my music back.

I don't want drugs. Screw the drugs. They killed my love for everything that ever meant anything to me, including myself."[66]

His stay in hospital gave him plenty of time to reflect coolly on William Blake's famous maxim: "The road of excess leads to the palace of wisdom, huh? Well, maybe, but what kind of excess and who said it's got to be chemical? And what sort of wisdom? At what price? And will somebody please tell me what's so excessive about being a drug addict anyway? It's the most limiting existence I can think of."[67]

What of the life of Jim Morrison and the lives of the other "geniuses" who died broken addicts? Sugerman's analysis is frank and sobering: "Jim Morrison never found what he was looking for. That intensely dramatic, charismatic search? It was all for nought. He got nothing. *We* got Morrison's life. But he lost it. He got zip. He got *dead*."[68]

And what would Morrison say to his protégé Sugerman as he lay in that hospital bed with a rotting liver and a damaged heart?

> You know what *I* think Morrison would have said? '*Experience*, feel the pain. Without pain there is no change. Without change there is no growth and if you don't grow, you die. Don't make the same mistakes I made. Make different ones. Don't be stupid. Grow. *Live*.' It was, if not Jim's voice directly, the truth nonetheless. Morrison always was a better teacher than role model.[69]

My own brief sojourn in *Morrison Hotel* was such that I was able to learn from the teacher without seeing him as too much of a role model. For Sugerman, who knew Morrison well and thought of him "as an older brother figure",[70] the influence was more thorough, hard-hitting and direct. His book shows very clearly why he was so susceptible to the influence of Jim Morrison and the Doors, and why he took that influence in the particular direction he did. But his book also provides a graphic and frightening illustration of what can happen if one remains in awe of one's heroes and lives one's life entirely within the tracks they have laid down.

Of Morrison's death, Sugerman comments: "It does not matter how Jim died. Nor does it particularly matter that he left us so young. It is only important that Jim Morrison lived, and lived with the purpose birth proposes: to discover yourself and your own potential."[71]

The message, then, is a Socratic one: Know Thyself – an endlessly challenging quest that is the ultimate in personal introspection. At the same time, an important part of coming to 'know thyself' is being open to others. Seen from this perspective, it is not, perhaps, surprising or ironic at all that I starting reading about Jim Morrison at a time of personal fragmentation. But, while having influences in itself is no bad thing, it's healthy to place our influences in a wider context, learn from them and move beyond them. Remaining in thrall to the influence and personality of a 'rock star', or any other 'idol' come to that, is no basis for personal development and growth. Hero-worship is a poor and limiting way of relating to other people. This is true even when our heroes are not such obviously flawed characters as Jim Morrison.

8

Blood on the Tracks

Discovering Dylan

It was probably inevitable that at some point in time someone was going to decide that I should listen to Bob Dylan. I was, of course, aware of him. I had heard some of his more popular songs, such as 'Blowin' in the Wind' and the Byrds' version of 'Mr. Tambourine Man', and, like others, I'd had a good chuckle at the Dylan character in the BBC children's TV programme *The Magic Roundabout*. It had never really occurred to me, however, that Dylan's music was for me. I suppose I associated him with an older generation – and, at any rate, the back catalogue looked so daunting that I really wouldn't have known where to start.

My introduction to Bob Dylan came through a college friend – Iwan. Iwan was from Hirwaun, near Aberdare in the South Wales valleys. He was another product (or 'refugee') of Coleg Harlech, and like many Harlech students he had a fascinating background. He had seemed destined for a life on the production line but, against all odds, his natural ability and intelligence began to fight their way through. He began reading and thinking hard and looking for ways to make some kind of change. Having endured several years of factory boredom and survived a born-again Pentecostal experience, Iwan found his way to Coleg Harlech, where an excellent grounding in humanities gave him the words and concepts he needed to articulate not only his dissatisfaction but his seemingly permanent state of existential angst. He spoke about Harlech as though it was both a blessing and a curse. It was a way out for him. It opened doors for him. And yet the camaraderie and friendships of Harlech created bonds that could not be easily replicated elsewhere, and this made adjustment to post-Harlech life difficult. What's more, the relative isolation drove him mad, inducing extra-curricular behaviour that was, at times, extreme. And, though inspiring, the education he received at Harlech simply fuelled his sense of injustice at the way our modern society chooses to organise its 'factors of production'.

It was pure chance that we met. I was studying politics (soon to switch to philosophy) at Swansea University. Iwan was studying history. I had chosen to take history and philosophy as subsidiary subjects in my first year. Iwan had chosen politics and philosophy. Out of maybe 200 first-year history students, Iwan and I were placed in the same tutorial group with just two other people. Being a mature student with an extreme nature and a strong working class background, Iwan found it difficult to relate to most other 'first years'. He was appalled by what he perceived to be the 'artificial intelligence' and superficiality of the 'bright young things' around him. He saw enough of a spark in me, however, for the two of us to become friends. For my own part, I found his sense of urgency, his perpetual motion, and the unusual mix of intensity and humour with which he approached everything to be utterly compelling. He was a man on the edge, a man struggling to keep his head above water, but a man who recognised and even delighted in the absurdity of it all. Though his path was his own, and he valued his freedom to move around above all else, he was quite prepared to take me under his wing from time to time. And though my path was my own, I enjoyed his company and learned much from his take on life and his undoubted experience.

As Iwan struggled to settle into university life (he recalls an occasion when our tutor started head-butting his desk in exasperation), we both came to recognise that although it's sensible to set your sights high, what mattered most in your first year was just getting through it. The first year did not count at all towards the final degree mark, so all you needed to do was avoid disaster and pass. Iwan therefore devised a clever essay-sharing system that helped participants to 'work smart' to maximise their chances of avoiding disaster. He called it "academic socialism": 'from each according to their ability, to each according to their need' (or, if you want to be cynical: 'from each according to their ability, to Iwan according to his need'). Let me give you some indication why such a system was helpful. In history there were around 40 small tutorial groups, each of which was set different coursework – around four or five essays – through the year. We calculated that across all tutorial groups and both history modules (modern and medieval) around 200 essay topics were covered. However, the course was assessed entirely by two examinations at the end of the year, with each exam paper containing only 16 questions. That meant that each tutorial group covered only 2.5% of possible topics through its coursework, and only about one in six of all the topics covered by all groups made it onto the examination papers. Or, to put it simply, the vast majority of topics you put hours and hours into researching and writing up in essay format would *not* appear on your end of year exam. It seemed crazy, and it was, and although the situation was less chaotic in our other subjects, there was nevertheless a compelling logic behind participation in Iwan's system: a combination of 'question-spotting' and essay-swapping allowed us to cover more topics, and increased our chances of being able to answer a sufficient number of questions at the right kind of level to pass the course. And so we sought out other high-calibre students – those, that is, whose essays were of 2:1 standard (60–70%) or higher – and arranged to share and discuss photocopies of each other's work. In reality it was always the case that you would prefer to write on topics you had researched yourself, but the process provided 'back up' answers for exams, just in case one's personal preferences or 'bankers' did not come up. Most importantly for Iwan, it also provided a kind of psychological safety net which made him feel more prepared and helped calm both his nerves and his mind.

Though Iwan lived most of the time in Aberdare and drove back and forth to college most days, the essay-sharing scheme and his need for contact necessitated fairly frequent visits to my room in Halls.

"Where's Cunty?" he affectionately asked my neighbour Matt one day, when Matt came out of his room to see what all the banging on my door was about.

"You mean the hippy?" asked Matt, equally affectionately. "He's out. I'll tell him you called."

This became something of a recurring experience for my hall mates.

"Oi, Mike," they'd shout down the corridor as I returned home, "that Cunty bloke's been looking for you again."

But for all his angst, self-preoccupation and fast-paced living, Iwan had a surprisingly insightful and caring side. His detachment from the rest of my college life made it easy for me to speak with him about all manner of personal matters. I found him to be a good friend and an invaluable source of advice. Iwan himself derived considerable succour from the work of Bob Dylan and, after assessing both my record collection and my personal disposition, he decided that I too "was ready" for "the Dylan experience". He turned up at my room one day with a pile of albums he wanted me to hear. He gave me a quick run-down on what he had brought, and then insisted that I play particular tracks as he offered words of elucidation and sang along loudly in mock-Dylan voice. And then he was gone, leaving me alone with *Bringing It All Back Home*, *Highway 61 Revisited*, *Blonde on Blonde*, *Blood on the Tracks*, *Desire* and *Street Legal*. I took his recommendations very seriously and resolved to work through the albums in chronological order. I'd never seen him so determined (other than when he was 'procuring' essays) and settled down to explore each album in turn. I was particularly intrigued by a rather uncharacteristically cryptic comment he had made when he showed me *Blood on the Tracks*. "Play it seven times," he said, "and it will stay with you forever." I put it to one side, and singled it out for special attention.

Between them, these six great albums exposed me to a wide range of Bob Dylan's gifts, but at first I wasn't sure what to make of him. The sleeve notes on *Bringing It All Back Home* (March 1965) and *Highway 61 Revisited* (August 1965), for example, the earliest of the albums, seemed to be no more than a mixture of stream of consciousness claptrap and in-jokes. It seemed silly and just a touch pretentious, and rooted the albums firmly in the madcap, mind-bending ethos of the mid-1960s. The odd line looked profound, but I wasn't into such throwaway wordplay and trivialisation: I was a philosopher in the making, and I was seeking clarity and understanding, not deliberate obfuscation. And yet, despite these initial reservations, I was soon won over by the great music and ear-catching lyrics within.

I particularly enjoyed the range and variety of songs presented on *Bringing It All Back Home*. 'Subterranean Homesick Blues' rocked with serious attitude (a precursor to modern rap, some would say). 'Maggie's Farm', delivered with a kind of shuffling acerbic innocence, seemed to offer reflections on class relations, and was given new resonance by the grip Margaret Thatcher and her Conservative government had on the UK at the time. 'On the Road Again' and 'Bob Dylan's 115th Dream' (Dylan's mock discovery of America) made me laugh. 'Mr. Tambourine

Man' exhibited a supreme lyricism that I'd missed in the Byrds' pop interpretation and that pulled me into Dylan's "skippin' reels of rhyme". And 'It's Alright, Ma (I'm Only Bleeding)' stood out as the song of a bruised warrior-poet. *Highway 61 Revisited* also had tracks which made an impression on me. I could see why so many had been moved and excited by the impassioned drawl of 'Like a Rolling Stone', and I enjoyed the scatty blues rock of 'Tombstone Blues', which, as far as I could tell, was trying to say something profound about poverty. 'Ballad of a Thin Man' was a stark reminder of the need to, in modern parlance, 'keep it real' and avoid getting too attracted or distracted by the bright lights and dizzy intellectual heights of academia. And I read somewhere that 'Desolation Row' was a modern version of T.S. Eliot's *The Waste Land* set to music. I had no idea what this meant or if it was true – but I was impressed that it could even be said.

As an album, *Highway 61 Revisited* is characterised by a kind of frantic, scratching, hard-edged rock-blues sound that it shares with some of the more raucous and up-tempo tracks on *Bringing It All Back Home*. It's a sound that perhaps receives its most perfect, most rounded and most refined expression on the *Blonde on Blonde* album (May 1966). In a later interview for *Playboy* magazine (March 1978), Dylan told Ron Rosenbaum:

> The closest I ever got to the sound I hear in my mind was on . . . the *Blonde on Blonde* album. It's that thin, that wild mercury sound. It's metallic and bright gold, with whatever that conjures up. That's my particular sound. I haven't been able to succeed in getting it all the time.[1]

Even listening today, *Blonde on Blonde* does seem to express perfectly the sound Dylan had been striving for – or, at least, moving towards – and it was, in a sense, the culmination of that period. It's a fantastic album, which, like its immediate predecessors, is delightful, inspiring, profound and incomprehensible in equal measure. I know from what I have read since that the pace and nature of Dylan's life, and his musical direction, were soon to change, but it is hard to see how he *could* have recorded another *Blonde on Blonde*. Tracks like 'Visions of Johanna', 'I Want You', 'One Of Us Must Know', 'Just Like a Woman' and 'Sad Eyed Lady of the Lowlands' are enduring compositions that sit comfortably among his best material, but all artists must keep moving, as times change, as they change, and as their experiences change. And that's what Dylan did.

Even without any biographical knowledge or grasp of Dylan's history, it was obvious from the cover alone that the time gap between *Blonde on Blonde* (May 1966) and *Blood on the Tracks* (January 1975) was significant. While the mid-1960s albums had presented confident, strident and full-on images of Dylan on their covers, on the front of *Blood on the Tracks* he is in muted profile, eyes hidden, with an artist's impression replacing the earlier photography. It shows us not so much 'another side of Bob Dylan' as just a glimpse. It provides a perspective, an interpretation, a sense that one is viewing an outward aspect of something that is darker, more personal and more complex. *Blood on the Tracks is* a more moody and introspective affair, but somehow I found it more immediate than the 1960s albums – less noisy, less demanding, warmer, more sympathetic and more welcoming. The gentle, summery jangle of 'Tangled Up in Blue' drew me in, and while the lyric at first comes on like a Picasso painting, time and context all jumbled up, the impassioned repetition of the title line at the end of each verse created a sense of cohesion that I wanted to explore further. There are ten songs here, simply and beautifully played, no unnecessary musical extravagance, and hardly any let-up in either quality or impact across the whole album. It's a stunning and intense work, dripping in raw emotion and demanding of attention, respect and reverence, whatever your musical background and whatever your usual tastes. (Biographer Robert Shelton called it "the spiritual autobiography of a wounded sensibility."[2]) "Play it seven times . . ." Iwan had said. It didn't take seven listens to get me hooked, but I'd soon played it more than seven times and it is an album that has, indeed, stayed with me ever since. I'll say more about it later.

Given my comments about *Blood on the Tracks*, one might think that it was an impossible act to follow. And yet, with the release of *Desire* (January 1976) Dylan recorded a unique and exotically tinged album that was a worthy successor. But where *Blood on the Tracks* was introspective and soul searching, *Desire* showed Dylan fully engaged again in life around him, with 'Isis', Mozambique', 'Romance in Durango', 'Black Diamond Bay' and 'One More Cup of Coffee' all suggesting travel, adventure and cultural and contextual shifts of one sort or another. What's more, Dylan stepped outside himself to collaborate with musical theatre director Jacques Levy on lyrics for seven of the album's nine tracks. That's not to say that there are no songs of personal significance on the album. Some of the adventures are adventures of the heart, and album closer 'Sara', a plea to his then-wife, is one of the most touching and personal songs ever committed to record. It is said that Sara herself turned up at the studio and watched him record the version that appeared on the album. She was visibly stunned, and, at least in the short term, the song seemed to have the desired effect, as the couple were temporarily reconciled. Changing his sound again to incorporate Scarlet Rivera's violin, the accordion playing of Dom Cortese and the backing vocals of Emmylou Harris, Dylan and the musicians he assembled here were on fire. Only the somewhat overlong and dirge-like 'Joey' slowed the pace and broke the vibe, with Dylan re-emerging as an inspired, and inspiring, electric and eclectic minstrel. Back, too, are Dylan's near-incomprehensible self-penned sleeve notes ("on the heels of Rimbaud"), with poet Allen Ginsberg providing more extensive notes which herald Dylan's new 'Songs of Redemption'. "These songs are the culmination of Poetry-music as dreamt of in the 50s and 60s," enthused Ginsberg, " – enough Person revealed to make Whitman's whole nation weep."

Worthy of particular mention is 'Hurricane', a whirlwind of an opening track with bite and power to spare. For those with long memories, this was Dylan back in protest mode. It's the story of a boxer, Ruben Carter, who, claimed Dylan, "coulda been the Champion of the world". Instead "Ruben sits like Buddha in a ten-foot cell" after being convicted of murder for reasons that Dylan claimed had more to do with the colour of his skin than the facts of the case. Dylan visited Carter in prison after reading his book and, convinced of his innocence, not only released 'Hurricane' as a single, but used the first leg of the Rolling Thunder tour to campaign on Carter's behalf. Dylan spits and snarls his way through the lyric, sounding as angry and fired-up as he ever had:

> *To see him obviously framed*
> *Couldn't help but make me feel ashamed*
> *To live in a land where justice is a game*

Scarlet Rivera's playing is especially potent, her agonised violin histrionics making you feel that every word Dylan sings simply *must* be true.

At one point in the lyric, the police try to convince a petty criminal to testify against Carter by offering him a deal and pointing out that Carter "ain't no Gentleman Jim". For years I was under the impression that 'Gentleman Jim' was Jimmy Driscoll, the great Cardiff boxer to whom I am related. Jimmy Driscoll was, in fact, my great, great grandmother's nephew and my grandmother's second cousin. My Nan's grandmother and Jimmy Driscoll's mother were sisters, making my Nan's father (my great grandfather) and Jimmy Driscoll first cousins. Jimmy Driscoll was known for his upstanding character and his loyalty and commitment both to his family and to good causes. Indeed, he even turned down a world title fight and returned to Wales from America in order to keep a promise he'd made to box in a fundraising bout for the Nazareth House orphanage. My Nan, now in her 90s, remembers being around him as a very young child. When he died of consumption at the age of only 44 in 1925, an estimated 100,000 people lined the streets of Cardiff in his honour. I always felt a strong sense of pride listening to 'Hurricane', for here was Dylan with fire in his belly, singing once more about injustice, and name-checking one of my relatives. I recently discovered, however, that the nickname bestowed on the great boxer by the American critics was 'Peerless Jim Driscoll', not 'Gentleman Jim Driscoll' and that the 'Gentleman Jim' referred to is probably James J. Corbett, the late nineteenth-century world heavyweight champion who is credited with bringing a measured, scientific approach to boxing. "Shame," I thought. But it's still a great track!

The last of the six albums Iwan had given me was *Street Legal* (June 1978). It contained some great songs, and the addition of gospel-sounding backing vocals gave it a lift and a kick. 'Changing of the Guard' waltzed in like it had been somewhere at the back of your mind all along, full of archetypes and rich imagery. The dark, sensualised, edgy blues of 'New Pony' left me feeling like I'd just heard a prophecy I didn't understand. 'No Time to Think', with its swirling, descending melody, its tarot imagery, its litany of 'isms', and some rushed and outrageous rhymes, assaulted both the senses and the mind. In something of a break from the action, I heard 'Baby Stop Crying' as a simple and tender song of concern. 'Is Your Love in Vain?' was a song I struggled with initially, given the ultra-conventional woman at its heart. Lyrically, 'Señor (Tales of Yankee Power)' was, and remains, a mystery to me, though it is musically strong and certainly *sounds* profound. The remaining tracks, 'True Love Tends to Forget', 'We'd Better Talk This Over' and 'Where Are You Tonight? (Journey through Dark Heat)', played out almost like footnotes to the more emotionally charged *Blood on the Tracks*. The yearning of the final track notwithstanding, they seemed to offer more relaxed and 'objective' observations on matters of the heart that are sometimes wise, sometimes practical and sometimes resigned. I could see why Iwan had given it to me.

Of course I was aware that Dylan's back catalogue extended well beyond these six albums, and I was keen to explore further. Inspired by the mainly acoustic Side Two of *Bringing It All Back Home*, I resolved to check out Dylan's more overtly folk past as soon as I could. The opportunity presented itself quickly when I picked up an old vinyl copy of *The Times They Are A-Changin'* (January 1964) at a college record fayre. Iwan was particularly pleased. "It's brilliant – especially on a day like this," he said, gesturing towards the window and the wet Swansea weather. "In fact, it's the one I'd have given you next."

It wasn't long before I'd also purchased *The Freewheelin' Bob Dylan* (May 1963). Again I was impressed with songs from both albums. 'Masters of War' (from *Freewheelin'*) and 'With God on Our Side' (from *The Times They Are A-Changin'*), for example, had retained strong relevance over the years, particularly given the recent Falklands War and the prevailing nuclear threat. (The more things change the more they stay the same.) 'Only a Pawn in their Game' (from *The Times They Are A-Changin'*) was bound to appeal to a young philosopher interested in exploring ideas of determinism and free will, while Dylan's solemn and angry delivery of another song dealing with class, race and injustice, 'The Lonesome Death of Hattie Carroll' (also from *The Times They Are A-Changin'*) gave it a power that remains undiminished. (The criticism of "you who philosophise" made me sit up and take note.) As with *Bringing It All Back Home*, I particularly enjoyed *Freewheelin'* for the range of songs and moods on offer. 'Don't Think Twice, It's Alright', for example, as well as having a great lyric, is one of Dylan's prettiest pieces of music, while the self-mocking caricature of 'Honey Just Allow Me One More Chance' and the joyful release of 'I Shall Be Free' brought a smile to my face.

It wasn't until later that I became aware how controversial it was when Dylan 'plugged in', apparently rejecting the more traditional American folk idiom for electric blues-rock. But at the time I was blissfully unaware of 'the voice of a generation''s abdication, the displeasure of the political left, the cries of 'Judas' and 'traitor', and the boos and walkouts that dogged his mid-1960s tours. Even if I had known, it wouldn't have bothered me much. Voice of a generation? Such labels were of little interest to me – you can't pin all your hopes on one person like that, whoever they are. It sets expectations way too high. But more than that, you simply can't delegate moral or personal thinking and expression in that way. You can't leave other people to do your thinking and talking for you any more than you can "let other people get your kicks for you".* Where personal matters are concerned, you have to think and talk for yourself. I could well understand Dylan not wanting to be pigeonholed, defined and burdened with people's expectations. I could understand why he couldn't see himself as *their* voice or *their* representative. I could understand, too, why he would shy away from the notion of being a 'protest singer' – it sounds so negative. To write a 'protest song' you must be protesting *against* something, something you don't like and want to change, and while it's clearly important that people are able to protest against injustice and brutality, no *artist* would want to be known primarily as a *protestor*. For one thing, anyone can protest and the validity of the message and quality of the art can easily become confused. But more than this, music is usually at its most powerful when it is used to express something positive and real in the life of its creator. And what is most positive and real in the life of the creator is not the song itself, but what lies behind it – that is, the response or impulse that drives the artistic expression of the writer's feelings. Calling songs 'protest songs' makes them sound too cold, too analytical, too calculated, too message-driven. From my vantage point in the mid-1980s I didn't care whether Dylan was playing 'protest songs' or not. I didn't care whether he was playing 'topical songs' or personal songs. I didn't care whether he was playing folk or blues or pop or rock, whether he was playing quietly or "fucking loud", whether he used hard, gritty descriptions of real people and events or madcap surrealist imagery. I didn't care what the music was called. All I cared about was whether it was any good – whether, that is to say, it moved me or spoke to me in some way. And in this respect, none of the albums I heard left me disappointed.

Even within these eight albums, Dylan's output seemed to have everything. There was wordplay, wit and humour, alternative perspectives and quirky comments, good-time rock and roll, great stomping blues tracks and serious iron-wrought songs of folk and country extraction. There was social observation, cries of injustice, compelling narratives, reflections on love, aching introspection and confessions of the soul. It was overwhelming. He showed you the world. He showed you things you didn't have the time

---

* A line from 'Like a Rolling Stone'.

or money or opportunity or eyes to see for yourself. He showed you things you hadn't seen and things you couldn't see. He showed you things far away and things that were under your nose. It was both exciting and terrifying.

♀ *Fiona and the Knob Boys* ♀

At some point in my first year at Swansea, I developed a crush on a girl who lived in an annex attached to the hall of residence where I lived. Her name was Fiona. She was an American studies student, big on James Dean, Bruce Springsteen, Bryan Adams, The Stray Cats, Dwight Yoakam, Dylan's *Nashville Skyline* and the Brothers Grimm. She came from Chepstow, but from the English side of the border. She was well-spoken but with a slight Gloucestershire twang. She was a quiet but graceful young woman who had long dark hair and a taste for unusual and slightly gothic-looking black and white striped nail varnish.

It was an infatuation I couldn't shake off, and, if anything, discovering Bob Dylan made it worse, as I kept finding lines that seemed to capture aspects of her character and the way I felt about her. She had a kind of self-contained creativity, for example, that seemed perfectly expressed by a line from 'She Belongs to Me' (*Bringing It All Back Home*)

> *She's got everything she needs*
> *She's an artist*
> *She don't look back*

I was similarly impressed with her ice-queen coolness, and the almost Buddhistic wisdom she seemed to exude as she went about her business. I thought of her every time I listened to 'Love Minus Zero/No Limits' (also from *Bringing It All Back Home*):

> *My love she speaks like silence*
> *Without ideals or violence*
> *She doesn't have to say she's faithful*
> *Yet she's true, like ice, like fire*

She seemed to simply glide around the college campus, the very picture of serenity, a young woman with the natural and happy aloofness of one who "knows too much to argue or to judge". How was I to know that her 'coolness' was at least partly explained by the fact that she was extremely short-sighted and couldn't see people coming? I spent six months thinking she had *chosen* not to see me.

I imagined, too, that she was the female presence of 'Isis', one of my favourite tracks from *Desire*, the "mystical child" whom the protagonist must leave behind in order to return to her, older and wiser, a year later:

> *She told me that one day we would meet up again*
> *And things would be different the next time we wed*
> *If only I could hang on and just be her friend*
> *I still can't remember all the best things she said*

Dylan's lines bestowed on her an enhanced mysteriousness, as in my own head I turned this living, breathing person into an unwitting earth goddess, a character of almost literary or mythological proportions. She became the perfect foil for my desperate hopes and projections of unrequited love. Man, I had it bad! I once bumped into her in Boots the Chemist in town and was so completely smitten and distracted by her presence that as we talked I followed her out of the shop with a big basket of shopping for which I hadn't paid. (I went back afterwards to impress her with my honesty.) I even convinced Iwan that we just had to have a copy of her essay on the Tang Dynasty in early medieval China. It had *never* come up before on the medieval history examination paper and "just has to come up this year". We read it, précised it, discussed it, learned it – it didn't come up. (But oh, what lovely handwriting!)

The Knob Boys were a group of second-rate public school boys and their cronies who, we were told, kept a log book detailing their sexual antics. We called them the Knob Boys partly to reflect this, but mainly because we thought they were a bunch of knobs. (Or, for those unacquainted with this particular colloquialism, dicks, pricks, cocks and penises. They were all of those things.) They ran their log book as a competition, awarding points to each other for various sexual achievements, the highest scoring of which was, so it was said, bedding a 16-year-old local virgin on the first date. The unofficial leader of the Knob Boys (the 'top knob') was Tim, who, after a period of enforced celibacy while recovering from a hernia operation, went on a 'slag-a-night' binge to rack up the points he needed to regain his rightful position at the top of the tree. Whether or not the young women they slept with wanted such frivolous and short-term engagements (I suspect that some did and some did not) their attitude was sickening. This wasn't 'free love' or anything approximating to it.

This was one group of people using another group of people in the most horrible and thoughtless of ways. By and large, my mates and I abhorred them, regarding them as the very antithesis of what we stood for (which, at the time and not for want of trying, was usually 'no sex'). Nevertheless there was a degree of 'cross-fertilisation'. Dominic, the public school boy in our own ranks, soon chose to cross the divide and become one of them, while the Knob Boys crowd included a chap called Prosser, a DJ and a massive Smiths fan who had previously been to sixth-form college with some of my own friends. (It was this 'cross-fertilisation', incidentally, that provided us with gossip and information about the log book.)

Incredibly, an endless stream of seemingly sensible and intelligent women surrendered to the Knob Boys' charms, taken in by their wealth, their good looks and the trappings of their well-bred upbringings. 'Real men come in a *Jiffy*' said one of their t-shirts, advertising a new brand of condom, but these 'real men' went in a jiffy too, leaving a trail of used and confused young women in their wake. The Knob Boys were not oblivious to Fiona's existence – and there was nothing they liked more than a challenge. But for all the attention she received from them from time to time, she seemed to have her head screwed on and had no trouble rejecting their advances. This seemed to genuinely baffle them and led to predictable charges of 'frigidity'. In the arrogance of their mindset, no woman could possibly refuse to roll over and become their temporary plaything unless there was something wrong with her! I watched all this from afar, secretly delighted by her resolve and her strength of character. She went up even further in my estimation.

For my own part, fearing rejection and acutely aware of my tendency to become incapacitated with nerves when talking to beautiful women, I had decided to woo her by adopting a low key approach that was cool and 'standoffish'. But with such an indirect method showing no signs of success and the end of the academic year looming, I decided that I had to tell her how I felt. I had planned to tell her one evening, when I expected her to be out at the same party as me. The environment would be just right. I would be able to speak to her alone but in relaxed surroundings, and I knew just what I would say. I thought of nothing else for days. And then disaster: she didn't turn up, and I had a miserable time. The next morning I woke early, feeling rotten but too anxious to stay in bed. I got up for a glass of water and, as I stood there drinking, pulled back the curtains to let in some daylight. I gazed across the courtyard towards

Fiona's annex – and there she was, coming out of the door and heading off campus with a big, fully packed rucksack on her back. I went into a panic. "Oh no!" I shouted, "She's leaving!" I knew I had to get to her. There was still a fortnight of term left and then a three-month summer holiday. I couldn't possibly endure all that time without having at least told her how I felt about her. I grabbed the smoky shirt I had worn the night before and hastily pulled on my jeans. With my shirt buttons done up in all the wrong holes and the laces of my trainers still untied I went sprinting after her, cutting an intense and slightly unhinged figure as I ran coatless through the drizzling rain.

"Fiona! Fiona!" I shouted as I got closer, "Where are you going?"

She was going home for a bit, she said, or maybe to visit a friend. I don't remember now. She would be back before the end of term, but she didn't see the point of just hanging around for a fortnight when there were other things she wanted to do. I offered to help carry her bags and she seemed grateful. We kept walking and talking. I was captivated, intoxicated. It was calming to hear that she was coming back, but I knew I had to say something: this was unbearable. All too quickly we reached the bus stop and I put down her bags. I could feel the nerves rising in my stomach. My heart was beating fast. It was now or never.

"Fiona," I said earnestly, breaking the flow of our previous conversation, "there's something I've been meaning to tell you."

She turned to face me and looked deeply into my eyes. Time seemed to stand still. In that instant I felt that I knew her, that I really, really knew her, that this was fate, that the situation was right, that we were right for each other.

"What?" she asked, "What is it?"

I paused. "Um, I just wanted to say that . . . um . . . that . . . um . . ."

Out of the corner of my eye I saw the bus pull up at the bus stop. There were only about half a dozen people in front of us in the queue. I tried again.

"I just wanted to say that . . . um . . . that . . . um . . . um . . . that you'll miss your bus if you're not careful."

"Oh yeah, thanks."

And she picked up her bags. And she got on the bus.

We never spoke of the bus stop incident. But we did become friends, of sorts. She sent me postcards from her holiday in Yugoslavia. She wrote to me in the summer holidays. In later college years she came round for tea or a meal occasionally. She wrote to me from Tennessee during her study year in the United States. When she left college she went to London to join the Civil Service, and even then we kept in touch. She phoned me on one occasion and proposed a visit. I was enthusiastic, though for reasons I don't now recall, it didn't come off. How come she couldn't see my feelings for her? I always used to wonder. Perhaps she did and liked to toy with me a little. Perhaps she liked me well enough as a friend but didn't want to give me too much encouragement. Perhaps I was a safety net of some sort in case relationships with other people didn't work out. Who knows?

○ *Outlaw blues* ○

Early one Saturday morning, Iwan came to see me needing a favour. "I need to get back to Aberdare today," he said, "but I've been banned from driving. Will you take me?"

"I haven't got a car," I replied.

"No," he said, "I mean in my car. Will you drive me to Aberdare in my car, this morning, now, in the next half an hour?"

"Am I insured?" I asked, vaguely recalling a conversation with my Dad about being able to drive other people's cars with their consent.

"Yeah," said Iwan reassuringly, "don't worry about that, anyone can drive my car."

"OK," I said. It sounded like an adventure. Little did I know.

Although the commuting between Swansea and Aberdare had helped Iwan's state of mind, in some ways it had proved impractical. He had overdone it on the beer one night, and was stopped by the police on his drive home. The resultant ban gave him a dilemma which he hadn't yet resolved. On this particular occasion he'd somehow managed to get his car to Swansea in time for a big Friday night out but, having stayed overnight at a friend's house, he now needed to get himself and his car back to Aberdare. I was pleased to be able to help him out. He had told me a lot about the estate on which he was brought up. In some streets, he said, up to one in three houses were now burned out and boarded up, and the words "Visitors Not Welcome" had been sprayed on the side of a house on the main road into the estate. There was even a story about people stealing the guard dogs from the factory at the top of the hill. I thought it would be good to see things for myself. And so we set off through Singleton Park to find the old Ford Escort he had parked just off campus in Brynmill.

"There's something else you need to know," said Iwan as I eased myself into the driver's seat.

"What's that?"

"The brakes don't work properly."

"What?"

"The brakes don't work properly. But don't worry. I'll guide you through things, and you can use the handbrake to stop."

"Are you sure that's OK?"

"Yeah, it'll be fine. I'm used to it."

And so began what I've thought of ever since as my 'Aberdare death drive'. Iwan guided and directed me like a mad conductor. "OK, on the gas . . . not too much . . . slowly does it . . . cover your handbrake . . . OK, off we go . . . watch it, there's a bend coming up . . . slow down . . . no more than 20mph here . . . whoa! whoa! steady on . . . ease off now, Mike . . . not too close to that fucker . . . that's good, well done . . . OK, foot back on the gas . . . you can accelerate a bit here . . . not that fast . . . ease off . . . ease off . . . watch 'em up ahead . . . they drive like maniacs around here . . . careful now, there's another bend in about half a mile . . . don't forget, take the bend slowly . . . slow right down . . . that's the way . . . faster . . . slower . . . faster . . . slower . . . are you still covering your handbrake? good . . . not too far to go now, you're doing well . . ." and so it went on for what seemed like an eternity. By the time we crept up to Iwan's parents' house I was exhausted and dripping in sweat. It reminded me of my first ever driving lesson – except this time I was manoeuvring a potential death-trap.

"You've got to get those brakes sorted," I said, figuring I'd earned the right to comment.

"I know, I know," said Iwan. "What are you doing next Friday?"

We went inside, where Iwan introduced me to his mother who made us a cup of tea. Suitably becalmed, Ian then gave me a quick tour of the area *en route* to a small, greasy-spoon café where we had lunch. Soon after, he packed me off to a nearby bus stop, giving me a crisp ten pound note and his original vinyl copy of Dylan's *John Wesley Harding* for my trouble.

"Really?" I said, "You're giving me your album?" I couldn't believe his generosity.

"Yeah, I think you deserve it," he answered, taking it back and studying the cover. He looked like he was mulling things over. Finally he looked up, smiled and once more thrust the album towards me: "Great album, great album. I think you'll like it."

It was (and is) a great album. Again, I couldn't make much sense of Dylan's sleeve notes – the so-called 'Three Kings' parable – but the songs themselves, what a revelation! The vibe was predominantly laid back and spacious, with wise, almost philosophical lyrics which goaded the listener to moral and personal reflection. Despite the light musical touch of the Nashville session men, the album seemed to have a kind of biblical weightiness. Little did I know at the time that *John Wesley Harding* was Dylan's response to what was, by most accounts, a serious motorbike accident and a brush with death, and little did I know that Dylan had once himself described *John Wesley Harding* as "the first biblical rock album".[3]

John Wesley Harding contained lots of lines and phrases (musical and lyrical) that appealed to me, and I delighted in its hints of a kind of understated and underlying personal contentedness. I found the album instructive in other ways too. Released in January 1968, it helped explain how Dylan moved from the mania of the *Blonde on Blonde* period to the inner rage and pain of *Blood on the Tracks*. Or at least, it helped me see that there had been significant change in Dylan's life and music between *Blonde on Blonde* and *Blood on the Tracks* and that *John Wesley Harding* was most likely one of a number of significant points on the journey. Lyrically, I particularly liked a verse from 'As I Went Out One Morning', when the singer encounters "the fairest damsel who ever did walk in chains":

> *I offered her my hand*
> *She took me by the arm*
> *I knew that very instant*
> *She meant to do me harm*

There were other tracks that held weight for me, including 'The Ballad of Frankie Lee and Judas Priest', 'I am a Lonesome Hobo' and, perhaps the album's best known track, 'All Along the Watchtower'. Most rock fans know Jimi Hendrix's version of 'All Along the Watchtower', and there are many who regard the Hendrix version as definitive. Even Dylan himself adopted Hendrix's interpretation and arrangement when he returned to the road after a lengthy touring hiatus in 1974. But personally, I prefer the restrained and solemn power of the original. The opening chords strike a note of threat and foreboding that is maintained throughout, giving the listener a strong sense of where Dylan had been and what lay ahead for him. In its own subtle way the Dylan version has more light and shade than even Hendrix's masterful histrionics managed to summon.

For several years, during the summer holidays, I had a job as one of a small team who organised and ran a summer school for children and young people with learning disabilities. We took over the regular school building, an environment with which the children were both familiar and comfortable, and used it as a base, offering a wide range of community and school-based activities to those who attended. Tŷ Gwyn Summer School effectively provided a respite care service for parents during the school holidays, but it also provided a fantastic experience for the kids, who often had little else to do but sit at home getting frustrated. We took between 50-60 children a week, splitting them into age-appropriate classes that catered for a range of abilities. In addition we had a 'special needs' class for children with more severe physical disabilities who required a greater degree of nursing care. Along with my old school friends Brendan and Anne-Marie, and colleagues Joanne, Matthew and Hayley, I worked as a class supervisor, responsible for the general management and supervision of a different class of children each week. Anne-Marie and Joanne were qualified special needs teachers, Hayley was a teacher, and we had additional medical and health professional support from an on-site specialist nurse and various therapists who came and went as dictated by the children's health and care requirements. The community-based elements of our programme – boat trips, open top bus trips, shopping trips, visits to sports centres, swimming pools, soft play facilities and the like – were made possible by the goodwill of volunteers from local school and college sixth forms, and the bus driving exploits of a group of Educational Welfare Officers who were contracted to work for the local authority but who were at a bit of a loose end outside of normal term time. Brendan and I had graduated from the ranks of the volunteers to become assistant organisers and class supervisors. Matthew was a law student and the boss's brother-in-law. In my first summer at the school, he was the cook.

The boss was a bloke called Steve, a special needs teacher whose regular job was teaching children with hearing difficulties. He had built the summer school up from scratch over a period of around a decade. He was a quick-witted, thin, intense looking guy – who was regarded as a near genius by those in the team who had worked with him for a long time. For a while I found it quite difficult to communicate with him. I often seemed to miss the significance of things he said, or failed to read his mood and requirements correctly. This was a source of some concern to me. All seemed to change, however, when one day we found ourselves standing in for the Educational Welfare Officers and driving the children home. As we waved the last one off, I left my post as 'door guard' at the back of the mini-bus, and moved alongside Steve upfront. We started talking about music.

"I like a lot of rock music," I said, "mainly heavy rock, but I like some other stuff too."

"Like what?"

"Blues. I like a bit of blues. And just recently I've really been getting into Bob Dylan."

Steve's eyes lit up. He became animated. Suddenly he was less guarded, less private and more willing to engage. Steve, it transpired was a massive Dylan fan – more extreme in his love of Dylan than Iwan, and a collector of bootlegs and rarities. We talked Dylan all the way back to the school. As we pulled up outside the main building, Steve turned off the engine. "Before you get out," he said, "answer me this. Leaving aside the obvious choices, the albums everyone likes, what's your favourite Dylan album?"

"Well," I said thoughtfully, trying to sound knowledgeable, "leaving aside the ones that everyone likes I'd have to say *John Wesley Harding*."

He looked at me and smiled. I guessed I'd got the answer right.

"I'm glad you said that," he nodded, "I think that too."

Class dismissed.

Whenever we found time to socialise and get to the pub there was a very cool, relaxed musical vibe around the summer school team. Steve and Matthew were both big blues fans and Matthew, in particular, was keen to lend me a lot of his classic blues stuff: Muddy Waters, Buddy Guy, Junior Wells, that sort of thing. The Rolling Stones, Van Morrison and Christy Moore were also popular choices within the team, but it was really the music of Bob Dylan that provided the most common ground and pulled our disparate tastes together. Brendan, too, enthusiastically embraced my newfound interest in Dylan and was keen to hear what all the fuss was about. In particular he warmed quickly to *Blood on the Tracks* and *Desire*. It was a beautiful summer that year, and he took to setting his stereo so that he was woken each day by the opening bars of 'Tangled Up in Blue' and Dylan singing: "Early one morning the sun was shining/I was laying in bed."

Working at the summer school and spending so much time with the children and the small, dedicated team of staff was a fantastic experience. More than anything else I have ever done, it taught me to recognise and accept individual difference. There were limitations on what many of the children would go on to achieve. Some of these reflected their own natures and abilities, but some reflected the way people with learning disabilities are viewed and the way we organise services for them. For the time we were all at Tŷ Gwyn Summer School together, we did not see limitations: we saw only children. What mattered was providing a rewarding environment in which everyone was safe, everyone laughed and everyone was happy. The children did have extra needs that required thought and attention and care, but that simply meant that as unique individuals they offered the rest of us new opportunities for meaningful human engagement. Working in that kind of environment, I came to appreciate better the value of even the smallest acts of contact or kindness – a smile, a hug, an extended hand. I have never known a place built on so much positive energy, selfless behaviour and joy. The children had a great time at the summer school. The adults and helpers did too. Over a six or seven week period it was exhausting work, but it was a powerful experience for all concerned, and it put our common vanity and often shallow hopes and desires well and truly into perspective.

It was during early preparation for the 1988 Summer School that I caught up with Dylan's back catalogue and was ready for, and open to, new Dylan releases. *Down in the Groove* (1988) was the first new studio album he had released since I had properly gotten into him. As the rest of us sat talking and drinking in The Claude public house, Steve arrived late, fresh from a first listen to Dylan's latest offering.

"What's it like?" we all wanted to know.

He responded by sharing with us the track-listing and drawing our attention to the unexpected inclusion of unusual covers such as 'Shenandoah' and 'Let's Stick Together'.

"Yes, but is it any good?"

"Too early to say," said Steve, looking away and supping sheepishly on his beer.

Unfortunately, with the exception of the single 'Silvio', it wasn't any good. In fact, it contained an extraordinary number of lacklustre tracks (mainly covers), including the rather weak 'Had a Dream About You Baby' which was pulled from the soundtrack of what writer Michael Gray has described as the "quaintly atrocious"[4] 1987 film *Hearts of Fire* (in which Dylan played the role of a washed-up rock star alongside Rupert Everett and *Kerrang!* darling Fiona Flanagan). I was unaware of the film at that point, though I found out later that some of it was shot in South Wales, including beach scenes which I'm told were filmed in Southerndown – a place where my parents and aunty used to take me, my sister and my cousins when we were young. Two or three years later I met a guy called Skim. He was another ex-Harlech boy, whose girlfriend shared a flat with my girlfriend of the time, Jo, when they were teacher training. Skim's girlfriend allegedly had powers of premonition and experiences of conversing with ghosts, and she told us stories that sent a chill down my spine. That old Harlech experience of mine – perhaps there was something in it after all. Anyway, it turned out that Skim was not only at Harlech around the same time as my friend Iwan, but was also a huge Dylan fan. Skim told me that when Dylan was filming *Hearts of Fire*, he had gone down to Southerndown with a friend of his to see if he could catch Dylan 'on location'. After much wandering around, he spotted a film crew in the distance and was beside himself with excitement when he noticed Dylan on the set. He edged ever closer, and during a break in filming finally mustered up the courage to approach his idol:

"Hey, Bob, I'm a big fan. Can I have your autograph, please?"

"Sure," replied Dylan, reaching out and taking the pen and paper. Dylan turned to Skim's mate. "And I suppose you want my autograph too?" he asked.

"No thanks, Bob," said Skim's mate, without any regard for Dylan's status or reputation, "I don't like your music."

But despite the disappointment of *Down in the Groove*, I *did* like his music. I had come to like his music very much. And yet, while Dylan's music was almost always challenging in some way, I was never particularly drawn to *him*. Speaking of the way he himself was influenced by his folk hero Woody Guthrie, he says in the sleeve notes to *The Freewheelin'*

Bob Dylan that: "The most important thing . . . I learned from Woody Guthrie [is that] I'm my own person." No one likes to think that they are not their own person, but it's quite a significant moment when we really start to learn what this means. Discovering the music of Bob Dylan freed me, in a way, from some of the powerful symbols and iconography of rock fandom. It helped me to develop a stronger sense of self than I previously had, and a desire to stand on my own two feet in both an emotional and a creative sense. In some strange way, it helped to restore a degree of balance and perspective both in the way I listened to rock music and in my expectations of it.

☿ Who is that man? ☿

As a Welshman, the resonance of the name 'Dylan' was not lost on me, and indeed it is commonly believed that Dylan (whose real name, of course, is Robert Allen Zimmerman) changed his name after acquainting himself with the poetry of Dylan Thomas. Dylan has often expressed frustration with those who read too much into the Dylan Thomas connection. "I've done more for Dylan Thomas than he's ever done for me," he once famously remarked. "Look how many kids are probably reading his poetry now."[5] He is probably right about that, too. When Robert Shelton set out to write his biography, Dylan urged him to "Straighten out in your book that I did not take my name from Dylan Thomas,"[6] and, indeed, alongside Dylan's own attempts to 'straighten things out' via a trickle of misinformation about the family origins of the name, Shelton also notes Dylan's likely familiarity with both the "frontier hero" Matt Dillon from the TV series *Gunsmoke*, and the legacy of the pioneering Dillion family from his Hibbing hometown.[7]

In Volume One of Dylan's autobiography, *Chronicles,* Dylan explains the matter thus:

> What I was going to do as soon as I left home was just call myself Robert Allen . . . that was who I was – that's what my parents named me. It sounded like the name of a Scottish king and I liked it. There was little of my identity that wasn't in it. What kind of confused me later was seeing an article in a *Downbeat* magazine with a story about a West Coast saxophone player named David Allyn. I had suspected that the musician had changed the spelling of Allen to Allyn. I could see why.

It looked more exotic, more inscrutable. I was going to do this, too. Instead of Robert Allen it would be Robert Allyn. Then sometime later, unexpectedly, I'd seen some poems by Dylan Thomas. Dylan and Allyn sounded similar. Robert Dylan. Robert Allyn. I couldn't decide – the letter *D* came on stronger. But Robert Dylan didn't look or sound as good as Robert Allyn. People had always called me either Robert or Bobby, but Bobby Dylan sounded too skittish to me and besides, there already was a Bobby Darin, a Bobby Vee, a Bobby Rydell, a Bobby Neely and a lot of other Bobbys. Bob Dylan looked and sounded better than Bob Allyn. The first time I was asked my name in the Twin Cities, I instinctively and automatically without thinking simply said 'Bob Dylan'.

. . . Spelling is important. If I would have had to choose between Robert Dillon and Robert Allyn, I would have picked Robert Allyn because it looked better in print. The name Bob Allyn never would have worked – sounded like a used-car salesman. I'd suspected that Dylan must have been Dillon at one time and that that guy changed the spelling, too, but there was no way to prove it.[8]

Whatever way you look at it, it would seem that the work and reputation of Dylan Thomas were not the whole story, and Dylan's irritation with those looking to oversimplify matters is understandable. He is clearly wrong, however, in his suspicions that "Dylan must have been Dillon at one time". The name Dylan is an old Welsh name, a very old Welsh name, with the first syllable pronounced more like the English 'dull' than 'dill', and the second syllable like the girl's name 'Ann'. In fact, 'Dylan' is the name of a minor character from the medieval collection of Welsh folktales now known as *The Mabinogion*. The earliest copy of the complete *Mabinogion* is found in the *Red Book of Hergest* (circa 1400), though fragments of many of the stories are found in the *White Book of Rhydderch* (circa 1325) and, similarly, fragments can be found in earlier documents again. Given the oral tradition in Celtic storytelling, it is likely that the origins of the stories go back much further. Dylan appears in the *Fourth Branch of the Mabinogi* ('Math Son of Mathonwy'), and I offer the reader the following extract from Jeffrey Gantz's Penguin Classic translation:

After the two nephews [Gwydyon and Gilvaethwy] had been cleaned up they went to see Math, who said 'Men, you have earned peace and you shall have friendship. Now advise me which virgin to choose. Gwydyon replied, 'Lord, that is an easy choice: Aranrhod daughter of Dôn, your niece and your sister's daughter.' The girl was sent for and when she arrived Math said, 'Girl, are you a virgin?' 'I do not know but that I am.' Math took his wand and bent it, saying 'Step over that, and if you are a virgin I will know.' Aranrhod stepped over the wand, and with that step she dropped a sturdy boy with thick yellow hair; the boy gave a loud cry, and with that cry she made for the door, dropping a second small something on the way, but before anyone could get a look at it Gwydyon snatched it up and wrapped it in a silk sheet and hid it in a little chest at the foot of his bed. 'Well,' said Math, 'I will arrange for the baptism of this one,' referring to the yellow-haired boy, 'and I will call him Dylan.' The boy was baptised, whereupon he immediately made for the sea, and when he came to the sea he took on its nature and swam as well as the best fish. He was called Dylan son of Ton, for no wave ever broke beneath him.[9]

The mysterious appearance (and prompt disappearance) of Dylan is described by Gantz as "an unintegrated tradition",[10] sufficiently "unintegrated" indeed, for Gantz, in his introduction to the tales, to ask the unanswered question "What purpose does Dylan serve?"[11] For our purposes, at least, the introduction of Dylan serves to demonstrate that in so far as 'Dylan' and 'Dillon' are related, then it is the latter which must be a corruption of the former. 'Dylan' *does* look better than 'Dillon' but one doesn't need to create the inscrutability: there really is magic in them there Welsh hills. Bob Dylan is from Minnesota, not Wales. He knows a lot of things – but we can't expect him to know everything.

○ *Going, Going, Gone?* ○

The question of Dylan's name change is obviously a superficial one. But beyond this, fans and commentators have for a long time asked, 'Who is Bob Dylan?' "This is not a meaningful question," writes Paul Williams (in the Introduction to the first volume of his mammoth three volume set, *Bob Dylan: Performing Artist*) "but it has a wonderful resonance and a remarkable endurance, all the same."[12]

In interviews included as special features on the DVD of his 2007 quasi-biopic *I'm Not There*, director Todd Haynes notes that most of Dylan's biographers concur in identifying 'change' as their overriding perception of Dylan – as hard as you try, you just can't pin the man down.

Dylan is, says Haynes, "the serial changer . . . this person who couldn't reside in the same skin at times for what seemed like longer than a few months."[13] When you look at Dylan's work, you find not one constant self but a "cluster of different selves" and this is "the key" to understanding Dylan.[14] Speaking of his film, Haynes says:

> In approaching a subject as complex and as rich as Bob Dylan, I realised that the only way to really get to the core of who he was, was to honour the changes that had defined his life, and by doing that I wanted to dramatise them and have different actors become these different phases of his life both creatively and personally.[15]

One often hears people say that 'finding yourself' and 'being yourself' are the keys to freedom, and yet for Dylan freedom appears to lie in his ability to escape whichever 'self' has most recently been presented through his music and objectified by a fawning public and a greedy press.

But is 'change' really the key to understanding Dylan himself, or is it simply the key to understanding his public manifestations? I'm not going to try to answer that question. It is well known that Dylan has at times provided journalists with misinformation about his upbringing and private life, and he has fiercely guarded his privacy – as he is quite entitled to do. I've no intention of trying to tell you who Dylan really is. Not only don't I know, but I don't think I even want to know and I don't think the answer matters anyway. I think Haynes is right when he says at one point that for most of us, all we *really* have and know of Dylan is the music.[16] And with a body of work so varied and extensive, surely the music is enough?

"I'm a mystery," Dylan once famously remarked, "only to those who haven't felt the same things I have."* If one views his songs as snapshots, expressions of feeling, or the presentation of a certain perspective, then there is no need to go further than this. There is no need to to delve too deeply into the personal life of the man behind the songs, nor to strive too hard to understand the minutiae of his creative processes. Great songs and great lyrics open things out for us. They make us feel that the world is a bigger place full of wonder and possibility, and that this world of wonder and beauty is accessible to us. They help us to see or feel or understand something that previously we didn't see or feel or

---

* See the booklet accompanying the *Biograph* collection (Columbia, 1985), p.34

understand, and to this extent they give us wings and help us fly. But too much breakdown and analysis can sometimes pull a song down and destroy what is special about it. (After all, if you trap a butterfly in a jar and start to poke and prod it around, you wouldn't expect it ever to be the same again would you?) For the most part great songs can speak for themselves, and if we let them, they will. I am not saying that there's anything wrong with thinking about songs, analysing lyrics or drawing on what's known of the artist to help us understand his work. Sometimes this can be helpful. All I am saying is that first and foremost we should give the songs room to breathe and let them do their thing. The problems only come when we try to push the analysis too far, or get too preoccupied with the detail of the creative process, or get too hung up on our need to know the artist, or get too determined to fathom *the* meaning of a song.

While Dylan the man may prove eternally elusive, the music is already out there for us all to experience. More than with any other artist, I've tried to take Dylan's music for what it is without, initially, either awareness of or interest in the context in which it was created. To an extent the same is true of the way I experienced the Doors – a band I also discovered 'retrospectively'. In both cases I did not, as a rule, put a great deal of time into trying to unravel the artistic and personal influences behind the words and music but simply allowed myself to react to what spoke to me. Nevertheless, my experience of Dylan was a 'purer', less visceral, more cerebral experience than my experience of the Doors, and my initial reactions to Dylan and to Jim Morrison were very different. While Morrison's words and persona do their best to draw the listener into a maelstrom of dark desire and sensual knowledge, Dylan has always seemed to me to provide an oasis of reflective calm.* That's not to say that Dylan didn't have his wild side. It's clear from reports of the mid-1960s period that Dylan worked hard and played hard in a way that could not possibly be sustainable and, indeed, only was sustained at the time with the help of "a lot of medicine". It's also clear that Dylan was a man who knew about living on the edge, but who always managed to pull back, whether by luck or design, before he fell off. He clearly knew the madness of personal and creative self-absorption, but never *quite* lost

---

* Dylan was, in the words of Howard Smith of *The Village Voice*, "more of a cerebral heartthrob". Quoted in Jerry Hopkins and Danny Sugerman, *No One Here Gets Out Alive* (Plexus, 1982), p.156

touch with the world. Dylan had been there, done it, and moved on before Jim Morrison had even got into his stride.

I listen to Dylan when I need to take a step back, or to the side, and gather myself. This is true of the way I listen to his songs about relationships, but it's also true of the way I listen to Dylan in general. This is the way I first encountered him and, though other people may relate to the work of Bob Dylan differently, I cannot imagine listening to him in any other way.

♀ If music be the food of love ♀

> If music be the food of love, play on
> Give me excess of it; that surfeiting
> The appetite may sicken, and so die

> (William Shakespeare,
> *Twelfth Night*, Act 1, Scene 1, 1-3)

The opening words of Shakespeare's play are those of the lovelorn Duke Orsino of Illyria whose cure for lovesickness is to overindulge his passion for music (the 'food' that nourishes love) in much the same way as overeating can quash one's appetite for food that, in appropriate quantities at least, nourishes the body.

It's tempting to speculate that Orsino's lovesickness has infected his powers of reason. If you overindulge your passion for food by overeating, you are likely to make yourself sick. If you overindulge your passion for music by repeatedly playing "that strain again", then you are likely only to become sick of the music. Only if Pavlov has been at work and the music and one's feelings for the loved one have become irreversibly associated, could boredom with the music transfer to the object of one's love. It would be interesting to test it out. First, find someone who fell in love with his partner while listening to Dire Straits's 'Romeo and Juliet' at the school disco and who subsequently always associated the song with his partner. (Perhaps they regard it as 'their song', having played it on their first anniversary and then at their wedding party and then at every significant event thereafter.) Then wait until his wife leaves him, lock him in a room and play the song incessantly over and over again until the boredom he starts to experience for the song transfers to his wife and overrides the feelings of desperation and hurt he previously felt. It's worth a go, isn't it?

Can music nourish love? At a basic level, the association with love is perhaps the most obvious and self-evident way in which music does weave its way into our lives, helping us to capture moments and moods of significance and memories of value. I didn't mean to be facetious above. Not *that* facetious anyway. Lots of couples have a song that reminds them of when they first met or fell in love or got married. Lots of people associate songs with particular times in their lives and particular memories, whether good or bad. I'm no different. Bon Jovi's 'Livin' on a Prayer' reminds me of my old college friends and worrying bouncers in Swansea nightclubs by riding high on people's shoulders playing air guitar. Ditto Europe's 'The Final Countdown'. 'Cool for Cats' by Squeeze reminds me of the first crush I ever had on a girl when I was about ten. Leo Sayer (no particular song, just Leo Sayer) reminds me of the first crush I had on a girl in school when I was 12, and almost any song by Crowded House reminds me of the early days of my relationship with my first wife. It's an extraordinary and wonderful thing that music can attach itself to our lives like this, and it's part of what makes us human that we respond to music in this way. But my interest here is not in music that simply *reminds* you of things that are only accidentally connected with it, nor even in the fact that this emotional connection between music and experience can be, and is, ruthlessly exploited by marketing men whose job it is to fashion public taste, push product and sell us 'the soundtrack to our lives' (as though we all live the same lives). My interest, rather, is in music that *itself* carries meaning; music that matters because of what it is, how it sounds and what it says.

Music can do more than just attach itself to incidents and memories in our lives. It can extend our conception and understanding of what's possible. It can help us to learn about ourselves. It can help us grow through triumph and success, and it can help us cope when things turn out wrong. We can't all be poets, musicians and artists, but we *can* all look to the fruits of their labours and find nourishment there. It is what we learn from music, not the killing of our appetite for it, that, potentially at least, can help us to cope with our lovesickness and other matters of the heart. And so, without further ado, if music be the food of love, play on . . .

◉ *Blood on the tracks* ◉

Over the years *Blood on the Tracks* has gained in stature and become generally regarded as one of the greatest albums, if not the greatest album, in Dylan's entire canon. Writer Paul Williams has called it a "Concerto for a Breaking and Opening Heart,"[17] while Michael Gray, author of perhaps the seminal scholarly work on the words and music of Bob Dylan, describes it as "an album of genius; of powerful emotional complexity, unerring fresh insight and the kind of maturity (horrible word) that manifests itself . . . as pure, strong intelligence."[18] *Blood on the Tracks* gives us, says Gray, "Dylan's scorching *urgency* at its very best."[19]

To be sure, in retrospect it is possible to see hints of what was to come on *Planet Waves* (January 1974). *Planet Waves* was, as biographer Robert Shelton notes, a "strongly autobiographical" album that explored "the many faces of love" and "marked a return to stinging, aphoristic expression."[20] Two songs in particular stand out for me as precursors of *Blood on the Tracks*. The barely repressed negativity of 'Dirge' foreshadows the all-out spleen-venting of 'Idiot Wind', while 'Wedding Song' provides a glimpse of how much Dylan realised he was losing when aspects of his private life started to go wrong. These songs in fact appear almost as two sides of the same coin. 'Dirge' is, in the words of Robert Shelton "an elliptical essay in morbid dependency" while 'Wedding Song' is "a total statement of redemption through love".[21] Dylan clearly had an active and at times troubled inner life – and was not the passive has-been some critics were suggesting he had become. If this wasn't clear from the subtitle of the album alone – 'Cast Iron Songs and Torch Ballads' – then it didn't take the listener long to discover that its creator was very much alive and kicking. He was kicking less forcefully than at other times in his career perhaps, but it's telling that not all the songs are kicking in the same direction. *Planet Waves*, though not without its share of filler, contains other gems in the form of the searching 'Going, Going, Gone' and the inspiring 'Forever Young'. The latter was written by Dylan for his son, apparently, and is included here in two guises, slow and wistful to close what at the time was Side One, and upbeat, drawling and country to open Side Two.

But it would be wrong of me to overegg the pudding. *Blood on the Tracks* grew from a number of sources and *Planet Waves* was just one of them. As Paul Williams notes, Dylan's 1974 tour with The Band, his first for seven and a half years, seemed to both settle accounts and raise new questions for him. Thereafter, Dylan "had a hard time resuming his life as a husband"[22] and subsequently developed a "tremendous need to speak to and about his wife and marriage".[23] But there was also the influence on Dylan of the classes he took with the artist Norman Raeben, who, he said, "put my mind and my hand and my eye together in a way that allowed me to do consciously what I unconsciously felt."[24] In Paul Williams's opinion: "If any of Dylan's record albums deserves to be singled out as a 'masterpiece', it is the one that most successfully combines conscious, deliberate creation (composition) with spontaneous expression (performance) – 1974's *Blood on the Tracks*."[25] While it may have been, in Dylan's words, "the blood behind the myth" that fuelled the songs, the implication is that *Blood on the Tracks* could not have come together as it did without Dylan applying to his songwriting techniques he had learned from Raeben.

A few years ago, while looking for information on *Blood on the Tracks* to share with a work colleague, I came across a review by Grey Cavitt of MusicTap.Net. It's absolutely spot on, and in places it's almost as moving as Dylan's album itself. Even my work colleague, who had always seemed resistant to my attempts to get her to listen to Dylan, told me that it brought a lump to her throat. With immense thanks to Grey Cavitt for writing such a stunning piece, I'd like to quote some extracts from it here. He writes:

Dylan is best known for plugging in folk music and for spurring on the spirit of the sixties with impossibly powerful protests that soon became modern psalms to many. Both of these qualities were gone by the end of the decade. Dylan had retreated from the front lines of political unrest, and he no longer sought to rig disparate styles into new sounds. He relaxed, releasing country albums, stretching out into a comfortable mode of music that combined many of his loves without shattering conventions or rocking the world. By the mid-70s, many critics treated him as a write-off or a washout. It seemed his star had finally flamed out.

On *Blood on the Tracks*, Dylan still avoided any novel mixing of genres or blatant fodder for political radicals. He simply focused all his energy on writing and performing folk-styled songs, and his undivided, honed genius, free of the very concerns that catapulted him into the public eye, produced the greatest album of the rock era.

... [T]hese songs are largely stains of tragedies distant, past, and unchangeable ... Yet ...the dominant mood here is melancholy and sorrow, not anger ...The music is lush, inventive, and beautiful, giving *Blood on the Tracks* a gently cathartic, redemptive power. Dylan is not pulling the listener into the pit of self-pity. He is making misery beautiful, and thus, bearable.

Dylan's earlier work is largely the limitless and exhausting wilderness of youth. In contrast, this album is the dark, quiet room surrounding an experienced, worn man reflecting on his life, the whirlwind romances and spitfire disunions, the promises of heaven and the realities of hell, and inside this knowing, cracked voice, a lifetime of experience, joys and regrets spill out until the room is flooded with bittersweet heartbreak and dim hopes of love. He was no longer a force moving millions, only a sad, lonely man who happened to be the greatest songwriter of his century. This album proved it.[26]

In March 1975, just a couple of months after the album's release, Dylan did a radio interview with Mary Travers (of Peter, Paul and Mary fame). When Travers remarked on how much she had enjoyed *Blood on the Tracks*, Dylan replied: "A lot of people tell me they enjoyed that album. It's hard for me to relate to that – I mean, people enjoying that type of pain."[27]

๐ "Pain sure brings out the best in people, doesn't it?" ๐

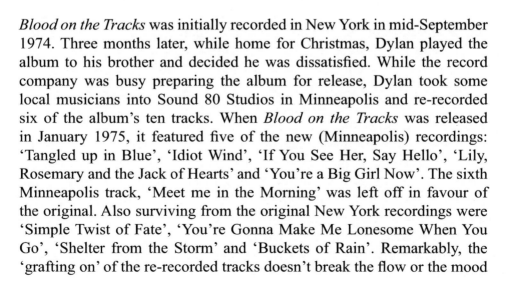

Blood on the Tracks was initially recorded in New York in mid-September 1974. Three months later, while home for Christmas, Dylan played the album to his brother and decided he was dissatisfied. While the record company was busy preparing the album for release, Dylan took some local musicians into Sound 80 Studios in Minneapolis and re-recorded six of the album's ten tracks. When *Blood on the Tracks* was released in January 1975, it featured five of the new (Minneapolis) recordings: 'Tangled up in Blue', 'Idiot Wind', 'If You See Her, Say Hello', 'Lily, Rosemary and the Jack of Hearts' and 'You're a Big Girl Now'. The sixth Minneapolis track, 'Meet me in the Morning' was left off in favour of the original. Also surviving from the original New York recordings were 'Simple Twist of Fate', 'You're Gonna Make Me Lonesome When You Go', 'Shelter from the Storm' and 'Buckets of Rain'. Remarkably, the 'grafting on' of the re-recorded tracks doesn't break the flow or the mood of the album at all. Not a single person I've ever played or lent this album to has ever commented or noticed. And even when you do know, it's still very difficult to hear the joins. (I had to do some research to find out for sure which tracks were recorded in which sessions.) *Blood on the Tracks* is, says Paul Williams, "a cycle of songs written together but performed in two separate, intense bursts,"[28] and as a collection of songs it retains an incredible cohesion.

Album opener 'Tangled up in Blue' is a catalogue of jumbled up yearning in which Dylan bounces from one emotional skirmish to the next, not knowing what to do except "keep on keeping on". His quick-fire, evocative descriptions create a landscape of changing scenery which brings the experiences he describes to life without removing the need for interpretation or closing down possibilities of meaning for the listener. The song is marked by shifts in time and context that can initially create a sense of dislocation. Commentators often remark on Dylan's shifting use of pronouns in this track, and while this is not really evident on the album version, which is sung as a first-person narrative, it is a striking feature of both the original New York recording and Dylan's 1975 *Rolling Thunder Revue* performances, which blend first person ("I") and third person ("He") perspectives. Commentators have also noted some lyrical differences between the New York and Minneapolis versions that seem to mess with the facts of the matter. Was the Italian poet referred to in verse five from the thirteenth or the fifteenth century? What jobs did the narrator really have? What were the occupations of the narrator's friends? Such changes will only really bother you if you took the lyrics too literally in the first place or you prefer to get cosy with one version and can't cope with the thought of there being others. (If this is the kind of listener you are, then this is a good example of the dangers of delving too deeply or seeking out discarded versions and alternative performances.) For me, 'Tangled up in Blue' has a depth that transcends (or is perhaps created by) the shifts in time and context, and I can live with the minor lyric changes (though I have to admit that I'm not too keen on the pronoun shifting). In the sleeve notes to *Biograph* (1985), Dylan explained that he was "just trying to make it like a painting where you can see the different parts but then you also see the whole of it."[29]

'Simple Twist of Fate' is a tender and achingly sad tale of lost love with a much more straightforward narrative than 'Tangled up in Blue'.

Again there's a significant pronoun shift, with Dylan telling the tale in the third person until the final verse:

> *People tell me it's a sin*
> *To know and feel too much within*
> *I still believe she was my twin*
> *But I lost the ring*
> *She was born in Spring*
> *But I was born too late*
> *Blame it on a simple twist of fate*

It is also evident from the recording that features on the *Bootleg Series Volume 5 – Bob Dylan Live 1975: The Rolling Thunder Revue*, that Dylan had already at this stage made some lyrical adjustments; adjustments that by and large carry through to the version presented on 1978's *Bob Dylan at Budokan* album.

'You're a Big Girl Now' finds Dylan "back in the rain", struggling to gain a sense of perspective as he sings to a lost love from atop a metaphorical (barbed wire) fence. The music is gentle and melancholic but Dylan's vocal is raw as he reaches out with long, pained 'oh's at the heart of each verse which turn resignation and acceptance into heartfelt plea.

'Idiot Wind' is an outpouring and release of anger and sadness that sounds like it's been brewing for years. The vocal is almost snarled, the lyrics spat out with both regret and a sense of catharsis:

> *You'll never know*
> *The hurt I suffered*
> *Or the pain*
> *I rise above*
> *And I'll never know*
> *The same about you*
> *Your holiness*
> *Or your kind of love*
> *And it makes me feel so sorry*

Of all the re-recorded tracks on *Blood*, 'Idiot Wind' is perhaps the one that changed most. Certainly it is evident from the take contained on the *Bootleg Series Volume 2* that there are significant lyrical differences between the New York and Minneapolis versions. But even more striking is the change in mood and tone. There are those who feel that between the sessions

Dylan had toned down his anger and bitterness. Personally, however, I find sorrow more than anything in the softer *Bootleg Series* version. The album version is loud, brash, 'in your face' and unquestionably angry.

In the context of the album, 'You're Gonna Make Me Lonesome When You Go' appears to provide a quick burst of warmth and sunshine as the singer finds a love that is "right on target" and that has "never been so easy or so slow":

> *Flowers on the hillside blooming crazy*
> *Crickets talking back and forth in rhyme*
> *Blue river running slow and lazy*
> *I could stay with you forever and never realise the time*

However, time does have a role to play. The lover is soon to leave and the singer will be lonely again. This is a song that seems to anticipate pain. It's a song that makes you *want* the short-term joy and the intensity of love in full knowledge of the pain that will follow. And it's a song that makes you feel that however much that pain might hurt, it's always worth it.

'Meet me in the Morning', the track which kicked off what was originally Side Two of the album, is a relatively straightforward blues track that offers something of a break from the album's intensity. Nevertheless, it has musical bite and carries a slightly ominous vibe, and again there is lost love at its heart. The sun has gone down and the singer is once more living in darkness.

'Lily, Rosemary and the Jack of Hearts' is a stunning, show-stopping Western allegory. Musically it's an extended and breezy country jaunt. Lyrically it's an edgy Dylan narrative which weaves its way through a complex web of yearning, hope, disappointment and desire as these express themselves in the lives of the narrative's four key characters – Lily, Rosemary, Big Jim and the Jack of Hearts. Dylan gives us just enough detail to bring the characters to life, but leaves it to the listener to develop the characters and fill in the blanks. We are told, for example, that Rosemary "had done a lot of bad things, even once tried suicide", but we don't know what kind of bad things she has done. We know that Lily had "come away from a broken home," and "had lots of strange affairs", and we know that at the end of the song she is "thinkin' 'bout her father, who she very rarely saw", but we know nothing more of these affairs or her relationship with her father than this. We know that Big Jim, a successful mine owner, has seen the Jack of Hearts somewhere before, but we have no idea of the circumstances in which their paths may have crossed. And while we know that the Jack of Hearts is an outlaw type whose charisma draws the attention of all, his identity remains a mystery. The relationships and characters described are trapped in time – but some of Dylan's observations and the interaction between the characters have timeless relevance.

'If You See Her, Say Hello" is one of the saddest songs you'll ever hear, but it describes a kind of sadness that's rich in generosity of spirit as the singer struggles to come to terms with heartbreak and loss. Dylan delivers an emotionally charged performance of what is, surely, one of the most personal songs he has ever penned:

> *If you get close to her, kiss her once for me*
> *I always have respected her, for doing what she did and getting free*
> *Oh, whatever makes her happy, I won't stand in her way*
> *Though the bitter taste still lingers on from the night I tried to make her stay*

'Shelter from the Storm' is the closest we get on *Blood on the Tracks* to the idea of any kind of salvation or redemption through love. Dylan sings of a time when he was "burned out from exhaustion", "poisoned", "hunted", and "ravaged". There are touches of 1960s surrealism in the lyrics (a "one-eyed undertaker", for example), and apparent references to the Passion of Christ that invoke thoughts of suffering and persecution. Clearly, the song reflects a time or times when the singer desperately needed shelter:

> *Suddenly I turned around and she was standin' there*
> *With silver bracelets on her wrists and flowers in her hair*
> *She walked up to me so gracefully and took my crown of thorns*
> *"Come in," she said,*
> *"I'll give you shelter from the storm"*

Again there is plenty of room for interpretation. What kind of shelter was provided and for how long? And was it provided by one woman or several? There is sufficient ambiguity to make it possible for us to ask these questions, though we have to look to our own lives, not to Dylan's, if we want to fathom their meaning. Dylan is singing of "another lifetime" and most of the song is set in the past. The last line, however, which beautifully combines optimism and regret, is set in the present and points to the future, and all but invites us to frame our own kind of answer. It's another stunning track on an album full of stunners. (There are at least half a dozen tracks here that would be the stand-out tracks on almost any other album you could mention.)

Finally, 'Buckets of Rain' is a charming and beautifully picked track that ends the album with a rueful and knowing smile. It's another fine mess the singer has got himself into: 'I'm miserable because you're not here', he seems to be saying, 'but I'm here for you . . . if you want me'. It's not exactly a happy ending, but it's a warmly delivered track that brings pleasant relief. There is a wry wit and a lighter touch at work here. 'Buckets of Rain' adds a sense of roundedness to the album, ensuring that we come out feeling calm and not raw.

It should, perhaps, be added that despite its general subject matter, *Blood on the Tracks* is not an album without wit and humour. Note for example the hillbilly overstatement in 'Lily, Rosemary and the Jack of Hearts': "The hanging judge was sober/He hadn't had a drink", or 'Idiot Wind's' sardonic nose-thumbing at those who suspect foul play when the singer inherits "a million bucks": "I can't help it if I'm lucky." Elsewhere it's hard not to smile at the thought of Dylan wittering on to no one in particular when he sings: "You're gonna make me give myself a good talking to" (from 'You're Gonna Make Me Lonesome When You Go'). Most memorably, there is the caustic payback line of 'Idiot Wind': "You're an idiot babe, it's a wonder that you still know how to breathe." The first time you hear it, you don't know whether to smile or wince. "*We*'re idiots babe," he sings at the end of that same song, "It's a wonder *we* can even feed ourselves." At times Dylan does a pretty good job of both singin' and smilin' through the tears.

Taken as a whole, *Blood on the Tracks* is a giant bucket of human emotions, containing as it does the joy and pain, the hope and disappointment, the gain and loss of a million and one heartfelt experiences – not just Dylan's experiences, but mine and yours. In the words of Paul Williams: "The triumph of the album . . . is its success at blending the totally personal and the totally fictional so thoroughly and with such originality that the end result is a tale told by and for Everyman (or woman)."[30] And there, at the heart of the album, is that all too human voice, cracked and flawed, inhabiting the songs like no artist I've ever heard before.

It could be argued that the key to understanding *Blood on the Tracks* lies in understanding which of Dylan's relationships and experiences inspired which songs (and which bits of which songs). But, as I warned above, too much knowledge here can be a dangerous thing. If you use what is known of Dylan's private life to try to 'decode' the songs, you won't find it so easy to relate to them yourself. I've always listened to *Blood on the Tracks* in a personal way and I would urge anybody else to do the same: just open yourself to the songs and respond to them as they are presented.

According to Michael Gray, the "creative genius" of *Blood on the Tracks* "is still very much an undiminished thing of the present."[31] It is this, and not the details of Dylan's personal life, that is the key. Bob Dylan has produced a wide range of material across the numerous phases of a 50-year recording career. It's not surprising, therefore, that different people will relate to different parts of Bob Dylan's output in different ways at different times of their lives. But the thing about *Blood on the Tracks* is that it doesn't depend on your age or your preoccupations during a particular time of your life. It's an album of all-encompassing relevance, and it grows with you. It moulds itself into your life, pouring itself into every nook and cranny it can find and embedding itself there. As a rock album, this makes it almost unique. It was relevant to me when I was 19, infatuated and looking for a girlfriend; it was relevant at 25 when I was frustrated and unhappy in a long term relationship; it was relevant at 34 when I was going through a soul-destroying divorce; and it was relevant after that when I was seeking and found love again. Rock fans often like to discuss lists of their favourite groups and albums, and they often push each other to name their ultimate 'desert island disc'. I don't anticipate being carted off to an exotic island location or having to surrender my record collection any day soon, but if I could only keep one album, it would be this one.

♀ Modern Times ♀

Since the release of *Time Out of Mind* (1997), Dylan has produced a run of fine and largely critically acclaimed albums that takes in 2001's *Love And Theft* (my favourite of the current era), *Modern Times* (2006), and the chart-topping *Together Through Life* (2009). That Dylan would re-emerge in the new millennium to consolidate his reputation, however, was no sure thing. A stunning comeback of weighty proportions *Time Out of Mind* might have been, but it was also Dylan's first album of original material for seven years. In-between times he had released two albums of stark solo and acoustic re-recordings of rootsy, traditional and largely American folk and blues tunes. Commercially, both *Good As I Been To You* (1992) and *World Gone Wrong* (1993) were flops, ranking among the worst charting of all Dylan's studio releases. Nevertheless, they are important albums for anyone wishing to understand Dylan's later resurgence. For most of the mid and late 1980s, Dylan had suffered from writer's block and produced a series of indifferent albums (for many the *Oh Mercy* album was a false dawn that only temporarily halted Dylan's decline). In the early 1990s Dylan returned to the "old songs", at first reportedly looking to run down his recording contract, but then, as inspiration hit, attempting to "personally get back to the music that's true for me".[32] In looking to reconnect with his musical roots, Dylan also struck an apocalyptic note: "Technology to wipe out truth is now available," he wrote in the sleeve notes to *World Gone Wrong*. "Not everybody can afford it but it's available. When the cost comes down look out! There won't be songs like these anymore."[33]

Dylan has done his best to preserve the songs and their "truth" – not just through his covers albums, but through the original material he has written and recorded since. His re-immersion in traditional American music heralded another shift in emphasis and a new phase of creativity. From *Time Out of Mind* on, Dylan has placed his music in a great American tradition, drawing on influences that, according to some commentators, go back beyond the Second World War to the 1920s and 1930s. Dylan's muse has returned and he has written new "old songs" for both our listening pleasure and our edification.

But Dylan's conscious reconnection with traditional American music is only half the story. In July 1987 Dylan toured with the Grateful Dead (the resultant *Dylan and the Dead* album appearing in 1989). According to Nigel Williamson, Dylan was profoundly influenced by the Grateful Dead's belief that "music is fundamentally a live rather than a recorded experience and . . . its power can only be fully realised in communion with an audience."[34] As rehearsals for the gigs with the Dead began, and Dylan came under pressure to revisit his back catalogue, it seems that he began to doubt the wisdom of the tour. But in *Chronicles Volume 1*, he describes an experience in a jazz club in San Francisco, and a later experience on stage in Switzerland, which together helped him to rediscover his zest for performing and to develop new ways of seeing and presenting his older material.[35]

Pretty soon Dylan seems to have reached a new awareness that taking his songs to people and performing live was right at the heart of who he was and what he did. Thus began what (despite Dylan's lighthearted protestations in the sleeve notes to *World Gone Wrong*) is commonly referred to as the Never Ending Tour, the first gig of which took place on 7 June 1988 in Concord, California. This new desire to perform seems to have saved Dylan from retirement. Prior to this, a long tour with Tom Petty had convinced him that he'd had enough. "I felt done for," he wrote in *Chronicles*, "an empty burned-out wreck . . . There was a hollow singing in my heart and I couldn't wait to retire and fold the tent."[36] Now, however, he approached the task with a new vigour. He'd found a way of reconnecting with his music and with his audience. Since then Dylan has maintained a demanding touring schedule, averaging around 100 gigs a year. Writer Nigel Williamson calculates that between 7 June 1988 and the end of 2003, Dylan clocked up 1,630 gigs. In the words of Williamson, in the art of performance Dylan "found a way of keeping in touch with his muse without the need for prolific songwriting."[37]

The notion of 'performance' and "the art of performance" is one that seems to be taking on an ever-increasing significance among Dylan commentators. This is due, in no small part, to the work of Paul Williams, whose three-volume set *Bob Dylan Performing Artist: 1960-1973; 1974-1986; and 1987-1990 and beyond* I have quoted from several times. Williams writes:

> I see Dylan as first and foremost a performing artist, as opposed to a composer or songwriter. He *is* a songwriter, of course, and a very good one; but in my view (and apparently Dylan's as well, according to comments he has made to interviewers throughout his career) his songwriting is best understood as an activity directed by, and in service to the needs of the performer.[38]

It is a view, indeed, that Dylan seems to endorse in the interview that informed Martin Scorcese's film *No Direction Home: Bob Dylan*. According to Dylan: "the ideal performances of the songs . . . come on stages throughout the world. Very few could be found on any of my records."[39]

It is also a view that is shared by Todd Haynes. In one of the interviews edited together as a special feature for the *I'm Not There* DVD release, Haynes says: "To me, Dylan is ultimately a performer. He's somebody who lives in the moment for the performance that he's making; lives and dies in that moment of creation, and when it's over it's dead and he needs to move on to something else that's alive and vital in the moment. Which is why he's always now these days in a state of constant performance and that the songs . . . from his canon that he reinterprets . . . always sound completely different, cos they need to be new and in the moment and alive again for him."[40]

I'm sure there is truth in all of these remarks, though despite the importance I have placed on 'the gig' in my experience as a rock fan, live performance is not something that has ever been part of the way that *I* have experienced Dylan. As you know from reading the early parts of this chapter, I discovered Bob Dylan through his recorded performances when he had already had a long career – and everything his music means to me has its source within those grooves. In fact, for a long time I deliberately avoided seeing Dylan live. Listening to Bob Dylan has always been a more solitary and personal experience for me, and I simply wasn't sure how this 'private' way of relating to his output would fare in a live context. I'd read reports of Dylan's unpredictability on stage too – dynamite one night, abysmal the next. I had no idea how long he would keep touring, or how often he would play somewhere close enough to my home to make a trip to see him manageable. I didn't want my first and possibly only experience of Dylan live to be a bad one.

I finally took the plunge on 27 June 2006. Dylan was playing Cardiff International Arena. It was, in fact, the fourth time he had played the venue since September 2000. The difference this time was that my life was more settled. I had a new partner (now my wife) who shared my love of music. It was too good an opportunity to pass up. It was easier to buy the tickets and go than agonise over the decision and sit at home feeling anxious and biting my nails while life took place elsewhere.

In the event, it was something of a mixed experience. The band looked good and sounded tight. From our balcony vantage point though, the quality of the sound wasn't great as, despite a full hall, the music echoed around us (a notorious problem at that particular venue). Dylan wasn't particularly animated either, though he clearly had presence. He played a keyboard, not a guitar. He didn't speak to the audience until the encore. When he did speak, a gasp and a ripple of excitement ran through the crowd as though we were truly in the presence of greatness ('He spoke! To us!' it seemed to say). Around two thirds of the setlist was culled from the 1960s, though Dylan offered radical interpretations of most of the songs as he brought the approach of his recent studio albums to bear. In some cases it took me at least 30 seconds to identify the songs! In truth the gig didn't really catch fire until the latter part of the set and the encores. For most of the time, it was an enjoyable and interesting experience rather than an involving and moving one.

The end of the show, however, *was* involving *and* moving, and was quite something to behold. As Dylan and the band brought a rousing version of 'All Along the Watchtower' to its climax, the lights went out and the hall was plunged into total darkness. When the lights came back on, the musicians stood on the edge of the stage to take the crowd's applause. Dylan stood almost completely motionless, slightly apart from the band and to their left. From where I sat I could see him gently rolling the fingers of one hand across something he was holding (his harmonica perhaps?). The applause was rapturous. Time seemed to stand still. Dylan looked out across the audience like a man surveying his life's work. He had just reprised 'All Along the Watchtower''s famous first verse:

> *Businessmen they drink my wine*
> *Ploughmen dig my earth*
> *None of them along the line*
> *Know what any of it is worth*

Somehow it seemed both pointed and fitting.

"It's nice to be known as a legend," Dylan writes in *Chronicles*, "and people will pay to see one, but for most people, once is enough."[41] I haven't decided yet whether at this stage of Dylan's career once is indeed enough for me. My memories of the end of that gig are strong and striking. It would be a shame to tarnish them.

○ Between despondency and hope ○

As Dylan prepared to release *Time Out of Mind* in May 1997, he was taken ill, complaining of chest pains and breathlessness. He had acquired a fungal infection called histoplasmosis, which in turn had caused a potentially fatal heart condition called pericarditis. When the album was released in September 1997 it became evident that both musically and lyrically the album was one of his darkest. "It appeared," says Nigel

Williamson, "that Dylan had been divining his own fate . . . as if he knew that something terrible was about to happen to him."[42]

Dylan's *Tell Tale Signs* album, Volume 8 of the excellent *Bootleg Series*, is accompanied by a warm and illuminating essay by Larry 'Ratso' Sloman (drafted in New York in 2008). Sloman notes that although *Time Out of Mind* was released to critical acclaim, "the prevailing critical sentiment was that the songs were despairing and bleak confrontations with mortality."[43] Sloman reports an interesting exchange between Dylan and L.A. Times music critic Robert Hilburn. Asked what he thought of the critics' assessment of the songs as "brooding and gloomy", Dylan replied:

> I don't know . . . would you expect me to make an album of felicitous content? Why on earth would you expect that? The space between despondency and hope can be as large or as small as we make it, depending on who we are . . . I try to put my songs right exactly in there, and hope for the best.[44]

The passage is striking. We all of us live our lives "between despondency and hope", but what a great way for a songwriter and artist to conceptualise his outputs and achievements. It got me thinking. Hasn't my life as a music fan oscillated between these two extremes, the balance shifting first one way, and then the other? When I swapped records and listened to music and went to gigs with my teenage friends, full of joy and energy and youthful enthusiasm, wasn't that hope talking? And when I first listened to music as a lonely individual, looking to records rather than friends for wisdom and support, wasn't that when I was nearer to despondency? And don't 'hope' and 'despondency' themselves have both personal and social dimensions? We have hopes not just for ourselves but also for our family and friends, our faiths, our nations and our ideals. And isn't it true that wherever hope is possible, despondency is possible too?

My experience of Bob Dylan has been one of using his work to help restore some kind of balance or equilibrium. When I needed to feel that I was not alone in my moral or political objections to the status quo, I could listen to the so-called 'protest' songs. If I'd lost my way and needed time to sort myself out, I could listen to tracks like 'Wedding Song', not just for its vision of pure love, but for the lyrical reassurance that sometimes it's OK to withdraw from social action and look after yourself. (We don't always have to labour under a duty or desire to "remake the world at large".) If events in my life gave me cause to reflect on relationships or to try to come to terms with feelings of loneliness or rejection, I could listen to *Blood on the Tracks*. If I started to wallow too deeply in self-pity, the 'truth' of the early folk songs and the latter day albums could bring me back to the world. If I just wanted to feel good about life, I could listen to *Nashville Skyline* or some of the more quirky, humorous tracks from the 'wild mercury sound' period, or the relaxed wisdom of *Love and Theft*. And so on.

Over time I've come to regard Dylan as an artist apart from all others. On numerous occasions in pub conversations I've left him off lists of my favourite artists and bands, and when his omission has been pointed out to me, I've realised that it's not because I've forgotten him, but because in some ways he has a different kind of significance for me than others discussed in these pages. At his best, as I've said before, he is peerless. His greatest works are timeless, transcending age and context, sitting there waiting for those who need them, sitting there in that gap between despondency and hope.

9

Islands are Mountain Tops

Do you remember the thrill and excitement of discovering rock music for the very first time? Do you remember that feeling of amazement and awe as the world seemed to open up in front of you? Do you remember the first time you heard a song that you just couldn't get out of your head? Or the first time you bought an album that you couldn't stop playing? Do you remember that feeling when music first wove its way into your life and you knew that somehow things would never be the same again? Do you ever wish you could recreate those moments or go back and live them again? Of course, you can never experience exactly the same thing twice because of everything you've learned and experienced in the meantime, but from time to time there have been bands or albums that have stirred something in me that has approximated to those early feelings; bands and albums that have reminded me of the past while offering something new and timely and relevant to the kind of person I have since become. Music, even rock music, is not just a young person's obsession: it has the potential to inspire and stimulate and inform even as we creep into middle age and beyond.

Anorak? What's wrong with that?

Not long after returning to Cardiff, after some years spent studying and working in Swansea, Sussex and Bangor, I found myself seconded to an enquiries team to provide politicians and their officials with briefing in advance of two high profile scrutiny sessions. One day, during a short coffee break, I told some of my colleagues about an interview I'd heard on the radio. "I have two favourite singers," the interviewee had said. "The first is Peter Gabriel, but I can't decide whether the second is Jim Morrison or Phil Collins."

"Why didn't he just say he had *three* favourite singers," I said, and everyone laughed. My colleague Phil, who had seemed to be too engrossed in his work to be paying much attention, turned round to face us:

"I don't know what his problem is anyway," said Phil, "it's obvious who should be second."

"I know," I said incredulously, "Jim Morrison."

"Jim Morrison?" Phil looked and sounded outraged, "Phil Collins, you mean."

We laughed. We had a clear difference of opinion, but it broke the ice. We had worked together for two weeks. Phil was a tall chap with long wavy hair that grew down over his collar and rested on his shoulders. Back in the day it would have been a sure sign that we shared some taste in music – but I had long stopped making such assumptions, and, to be honest, it had never even occurred to me to quiz him on his musical preferences. Before long, however, we discovered that, musically speaking, we did indeed have a good deal in common. While there were clear differences between us – Phil was a bigger fan than me of the major 1970s progressive rock bands, and branched out into what he called "intelligent contemporary pop" – our tastes converged when it came to early 1980s British rock and, in particular, the 1980s progressive rock revival. We spoke at length about bands like Marillion, Twelfth Night, IQ, Pallas and Pendragon. But whereas my preoccupations had changed a little and my attention had wandered – I had moved to North Wales, got married, had a child and started listening to Welsh folk music – Phil had kept his finger on the prog rock pulse, purchasing magazines, new releases and archive recordings like they were going out of fashion (had they ever been in fashion). He had built an astonishing CD collection and a near-encyclopaedic knowledge. I soon came to refer to him as 'Phil the Collector' and he told me that even friends of his who had maintained an interest in rock music regarded him as 'The Keeper of the Keys'. Clearly I had a lot of catching up to do.

One day, as we chatted over coffee, Phil invited me to accompany him to a small club in Cardiff called Jumpin' Jacks. It was early April 2002 and Marillion were playing a 'warm-up' gig to run through the 1994 'concept album', *Brave*, which they were due to play in its entirety at the first 'Marillion Worldwide Convention'. I hadn't heard Marillion for some time, and I was both intrigued and tempted, but home circumstances made it very difficult for me to make impromptu decisions to go out for the night. Not without regret, I declined the offer – and didn't understand the significance of what I'd turned down until sometime later.

It is true that I hadn't heard Marillion for some time, but let me provide a little more background. Although Marillion were one of the bands I'd lived for in the early and mid-1980s, by the end of the decade I had come to feel that I had outgrown them. Or, more to the point, I came to feel that I'd out-grown the lyrical preoccupations and writing style of original frontman Fish. That's when I *started* to lose interest. There is more to the story than that, though. In late 1988 Fish and Marillion parted company, citing irreconcil-able musical and lyrical differences as the cause of the split. Given the domi-nant presence and style of the inimitable frontman, it was unclear for a while – to fans at least – whether the band would or even could continue. And yet what choice did they have? They could change their name and risk losing a large proportion of the fan base they had worked so hard to establish, or they could try to find a new singer. They decided on the latter option. If the change was to be a success, it was clearly important that they did not fall into the trap of trying to imitate the inimitable. And so Fish's replacement, Steve 'h' Hogarth, was a different sort of character altogether. Most notably, he was a *singer* rather than a frontman, and a genuine musician to boot. Creatively speaking, this was to stand the band in good stead over time. However, it would take an album or two for the new line-up to really settle down, and I was an impatient young man. If I'm perfectly honest I didn't really take to Hogarth back then. There was a touch of 1980s 'new romantic' about him that I found off-putting, and, although I gave it a go, I found the first Hogarth-era album, *Seasons End* (1989), to be a pretty bland, tentative and understated affair. *That's* when I finally lost interest in Marillion.

Now, Marillion are one of those bands whose progress has been hampered by the baggage that they carry. Part of this is the association of the band with a particular point in time when they enjoyed considerable chart success with a run of hit singles – 'Kayleigh' and 'Lavender' are the best known – from their *Misplaced Childhood* album (1985). The other part is the deeply unfashionable 'progressive rock' tag they have carried, that might have seemed appropriate enough when they 'hit the streets' back in the early 1980s, but which soon came to be something of a millstone around their necks. This has always struck me as unfair. Even if one does accept the applicability of the label, progressive rock is itself a much misunderstood and maligned art form. While its excesses are not really to my taste – in fact I find the worst excesses of progressive rock almost unbearable – it's almost always a mistake to judge anything, whether it's music or politics or fashion or religion, by its most extreme advocates and its worst practitioners. The view of progressive rock propagated by the mainstream media, in other words, is not the whole story. Let me explain what I mean.

In early January 2009, BBC4 broadcast two programmes on progressive rock – *Prog at the BBC* and *Prog Brittania* – on the same night. While it was great to see the BBC devoting some airtime to the genre, and while both programmes contained some interesting footage, both faded badly with no more than a cursory acknowledgement of the reach and influence of many of the bands featured. The viewer was left with a picture of progressive rock which promoted the orthodoxy that:

- progressive rock was killed by punk;
- progressive rock is about demons and wizards, myths and legends, fantasy and fiction;
- progressive rock has no social relevance; and
- progressive rock musicians are frustrated jazz musos who really should have kept away from rock and roll.

All these statements are misleading generalisations which led me to marvel at the way the genre continues to be treated. Punk *did* dent the pretentions and ambitions of some of the progressive rock giants, but many of them survived the brattish assault on their musical values and emerged stronger and more refined for it. (They 'progressed' in fact – isn't that what 'progressive rock' bands are supposed to do?) Bands like Pink Floyd, Genesis and Yes continue to this day to sell albums by the shed load, with both their pre-punk and post-punk recordings retaining appeal. And what of the bands that formed a second wave of British progressive rock in the 1980s? The aforementioned artists, Marillion, Twelfth Night, Pallas, Pendragon and IQ, may not have packed the commercial clout of their predecessors, but that they emerged alive and kicking in a post-punk era, and that most of them are *still* alive and kicking almost 30 years later, is often conveniently overlooked by those who like to oversell the impact of punk. In some cases the new bands brought with them a sense of gritty realism that one also found in ambitious metal bands like

Queensrÿche, and that's been further developed by modern prog metal bands like Dream Theater and Opeth. And what of the emergence of other musically ambitious bands like The Mars Volta, Gorky's Zygotic Mynci, Porcupine Tree and perhaps even Radiohead, all of whom have adopted the musical thoughtfulness, ambition and desire to push boundaries that has always characterised the best progressive rock? It should be clear from this list alone that progressive rock does not lack social relevance – and if one adds such luminaries as Pink Floyd and Rush to that list, with Roger Waters's bleak lyrical reflections and Neil Peart's allegorical writing to the fore, then it's clear that it never did. Similarly, one will recognise instantly that while some progressive rock bands have chosen to express themselves through themes and imagery incorporating myths, legends and science-fiction fantasy, others simply have no interest in this sort of thing. As for the 'frustrated jazz muso' line, I strongly suspect it's a generalisation based on the tastes and subsequent history of a relatively small subset of progressive rock musicians.

As far as Marillion are concerned, there never really were dungeons and dragons, despite the Tolkien-inspired name. Admittedly, there was 'Grendel' – an 18-minute epic based on the Beowulf legend, which was released as one of two B-sides on Marillion's first 12-inch single – and there was a jester, a princess (of sorts) and an occasional touch of whimsy with the odd reference to literary figures such as Chaucer and Shakespeare, but there's not much of that these days and there hasn't been for many years. Similarly, while the early albums do contain some overwrought and verbose lyrics, and there are some distinctively prog meanderings that owe a lot to the influence of one or two bands in particular, it's not really fair to make assumptions about a 30-year recording history based on a knowledge of just the first couple of albums. In fact, it's truly staggering to see how media misconceptions and misrepresentations have hindered a band which, in my humble opinion, deserve far greater artistic recognition than they get. So deeply entrenched are the misconceptions that the band has at times resorted to fighting them explicitly. One finds the following, for example, on the cover of the 2006 *Crash Course* sampler: "Marillion are used to fighting misconceptions. Marillion are not what you think they are. No, really, they're not. Just remember that whatever your pre-conceptions are about this band, chances are they are wrong."*

---

* *Crash Course: An Introduction to Marillion* (Racket Records, 2006)

Perhaps it is true that when I gave up on the band around the time of *Seasons End*, I too became guilty of letting assumptions get in the way of my listening habits. I knew that the mainstream anti-prog prejudice didn't apply to Marillion, and yet, in feeling that I'd outgrown the Fish incarnation of the band, I was perhaps too ready to write Marillion off as a band who had nothing new to offer. As I've discovered since, however, the truth is that, creatively speaking, Marillion had barely got going. As Marillion have grown older their music has matured, and, as you might expect – if you consider the matter without preconceptions – the things they write about and the ways in which they express themselves have evolved. The musical turns they have taken since *Seasons End* have, for the most part, been far more to my taste than their initial hurrah with Steve Hogarth (though I do like *Seasons End* more now), and, like a fine wine, they seem to get better and better with age. Much of their best material comes from the second half, not the first half, of their careers. Faced with this information, you can do one of two things. You can sit back as I did and write them off as a spent force – a band who were of their time or perhaps a little after it – or you can put your preconceptions to one side and have a flutter on one of their recent albums. If you take the former view, then you risk missing out on one of the most wonderful bands ever to plug in and rock out.

In this respect, Phil the Collector was my saviour. Phil was convinced that I'd simply given up on the band too soon. I think he could see why someone might feel they had grown out of Fish-era Marillion, but he also felt that if I'd liked the music in the 1980s, there was certainly no reason why I shouldn't have a listen to what they'd done since. In particular, he thought I might appreciate *Brave*. Undeterred by my having politely declined his Jumpin' Jacks invitation, one day he brought the double live CD *Made Again* in to work and insisted that I borrow it. The first disc contained a kind of 'greatest hits' set – a mix of Fish and early Hogarth-era material. The second disc, however, contained a live version of the whole of *Brave*. I remember listening to it at home as I did the ironing. I enjoyed the first disc far more than I'd expected. *Brave* itself was something that I realised I'd need to listen to a few times. But I liked the overall sound and feel of it and made a note to keep my eye out for a cheap copy. Phil was surprised when I gave his CD back to him so quickly, concerned that I either hadn't liked it or hadn't given it a chance. "No, I do like it," I assured him, "I just don't want to become too familiar with it before I buy a copy of my own."

Inspired both by Phil's enthusiasm and my positive experience with *Made Again*, I dug out my copy of *A Singles Collection* – a 1992 EMI compilation of 'hits' from both the Fish and early Hogarth periods, which I'd picked up cheaply around the time I started buying CDs. Much to my surprise, I discovered that most of my favourite material on the disc came from the second album with Steve Hogarth, *Holidays in Eden* (1991). Tracks like 'Dry Land', 'No One Can' and 'Cover My Eyes' were well-crafted, mature tracks with simple but touching lyrics and memorable hooks. I was slowly being reeled back in.

But what finally convinced me to check out the band properly was seeing Steve Hogarth on a HTV Wales programme about the state of the music industry. Hogarth took part in a live studio debate with, amongst others, former Stereophonics drummer Stuart Cable and Red Dragon DJ Jason Harold. Hogarth noted, with frustration, the difficulty that bands like Marillion have in achieving radio airplay and taking their music to a wider audience. The programme included documentary footage of the band at work in their Racket Club recording studio, and an interview with them about their novel response to the problem of mainstream rejection. It was the first time I'd really heard about Marillion's innovative approach. Here was a band who bucked the trend of multi-national corporate consumerism by 'doing it for themselves' – with a little help, of course, from their friends, or, to be more accurate, from their solid and loyal fan base. Marillion had developed an online community of fans who effectively financed the making of new albums through a pre-order system. It was a stroke of genius. Money from the fans essentially removed the need for record company advances, leaving the band free to make the music they wanted to make in their own time, and allowing them to strike a favourable distribution deal with a 'major' once the record had been made. This new way of working gave them complete artistic freedom over their output and necessitated a closer than usual relationship with those who coughed up money for pre-order payments months before an album was even made. The nature of this relationship clearly made being a paid-up Marillion fan something a bit different. In return for their trust and commitment, the fans got not just a *sense* of involvement, but constant information from the band about progress and a special, collectable, deluxe limited edition version of the album that would never be available again once the initial print run had sold out. Those pre-ordering before a cut-off date also got their names in the album credits. It's a way of working that has allowed Marillion not just to survive in the new millennium, but slowly and surely to start to thrive again, with each recent album selling in sufficient quantities worldwide to keep the band going and finance "a better way of life".

After seeing the HTV programme I went online and pre-ordered a copy of the forthcoming album *Marbles*. Unable to wait an estimated four months to hear some 'new' Marillion music, however, I also ordered a couple of the two-disc remasters of some of the Hogarth-era EMI albums that I had missed: *Brave* (1994) and *Afraid of Sunlight* (1995). I was so impressed with these albums that more orders soon followed as I steadily worked my way through the entire back catalogue, exploring solo albums and side-projects too, purchasing Jon Collins' excellent biography *Marillion/Separated Out*, and even rejoining The Web – the Marillion fan club.* I quickly learned more about the band – their departure from EMI, their subsequent deal with the smaller, independent label Castle Records, and the run of lower-budget but very commendable releases that followed before Marillion took the bold steps that established the new way of working that has served them (and us) well to this day.

The first pre-order experiment came with 2001's *Anoraknophobia* – a lively and colourful package that sparkles with freshness and exciting ideas, musically, visually and conceptually. It's a special album indeed, whether you have the limited edition pre-order version or the standard retail release. The groundwork for the experiment was laid an album earlier, however, when Marillion used the offer of a free bonus disc with the *marillion.com* album (1999) to build up their fan database. To get the bonus disc fans had to complete and return the 'mail-off' inlay card included in the album booklet. According to biographer Jon Collins this added around fourteen thousand more e-mail subscribers to the Marillion eWeb mailing list.[1]

Between them, the database and the band's growing use of the Internet made the pre-order experiment possible. It even enabled the band to run the idea by fans to test out its likely feasibility. In the event, the pre-order was a stunning success. The band set an "optimistic" pre-sales target of 10,000 and secretly hoped for 8,000. In the end, 12,674 people bought the album months before it existed. "That's a serious hard-core family,"

---

* Each Christmas the band send out a one-off CD or DVD to all fan club members featuring unreleased tracks, live performances, remixes, acoustic versions and so on. The quarterly magazines are pretty good too!

wrote Steve Hogarth in the sleeve notes to the special pre-order edition of *Anoraknophobia*, "and it's growing. This is the 21st Century and everything is hype – but not this. This is about passion. See you on tour. (Wear anything you like.)"[2]

Even the title of the album expressed the band's newfound confidence as they grabbed hold of mainstream media (mis)conceptions and had a little fun with them. "Call us 'anoraks', call us anything you like," the band seemed to be saying, "– we don't care!" Hogarth further elaborated on the *Anoraknophobia* concept:

> It occurred to me about a year ago watching *Never Mind the Buzzcocks*, or something like that, that we're starting to live in a 'take the piss' culture, and that having a cheap shot or ripping the piss out of somebody has become a national sport in this country, and all the easy targets are people who believe in something and have a passion. Our fans are the easiest people in the world to point the finger at and call anoraks, and the thing about these guys that are sitting there – the Mark Lamarrs and the Angus Deaytons of the world – whether you love or hate them, is that they never actually stand up and declare what they believe in themselves, because if they were to do that, then everybody else would point and laugh at them.
>
> So really to declare a passion is to expose yourself to ridicule, and I personally would much rather have a world full of people that were passionate and believed in something and cared about something, than a load of two-dimensional types who stood around smirking and pointing at other people. I really just wanted to say, "We know you're all anoraks, and there's nothing wrong with it! We're anoraks too!" The point of the title *Anoraknophobia* was no fear of it. Anorak-no-phobia.[3]

The album photo shoot showed the band bespectacled, wielding coat-hangers, and decked out in hooded anoraks adorned with button badges. The cover introduced the world to a little graphic anorak man called Barry. The retail version of the album replaced the more extensive text of the pre-order edition with space for the members of the band to list their more 'anorak-type' likes and dislikes. We now know, for example, that: Steve Hogarth's likes include "Hormone Rooting Powder"; drummer Ian Mosely likes "Parrots (especially African Greys that can't talk)"; bass player Pete Trewavas's dislikes include "Umbrellas and Wellington Boots"; guitarist Steve Rothery likes "anything with flashing blinking lights"; and keyboard player Mark Kelly's favourite food is a "Whopper

With Cheese". Whichever version of the album you buy, it's bright and vibrant – it *feels* like a great album, and there's plenty here to bring to a smile to your face. On a more serious note, having total control of their own project enabled the band to use the album booklet to voice support for a number of good causes, including UNICEF and Comic Relief.

Observant readers will notice that although I didn't rediscover Marillion until early 2004, I quoted above from the special pre-order edition of a 2001 album. How can this be? Well, *Anoraknophobia* has quickly become one of my favourite Marillion albums. On first hearing it I thought: "Bloody hell, this is the best rock album I've heard for 20 years," and, some years on, my views haven't changed much. Until recently the pre-order edition of *Anoraknophobia* remained one of only two Marillion products I wanted that were missing from my collection (the other, in case you're interested, is an original vinyl copy of *Brave*). I asked on the Marillion Online Forum whether anyone had a spare. A chap in Canada told me to e-mail him. "How much do you want for it?" I asked, expecting an absurd request of online auction proportions. "Nothing," he replied "but I see you're from Wales. Just send me a Wales t-shirt for my two-year-old daughter." So I did, and received not just a copy of the *Anoraknophobia* pre-order, but an unexpected copy of his own album, Mackey+ *Soundbathing*, which is based on an interesting idea of presenting songs in both their original stripped down state and in a fuller format with added instrumentation. Obviously one can find plenty of instances of touching generosity in all sorts of places (if you look hard enough) and just as obviously not all Marillion fans would have parted with such a unique product for such little return, but Graham Mackey's generosity is indicative of the general vibe around the band these days. Being a Marillion fan does bring with it a sense of being part of something special. It's a good feeling, a feeling I had around bands when I first discovered rock music, a feeling that music *can* bring people together in positive ways – ways that transcend the humdrum of everyday existence.

So what about the music? I haven't really said anything about the music yet, and 'a new way of working' isn't enough in itself to get people to buy your CDs – not when you're an unfashionable ageing rock band with a progressive rock heritage anyway. Ultimately, of course – to quote Tommy Vance again – it's the music that matters. So what is it about Marillion's *music* that inspires such loyalty and commitment among the fan base? What is it about this music that touches people across the world and allows it a place in the new millennium? And what is it about this music that drew *me* in again and has sustained my interest 21 years after I first got into the band, and about 14 years after I initially 'got out of them'? I'll have a go at answering the third question in the hope that something in my experience provides at least a partial answer to the first two.

🎺 Such a brave, brave girl 🎺

My daughter Alys was diagnosed with Type-1 (insulin-dependent) Diabetes on 18 November 2002. She was four years old. She had been wetting the bed a lot and getting very sleepy, both of which were unusual for her, and then she started losing weight dramatically. I had taken her to the doctor's soon after the bed-wetting started, but they had failed to diagnose diabetes and, instead, had referred her to a children's clinic for further assessment. As I sat chatting to the doctor, Alys drew one of her 'maps' on a blank piece of paper. It showed me standing next to my house, and her mother standing next to hers. We both had sad faces. Alys drew herself in-between us with a big smile on her face. Children can be so perceptive – and can make you feel the full force of things you have done. Alys's mother and I had recently divorced after a rollercoaster marriage that had been full of highs and lows – mainly lows – and had never reached a stable state of peaceful co-existence. By the time of her diabetes diagnosis, Alys had moved from North Wales (the place of her birth) to South Wales, had been to four different nurseries, and had seen her parents separate. Through all the change, she had remained a happy, resilient child. But the diabetes diagnosis rocked us all. There was no history of any type of diabetes on either side of the family; this was a bolt from the blue. It seemed as unfair as it was sudden. It was the grown-ups, Alys's mother and I, who had messed up our relationship and broken up the family home. Why was Alys the one being punished with this god-awful life sentence?

Just as the doctor had initially missed the diabetes (they are *general* practitioners, and human beings, after all), so, as I sat in the surgery again, I had to push for the doctor to perform the necessary test to confirm the likely presence of diabetes. "Take her home and keep an eye on her for 48 hours," the doctor had said, "and bring her back if there is no change. There are lots of nasty bugs around." But I was insistent. I had been looking up the symptoms in my *Family Doctor* book and was convinced I knew what was wrong. The doctor agreed to test her urine – just to shut me up I think – and within an hour or so Alys had been admitted to the high-dependency ward of the paediatric unit at the University Hospital of Wales. As is often the case when an early diagnosis is missed, she had developed ketoacidosis, a potentially life-threatening complication marked by excessive ketones in the body. Her mother and I stood by helpless as our beautiful daughter lay wired up to insulin and saline drips for three days. Meanwhile, more accurate tests quickly confirmed that Alys did indeed have Type-1 Diabetes.

Type-1 Diabetes is a condition that can be managed – but it requires daily insulin injections of one kind or another and daily 'pin-prick' tests to monitor blood glucose levels and inform insulin dose adjustment. It can be a strain for parents and child, with constant vigilance and adherence to a strict routine required to keep blood-sugar levels as close to 'normal' or, at least, 'recommended' levels as possible. The consequences of failing to monitor glucose levels appropriately and getting the balance of insulin, exercise and diet wrong can be dire. If blood-sugar levels fall too low or too quickly, unpleasant *hypo*glycaemic symptoms will be experienced. Failure to treat these symptoms can lead to coma and, in extreme cases, even death. But if blood-sugar levels are allowed to stay too high, *hyper*glycaemic symptoms can make the sufferer very sick and at risk of ketoacidosis. What's more, the long-term consequences of running higher than normal blood-sugar levels (risks endured by all those with diabetes) are horrendous, with vascular damage leading to potential blindness, kidney problems, heart problems and problems with the hands and feet (which, in some cases, can lead to amputation). There's nothing quite like a family crisis and the onset of a dangerous medical condition to focus the mind on the fragility of human existence.

One effect of Alys's diabetes was to plunge her parents into a state of emotional confusion. Should we give things another try "for Alys's sake"? We had found being together insufferable, and the tension and arguments that followed made it obvious that any such attempt at reconciliation would be doomed to failure and would not be in anyone's interests. In truth neither of us really knew what we should do or what was for the best. We both experienced an extraordinary sense of guilt about Alys's condition. If it's in the genes it's in the genes, and there's very little you can do about either that or some of the environmental factors that seem to be implicated in the 'triggering' of the sufferer's 'genetic predisposition'. But you don't think like this when you're in the early throes of life with diabetes. If only we'd been more accepting of each other. If only we hadn't argued so much. Remember that time when we were shouting at each other and she walked into those brambles? If only we hadn't moved around from place to place. If only we'd created a more stable environment. If only we hadn't given Alys so much to cope with. If only . . . These are the kinds of thoughts you use to torture yourself. But things do get better, they do settle down, and it helps if you have a sensible and adaptable child who is determined to let nothing, not even diabetes and her parents' failings, get in the way of her enjoyment of life. That said, even now, years on, I sometimes watch her sleeping and, overwhelmed with love for her and, still harbouring some guilt, quietly cry my frustration away. It *is* such a shame for her. It *is* sad for her that she has been condemned to a life of needles and pins. It *is* a nuisance and a burden that she has to think ahead and plan carefully whenever she wants to do things that other children take for granted. "I've tried everything to get rid of it," she told me soon after her diagnosis, "but it just won't go away."

Both before and after her diagnosis, since the breakdown of my relationship with Alys's mother, Alys has lived with me most of the time. In fact, she lives with me through the week and roughly one weekend in four. She stays with her mother all other weekends. We split school holidays, and Alys also spends a week with both sets of grandparents every summer. My relationship with Alys's mother is now amicable enough. She has remarried and has another daughter. A couple of years ago my partner Chrissy moved in with me and Alys, and Chrissy and I have also married. While life is busy and not without the usual stresses and strains, generally it is good. We are alright.

At the time I first rediscovered Marillion, however, I was very emotionally raw. It had been just over a year since Alys had been diagnosed and her mother had finally left for good – and it had been a difficult year. I had tried to take everything in my stride, to keep things going, to present a calm exterior, to keep things as 'normal' for Alys as possible, but inside the ravages of divorce and diabetes had left their mark. I had met Chrissy, who brought freshness and love and healing with her. On the outside I looked fine. But Chrissy started to smooth out the tangles and the knots and get me feeling better on the inside. She also brought with her an infectious enthusiasm for the history of rock music – unusual for someone of her age – that brought me back to myself and helped to wake me up. I started listening to a lot more rock music again. And then . . . Marillion. It's true to say that I was not expecting to be moved by any band in the way that I was, and the experience of rediscovery was cathartic in the extreme. At the heart of that experience was one of the albums I mentioned above – 1994's *Brave*.

Brave is, for want of a better term, a concept album. That is to say, it has a story that unfolds as the album progresses and reaches a conclusion (or two) as the album ends. There are lyrical and musical themes which give the album a flow and cohesion. Initially, it came as a great surprise to me that Marillion had taken this route so soon after the self-consciously more commercial *Holidays in Eden*, but as I listened to the studio remaster of *Brave* for the first time I could hear that it had depth and guts, and I prepared to engage.

Brave is based around a news report that Steve Hogarth heard on GWR radio. The police in Bristol had found a young woman on the Severn Bridge who wouldn't or couldn't tell them anything about herself. In desperation they had launched an appeal to try to uncover the girl's identity. As the band started writing material for the album, a lyric contributed by sometime collaborator John Helmer reminded Hogarth of the radio broadcast and gave the band a theme. As the songs for *Brave* developed, it became a fictional account of what might have happened to someone to lead them to the point of jumping off the Severn Bridge in such a messed-up and distressed state.

The Helmer lyric was for a song called 'Runaway', and as I listened to *Brave* it was this track that was the first to really speak to me. "Did you cry when they dragged you home?" sings Steve Hogarth with astonishing sensitivity. "Were they deaf to the prayer behind your lies? Was a runaway girl all they chose to see?" It's a moving lyric that is beautifully sung, but it's Mark Kelly's keyboard runs and Steve Rothery's suitably anguished guitar work that really tug at the heart strings, reaching out and pulling you in as the words ask you to contemplate any number of imagined horrors – all the things that can happen when parenting goes wrong; all the things you'd want to protect your own daughter from – living rough, mixing with undesirables, engaging in harmful pursuits and dubious 'pleasures'. Throughout, the girl's unhappiness is palpable. You can almost touch it. You can almost smell the dank mattresses and unwashed clothes. You want to reach out to her and hold her and tell her that it will be alright. Before

I knew it I was a quivering wreck, tears streaming down my cheeks. It's a wonderful band performance that turns words and thoughts that are sad and dark into something beautiful.

There are hints of parental abuse in the lyric, one suggested reason why the girl has run away and can't go home, but it's not really sadness or anger at the thought of abuse that moves me most in this song – I just can't relate to parents wilfully hurting their children at all. What moves me most is simply the picture of an unhappy, lonely, isolated girl who feels unloved and unable to go home, and this picture makes me anxious. What if despite all our efforts as parents things go *this* wrong? What if you make mistakes so big that you lose the ability to communicate with your child? What if despite trying your very best you fail to keep your children safe? The weight of parental responsibility suddenly seemed enormous, and, listening to this song, I buckled under it. I became instantly and acutely aware of some of my own faults and limitations; of the need to try hard, and then to try harder and to take nothing for granted; of the need to love my daughter, to love her unconditionally, and to keep on loving her, whatever life brings. I don't mind admitting that it was months before I could listen to this song without tears welling up in my eyes.

Brave is a dense and multi-faceted album that has many other striking moments. There is a powerful reminder, for example, that nothing is as 'Hard as Love' (a track in which the band cut loose and rock out, with Mark Kelly mustering a passable Jon Lord impression during a notable but brief 'Purple passage'). And there's a moving track towards the end of the album called 'The Last of You', in which the angry child herself finally finds the strength to cut loose and rages at a seemingly repentant parent. 'The Last of You' itself segues out of 'The Great Escape', a track which finds the young girl standing on the bridge contemplating "the dignified walk away". "They shower you with flowers when they bury you," sings Hogarth . . . when it's too late, that is – when you have no further need for kindness or love or fragrance. It is a chilling line.

While all of this sounds extremely grim, it's worth noting that *Brave* is an album with two endings. Side Four of the original vinyl album was produced with a double groove. One groove ends with an optimistic track called 'Made Again', the opening guitar part for which was written by Steve Rothery for the birth of his own daughter. I like to think that this ending opens the possibility that at the point of no return, and against all the odds, the girl on the bridge somehow finds the strength and resolve she needs to overcome her pain and turn back. The second groove, however, features an alternative version of 'The Great Escape' and seven minutes of lapping water sounds, suggesting that the troubled girl has jumped and chosen to end her ordeal tragically. Which ending you experience is an entirely random matter, depending on which groove the needle picks up when it first hits the record.

As I sat writing about *Brave* and 'Runaway', a John Mayer track from his *Heavier Things* album came on the radio. It's called 'Daughters'. It urges parents to be good to their daughters as their upbringing makes a difference to the kind of lovers and mothers they later become. Somehow it seemed very appropriate.

Hope for the future

As I started working my way chronologically through all the albums I'd missed, it didn't take me long to realise that *Brave* wasn't the only album in the back catalogue worthy of attention. In fact, every one of these albums turned out to have something to offer, each having its own sound and identity, and each taking a different creative turn.

Perhaps the strongest of the 1990s albums was 1995's *Afraid of Sunlight*. Commenting on its predecessor, Steve Hogarth noted in the sleeve notes to the EMI *Brave* remaster that: "*Brave* is all about the spiritual aspect of life dominated by the non-spiritual,"[4] and in a sense *Afraid of Sunlight* continues the theme. This time, however, with *Brave* having exhausted both the band's emotional resources and the patience of their record company, they settled on a way of expressing the theme that was somewhat closer to home. As Hogarth explains:

> Both EMI and Marillion were still reeling from the relative commercial disappointment of the *Brave* album. We thought it was a masterpiece. We just couldn't understand how the world hadn't noticed . . . The *Brave* album and the tour that followed it had made mincemeat of my psyche and I was pretty much a lost soul. Racked by self-doubt and emotional turmoil, I was feeling my life coming unstitched before my eyes. Little wonder then that [*Afraid of Sunlight*] was to repeatedly examine show-business and the damage done. We did this through the eyes of the boxer, the footballer, the rock 'n' roller and the speed-king. All had famously self-destructed. You should be able to guess their names . . . I think it's the best record we've made.[5]

Best record or not, it turned out to be their last for EMI, as the band took the independent route and signed up for a run of albums with Castle Records. Their first studio album for Castle, *This Strange Engine* (1997), was, creatively speaking, a pivotal release that both heavily referenced their past *and* pointed in new and exciting directions for the future. At the heart of the album is a wonderful track called 'Estonia' that was inspired by Steve Hogarth's chance meeting with the only British survivor of the Estonia Ferry disaster. "This is one of our most powerful songs," guitarist Steve Rothery told the The Web UK Magazine,[6] and for sure it deals in raw emotion. But it also deals with the limits of human knowledge, and the meaning we find in our immediate relationships with those we love. Some might see it as the ultimate 'funeral track'; a heartfelt meditation that offers words of wisdom and comfort for anyone mourning the passing of a loved one:

No one leaves you when they live in your heart and mind

People are kept alive in the memories and conversations of those they have known and influenced, and in this way they stay with us even when they are not around anymore. I sometimes catch a glimpse of my grandfather in myself . . . a kind of (positive) shadowy presence in some of my thoughts and deeds . . . me but not me . . . and it makes me realise that in a sense he is still living . . . in me . . . through me . . . and through the lives and memories of many of the people that he touched. As Steve Hogarth said of 'Estonia': "I believe that people live on in the hearts of those who cared about them."[7]

But Marillion are not all heaviness and shade on this album. *This Strange Engine* introduced a welcome range and variety into their songwriting, with weightier numbers like 'Estonia' and the lengthy, autobiographical title track nestling comfortably alongside joyful tracks like the delightful mock-Salsa (I kid you not) of 'Hope for the Future', and the breezy fan tribute '80 Days', with Rothery's acoustic guitar work on both the latter track and album opener 'Man of a Thousand Faces' betraying a strong Crowded House influence. The album also features the upbeat and punchy 'Accidental Man', with its tip of the hat to 1980s indie, and an exquisite keys and vocals only version of the compelling 'Memory of Water'. It is an album full of possibilities. In range and potential, at least, and as a vehicle for showcasing the band in all its guises, *This Strange Engine* is to the Marillion back catalogue what, say, *A Night at the Opera* is to Queen's. There is something for everyone.

The next album, *Radiation* (1998), found the band in an even more overtly experimental mood. From the quirky comedy of opener 'Costa Del Slough', through the guitar-driven 'Under the Sun', the Beatles pastiche that is 'Three Minute Boy', the heart-rending sadness of 'Now She'll Never Know', the brooding slow blues of 'Born To Run', and the terrifying goth-rock of 'Cathedral Wall', this is an album full of surprises. As bass player Pete Trewavas has explained: "What we tried to do with this album was to change people's preconceptions of us and indeed our own ideas of what we were and what we could and should do musically."[8] The following year found their sound changing again with 1999's *marillion.com*. Trewavas explains: "If the idea for *Radiation* was to be different then the thinking behind *Dotcom* was to define the changes we wanted to bring to our sound: being a little more musical yet still keeping our new found energy."[9]

If anything, *marillion.com* seems to have an overabundance of energy, with the band sounding so creative that at times their ideas are in danger of tripping over each other. Once again variety and experimentation are at the core of the album, with a lighter, brighter production (a real team effort) making this one of the most accessible of all Marillion albums. Pick of the tracks for me are: 'Rich', in which Marillion meet the Doors and drag 1960s psychedelia into the late 1990s; the similarly upbeat 'Deserve', which brings to mind The Psychedelic Furs and features some great saxophone playing from Ben Castle (son of Roy); the two slower tracks 'Go!' and 'Enlightened', both of which invoke cool and serene 'memories of water'; and last, but not least, the magnificent but achingly sad 'trip hop' groove that is 'House', perhaps the most surprising track Marillion had recorded since the wonderful weirdness of *Afraid of Sunlight*'s 'Cannibal Surf Babe'.

The scope and range of these albums, and the band's desire and willingness to explore different musical styles, would have been unimaginable for Marillion as they were in the 1980s. They were now so far removed from both the progressive rock stereotype and the 'chart band' of 1985 that the hinderance of the 1980s baggage would have been laughable had it not created such blind prejudice and misconception. For my own part, I was staggered at what I was hearing, and a little bit cross with myself for having missed all this great music over the years, and all the gigs and friendships that would certainly have followed.

Waves and numbers

And that was before I'd even heard *Anoraknophobia*! If *Radiation* and *marillion.com* had a common fault, it was that for all the excitement and variety they brought to the band's music, they lacked coherence as albums. That was addressed on *Anoraknophobia*, which in many ways can be seen as the culmination and logical outcome of the experimentation and change of the Castle years. *Anoraknophobia* maintains the energy and element of surprise, but presents a tight, supremely confident band firing on all cylinders, and a consistency of sound and feel from start to finish. It's no coincidence that it was generally well received both by fans and parts of the music press. Biographer Jon Collins describes *Anoraknophobia* as: "a uniquely-funded, history-making, foot-tapping, gut-wrenching, heart-breaking, soul-shaking, brain-engaging, funk-tastic, soaring, grooving, glorious great beastie of an album."[10] But don't just take his word for it (or mine for that matter). A Channel 4 teletext review (April 2001) gave *Anoraknophobia* eight out of ten, citing Doves, U2, Radiohead, Massive Attack and The La's as unlikely and unexpected reference points and urging its readers to "embrace the anorak", while heavy metal magazine *Kerrang!* found the material sufficiently palatable to award it four stars out of five in May of the same year. Perhaps the most striking review, however, was by Robert Adams of *Rock Sound*, who, in giving the album five stars out of five, wrote:

> I haven't listened to Marillion since I was a kid in the mid 80s. After listening to *Anoraknophobia* I had to check the sleeve to make sure that this was the same band I remember from my spotty youth . . . Leave your preconceptions of the band at the door and buy this album now, it's that good. Play 'Quartz' to your friends and rake in loads of cash betting them they won't recognise who it is. It sounds like Massive Attack, full of rolling, funky bass lines and subtle guitar touches. The biggest thing holding Marillion back is the name and all the baggage it carries. Marillion are relevant in 2001. I am on the floor having been felled by an enormous feather. A phoenix-like rebirth.[11]

In the passages above, references to unexpected influences abound, and yet, let us be absolutely clear, even when the band have opened themselves and their music up to new influences, even where they've taken detours and explored new avenues, there is something unmistakably *Marillion* that runs through their music. Influences are reference points, nothing more, and the band's unique talent is their ability to blend the skills, influences and characters of all five members in a distinctive and often powerful way. There are no throwaway tracks or throwaway moments on recent Marillion albums. The music always means something. Even the lightest, poppiest moments have strength and depth and come from somewhere real. Take 'Map of the World' for example, from the aforementioned *Anoraknophobia*, a melody-rich track which was fine-tuned with the help of Nick van Eade of Cutting Crew fame.

'Map of the World' is an inspiring tale of liberation, a wonderful fillip for anyone who feels shiny and smart on the outside but lonely on the inside, anyone in a tedious nine-to-five office job, or indeed anyone who is just tired of the daily drudgery and feels that life is passing them by. "Strange how much pain you can hide away beneath a well-cut suit," sings Hogarth, and his words hit home (not that my suits are particularly "well-cut"). We rush around with a "buy, buy, buy" mentality, trying to keep going, trying to have a good time, trying to keep the truth hidden from ourselves, forgetting our dreams, "runnin' on empty" and "sleepwalking through the danger signs." The girl in the song sees all this, and plans and saves and waits until at last she can get away from it all. And this is her day, "this is day she walks", this is the day she leaves the lie behind and sets off to see the world:

> She'll empty the sand from her shoes
> In paradise
> Sail out across the bay
> She'll dance under an island sky
> Until the break of day

Is it a pop song? It's certainly the most 'poppy' track on the album, but "it's too dark to be a pop song," (as Steve Hogarth told the audience at the 2009 Marillion Weekend). At any rate, it's predicated on a strong Rothery riff, it's razor-sharp around the edges, and during the instrumental section the band drive it hard and fast into clear 'rock' territory. Whatever you call it, it's an outstanding track on an album full of outstanding tracks.

Like its predecessors, *Anoraknophobia* offers songs that draw on a range of influences and musical traditions: there's the catchy rock of 'Between You and Me' (majestically introduced by Mark Kelly's piano); the laid back and bluesy 'Fruit of the Wild Rose'; the funky, bass-driven and at times savage 'Quartz'; the hard rock circus freakery of 'Separated

Out'; and the bonkers trip that is 'If My Heart Were a Ball it Would Roll Uphill'. There are two songs, however, that deserve a special mention for their potential to engage and affect the listener.

The first of these is 'When I Meet God'. The lyric initially finds Hogarth in despairing mood, unable to cope with the sentience and conceptual sophistication that have left him reflecting bleakly on a broken life and a broken world. He has tried all the usual consolations – alcohol, sex, companionship – but they have failed to alleviate the hurt and sense of helplessness he is feeling. And what about the gods? Why did they make us like this? Why do they let things go so wrong? Why do they allow so much suffering? What on earth are they playing at? "What kind of mother leaves her child in the traffic?" sings Hogarth. It gets me every time. And yet, from the depths of despair, a solution does slowly emerge. The very sentience and conceptual sophistication that deliver such crushing emotional lows also enable us to find meaning and beauty and joy in our world, and to appreciate and drink in the magic of life around us, the magic of waves and numbers: "such beautiful numbers/And oh, such waves." Producer Dave Meegan contributed to the emotional bite of the song by adding news clips of events involving atrocities committed against children, but Meegan is lavish in his praise for the band:

> The band does a great job musically behind it again, but you can't avoid
> the words, and I think that's when Marillion really works, when there's
> that marriage between the words and the music.[12]

'When I Meet God' is, indeed, a great example of words and music working together to create an artistic whole that is greater than the sum of its parts.

But even 'When I Meet God' is arguably trumped by what, for many, remains the jewel in *Anoraknophobia*'s crown: 'This is the 21st Century'. The lyric, one of Hogarth's best, presents dual and duelling threads that weave in and out of each other before eventually coming together like the entwined bodies of the song's characters. The first thread deals with the singer's ruminations on the cold logic of philosophers and other intellectuals who have attempted through their theoretical or scientific endeavours to 'demystify' the Universe. The second thread provides a narrative account of his journey to visit a lover and the mixed-up confusion and sadness at the state of the world that he expresses to her when he gets there. It takes the love and the wisdom of a good woman to resolve both the tension in the lyric and the conflict in the head of its creator:

> *This is the 21ˢᵗ Century*
> *Can't you get it through your head*
> *This ain't the way it was meant to be*
> *Magic isn't dead*
> *Come to bed*
> *Come to bed*
> *And rest your heavy head my love*

"Would you want to have kids growing up into what's left of this?" The singer asks his lover, partly calmed by her but still troubled.

> *She shook her head*
> *She said "Can't you see*
> *The world is you*
> *The world is me"*

My wife, Chrissy, a literary type, regards this song as one of Marillion's very best. When I asked her why she likes it so much, she said: "It's genuinely romantic, and it's not easy to write something that's original and genuinely romantic these days." There's far more than romance here, though. In an interview with *The Web UK Magazine*, Dave Meegan refers to the "great darkness" in the song,[13] and one might initially think that Hogarth is simply finding Morrison-esque consolation in physical love. But Hogarth as a writer is consistently more positive and more spiritual than this. The song's conclusion – that we are all as much a part of the world, and what it is, and what it might become, as anyone or anything else – is both moving and inspiring, and the suggestion that the answer to the singer's troubles lies in a very pure form of love is also a powerful message. This is far more than 'finding consolation in love' – this is love as a means of building bridges . . . love as a way of radiating out and touching others . . . love as eternal optimism, life's great gift and great redeeming feature, a sign of what humans can and should achieve, a sign of what humans can and should *be*. I am reminded of a discussion I took part in many years ago with my punk friend Marv. One of our discussants noted that while anarchy was the only political ideology that gave us hope of being truly happy, it was also the most impractical of political theories and the most unlikely to be realised. "But it happens in my bedroom," said Marv. It was a typical Marv witticism but I thought it insightful and profound in its own way. 'O'r fesen, derwen a dyf', as the Welsh saying goes – from an acorn an oak tree grows. 'This is the 21ˢᵗ Century' is a trippy and modern sounding track. Once again the words and music work in perfect harmony. The band produce a suitably brooding soundscape that is subtle and sympathetic, aggressive and mechanistic by turns. And despite the chink of light offered by the closing lyric, the harsh, extended guitar-driven outtro leaves one in no doubt that retaining one's optimism and one's sense of what is possible will often be difficult in the face of pressures that seem to want to close life down.

🎱 A handful of Marbles 🎱

And so, by the time the pre-order deluxe edition of *Marbles* landed on my doorstep in April 2004, I already had a head full of songs by a band who had made music come alive for me in a way that hadn't happened for a very long time. *Marbles* itself was a double album, and came with the discs embedded in a beautifully presented 128 page hardback book and slipcase. Extensive photography from Carl Glover supported and embellished the lyrics, providing a visual dimension to an extraordinary aural and conceptual work.

With Dave Meegan back in the producer's chair, as he had been for *Brave*, *Afraid of Sunlight* and *Anoraknophobia*, the band created an album to rival their finest. Meegan has spoken at length about his own efforts to capitalise on the creative burst that put Steve Hogarth and his lyrics right at the heart of *Marbles*. As a result, he says, the band produced "a very male album" dealing with themes and situations that all men "either . . . had experienced or will experience."[14] "Men nowadays do have hearts and are quite able to admit it," says Meegan, "and Hogarth is one of the first to fly the flag."[15]

But despite the central place given to Hogarth's words and vocal performance, *Marbles* is truly a band effort, something Meegan recognises when describing guitarist Steve Rothery's distinctive contributions to the songs. "If Steve's going instinctively," he says, "he's enhancing what h is singing brilliantly – way better and like no one else, and that's the magic of the band anyway. It's when that happens."[16]

Marbles is indeed full of magic. It does not, perhaps, hold the surprises of *Anoraknophobia*, and, if anything, is a more introspective album, but it's crammed with tracks of ambitious composition and stark beauty. And once again the band manage to touch the odd nerve, making the personal universal with unerring ease, and squeezing emotion out of words and notes that in isolation, or in the hands of lesser bands, might look and sound so ordinary. There's clearly a strong degree of subjectivity in the way we respond to music, but for those who remain unaware of *Marbles*, let me elaborate a little on the songs that mean most to me.

'The Invisible Man'

From the opening line of *Marbles* ("The world's gone mad/And I have lost touch"), it's clear that Marillion mean business. 'The Invisible Man' is a weighty, emotionally wrought affair that deals with dislocation, empathy, impotence and frustration. It has an intense lyric, "the most intense thing I have ever written,"[17] says Steve Hogarth, that works at both a general and specific level.

The song starts with a man who is losing his bearings, who feels lost, out of place, out of time. He moves around seeking contact and validation, "Hovering/Witnessing/Sheltering in doorways of Venice, Vienna, Budapest, Krakow and Amsterdam", but moving on before he can form relationships or engage in any meaningful way with those he observes or meets. As this experience begins to erode his very sense of self, he comes to feel utterly detached from the world and powerless to act on it. "My body has gone/But my eyes remain," sings Hogarth, "I have become the invisible man."

Commenting on this 'symbolic invisibility', Dave Meegan alludes to the bandage-wearing 'invisible man' of the H.G.Wells novel and later screen and television adaptations – a man who, after a 'scientific' proce-dure goes wrong, must wear bandages to be seen as he is left invisible underneath. In the Marillion song, however, when the bandages come off "it's actually the inside of Steve and this is what he feels and experiences . . . and you go 'Oh my God! This isn't easy to listen to, and this is a bit like my life'."[18] Those familiar with the *Marbles on the Road* DVD[19] will have noted the 'blue wash' effect that, intentionally or otherwise, enhances the sense of detachment and dislocation. Musically, the band draw on all their experience to make the listener feel the 'tightness' of the singer, the tautness of his emotions, his brittleness and fragility . . . like a guitar string wound almost to the point at which it snaps.

With Hogarth's "invisible pulse silently thumping," the beat quickens, and he is moving again, wandering dangerously across busy roads, shouting his name in public places, following those he wants to help. The lyrics invoke feelings of helplessness and frustration and invite us to import our own memories and experiences. Ian Mosley's drums drive the band on as the tension builds and builds. The singer has become a ghost – tortured and haunted, desperate for release but now unable to throw off the cloak of invisibility. As the drama searches for a climax, the singer is defiant: "I will scream again: 'I am perfectly sane, I am perfectly sane'" but for now, at least, he remains the invisible man.

Hogarth, one might speculate, is speaking from within an anxiety-ridden state of being with which he is familiar, with both life on the road and modern technology contributing to the sense of invisibility and impotence that he describes. As he explained in an interview for the fan club magazine:

> One of the most remarkable aspects of modern living is that we're so conscious of other people's pain. We can turn on the television, and we can witness some massive injustice that's going on in some other part of the world . . . if someone gets murdered in Australia, we probably find out about it! And that's . . . an awful lot for us to deal with. If somebody starves to death in Ethiopia we find out about it, and we feel somehow vaguely guilty, that it's slightly our fault or that we should be doing something. And we're right, we should be doing something! But on the other hand, it's quite peculiar that that should be preying on our minds because we're just not wired up to have to cope with those things. In that sense . . . we are each and every one of us 'invisible men' because we witness things that we can't change, and we feel things that under normal, natural circumstances we would never have to feel . . . And in many ways, for me, that whole thing is multiplied up by a factor of hundreds, because I travel so much and I meet so many people . . . 'The Invisible Man' is sort of about that. It's about how conscious I've become of other people's lives, to the point where I almost feel like I'm everywhere at once, witnessing everything at once without being able to do anything about it. That's about as near as I can go to . . . beginning to scratch at the surface of what 'The Invisible Man' is about.[20]

At the general level, then, 'The Invisible Man' is about watching things happen, watching the world change for the worse but being powerless to do anything about it. At a more concrete and specific level it's about watching bad things happening in the life of another person (or persons) but being unable to intervene and help. The invisible man is the man who sees and feels all the pain around him but who can do nothing to put a stop to it. At a more introspective level again, it's a song about losing one's sense of self, or rather the struggle to keep oneself together and retain one's sense of self in the face of this growing feeling of impotence, detachment and insignificance.

I imagine that anyone choosing to scratch away at the surface of the song will find other, more personal ways of relating to it. For my own part 'The Invisible Man' reminds me of some of the feelings I tried to cope with as a teenager – that feeling that that no one is taking any notice of you, that nothing you do seems to matter or make a difference to anyone, that other people see you as worthless. This is not just a feeling of being unable to help, but a feeling of being rejected, for whatever reason, by those you want to help – and a feeling that an impenetrable wall has sprung up between you and other people. Hence the retreat into one's mind and the sense of the fading away or dissipation of one's physical self; hence the feeling of being an outsider; and hence the feeling that one might as well be invisible for all the good one is doing:

> *Talk to me*
> *Acknowledge me*
> *Confide in me*
> *Confess to me*
> *Or leave me be*

'Fantastic Place' and 'Don't Hurt Yourself'

'Fantastic Place' and 'Don't Hurt Yourself' are "medicines for the soul". "They're like medicines for my own soul," says Steve Hogarth, "but I knew when I was writing them they could be medicines for everybody."[21]

On the full two-disc version of *Marbles*, 'Fantastic Place' and 'Don't Hurt Yourself' are on separate discs, spreading the medicine across the album. On the one-disc retail version, however, they sit together right at the heart of the album, flanked by the vignettes that are 'Marbles II' and 'Marbles III'.

'Don't Hurt Yourself' is a superior slice of high-quality melodic rock. Although it entered the UK singles chart top 20, this was largely due to the initial purchases of established fans, and the song quickly fell back out of the charts. A bit of mainstream radio airplay, though, and I've no doubt that this song could have brought Marillion a whole new audience. Musically, the highlight is some exquisite guitar work from Steve Rothery, here at his sweetest and most soulful. Lyrically, it's a track that encourages us to put our troubles and preoccupations into perspective, recognising that we do not have to be constrained by the past or trapped by our pain. All things come into being and pass away. It's always possible to put the past behind us and move on: "Each day's an open door."

'Fantastic Place' has slowly emerged as one of the most highly regarded tracks from the *Marbles* album and is clearly a track that provides soul food for an awful lot of people. Personally I think it's one of the most perfect songs ever written. While the first two verses suggest a relationship gone bad, from the first chorus on it provides a profound sense of hope and escape. Hogarth sings the first two verses like a broken man . . . and the rest of the song as though his life depends on it.

> *Take me to the fantastic place*
> *Keep the rest of my life away. . .*
>
> *Take me to the island. . .*
> *The moment outside of real life*

The lyrics suggest that Hogarth has found his fantastic place, and it's a place (physical or metaphorical) he shares with someone who sets his soul dancing, allows him to 'leave himself' and, for a while at least, makes him happy. From broken man to fulfilment in love in the space of a few short verses . . . but it's a love that seems so perfect and intense that it's not without risk:

> *Take me to the island*
> *I'll tell you all I never told you*
> *The boy I never showed you*
> *More than I gave in my life*
> *Take me by the hand*
> *You'll either kill me or you'll save me*
> *Take me to the island*
> *Show me what might be real life*

The song builds and builds to a breathtaking Steve Rothery 'cliff-top' solo. Producer Dave Meegan wanted to get "an emotional solo not a musical solo" from Rothery, and boy did he succeed. I've been in the front row when they've performed this live and seen Steve Hogarth look utterly and completely emotionally drained at its conclusion – as though he's not only put everything into the song but, temporarily at least, left himself there.*

According to Hogarth: "'Fantastic Place' is about escaping your everyday life," whether that means escaping to "a place in your mind . . . a specific place . . . or . . . a specific person."[22] It's this indeterminacy that gives the song an openness that allows each and every listener to relate to it in his or her own way. Islands are mountain tops. Medicine for the soul, indeed.

'Neverland'

Just when you're expecting *Marbles* to start winding down and play itself out, along comes 'Neverland', the lengthy album closer that lifts us above the dull routine of everyday life and helps us find joy in the apparently mundane. You look up from the kitchen sink, tired, weighed down, and there, in front of you, is the sunset. It's beautiful, your partner sees it too, you look at each other, and you smile.

An opening, swirling whoosh gives way to a grand Kelly piano intro that instantly puts this track on a plateau. The piano playing yields to some rich synth chords over which Hogarth, fragile and wracked with self-doubt, starts to sing:

> *When the darkness takes me over*
> *Face down, emptier than zero*
> *Invisible you come to me*
> *. . . quietly*

The love and generosity of his partner soothes him:

> *Stay beside me*
> *Whisper to me "Here I am"*
> *And the loneliness fades*

---

* Check out Disc One of the *Marbles on the Road* DVD (Racket Records, 2004) at 49:18

Kelly's gentle piano returns, and then . . . bang . . . the whole band crash in, as Hogarth, still melancholic in delivery, acknowledges his debt to his partner and the effect her love has had on his life:

> *Some people think I'm something*
> *Well you gave me that, I know*
> *But I always feel like nothing*
> *When I'm in the dark alone*
>
> *You provide the soul, the spark that*
> *Drives me on*
> *Makes me something more than*
> *Flesh and bone*
>
> *At times like these*
> *Any fool can see*
> *Any fool can see*
> *Your love inside me*

From there, 'Neverland' builds in typical Marillion fashion with Rothery's precision soloing developing the musical theme and raising the stakes a notch or two. A quieter acoustically picked solo at around 4:25 yields again to the power of the full band, spurring Rothery on to some searing lead work that reaches for the stars, or the fairy twinkles at least. Producer Dave Meegan is gushing in his praise:

> It's so emotional, you know? It's just the notes but . . . only guitar legends can do that really. Usually it's left for a singer to hit those emotions. It's very hard for a pure musical thing to do it but if Rothery wants to do it, he can go straight for the heart just as easy as Hogarth can.[23]

But it's not all about the singer and the guitar player. Collectively the band create a sense of flight, a sense of ethereal otherness that helps us find magic in the simple things we usually take for granted.

Experienced live with strobe-lighting effects and ticker tape it's almost impossible not to get completely lost in 'Neverland'. Looking around you see people singing at the tops of their voices, doing their best to hit and feel every note. You see others simply standing awed in silent contemplation, and you see couples embracing, basking and rocking gently in the glow and flow of the music. For most bands this would be their creative peak. For Marillion it's just one outstanding moment among many.

🎵 *Something else* 🎵

If the reader will indulge me for just a few moments longer, there is one other song I'd like to mention. Although a studio version did not appear until 2007's *Somewhere Else*, 'Faith' was written before *Marbles* was recorded and in fact was played by the band at the Marillion Weekend in both 2003 and 2005. "This song is about something deeper than knowledge," said Steve Hogarth on stage in Minehead in 2005.

"Beer!" shouted some joker at the front.

"Drugs!" shouted another.

But, joking aside, it's a beautiful track that deserves a wider audience. "Feel inside the atoms where the science breaks down," sings Hogarth, and I am instantly reminded of some remarks of the great philosopher Ludwig Wittgenstein. At proposition 6.52 in his *Tractatus Logico-Philosophicus* (first published in English in 1922), Wittgenstein says:

> We feel that even when all possible scientific questions have been answered, the problems of life remain completely untouched.[24]

These remarks say something about the nature of human life and the nature of human happiness. For Wittgenstein, at the time he wrote the *Tractatus*, they also said something about the nature of language and logic. The view of language he held led him to conclude that we can only speak meaningfully of factual and scientific matters, and cannot speak meaningfully of "mystical" or "transcendental" or "higher" matters. Such things "*make themselves manifest*" he says in proposition 6.522, but "cannot be put into words"[25]

While this uncompromising position does help one to appreciate the difficulty of adequately capturing matters of value with words, Wittgenstein's views did change. His later views, most famously expounded in his posthumous work *Philosophical Investigations* (1953), encourage us to explore the "grammar" of our language carefully as a means of dissolving philosophical confusion, but they also provide a technique (let's call it 'conceptual elucidation') for exploring the ways people naturally speak about matters of value. At times, Hogarth's own insight and 'conceptual elucidations' scale extraordinary heights. There are philosophers who might well quiz him on the front-end epistemology of 'Faith', but personally I'd rather focus on the science breaking down, and Hogarth's conclusion that "if you don't believe in love, you'd have to make it up". Wittgenstein himself might well have reached a similar conclusion. Reflecting on his relationship with a loved one, he wrote: "*Love*, that is the pearl of great price that one holds to one's heart, that one would exchange for *nothing*, that one prizes above all else. In fact, it shows – if one has it – what great value *is*."[26]

Sheltering in doorways in Venice ... and Amsterdam

It's 3.30am. The taxi is late. I phone the company. They left us off the schedule, but they send someone straight away and get us to the airport just in time . . . or so we think. The plane is delayed by 50 minutes . . . we are told. But we board more quickly than this. We will miss our connection to Venice . . . we are told . . . but the pilot seems to make up just enough time to make the transfer do-able – if we run and if our luggage makes it. We are pointed in the right direction and we run. A KLM girl gives us a lift part of the way on a buggy. She saves us five minutes. We run . . . fast . . . and follow her directions. "Gate closing" says the screen. "Passengers for KLM flight 1653 go to Gate B25 immediately," says an announcement in a strong Dutch accent. We keep running. Down the stairs. We get there. KLM staff smile and hurry us along. "Our luggage?" I ask. "The computer says it's OK," smiles the desk attendant. We make it and collapse into our seats. We have escaped. Our adventure has begun.

We enjoy the flight and the KLM sandwiches. We reach Marco Polo. We follow the directions I have printed from a website. Out of the exit, along the walkway, seven minutes to the water taxis and the Alilaguna. We buy tickets and wait . . . and wait. The boat arrives. The 'captain' and his mate go off for coffee. They come back when they feel like, just like it says they will on my print-out. Later than scheduled we set off for Venice . . . only four of us on the boat, all bound for Rialto. We are lucky – the boat for the Piazzale Roma was overflowing. I sit quietly, holding Chrissy's hand and watching the joy on her face as we approach this miraculous city whose very existence challenges the imagination. We disembark and drag our heavy cases over the famous bridge. Busy shops, tourist tat, masks and people. We smell mulled wine and Lush soap and then the fish from the Pescheria. Our map lacks detail so we just keep walking, exploring the narrow streets and signs and bridges – so strange but so charming. We feel the history and magic of Venice in every nook and cranny. Finally we find our hotel – at last a chance to rest and gather ourselves.

We take coffee on the terrace, gaping at the Grand Canal in disbelief as it laps against the wooden beams around us. It's magnificent. We head back to Rialto with a better map given to us by the hotel concierge. We sample one of the many 'tourist' menus – clams and squid and veal. We sit in the glow of the table heater, just along from the famous bridge, still on the banks of the famous canal. Vaparetti and Gondolas. Waiters falling over themselves to please us. We've stepped into another world. In fact we've stepped into another two other worlds: the Venice that was, hints everywhere of past lives and former glories – and the Venice that is, the Venice of the tourist . . . of Chrissy and me and thousands of others who come for just a few days and wish to claim her as their own. We sense that there are more than two worlds and we hope we will see something of the hidden Venice . . . real lives not far away but off the beaten track. We go back to our hotel – once the residence of the artist Giacomo Favretto – to read maps and books and get some sleep.

We wake up early . . . but an hour later than expected. I forgot to change the time on my phone alarm. Breakfast is wonderful – hot scrambled eggs and ham and sausages, fresh pears and prunes and fruit juice and croissants and coffee and more coffee. The weather is beautiful; we can't believe our luck. We eat and drink our fill and walk to Ferrovia . . . more narrow lanes and small bridges over small canals. Everything looks so special and so lived-in. We pass small baker's shops with cakes too delicious for words. If only I wasn't so full of breakfast! At Ferrovia we buy travel cards for the Vaparetti and hop on the No.1 which follows the Grand Canal all the way to San Marco. San Marco is busy but magnificent. We climb the bell tower . . . well, we want to . . . but they make us take the lift and charge us heavily for the privilege. The views are stunning. We take photos and look across the Venetian lagoon. We see the road and train lines which bind Venice to mainland Italy. It somehow seems a shame. We leave the tower and walk around the Piazza. We find cappuccino 'al banco' for only €1,50 and gelato for only €2 for 2 scoops and 2 flavours each: melon, banana, rum and raisin, tiramisu. We look for Harry's Bar – where Hemingway drank – but can't find it . . . so we just walk . . . past the Bridge of Sighs and out along the Riva degli Schiavoni. We find the Hotel Gabrielli Sandwirth – the exterior used in the classic film *Don't Look Now*. We keep walking, further and further from the other tourists. It's quieter and beautiful. Hotels and churches shimmer behind us as sunlight glistens on the water and brings everything alive. We stumble into Viale Giuseppe Garibaldi, and marvel at the sign telling people not to throw their pet tortoises and fish into the pool around his statue. We explore the Giardini Pubblici and, tiring now, decide to catch a Vaparetto back to San Marco. It's almost 4pm. We find a café-cum-restaurant on the Piazza San Marco which is showing the Wales-Italy rugby international live from Rome. We eat pizza and watch the game. I drink wine, and need it as Wales toil to a laborious and hard-fought victory. We hear North Walian accents at the back of the restaurant, and a little Cymraeg. An Italian family – father and son – watch the game too, and an Italian gentleman wanders in from the bar every now and then to express his amazement that the Italians are still in with a chance of winning. What a place to watch your rugby!

We window-shop as we stroll back to Rialto and make our way home for more coffee on the hotel terrace. Suitably rested, within half an hour we are out and about again. We walk to the Pescheria, now cleared and hosed down, and pick up a Vaparetto to see the Grand Canal by night. We pass countless palaces, lit up to show another side of their beauty. We ride on to the Lido – it's getting cold but we are unable to resist the charms of the night time water. Then back to Ponte di Rialto, which shows itself defiant and stoical by night: no tourists, no business, just an old bridge, a very old bridge, keeping its tales to itself and absorbing history like the old Welsh hills. We follow the increasingly familiar route back to our hotel and we sleep. I am already looking forward to breakfast.

The next day is Sunday and again it is beautiful. Our breakfast room overlooks the Grand Canal, just opposite the magnificent presence and eastern arches of the Ca' d'Oro (the 'House of Gold'). It's not yet 8am, but the sun is already beating down on the city, and we stand awhile watching the Canal from above, listening quietly to its early morning noises. We walk to the Piazzale Roma, taking a new route and finding little shops and newsagents which appear to be used more by Venetians than tourists. We catch a Vaparetto to Murano. On route we pass St Michael's Island – Venice's cemetery. Old ladies get off to visit their dead. The rest of us, cameras in hand, carry on to Murano itself, where we watch a glass-blowing exhibition and throw some coins in a bowl for the glass master. We wander around and find a wonderful church. The Virgin Mary watches over us with child and rosary in hand, as I photograph Christ on his cross, intrigued by the human skull at his feet. Death and water . . . death and water . . . Despite the ostentatious facades, Venice and her islands know about the fragility of life and the dark power of death to ravage and tear asunder. There are small acknowledgements of this everywhere in Venice's art and architecture.

We ride the No. 42 back to San Marco. This time we do find Harry's Bar. It's small and busy and very expensive. It seems to have no nice views and, as far as we can see, it is not a place of any particular inspiration. It seems to be famous for being famous; famous just because Hemingway drank there. We decide it's not for us and go back to our Piazza café – the Aurora – for more cappuccino 'al banco' and more ice cream. We window shop some more. Chrissy likes the masks. Sometimes it's easy to tell the tourist tat from the craftsmanship – sometimes it's not.

Back at the hotel we sit on the terrace again reading and writing. It's 6.15 in the evening and the church bells are still ringing out. Along with the lapping water, and the buzz of the weekend tourists, these have formed part of the soundtrack of our day. But it's quieter now, save the bells and the occasional Vaparetto, and it's time for food. We go to a small Trattoria – the Al Nono Risorto – that we spotted near our hotel earlier that day. The food is excellent, the service good and friendly, and the atmosphere just a little bohemian. A colourful peace flag ('Pace') hangs to the left of the bar. It's our kind of place. Happy and relaxed, we go back to the hotel where we sizzle like Julie Christie. Well, Chrissy sizzles like Julie Christie. I'm mainly grateful . . . like Donald Sutherland.

Monday is another beautiful morning. We set off early for the San Stae Vaparetto stop and once again pick up the bus for San Marco. On the way we photograph the Palazzo Grimandi – scene of the grizzly climax of *Don't Look Now*. ("At least he had that night with Julie Christie," I think to myself, entirely inappropriately.) We reach San Marco before the Basilica opens and so go in search of the Campo San Moisè and the Bauer Grimwald – the hotel where the aforementioned sex scene was filmed. We find it quickly, and we also find the church of San Moisè which takes our breath away. The relatively unassuming church is easily missed, perhaps because of its proximity to extraordinary opulence, but inside it's truly stunning. I'm moved almost to tears. 'To the glory of God' – the Italians understand what that means. I feel like a Catholic again. We make a donation and move on to the Basilica, which, for all of its gold and grandeur, doesn't move us in the same way. Nevertheless we sit quietly in front of a small shrine to Mary for a while. I say a prayer – a 'Hail Mary' – and a lump comes to my throat. We move on. We take cappuccino 'al banco' one last time in our 'favourite' San Marco café. If we conceive a child here Chrissy wants to call her Aurora . . . or Giacomo, if it's a boy. We play with some children's names and laugh at the mix of Welsh, English and Italian. We walk to San Zaccaria and catch the No.2 Vaparetto to San Basilio via Giudecca. We have one more *Don't Look Now* location to find – the church of San Nicolò dei Mendicoli, which is tucked away in the Dorsoduro district.

We find it quite easily, and we love the feel of the area: laid back and friendly with lots of young people – students – cosy cafés and unusual-looking university buildings. We are delayed by doughnuts with lemon cream and enjoy just sitting in the warm sun. When we reach the church it is closing. But we photograph it from the outside and walk to Santa Marta to take a Vaparetto back to the Grand Canal. Some coffee and a spot of Vaporetto-hopping later and we are at San Marcuola in the Cannaregio district. Soon we reach the Jewish Ghetto, and are stunned by the plaques on the walls that remember the history and the suffering of Venice's Jews. We take some time to take it in, and listen to some cheery buskers, before heading back to the Grand Canal via bustling shopping streets that somehow seem more 'real' than those around the Rialto and San Marco. We pay 50 cents each to cross the Grand Canal by Traghetto – the cheapest thing we've found in the whole of Venice. Venice, as we thought, and as you'd guess from its masks, has many faces. I'm pleased that today has allowed us to see a few more of them.

We leave the next morning. A brisk walk to San Stae, a waterbus to Piazzale Roma, a 'normal' bus to Marco Polo airport and we're on our way. We enjoy cappuccino and wait for the plane. There are no delays. As we rise, bound for Amsterdam, I look out of the window. Venice and its islands lie beneath us, as miraculous from the sky as from the sea. I can see snow-capped mountains ahead – hanging there in suspended disbelief like a tiramisu dream. Briefly we occupy a weightless wonderland somewhere in-between the mountains and the lagoon. It is truly a fantastic moment: one of many in a truly fantastic place.

From Schipol airport, we catch the train to Amsterdam's central station. It's surprisingly easy, despite the guidebook warnings about thieves and pickpockets that make it sound like we are putting our lives on the line. Our hotel is just a few minutes' walk from the station. It's luxurious and extremely comfortable, though it does lack the character of our Venice hotel. We wander around the busy afternoon streets of Centrum just to get our bearings. We pass coffee houses and cannabis paraphernalia shops. "Welcome to Amsterdam," we say with a chuckle, and how nice it is to be here. Back at the hotel the restaurant is closed so we order room service. In the night we go out and visit the Sex Museum on Damrak. It's well put together and very entertaining. We remark on how little human sexuality has changed over the centuries: we are all the same underneath. Chrissy finds a video she likes the look of in a shop window. It features attractive female pirates. On closer inspection, it just looks like porn. The costumes don't stay on for long – the actresses, too, are all the same underneath.

The next day we wake early and, after a hearty breakfast, set off in search of the Anne Frank house. The house and its story are fascinating, beautifully preserved and presented, and very, very moving. I walk around on the verge of tears. We see the 'Secret Annexe', the walls of Anne's room which retain the pictures she put up to cheer the place up a bit, and we even see her original diary which is laid open to view. I read how she longed to whistle and ride a bike and breathe fresh air and feel free and, not for the first time on this journey, a lump comes to my throat. I read some words of a family friend which say that life is unpredictable and uncontrollable, that it picks us up like small rocks on the river bed and sweeps us along and drops us down just where it pleases. I watch a video of Otto Frank speaking some years after the war, reflecting on his daughter's work. He says that some of what he read in her diary surprised him, particularly the range and depth of her feelings. He concludes that parents never really know their children, even when they get on well with them. I am deeply moved by the dignity and wisdom of this man who came so close to saving his family from their terrible fate. Once again, I'm overwhelmed by the frightening responsibility that being a parent confers on us. I hear the piano tinkles of 'Runaway' in my head. "Did you cry when they dragged you home?" I weep, just a little, and do my best to hold back my tears.

We take coffee in the museum's café to reflect on what we have just experienced, and to recover a little. We write in the visitors' book and 'leave a leaf' on the Anne Frank internet tree. Back outside we photograph the house to help preserve the memory of our visit. We will talk to Alys about Anne Frank. She has studied World War II in school recently. We know she will be interested. We find a book we think she'll like, *Anne Frank's Story* by Carol Ann Lee – a book written specially for children.

We move on, and pick up what our guidebook says is the "ideal Canal walk", and we take in more of Amsterdam's sights. We walk all afternoon and get back to the hotel in time for dinner in the exquisite Dorrius restaurant. We eat duck and astonishing desserts and like it so much that we book for the next evening too.

After dinner we head off for a tour of Amsterdam's infamous Red Light District. We are taken to the Prostitute Information Centre where we are given a drink and treated to a presentation by the ex-prostitute who set up and runs the Centre. She is 40 years old now and has a daughter the same age as Alys. She has not worked as a prostitute for nearly 20 years but works tirelessly to support the women who choose to work the windows and clubs of Amsterdam, and to educate visitors. She is strong and self-assured, intelligent and clear when she speaks, open and honest when she answers questions. We like her very much. "We are not waiting to be saved," she says when explaining how the prostitutes feel about those who pity them and want to rescue them from their 'plight'. "Yes, there are risks and dangers, but we like the work. It is our right to work in this way. And here, in Amsterdam, it is well regulated." She explains how the prostitution system works, and what is done to protect the girls and keep them as safe as possible. We leave understanding a bit more. We tour the streets, some of Amsterdam's oldest, our tour guide pointing out all the famous sights – historical and sexual. We look at the girls in the windows. Some pout and tempt. Some have faces full of fun and mischief. Some look sad when you catch them off guard.

The main streets are colourful and vibrant. There's a 'fairground' vibe that says 'Funfair for adults. Everyone's just having a good time'. But there are also smaller, seedier streets, there are rough looking men, and there are flickers of boredom and contempt on some of the girls' faces that hint at the darker side of this nightlife. Some *look* just a little bit too young for comfort. You can't photograph the girls, we are told. Some of them hide their profession from family and friends – they don't want their photos circulating on the internet. And with 'management' on the look-out, you take photos at your peril. I'm not sure what to think. Is this liberation, freedom? Is it innocent pleasure? A woman's right to work? Or is it love being kicked around and abused, the world in moral and spiritual decay? How am I supposed to know?

The next day we breakfast well again and leave the hotel early. We walk down Nieuwezijds Voorburgwal to the Begijnhof – a courtyard of peace and tranquillity that is hard to find but accessible through a large wooden door that leads you down some steps and under an archway. The Begijn were a small community of Catholic women who either lost their husbands or chose not to marry. They dedicated themselves to living good lives and doing good works without taking the formal vows of nuns. Only two wooden houses still exist in Amsterdam and one of them is here – No.34. The other one is at the end of Zeedijk, which we are told is the most dangerous street in the Red Light District after dark. What a contrast of lifestyles and locations!

We keep walking, down Leidsestraat where we buy cakes, and on to Vondelpark. We go to see the Filmmuseum, which turns out not to be a museum at all in the sense we expect, but we look around at the information boards and the things in the shop before walking some more in the large, open spaces of the park. We find the House of Bols and head inside for an experience of sensory delight which concludes with some wonderful cocktails and liqueurs. Chrissy chooses a Toffee Apple Martini cocktail, I choose Braambos and 'Starry Night', and we share coffee, lychee and parfait amor liqueur shots. We chat to the assistant in the shop about languages and Holland. The ability of the Dutch to acquire languages is impressive. Many of the Dutch people we have met speak good English. When we leave we are a bit 'squiffy'. We find a place to sit between the Van Gogh Museum and the Rijksmuseum for lunch, then stroll back slowly across canals and past the flower market. We head back through the Red Light District to find the Buddhist Temple in Zeedijk that we saw, briefly, the night before. It is another haven in stormy seas. More contrast. It's a temple of the mind in a place where most worship the pleasures of the flesh; a sign of the presence of the divine at the heart of the sleaze; a place of hope and release for those who need hope and are seeking a release.

We stumble across the first ever drug-selling coffee house in Amsterdam – the Bulldog – now part of a chain which our guidebook tells us is "brash and commercial". We go in for coffee (really) and like the atmosphere. We walk back to the hotel via Dam Square. We eat caramelised shoulder of lamb in the Dorrius restaurant. It's superb – the finest food of our entire holiday. We head out again to find an Irish pub called The Tara on Rokkin. We have heard that Marillion fans will be gathering there from 7pm onwards. It's Thursday 19 March, the night before the 2009 Marillion Convention at Port Zélande on the South West coast of Holland. We arrive at The Tara at about 8pm. We meet some fellow fans from England and Wales, including a group who call themselves the Crazy West Country Pumpkins, and we bump into our Greek-Cypriot friend Antonis again (always a pleasure). As the pub blasts out Marillion's *Seasons End* album the mood is good. Marillion Weekends are always special. People travel from all over the world to be there. Some travel much further than we have.

🏝 *These strange conventions* 🏝

The impact of Marillion's music, and what I perceived as 'points of contact' between the themes of some of the songs and my life as an adult, made me want to see the band live again for the first time in almost twenty years. The first opportunity came on the *Marbles* tour in July 2004, when, along with Chrissy, Phil the Collector and Phil's friend Andy, I caught their Newport Centre show. Two days later and Chrissy and I were off to London. We had won the 'Golden Mug' competition when ordering a Marbles coffee mug from the band's website, and this won us 'Access All Areas' passes to a gig of our choice. We choose the Saturday night gig at London's Astoria (10 July 2004), one of the two shows used for the *Marbles on the Road* DVD. I was struck on both occasions by the quality and passion of the band's performance. Since then more gigs and Marillion-related events have followed: we caught Steve Hogarth at Bush Hall, London, on his 'h natural' tour (27 February 2006); we won tickets to attend the *Somewhere Else* listening party at the Zodiac Club in Oxford (12 March 2007); we caught the band three times on the *Somewhere Else* tour itself, in Bristol on 8 June 2007 (with friends Brendan, Ed, Phil the Collector and Andy) and at the London Forum on 15 and 16 June; we saw the band's Cardiff University show (4 December 2007) on the Snow-Where Else Christmas tour; and we caught the Bristol gig in November 2008 (with friends Kim, Harrison, Phil the Collector and Andy) on the first leg of the *Happiness Is the Road* tour.

In addition there have been the Marillion Weekends, the four-day conventions at which the band play three completely different two and a half hour sets on successive nights (and discussion about which – as reported way back at the start of Chapter 2 – triggered this entire book). The first such event took place at Brean Sands in England in April 2002, with a second following in Minehead a year later. The first one Chrissy and I attended was the 2005 event, also in Minehead. Now, with the Marillion Weekend growing in scale, ambition and popularity, it has settled into a bi-annual groove, with the last two held at the Center Parcs resort in Port

Zélande on South West coast of Holland (in February 2007 and March 2009 respectively), and the band holding a follow-up event to the 2009 Weekend in Montreal, Canada.*

The Marillion Weekend has become a truly wonderful and international affair. One meets an astonishing range of people from an astonishing range of backgrounds and nationalities. Indeed, the Marillion Weekend 2009 in Port Zélande was attended by nearly 3,000 people from 45 different countries: Argentina, Australia, Austria, Belgium, Brazil, Canada, Cyprus, Czech Republic, Denmark, Egypt, England, Finland, France, Germany, Gibraltar, Greece, Guatemala, Hong Kong, Hungary, Iceland, Iran, Ireland, Italy, Japan, Libya, Lithuania, Luxembourg, Malta, Netherlands, New Zealand, Northern Ireland, Norway, Poland, Portugal, Romania, Russia, Scotland, South Africa, Spain, Sweden, Switzerland, Singapore, USA, Wales and Venezuela. If you are looking for an example *par excellence* of how music can bring together and unite people even in the modern age, this is it.

The band themselves, along with musicians from the supporting acts, stay on site for the Weekend, spending as much time mingling, chatting, signing autographs and posing for photographs as their schedules allow. In addition, it has become customary for the band to use the occasion to raise some cash for good causes through the now customary 'Charity Book Raffle'. The Marillion Weekend 2009, for example, raised over £4,500 for Project Enlighten, a non-profit organisation established by two fans – Asad Rahman and Olivia Lorge – which aims to support and empower poverty-stricken children, with a current focus on South East Asia.† Project Enlighten runs entirely on the goodwill of volunteers, with no one, not even the organisers, taking a wage for their good work. The 'charity book' itself is a large book containing signatures, messages and handwritten lyrics from the band along with messages and sometimes photographs of many of the attendees (entrants and contributors to the raffle fund) in whatever language they choose to write. It's a marvellous prize. Previous beneficiaries of the raffle have included Diabetes UK.

The Marillion Weekend is a fantastic few days – a real chance to step outside one's day-to-day routine and experience the power and joy of rock music in one of its most positive manifestations. But once again,

---

* Since this book was written, three 2011 Weekend events have also taken place at Port Zélande, Montreal and Leamington (England).

† For more information, see www.projectenlighten.org.

you don't have to take my word for it, nor the word of other conceivably 'biased' Marillion fans – look instead at what some of the other musicians who have attended say about it.

Steve Thorne, for example, played at the 2007 Weekend on the back of his critically acclaimed *Emotional Creatures Volume 1* album and the imminent release of *Emotional Creatures Volume 2*. He had managed to persuade a wide range of progressive rock luminaries to guest on the albums including: Geoff Downes (Yes/Asia); Tony Levin (King Crimson/Peter Gabriel); Nick D'Virgilio (Spock's Beard/Genesis/Tears for Fears); Gavin Harrison (Porcupine Tree); Pete Trewavas (Marillion); and Martin Orford, Paul Cook and John Jowitt (all IQ). (Apparently he managed to persuade Geoff Downes to play on the first album for a curry, and to play on the second album for two curries.) For his Marillion Weekend appearance, however, he played solo (guitar and vocals), making extensive use of backing tapes for the material pulled from the *Volume 1* album. Despite being 'unbanded', he threw absolutely everything into his performance, impressing most of those present with his passionate display. On returning home, he posted the following entry (dated 06.02.07) on his website:

> "I have to say, that all three nights Marillion played a blinder. I hadn't seen them perform for a while, so it was a real treat for me. When the time came for me to play, I was quite nervous, however after the first track, I realised that the audience were a very warm crowd and I even spotted a few people singing along. . .. That really lifted my spirits and put me at ease, and made the whole experience an enjoyable one.
>
> On Sunday, I spent a few hours meeting with people and signing albums they had bought . . .
>
> The journey home was uneventful, but it gave me a chance to reflect on a memorable weekend. Marillion were brilliant, the food and facilities were 'top drawer' but what struck me the most, was the friendliness of the Marillion community. Whole families had attended this event and everyone was having such a great time. I got the chance to meet and speak with some really friendly people including Stephanie and Lucy* who played a massive part in ensuring the whole event ran smoothly. It was great to be invited, and it was one of my most memorable birthdays."[27]

---

* Stephanie Bradley and Lucy Jordache – organisational and managerial lynchpins of the Marillion organisation.

Similarly, while young English band A Genuine Freakshow rather succinctly described their appearance at the Marillion Weekend 2009 as "definitely the high point of our musical careers so far,"[28] Matt Cohen of The Reasoning, one of the great hopes of the current British prog rock scene, has commented more expansively on the experience. He told me:

> The Marillion Weekend was an eye-opening experience and one that I will genuinely never forget. We had been lucky enough to support Marillion at the Colston Hall in Bristol, which was mind-blowing, but to play at one of their hallowed conventions was a real dream come true. The trip over was just brilliant and everyone was buzzing with lots of beer being consumed, as is the law when on the road, so, by the time we hit Port Zelande at some ridiculous time of night, the only thing left to do was party some more.
>
> The sun shone all weekend, and everyone there just laughed, chatted, drank and generally enjoyed the fact that the whole weekend was about music and friendship – and we made many new and wonderful friends. The day of the gig was incredible. We rocked up to the venue, unloaded our gear and walked on stage. Words just cannot describe that feeling but 'joy', 'nervousness', 'excitement' and 'Jesus' all spring to mind. The show rocked and the audience was genuinely one of the best we have ever played to. They party like no-one else and made us feel so welcome and at home. After that it was many drinks and an incredible Marillion set.
>
> From then on, we just hung out at the various discos and parties happening around the place just laughing loads, sharing stories and savouring the whole atmosphere and experience. It's just a shame it couldn't have lasted for another 2 weeks.

🛸 Happiness is the Road 🛸

In his fine book *Rat Salad: Black Sabbath The Classic Years 1969-1975*, Paul Wilkinson writes:

> The truth is that unlike today, music in the late sixties and early seventies emanated from a creative movement independent of its parent, corporate ownership. In those days records were made to shift consciousness and opinions, not units. Music was crafted with toil and skill, rock music particularly so, and it offered an escape from the environment, a place for either contemplation or communal revelry. Now, music *is* the environment. It is everywhere: it is used to sell everything from toilet tissue to politicians, nappies to pensions. Its manifold genres and sub-

genres multiply, divide, expand and fragment with all the inexorable energy and devious reinvention of a virus.[29]

I didn't discover rock music until the very end of the 1970s and early 1980s and would argue strongly that for some bands, at least, the creative and consciousness-shifting qualities that Wilkinson describes have extended well beyond the late 1960s and early 1970s. Wilkinson has a point, but the picture is not quite as gloomy as one might suppose. With Marillion, for example, I discovered and then re-discovered a band who *still* craft rock music "with toil and skill", and who continue to offer opportunities for both "contemplation" and "communal revelry". Marillion, indeed, are a band who manage to bring the introspective and social aspects of being a rock fan together to stunning effect, crafting songs that connect with matters of importance in our lives while providing opportunities for us to share and celebrate the music with like-minded individuals from all walks of life and from all over the world. In that sense they are an old-fashioned band – a band who, in times that often seem troubled and even soulless, continue to make music that is fresh, vital, and meaningful; a band who show that there is still a place for integrity in rock music; and a band who show that it's still possible for music to help us "find a better way of life". Reflecting on the band's creative endeavours and their relationship to 'the mainstream', biographer Jon Collins concludes: "There will be more music, and, whether it is adopted by the mainstream or not, it will be great music. There will be more gigs, and they will be great gigs. There will be new ways for fans to participate in what is a truly unique relationship, forged over many years, with a band of fellows whose hearts are so absolutely in the right place that it hurts."[30] He wrote that in 2002. Since then there have been numerous tours, numerous Marillion Weekends, three studio albums of new and original material, and numerous live CDs and DVDs.

In 2008 Marillion released their fifteenth studio album, *Happiness is the Road*. Like *Marbles* it was a double album. CD1 contained a series of thematically linked tracks and was called *Essence*, while CD2 contained a more varied collection of additional material and was called *The Hard Shoulder*. It showed that, far from Marillon's well of creativity drying up, they are still brimming with ideas, lyrically and musically, and are still attempting to create music of breadth and significance. Reviewing the album for *Classic Rock* magazine, Phillip Wilding described the album as possibly "their most inventive and enduring yet . . . beautifully played, expertly rendered, touching and telling".[31]

The lyrical theme of *Essence* was reportedly inspired by Steve Hogarth's visit to a doctor in Holland, a man who turned out to be a doctor "of the body and the soul", and Hogarth's subsequent reading of a book recommended to him by the doctor: *The Power of Now* by Eckhart Tolle. From that book Hogarth took the message "you shouldn't become a slave to the past or future and deny the present moment"[32] The track 'Happiness is the Road', the final track on *Essence*, develops this theme, blending Hogarth's experiences with the old adage 'life's a journey, not a destination'. "Happiness ain't at the end of the road," the song concludes, "Happiness is the road." Discussing the album with the Web UK team in August 2008, Hogarth says: "Lyrically the whole of CD1 is really coming from different directions to the same thing, time and moment. The song 'Essence' is about trying to grab it. 'Trap the Spark' is about if you find it you can't hold it. It's like a spark that you can't hold in your hand. It's about the impossibility of maintaining the perfect moment. The point is that you should try to do it anyway. That's what it's all about."[33]

Sometimes experiencing music can itself be a perfect moment – it *is* the spark! But even when words and music refer to something outside of themselves, they can often help us to appreciate or reflect on some matter of value by holding an insight or an experience or a feeling still a while, pointing us towards it, and allowing us, however briefly, to see it or approximate to it.

There are particular tracks on *Happiness in the Road* that do these things superbly. 'Asylum Satellite #1', from *The Hard Shoulder*, for example, is a beautiful track which invites listeners to both lose themselves in the music and reflect on with the way society deals with groups of people whose thoughts don't quite fit. For those who like to hear musicians playing together to achieve an effect that is greater than the sum of its parts, this song approaches musical perfection, providing, as it does, some achingly beautiful moments that lift you out of yourself and set you adrift in musical heaven.

Elsewhere, the pairing of 'Dreamy Street' and 'This Train is My Life' at the start of *Essence* is truly sublime. The lyrics to 'Dreamy Street' were written in Bristol on the *Somewhere Else* tour, in one of the cafés near to where Chrissy, Ed and I saw Steve Hogarth wandering around. They always remind me of that day – sitting in the sun, sipping on a cold lager and sharing time with friends I see far too infrequently. 'Dreamy Street', in fact, offers an almost Zen-like statement of dreamy contentedness before segueing wonderfully into 'This Train is My Life'. Lyrically, the contrast between 'This Train' and the short and gentle album opener couldn't be greater. For those of us who worry that life is passing us by, the "speeding" train and "stroby stations" provide a fine metaphor. Metaphor it might be for us, but the lyric is borne of the singer's life on the road, a fact which gives it a particular force. Even as life hurtles along at pace, however, the lyric introduces a ray of light – the possibility of sharing the journey with someone who can make it better and who, perhaps, offers some hope of slower, calmer, more tranquil times ahead:

> *So take my hand*
> *Squeeze it tight*
> *Make some light*
> *In the darkness*
> *I'm glad you came on this trip*
> *Don't lose your grip*
> *Don't lose your grip*
> *This train is my life*
> *This train is my life*
>
> *Travel with me*
> *And we'll see . . .*

It is classic Marillion, with the band wringing every last drop of meaning out of Hogarth's lyric. Rothery's solo is particularly worthy of note and is, as most of them are, exquisite.

Postscript

On 24 November 2009, Chrissy and I had a beautiful baby daughter. She came about a week and a half early. Venice? Amsterdam? The Marillion Weekend? We've done the maths. We called her Anwen Aurora.

10

High Voltage Rock 'n' Roll

It's Saturday 24 July 2010, the first day of the 'inaugural' High Voltage Festival – the festival that's been 'curated' by *Classic Rock* magazine in conjunction with sister magazines *Metal Hammer* and *Classic Rock Presents Prog*; the festival that's been developed "*by* rock fans, *for* rock fans". Chrissy and I have forked out for a VIP Rock Star Package which includes three nights bed and breakfast at the Crowne Plaza Hotel in London's Docklands and shuttle bus transport to and from the venue. We are waiting with about 30 other people and the High Voltage Festival rep in the hotel foyer. The shuttle bus hasn't turned up. Finally three taxis arrive and some of our party get in and drive off. We wait, full of both excitement and impatience. Eventually two other taxis turn up and we get into one of these.

Our taxi driver drops us off in a side street near Victoria Park. We find our way into the park and at the first gate we see we ask advice. We are told to keep walking and follow the perimeter fence all the way to the main entrance some 10–15 minutes away. We do as we are told and before long we can hear Kim Seviour's dulcet tones, as Touchstone open the festival on the Prog Stage. We join the queue as we near the main entrance, but before long, thankfully, we realise that there is a separate entrance and a much shorter queue for VIPs and holders of early bird queue jumper tickets. "Make sure you arrive at High Voltage early," says the official programme in the Touchstone section. Well, we tried!

By the time we are inside, New Device have kicked off proceedings on the Metal Hammer Stage. They sound good and we linger to listen to a track or two. The festival line-up is so strong that this is likely to be the first scheduling clash of many – and although we are going to fill up two long days with music and see a large number of bands, there will inevitably be bands we will miss or ones that we wish we could watch for longer.

We head over to get our first glimpse of the Prog Stage with its oh-so-appropriate purple colouring and its curious 'wizard hat' design. It looks cool, and Touchstone sound good. We watch them for a while and then, as instructed in our pre-festival information, head up through the festival site to register at 'VIP Reception' and collect our programmes, t-shirts, laminated passes and goody bags. As the VIP Area is up behind the Main Stage we get a chance to take in the whole festival site before it gets too busy. And what a sight it is! Three fantastic-looking stages, funfair rides, food stalls and bars aplenty, retail stalls, a real ale tent, a classic car exhibition, the Eagle Vision Cinema . . . we feel so privileged just to be here.

We find the VIP Area and VIP Reception and pick up our gear. We ask about our return shuttle bus transport. "Be back here at 11.30pm," we are told.

We buy iced water and chill a while – sitting on comfortable seats and taking in the 'VIP' facilities. The VIP Area is adjacent to the more exclusive Classic Club, and we see a number of *Classic Rock* magazine journalists meeting and greeting assorted musicians and, one assumes, other valued guests. I bump into an old school friend, Pete – the self-same Pete from Chapter 3, whom I haven't seen for probably 20 years. He works for Olympus Cameras now. He lives in Cambridgeshire and advertises his company's wares in *Classic Rock*. He's here at the magazine's invitation. It's good to see him.

So busy are we, chatting and enjoying our surroundings, that we completely miss Pendragon and the Black Spiders, but we wander off to get some lunch and catch the start of The Union – the first band on the Main Stage. It's a running joke between Chrissy and I that we've seen Thunder loads of times without even trying. They always seem to pop up on the bill somewhere. "Well, they can't this time," I told her, "they've split up." I was only half right. Soon after we'd had this conversation, Thunder guitarist Luke Morley's new band The Union were announced on the High Voltage bill! Their debut album received an excellent nine out of ten review in *Classic Rock* and, actually, they sound pretty good as we munch on our burgers, salad and risotto cakes.

We wander back down the site for a taste of Dutch proggers Focus and notice for the first time some possible 'sound bleed' problems as biker band Orange Goblin kick into action on the Metal Stage and intrude a little on Focus's gentler and more cultured approach. Much depends on where you stand, but before long we give in to the metal ("the power of metal compels you" – as it says on one girl's t-shirt) and go for a closer look at Orange Goblin. I have recently bought their *Healing Through Fire* album and quite like it. But it's a bit too raw for Chrissy's tastes, so we stay for just a couple of tracks. At any rate, we want to catch the start of The Answer's set back on the Main Stage. The Answer are one of heavy rock's bright new hopes – and they certainly look and sound the part. 'Classic' rock indeed, delivered with verve and a real sense of purpose. These guys mean it. The sun is beating down. The audience is starting to grow. It's real festival weather and it's real festival music.

We stick around for a while, but 20 minutes or so into The Answer's set we are heading progwards again. All of the bands we've tasted so far have been entertaining and well worth hearing, but 3:40pm sees the arrival on stage of the first of our 'top bands', that is, the first of the bands that for us are absolutely essential viewing – our main course, if you will. We LOVE Bigelf and Professor Diablo's (Damon Fox's) organ. Bigelf's *Cheat the Gallows* album was our favourite album of 2009, and we can't believe we are getting the chance to see them play live. For the uninitiated, Bigelf channel a fascinating range of rock influences – ELO and Beatles melodies, massive Sabbath-style riffs, Deep Purple and Uriah Heep organ/guitar interplay, early Queen quirkiness and vocal harmonies, occasional Pink Floyd vibes and mood swings – and wrap them all up in their own unique mix of mapcap psychedelia and modern heaviness. If you listen carefully, you can hear echoes of almost any major 1970s act you care to mention including Bowie, 10cc and Marc Bolan. But this isn't mere homage to the past; this is *Bigelf*. They may wear their influences on their sleeves, but they make of them something fresh and exciting. This is rock music played as it should be played, with joy, passion and abandon. "I'd like to say how great it is to have Focus open for us," says Damon Fox with a big ironic grin and considerable affection for the Dutchmen. As planned we stay for the whole set and are utterly enchanted. "The Evils of Rock 'n' Roll?" There ain't nothin' evil here.

Unfortunately Bigelf overlap a little with Gary Moore, who is also high up on our list of 'must sees', so after Bigelf we rush back up to the Main Stage to catch the bulk of his set. Just as we get there, we bump into another rock buddy – a guy named Steve, whom I met through friends at a Porcupine Tree gig in Bristol in October 2009, and his friend Jon. We each knew the other would be here and made a tentative and informal agreement to look out for each other. But there are several thousand people milling around the main arena by now, so what were the chances of us actually meeting up?

Gary Moore delivers a solid if unspectacular set, though it's great to hear old classics like 'Empty Rooms', and the song that, reputedly, was the last track Phil Lynott committed to vinyl – 'Out in the Fields'. It's also good to see Gary reunited with keyboardist/guitarist Neil Carter, whose contributions to UFO in the early 1980s I've always regarded as underrated.

The end of Gary Moore's set is the cue for a wander and a chance to catch half an hour or so of Dweezil Zappa and his band playing a set of father Frank's compositions. The music is cool, jazzy and ambitious. We drink cold lager and lie in the sun. They end with 'Peaches En Regalia' which pleases Chrissy no end. Fantastic! We wish we'd seen more.

We realise we've missed Hammerfall and Cathedral. I don't know Hammerfall, but it's a bit of a shame about Cathedral. I've recently bought a Cathedral album, *The Garden of Unearthly Delights*, and enjoyed it, and would like to have seen what sort of stuff Lee Dorrian is pumping out live these days. It's a long time since I helped smuggle him in to see Metallica, and I wonder whether he'd even remember me. No matter. Foreigner are on the Main Stage, and we catch just a track or two as we hunt down and devour fresh fish and chips. We are surprised how hard they rock (Foreigner, not the fish and chips) but the Metal Stage beckons again, and I feel my excitement levels rising as we anticipate the 'Heavy Metal Thunder' of Saxon.

26 November 1980 – that's when I first saw Saxon; my first ever gig. And here they are, 30 years later, still pulling an audience and still sounding great. They've had their ups and downs and line-up changes over the years, but they, like the genre, are enjoying something of a resurgence, and it shows in the freshness and confidence of their performance. They rip through a host of old classics – '747 Strangers in the Night', 'To Hell and Back Again', 'Princess of the Night', 'Motorcycle Man',

'Crusader', 'Denim and Leather', '20,000ft' – and chuck in a couple of more recent tracks for good measure. Frontman Biff can still hold a crowd. His voice has held up astonishingly well, and his stagecraft is exemplary. Of particular note is his asymmetrical splitting of the crowd during the customary 'Wheels of Steel' singalong, a split necessitated by the angle at which the main thoroughfare hits the Metal Hammer Stage field. This creates an imbalance as more and more people join the crowd on the right hand side without realising how much space is over on the left. "Normally I'd split you down the middle," Biff explains, "but there's more people on this side than that side." He slices the crowd with his arm like he's cutting a garlic baguette. "This has never been done before," he announces with a chuckle. It's an exquisite feel-good moment in a set full of feel-good moments. I never thought I'd feel so emotional listening to Saxon! Enthralled and happy, we stay for the full set, unfortunately missing Asia (and Carl Palmer's first appearance of the weekend) but bumping into some of the Crazy West Country Pumpkins, including our friend Andy (nicknamed 'The Colonel' after his liking for KFC) and his girlfriend Pam. Rabid Marillion fans to a man (and woman), a number of them are also Black Sabbath/Ronnie James Dio fans, and so we stick with them when Saxon finish and rush back up to the Main Stage to see Heaven and Hell.

The Heaven and Hell set is a special one-off performance to celebrate the life of Ronnie James Dio who sadly lost his battle with stomach cancer on 16 May 2010. Initially the band withdrew from the bill, but they were reinstated having decided to play the High Voltage Festival as a tribute to Ronnie. This is a chance for band and fans alike to pay their respects in the best way they know how – by rocking out and immersing themselves in some of the truly sensational music that Ronnie made with Tony Iommi, Geezer Butler and Vinnie Appice, originally as a *bona fide* Black Sabbath line-up and more latterly under the Heaven and Hell moniker. Vocals are handled by former Deep Purple (and briefly Black Sabbath) man Glenn Hughes and Dio-fan Jorn Lande from the band Masterplan. It must be an emotional occasion for all the band, but Glenn Hughes in particular looks almost completely overwhelmed, and at times seems in danger of falling to pieces.[*] Somehow he holds it together and turns

---

[*] *Classic Rock* magazine's later review of the festival refers to Hughes's "Hollywood-style melodramatic gestures" (*Classic Rock* magazine, issue 149, September 2010), but I put his behaviour down to the emotion of the occasion.

in a vocal performance of which he can be truly proud. The occasion is also notable for a moving and heartfelt statement from the stage by Ronnie's widow Wendy – a poignant moment and a poignant set, as the band storm purposely through a fine selection of tracks including 'Mob Rules', 'Voodoo', 'Children of the Sea', 'Turn up the Night', 'Country Girl', 'Falling off the Edge of the World', 'I', and, of course, the track that may well now become Ronnie's epitaph, 'Heaven and Hell'. The set also includes the modern Heaven and Hell classic 'Bible Black', and the band encore with a rousing and chaotic version of 'Neon Knights', joined by Phil Anselmo of Pantera/Down who tears around the stage with the enthusiasm of an over-excited and over-emotional fan. And then they are gone, leaving the giant screens on either side of the stage to pay their own tribute to Ronnie James Dio – one of THE definitive voices of heavy rock; the man whose vocals and songwriting skills gave us three of the genre's best loved albums in *Rainbow Rising, Heaven and Hell* and *Holy Diver*, and many other great albums besides; a man who has influenced many and whose legacy will live on. Many thousands of us look at the screens and realise that we have witnessed the end of something very special. That great band I saw at Sophia Gardens in January 1981 is no more. The set was a fitting tribute and a fine celebration – but . . . suddenly I feel sad and empty. Heaven and Hell's, and more particularly Ronnie's, departure has left a big black hole.

Chrissy and I left the Pumpkins during the Heaven and Hell set, sitting for a while in the Grandstand and then making our way closer to the front to get more involved and to pick up the vibe of the performance from the heart of the crowd. Performance over, we head back to the Metal and Prog Stages to catch the tail end of the Black Label Society set and listen to a little Transatlantic, the prog 'supergroup' whose members include drummer Mike Portnoy of Dream Theater and bassist Pete Trewavas of Marillion. Black Label Society surprise us with a flame-throwing and ticker tape finale, while Transatlantic sound clear, polished and professional. Portnoy's drumming is particularly impressive – crisp and inventive. In both cases I wish I could have heard more. But headliners ZZ Top are soon due on the Main Stage, so it's back up we go to find a suitable viewing point deep within the gathering and expectant throng.

From the moment ZZ hit the stage they are superb. Their infectious brand of 'abstract', Texas-flavoured blues-rock is as joyful and engaging today as it's always been. Their characteristic humour is evident throughout. "We've been fixin' to come and see you here for 40 years," says the apparently ageless Billy Gibbons. "Same three guys right here," he says, gesturing to band mates Dusty Hill and Frank (no) Beard, "same three chords right here," he jokes, raising his guitar. We lose ourselves in the music as the band run through a selection of blues rock classics from across their back catalogue, even incorporating a tribute to Jimi Hendrix. Right on cue, Chrissy dons her cheap sunglasses. She has carried them around all day just for this moment. About two thirds of the way through the set I see a big biker guy fighting his way back through the crowd, presumably *en route* to the bar or the gents. He catches my eye and stops to talk to me. His voice is cracking with emotion, and he sounds overwhelmed as he pauses for breath and sweeps back his hair from his sweat-drenched forehead. "Man," he says, finally gathering himself, "does it get any better than this? These guys are just . . . just . . . they're just blues-rock masters." Masters of Sparks? Sultans of Swing? They end on a high with a run-through some of the hits from their *Eliminator* album and a kick-ass version of 'Tush'. After the emotion of Heaven and Hell, ZZ's set provides a suitably warm and rousing conclusion to a fantastic day. The Gods of Rock had looked down favourably as the sun shone hard and we ate and drank our fill. We joined together with thousands of other music fans and, in memory of Ronnie James Dio, we rocked!

Post-gig, we head straight back to VIP Reception. We're there at about 10:55pm. It's 35 minutes until the 11:30pm time we've been given, but we figure we can chill out and have a drink and see who else is around. Just as we are about to sit down, and I start eyeing up the bar, we hear our High Voltage Festival rep calling for people for our hotel. We are led straight to our shuttle bus which whisks us off faster than you could sign an autograph and pull a groupie. We are back in our hotel room drinking coffee and running a warm bath by 11.20pm!

Thankfully, by the following morning the transport hiccoughs of the previous morning appear to have been overcome. This time the promised shuttle bus *does* turn up. There are two reps today, and they keep a list of the order in which people have arrived at reception and registered with them, filling up the bus on a 'first come first served' basis. We are in the first dozen or so to arrive, so we get on the first bus, along with a friendly couple from Essex who are particularly looking forward to seeing Emerson, Lake and Palmer, and a cool, leather-clad and behatted couple from Ammanford, West Wales. This time we are driven into the park and up to the Artists' Gate, where we stroll casually past the artists' tents and straight into the VIP Area. This is what should have happened yesterday too. We are inside ten minutes or so before the main gates open, and it gives us a chance to take a few snaps and replenish our water bottles before we head down to the Prog Stage for the first band of the day, The Reasoning.

The Reasoning are a female-fronted, Cardiff-based modern progressive rock band with strong guitars and metal overtones. We have seen them several times before but never at an outdoor festival, and we are rooting for them. We have a giant inflatable leek which Chrissy has discussed with bass player Matt Cohen and which we intend to hurl up on stage. "Throw it at Dylan," (one of the guitarists) said Matt, "he's wanted a leek for a while." Although we don't quite make it to the stage itself before the gates open, our early entry still enables us to get pretty close to the front. Once again, we catch up with the Pumpkins. We watch the band with Andy and Pam, though we notice that others from the gang are right at the front, including Wayne who was the cover model for The Reasoning's 2010 album *Adverse Camber*.

The band play a strong set. We wave our leek around a bit, then pass it to Mark – one of the Pumpkins at the front – who launches it towards the stage. "Ooh, look, someone's sprung a leek," says singer Rachel Cohen mid-sentence, but it hits the edge of the stage, falls the wrong side, and gets tossed back into the crowd by a roadie or a cameraman. Somehow it finds its way straight back to me! This has happened before, when The Reasoning played at the Marillion Weekend in Holland. Someone came up to me at the end of The Reasoning's set and said: "I think this is yours." I can't get rid of the bloody thing!

At the end of The Reasoning's set we head back up towards the VIP Area to buy iced water, and then to the Main Stage. It's another beautiful day; the Rock Gods are smiling again. We take in full sets from the Quireboys and UFO. "Here's a song I wrote 20 years ago . . .. when I was 16," says Spike of the Quireboys, flashing a V-sign and a cheeky grin at those down the front guffawing at his memory for age and numbers. The Quireboys put in a fantastic shift, and we notice several *Classic Rock* magazine luminaries, including Editor-in-Chief Scott Rowley and long-time rock scribe Malcolm Dome, venturing out to watch them.

Between bands we go to the Eagle Vision Cinema, where we look at photos in the Mick Hutson (rock photographer) exhibition and sign the Ronnie James Dio condolences book.

UFO get a very warm welcome and are very fondly received. They are clearly fired up and ready to rock, and the crowd will them on, desperately keen to see them do well. The first track suggests they will, but then guitarist Vinnie Moore experiences the kind of technical problems that must be a musician's worst nightmare.

"I'm not gonna talk much," says singer Phil Mogg, "to save time. This is 'Only You Can . . .'"

"ROCK ME" shout the crowd.

Mogg turns to Vinnie who appears to launch into the riff . . . but his guitar remains silent. Cue frantic roadies and guitar technicians, as it takes, by my reckoning, a good five to seven minutes to get Vinnie going properly again, during which time Mogg is left to regale us with a mixture of family history and smart one-liners – more talking than he probably gets through in a full night's headlining! His performance speaks volumes for his experience and professionalism, and the rest of the band, even the clearly frustrated Vinnie, manage to keep their cool too. Eventually they get going again, but sadly the gremlins return to haunt them at inopportune moments throughout their set. The guitar cuts out, for example, at the crucial pay-back moment, right at the start of the inspired second solo in 'Love to Love'. It would be unfair to use this incident to compare Moore unfavourably with the solo's originator, Michael Schenker, but it does remind me of the rock perfection of this very moment on the *Strangers in the Night* album – an expression of genius to which, I suspect, even Schenker himself only approximates most of the time. Then, during 'Rock Bottom', as Mogg delivers the last vocal line before the solo spot and turns to Moore with fingers crossed on both hands, the guitar cuts out again, robbing Moore of the chance to take full advantage of a prime showpiece opportunity. Aware of the guitarist's difficulties, the band simply keep the rhythm going, and when Vinnie is able to come in again he busts a gut to make up for the problems, shredding like a good 'un, and letting rip with a passion and fury that's clearly fuelled by his frustration. It's a shame for UFO, but at festivals these things can happen. They drew a big crowd and the show could have been a triumph. As it was, they were simply very, very good, ending appropriately enough with a upbeat version of 'Doctor, Doctor' that sent shivers down my spine and even had me suppressing a tear or two of joy.

With UFO finished, we stroll through the food stalls. Refuelled by fried noodles and vegetables in Japanese sauces, we make our first visit of the day to the Metal Hammer Stage. We've missed South Wales band Lethargy and Norwegians Audrey Horne, both bands I'd like to have seen, but we do have a quick look at High on Fire. We had been hoping to meet up with my punk friend Marv. He lives in Norwich now and is a qualified electrician, but he continues to play in various bands and be inspired by music. His tastes, he tells me, have, if anything, become even more extreme than they were in our youth (and that's saying something). He's still mates with Lee Dorrian, and he's mates with Jimmy Bower too, who drums for Down who are headlining the Metal Stage later. Marv was hoping to meet up with Jimmy, but it hasn't come off. So, instead of being here with us in London, he's doing the laundry back in Norfolk. (What a waste of a red Mohican!) High on Fire are one of the bands who interested him though, and so we pop over to see what they are like. In truth they're a bit too vicious for me. "If being pummelled to a bloody but cheerful pulp sounds like fun to you, then High on Fire would very much like to make your acquaintance," says the Official Programme, but it doesn't sound cheerful or fun to me. Loud, heavy and even thrashy I can handle, but I hate it when the overriding experience of listening to music is one of an overloud bass sound pounding through your entire body and shaking you to the core. But each to their own, I suppose. I'll leave it to someone else to tell them that the artwork on their *Snakes for the Divine* album makes it look like a Meatloaf record.

In prioritising the Quireboys and UFO, we have missed Wishbone Ash (playing their classic *Argus* album) and Steve Hackett, and we missed Steve Hackett's encore appearance with Transatlantic (for the Genesis classic 'The Return of the Giant Hogweed') the night before too. We are also going to miss Bachman Turner's Main Stage performance. Again it's a shame, but it's time for a return to the Prog Stage (via the cold lager sellers) for another of our favourite bands – Magnum.

Like Marillion, Magnum are a band who have, for most of the time at least, carried on working beyond their 1980s commercial heyday, producing some inspired and exceptional music. They are currently enjoying a purple patch, with the recent run of albums from 2004's *Brand New Morning*, through 2007's *Princess Alice and the Broken Arrow*, to 2009's *Into the Valley of Moon King* providing ample evidence that Tony Clarkin remains one of the best songwriters around and that, creatively speaking, Magnum are still a force to be reckoned with. It's perhaps only a little surprising, therefore, that they choose to play a set that draws heavily on their recent work – with only the occasional meander into their extensive back catalogue, and even then to pick up 'Les Morts Dansant' and 'All England's Eyes' (both from the *On a Storyteller's Night* album) rather than more obvious crowd pleasers. There are no doubt those who will argue that they chose the wrong set for the occasion, but even without the 'classics' they seemed to go down well, and I'm filled with admiration for the confidence they show in their newer material. Nevertheless, they do finish their set with 'Kingdom of Madness' from their very first (and possibly most proggy) album – an unexpected choice which has everyone in the crowd near me in raptures. Nice one, lads!

After Magnum it's back to the Metal Hammer Stage to catch the start of Clutch's set. Clutch are a fairly new band to me, but it's great to see that heaviness in rock music does not necessarily mean that there is no room for blues. I have a theory that from the early 1970s onwards, each new generation of bands has become more and more focused on speed and heaviness at the expense of other musical ingredients. This has increasingly diminished the influence of the blues on the music and as a consequence a lot of modern metal music, however technically advanced and dextrously played, sounds to me like it has lost its soul. Clutch are a clear exception to this, and from what I see of them live, they stomp and brood as gloriously on stage as they do on record.

Chrissy and I watch the first couple of Clutch tracks together, but then we have the kind of mad hour that you can only have at a festival. While Chrissy 'retires' to the VIP Area to watch folk-rock heroes (and Rick Wakeman's first band) The Strawbs, I drift slowly back to the Prog Stage to watch some of Uriah Heep playing their classic *Demons and Wizards* album. No matter that guitarist Mick Box is the only member of the current band who was there when the album was first recorded, the current line-up has, drummer aside, been largely intact for most of the last 20 years, and the 'special guest' addition of former Whitesnake guitarist Micky Moody adds to the attraction for many. I then rush up to the Main Stage to watch a bit of Joe Bonamassa – blues-rock guitarist extraordinaire and a top notch performer to boot. Joe is also high up on our list of 'must see' artists, but there are simply so many good acts on the bill that we are even having to miss artists we'd happily pay to see on their own.

I listen to two or three Joe Bonamassa tracks and then join Chrissy in the VIP Tent for a sizable chunk of The Strawbs's set – and very enjoyable it is too. But there's no rest for the wicked, and I'm soon back at the Main

Stage for the end of Joe Bonamassa's set, before rushing back down to the Metal Stage to watch the mighty Opeth. Chrissy stays to watch the rest of The Strawbs, joining me later once she's had time to collect their signatures and have a quick chat with Spike of the Quireboys.

Opeth are one of the 'modern' bands on the bill who are perhaps nearing, or at, their commercial peak. More notably, they are one of only a few bands you can think of who can bridge the considerable death metal/progressive rock divide and claim fans from both genres. While their early albums were full-on metal, their more recent works have shown astonishing subtlety, musicality and, yes, beauty. In fact, they were originally scheduled to play on the Prog Stage at High Voltage but were moved to the Metal Stage "due to overwhelming public demand" when New Wave of British Heavy Metal stalwarts Venom fell off the bill. On this occasion, they have clearly chosen music to suit the stage as they power through a set of predominantly (very) heavy tracks. Just as clearly, it is not true that "The name of this band is Poison," as mainman Mikael Åkerfeldt repeatedly claims, and nor is it true that Åkerfeldt is really "Brett Michaels without my big fucking suit". Like Phil Mogg, Åkerfeldt feels obliged to apologise for not talking much between the songs and is intent on cramming as much music as he can into his allotted time. "If you've seen us before," he says, "you know that usually I like talking a lot of shit."

We stroll past the Prog Stage and hear Argent playing their Uriah Heep-covered classic 'Hold Your Head Up'. We miss the rest of their hits, but wander up through the food stalls to seek out some pancakes with sugar and lemon. We listen to Joe Elliot's Down 'n' Outz while we eat – essentially Joe Elliot and the Quireboys playing covers of songs by Mott the Hoople splinter bands (really!) Their presence on the bill has caused some disquiet but I've enjoyed listening to the album they gave away with *Classic Rock* magazine. Whatever one thinks about offering the 'Special Guests' slot to a covers band, and a *new* covers band at that, Down 'n' Outz play good quality, solid rock music, and they play it very well. Later they are joined on stage by Mott the Hoople original Ian Hunter, but there's controversy as they overrun and have their power cut, just as a frustrated Hunter is starting to get into his stride.

We miss the drama, as we've already headed back to the Prog Stage for Sunday night headliners Marillion. We find the Crazy West Country Pumpkins, or at least some of them, and some other Marillion fans who call themselves the Parrotheads, and stand with them around a big Pumpkin flag that flies high, wide and handsome halfway between the mixing desk and the stage. Despite some initial technical glitches that seem to afflict keyboard player Mark Kelly and, especially, bass player Pete Trewavas, it's another fine Marillion set, centred, as promised in the Official Programme, on the band's "progressive and experimental works." On this occasion that includes 'The Invisible Man' (from *Marbles*), the epic and autobiographical 'This Strange Engine' (from the album of the same name) and the 'This Town'/'The Rakes Progress'/'100 Nights' trilogy from *Holidays in Eden*. Original singer Fish is reportedly in the audience too. We have seen him several times in the VIP Area walking round with a warm handshake, a smile and a big camera. He's looking pretty good following a recent throat cancer scare, and I wonder whether we'll see him on a future High Voltage bill.

At the start of the second track, 'Cover My Eyes', around 180 giant pumpkin balloons are released pretty much simultaneously and fly up into the air. That's how many balloons I am told have been randomly distributed through the crowd. At indoor gigs these balloons can hang around for ages. On this occasion the wind disperses them quickly and I can see large numbers of them gathering in the adjacent field. There are those who have no truck with this kind of nonsense, and I can see their point of view. After all, it's got nothing to do with the music. But I kind of like the fun and colour that the Pumpkins add to Marillion gigs. It's absurd, of course, but that's what makes it fun.

As good as Marillion are, they seem to suffer a bit crowdwise as Main Stage headliners Emerson, Lake and Palmer are back together for the first time in 15 years to play a 40th anniversary concert. Though a significant and appreciative hardcore stay for the full set, I am aware of people behind us gradually peeling off. Even a few people wearing Marillion t-shirts disappear a little early!

For some, the reformation of ELP is progressive rock heaven and their main reason for attending the festival. For Chrissy and I, it's something of a bonus. Arriving at the main field some half an hour into the set, we watch in relaxed mood, eating chips and wandering around for a varied perspective on the performance and the crowd reaction. Neither of us are big ELP fans but it's a fabulous spectacle, with a stunning light show, a great sound and a well chosen set list. Like many others we particularly enjoy the 'Fanfare for the Common Man' finale, with Carl Palmer's mad drumming extravaganza and Keith Emerson's destructive keyboard theatrics to the fore amid explosions, fireworks and rapturous applause. It's a great end to a wonderful festival – and hopefully it will be the first of many years of High Voltage rock 'n' roll.

Perhaps the mainstream media will continue to remain cynical and cautiously suspicious of events like the High Voltage Festival and many of the bands who play there. A couple of days before the 2010 Festival, for example, Sky News used a piece focusing on the progressive rock element of the event to mischievously quote (or, for all we know, misquote) John Lydon (Johnny Rotten of the Sex Pistols) on the cultural hollowness of trying to return to the past (as though that were the point of the High Voltage Festival). But if ELP, whom many regard as an exemplar of 1970s progressive rock excess, and ZZ Top, that li'l ol' blues band from Texas, can still pull a crowd, then it's clear that despite ongoing mainstream rejection, rock music – classic rock music – and the myriad genres and bands it embraces, still means an awful lot to an awful lot of people. And that's before we consider some of rock's biggest, most enduring and most revered bands – Iron Maiden, AC/DC, The Rolling Stones, Bon Jovi, Metallica, Aerosmith and the like – who continue to sell large numbers of records and draw huge crowds at festivals, stadia and arenas the world over. Whether the turnout at High Voltage was sufficient to ensure this particular event a safe and comfortable passage to the future remains to be seen, but without doubt the 2010 Festival brought heavy metal, heavy rock and progressive rock bands together with stunning effect, showcasing a fantastic range of styles of rock music.* It featured old bands and new bands, young bands and old hands. The vibe was fantastic, and I couldn't help but be struck by the wide age-range of those attending the festival and what appeared to be a very healthy gender mix. Black Label Society may have little in common with Marillion, nor Orange Goblin with Bigelf, nor the Quireboys with ELP, but one thing that all bands on the bill and all fans at the event continue to share is an uncompromising love of rock music, and a rock tradition, that transcends fashion and commercial trends. This book has been written for them, and for "true music lovers" everywhere.

---

* The festival was held in 2011 with an equally enjoyable bill and, it seemed to me, larger crowds than the previous year. At the time of publication the 2012 event appeared likely to become a scheduling victim of the London hosting of the Olympic Games.

Notes

Chapter 1

1 Seb Hunter, *Hell Bent for Leather: Confessions of a Heavy Metal Addict* (Harper Perennial, 2005), p.1.
2 Ibid., p.6.
3 *Classic Rock* magazine, response to 'Star Letter', issue 149, September 2010.
4 Vincent Budd, sleeve notes to Jon Lord's *Windows*, 35ᵗʰ Anniversary Edition, Purple Records (2009), p.5.
5 Nick Hornby, *31 Songs* (Penguin Books, 2003) pp.25–6.
6 Ibid., p.28.
7 Ibid., p.29.
8 Quoted by Michael Gray, *Song and Dance Man III: the Art of Bob Dylan* (Continuum, 2002), p.161.
9 Paul Williams, *Bob Dylan Performing Artist 1974–1986: The Middle Years* (Omnibus Press, 2004), p.32.

Chapter 2

1 Joel Gilbert, *Rolling Thunder and the Gospel Years: A Totally Unauthorised Documentary*, Section 17: 2 hours 29 minutes.
2 Both extracts from an interview with Ron Rosenbaum for *Playboy* magazine, March 1978, published in Jonathan Cott, ed., *Dylan on Dylan* (Hodder and Stoughton, 2006), p.207.
3 Interview reproduced in Jonathan Cott, ed., *Dylan on Dylan*, pp.139–60; this extract p.148.
4 Scott Rowley's editorial, *Classic Rock* magazine, issue 110, September 2007, "the Drugs Issue".
5 Andy Fyfe, *When the Levee Breaks: The Making of Led Zeppelin IV* (Unanimous Ltd., 2003), p.161.
6 Ibid., p.163.
7 Quoted by Mick Wall, *A Biography of Led Zeppelin: When Giants Walked the Earth* (Orion Books, 2008), p.336.
8 Quoted by Stephen Davis, *Hammer of the Gods: Led Zeppelin Unauthorised* (Pan Books, updated 2008 edition), p.321.
9 Andy Fyfe, *When the Levee Breaks: The Making of Led Zeppelin IV*, p.124.
10 *Mojo* magazine, December 2007, p.82.

11 Quoted by Stephen Davis, *Hammer of the Gods: Led Zeppelin Unauthorised*, p.321.

12 Andy Fyfe, *When the Levee Breaks: The Making of Led Zeppelin IV*, p.22.

13 Ibid., p.69.

14 Ibid., p.71.

15 Ibid., p.128.

16 Ibid., pp.129–30.

17 Ibid., p.9.

18 Quoted by Joel McIver, *Justice For All: The Truth About Metallica* (Omnibus Press, 2006), p.240.

19 Ibid., pp.290–1.

20 Ibid., p.143.

21 See http://www.homeoffice.gov.uk/drugs/ for up to date information.

22 Quoted by Joel McIver, *Sabbath Bloody Sabbath* (Omnibus Press, 2006), p.308.

23 Lemmy, *White Line Fever* (Pocket Books, 2003), p.94.

24 Ibid., p.99.

25 Ibid., p.103.

26 Ibid., p.103.

27 Ibid., p.62.

28 Ian Gillan, *Child in Time: The Life Story of the Singer from Deep Purple* (Smith Gryphon Limited, 1993), p.183.

29 Quoted in *Classic Rock* magazine, issue 105, May 2007.

30 *Classic Rock* magazine, December 2002, issue 47.

31 Quoted in Jerry Bloom, *Black Knight: Ritchie Blackmore* (Omnibus Press, 2006), p.95.

32 Ian Gillan, *Child in Time: The Life Story of the Singer from Deep Purple*, p.65.

33 Mick Wall, *Iron Maiden: Run to the Hills* (Third Edition, Sanctuary, 2004), p.11.

34 Ibid., p.193.

35 Paul Di'Anno, *The Beast* (John Blake Publishing Ltd., 2002), pp.7–8.

36 Ibid., pp.8–9.

37 Mick Wall, *Iron Maiden: Run to the Hills*, p.194.

38 Lemmy, *White Line Fever*, p.134.

39 Interview with Chris Welch, sleeve notes to *The Definitive Anthology: An Ecstasy of Fumbling*, p.16.

40 See sleeve notes to the EMI two-disc remaster of *Misplaced Childhood*, p.10.

41 Ian Gillan, *Child in Time: The Life Story of the Singer from Deep Purple*, pp.68–9.

42 Lemmy, *White Line Fever*, p.287.

43 Quoted in Nigel Williamson, *The Rough Guide to Bob Dylan* (Rough Guides Limited, 2004), p.47.

44 Quoted by Joel McIver, *Sabbath Bloody Sabbath*, p.12.

45 Quoted in Nigel Williamson, *The Rough Guide to Bob Dylan*, p.150.

46 Andy Fyfe, *When the Levee Breaks: The Making of Led Zeppelin IV*, p.191.

47 M.O'C. Drury 'Conversations with Wittgenstein' in Rush Rhees, ed., *Recollections of Wittgenstein* (Oxford University Press, paperback, 1984), p.157.

48 Ray Monk, *Ludwig Wittgenstein: the Duty of Genius* (Jonathan Cape, London, 1990), p. 451. See also: Paul Johnson, *Wittgenstein and Moral Philosophy* (Routledge, London and New York, 1991), p.14.

Chapter 3

1 From the interview with Lemmy in Penelope Spheeris's film *The Decline of Western Civilisation Part II: the Metal Years*.
2 Quoted in Joel McIver, *Sabbath Bloody Sabbath* (Omnibus Press, 2006), p.283.
3 Quoted in Mick Wall, *Iron Maiden: Run to the Hills* (Third Edition, Sanctuary, 2004), p.356.
4 Jerry Bloom, *Black Knight: Ritchie Blackmore* (Omnibus Press, 2006), pp.264–5.
5 Both extracts from Joel McIver, *Justice For All: The Truth About Metallica* (Omnibus Press, 2006), p.158.
6 Quoted in Kate Crockett, *Y Sîn Roc* (Y Lolfa, 1995), p.28, my translation.
7 In Menna Elfyn and John Rowlands, eds, *The Bloodaxe Book of Modern Welsh Poetry: 20ᵗʰ Century Welsh Lanaguage Poetry in Translation* (Bloodaxe Books, 2003), p.24.
8 Quoted in Kate Crockett, *Y Sîn Roc*, p.25, my translation.
9 In Menna Elfyn and John Rowlands, eds, *The Bloodaxe Book of Modern Welsh Poetry: 20ᵗʰ Century Welsh Lanaguage Poetry in Translation*, p.23.
10 From 'The Unbearable Politeness of Being' in Twm Morys, *Ofn Fy Het* (Cyhoeddiadau Barddas, 1995), p.47.

Chapter 4

1 Derek Lawrence, sleeve notes to *Green Bullfrog* (Connoisseur Collection, 1991), p.12.
2 Quoted in Jerry Bloom, *Black Knight: Ritchie Blackmore* (Omnibus Press, 2006), p.132.
3 Ibid., p.147.
4 Ibid., p.147.
5 Ibid., p.169.
6 Putterford's review is reproduced on p.3 of the sleeve notes to the 2005 'Expanded Edition' of *The Eleventh Hour* (Castle Music/Sanctuary Records).
7 Sleeve notes to the 2005 'Expanded Edition' of *The Eleventh Hour* (Castle Music/Sanctuary Records), p.6.
8 Sleeve notes to the 2005 'Expanded Edition' of *Chase the Dragon* (Castle Music/Sanctuary Records), p.7.
9 Sleeve notes to the 2005 'Expanded Edition' of *The Eleventh Hour*, p.5.

Chapter 5

1 See Mick Wall, *Iron Maiden: Run to the Hills* (Third Edition, Sanctuary, 2004), p.246.
2 See Joel McIver, *Sabbath Bloody Sabbath* (Omnibus Press, 2006), p.38.
3 David Tangye and Graham Wright, *How Black Was Our Sabbath: An Unauthorised View From The Crew* (Pan Books, 2005), also p.38 – spooky!
4 Quoted in Jerry Bloom, *Black Knight: Ritchie Blackmore* (Omnibus Press, 2006), pp.215–16.

5 Ibid., p.216.

6 Joel McIver, *Sabbath Bloody Sabbath* (Omnibus Press, 2006), p.90.

7 See the sleeve notes to the Union Square Music 4CD *Simply Gregorian* collection, 2006.

8 Andy Fyfe, *When the Levee Breaks: The Making of Led Zeppelin IV* (Unanimous Ltd., 2003), p.78.

9 Ibid., p.78.

10 Vokey, John R. and Read, Don, November 1985: "Subliminal messages: Between the devil and the media", *American Psychologist* 40: 1231–9.

11 Andy Fyfe, *When the Levee Breaks: The Making of Led Zeppelin IV*, p.124.

12 From an interview with J.D.Considine, 'Life in a Lighter Zeppelin', December 1983, published on the *Achilles Last Stand* website: http://www.led-zeppelin.org/.

13 See Joel McIver, *Sabbath Bloody Sabbath*, p.56.

14 Hugh Gilmour, sleeve notes to Black Sabbath, *Volume 4*, Sanctuary Records reissue (2004), p.2.

15 *Classic Rock* magazine, issue 106 (June 2007), p.42.

16 Quoted in an interview carried in *Classic Rock* magazine's *Decades: The 1970s*, p.48. See also *Classic Rock* magazine, issue 106 (June 2007), p.39.

17 See Mick Wall's interview with Geezer Butler carried in *Classic Rock* magazine, issue 106 (June 2007), p.42.

18 Interview with *NME*, 4 April 1970, quoted in David Tangye and Graham Wright *How Black Was Our Sabbath: An Unauthorised View From The Crew* (Pan Books, 2005), p.39.

19 Ibid., pp.37–8.

20 Ibid., p.38.

21 Quoted by Joel McIver, *Sabbath Bloody Sabbath*, pp.82–3.

22 Quoted by David Tangye and Graham Wright, *How Black Was Our Sabbath: An Unauthorised View From The Crew*, p.39.

23 Quoted by Joel McIver, *Sabbath Bloody Sabbath*, p.83.

24 Ibid., p.73.

25 Mick Wall, *Ozzy Osbourne: Diary of a Madman* (Zomba Books, 1985), p.23.

26 Quoted by Joel McIver, *Sabbath Bloody Sabbath*, pp.84–5.

27 Copies of Geoff Mann album reviews are accessible on the official Geoff Mann website at: http://www.geoffmann.co.uk/.

28 *Night Moves*, issue 16, March 1984. Thanks are due to my friend Phil Morris for digging out this quote for me.

29 Brian Devoil, sleeve notes to Twelfth Night *Live and Let Live* (Cyclops reissue – CYCL050), p.3.

Chapter 6

1 Ludwig Wittgenstein, *Tractatus Logico-Philosophicus* (London: Routledge and Kegan Paul, 1961), trans. D. F. Pears and B. F. McGuiness. The book is structured by numbered paragraphs which are often referred to as 'propositions'.

Chapter 7

1 Jerry Hopkins and Danny Sugerman, *No One Here Gets Out Alive* (Plexus, London, 1982), pp.182–3.

2 Quoted by Joel McIver, *Sabbath Bloody Sabbath* (Omnibus Press, 2006), p.28.

3 Ibid., p.373.

4 Friedrich Nietzsche, *Beyond Good and Evil* (Penguin Books, 1986), Part 4: 'Epigrams and Interludes', Section 99, trans. R.J. Hollingdale.

5 Doug Sundling, *People Are Strange: The Ultimate Guide to the Doors* (Sanctuary Encore, 2005), pp.9–10.

6 Quoted in Jerry Hopkins and Danny Sugerman, *No One Here Gets Out Alive*, p.143.

7 Ibid., p.164.

8 Danny Sugerman, Foreword to Jerry Hopkins and Danny Sugerman *No One Here Gets Out Alive*, p.viii.

9 Ibid., p.vii.

10 From a letter to Paul Demeny, 15 May 1871, quoted in Arthur Rimbaud, *Collected Poems*, introduced and edited and with translations by Oliver Bernard (Penguin Books, 1987), pp.10–11.

11 Quoted in Jerry Hopkins and Danny Sugerman, *No One Here Gets Out Alive*, p.107.

12 Ibid., p.143.

13 Ibid., p.vi. The source is given only as 'Los Angeles 1969'.

14 Doug Sundling, *People Are Strange: The Ultimate Guide to the Doors*, (Sanctuary Encore, 2005).

15 Quoted in the booklet that accompanies *The Doors Box Set* (Elektra/WEA, 1997), p.44.

16 Barney Hoskins, sleeve notes to the *Strange Days* reissue for the *Perception* box set, p.5.

17 Ibid., p.8.

18 Quoted in Doug Sundling's book *People Are Strange: The Ultimate Guide to the Doors*, p.43.

19 Ibid., p.28.

20 Jerry Hopkins and Danny Sugerman, *No One Here Gets Out Alive*, p.152.

21 Doug Sundling, *People Are Strange: The Ultimate Guide to the Doors*, p.109.

22 Ibid., p.32.

23 Ibid., see pp.165–6.

24 Quoted by Doug Sundling, *People Are Strange: The Ultimate Guide to the Doors*, pp.32, 41.

25 Quoted by Ben Fong-Torres, sleeve notes to *The Doors* reissue for the *Perception* box set (Elektra/Rhino, 2006), p.9.

26 Doug Sundling, *People Are Strange: The Ultimate Guide to the Doors*, p.61.

27 Ibid., p.82.

28 Ibid., p.61.

29 Ibid., p.88.

30 Ibid., p.86.

31 Jerry Hopkins and Danny Sugerman, *No One Here Gets Out Alive*, p.294.

32 Bruce Botnick, sleeve notes to *The Soft Parade* reissue for the *Perception* box set, p.5.

33 Doug Sundling, *People Are Strange: The Ultimate Guide to the Doors*, p.83.

34 David Fricke, sleeve notes to *The Soft Parade* reissue for the *Perception* box set, p.9.

35 Quoted in Doug Sundling, *People Are Strange: The Ultimate Guide to the Doors*, p.84.

36 Ibid., p.77.

37 Ibid., p.97.

38 Ibid., p.117.

39 Ibid., pp.109, 97, 114.

40 Ibid., p.109.

41 Ibid., p.124.

42 Ibid., pp.126–7.

43 Bruce Botnick, sleeve notes to the *L.A.Woman* reissue for the *Perception* box set, p.4.

44 Ben Fong-Torres, sleeve notes to the *L.A.Woman* reissue for the *Perception* box set, p.9.

45 Reported by Sundling himself, *People Are Strange: The Ultimate Guide to the Doors*, p.83.

46 Bruce Botnick, sleeve notes to the *Morrison Hotel* reissue for the *Perception* box set, p.3.

47 David Fricke, sleeve notes to the *Morrison Hotel* reissue for the *Perception* box set, p.11.

48 Ibid., p.5

49 Jerry Hopkins and Danny Sugerman, *No One Here Gets Out Alive*, pp.269–70.

50 Dylan Jones, *Jim Morrison Dark Star* (Bloomsbury, 1991), p.169.

51 This part of the interview, and others, are reproduced in the 1991 film: *The Soft Parade: A Retrospective* (MCA Home Video, Inc.).

52 Ibid., 33:04.

53 Quoted by Dylan Jones, *Jim Morrison Dark Star*, p.140. Unfortunately Jones does not provide a source.

54 Quoted in Jerry Hopkins and Danny Sugerman, *No One Here Gets Out Alive*, pp.316–17.

55 Ibid., p.183.

56 Ibid., p.183.

57 Ibid., p.210.

58 Ibid., pp.344–5.

59 Ibid., p.360.

60 Ibid., p.181.

61 Danny Sugerman, *Wonderland Avenue* (Abacus, 1997), p.39.

62 Ibid., p.41.

63 Ibid., p.183.

64 Ibid., p.183.

65 Ibid., pp.412–13.

66 Ibid., p.457.

67 Ibid., p.455.

68 Ibid., p.454.

69 Ibid., pp.455–6.

70 Ibid., p.443.

71 Danny Sugerman's Foreword to Jerry Hopkins and Danny Sugerman, *No One Here Gets Out Alive*, p.ix.

Chapter 8

1 Interview with Ron Rosenbaum for *Playboy* magazine, March 1978, published in Jonathan Cott, ed., *Dylan on Dylan* (Hodder and Stoughton, 2006), pp.199–236. This quote p.208.

2 Robert Shelton, *No Direction Home: The Life and Music of Bob Dylan* (Penguin Books, 1987), p.440.

3 Quoted by Robert Shelton, ibid., p.389.

4 Michael Gray, *Song and Dance Man III: The Art of Bob Dylan* (Continuum, 2002), p.13.

5 Quoted by Nigel Williamson, *The Rough Guide to Bob Dylan* (Rough Guides Limited, 2004), p.10.

6 Robert Shelton, *No Direction Home: The Life and Music of Bob Dylan*, p.50.

7 Ibid., p.49.

8 Bob Dylan, *Chronicles Volume 1* (Pocket Books, 2005), pp.78–9.

9 *The Mabinogion*, translated with an introduction by Jerry Gantz (Penguin Books, 1976), p.106.

10 Ibid., p.97.

11 Ibid., p.27.

12 Paul Williams, *Bob Dylan Performing Artist 1960–1973: The Early Years* (Omnibus Press, 2004), p.xii.

13 'A Conversation with Todd Haynes', included as a special feature with *I'm Not There* (VIP Medienfonds 4 GmbH & Co KG, 2007/Paramount Pictures 2008); this quote 2 minutes and 20 seconds (2:20) into the 'conversation' with Haynes.

14 Ibid., 4:20.

15 Ibid., 7:52.

16 Ibid., 0:55.

17 Paul Williams, *Bob Dylan Performing Artist 1974–1986: The Middle Years* (Omnibus Press, 2004), p.23.

18 Michael Gray, *Song and Dance Man III: The Art of Bob Dylan*, p.9.

19 Ibid., p.181.

20 Robert Shelton, *No Direction Home: The Life and Music of Bob Dylan*, pp.435, 434, 434.

21 Ibid., p.436.

22 Paul Williams, *Bob Dylan Performing Artist 1974–1986: The Middle Years*, p.17

23 Ibid., p.22.

24 Quoted by Williams, ibid., p.22, but commonly quoted by Dylan's biographers.

25 Ibid., p.21.

26 Grey Cavitt, http://www.musictap.net/Reviews/DylanBobBloodOnTheTracksSACD.
html.

27 See John Bauldie's notes to the *Bootleg Series Volumes 1–3 [Rare and Unreleased
1961–1991]* (Columbia, 1991), p.48; Nigel Williamson's *The Rough Guide to Bob
Dylan*, p.288; and Robert Shelton's *No Direction Home: the Life and Music of Bob
Dylan*, p.444.

28 Paul Williams, *Bob Dylan Performing Artist 1974–1986: The Middle Years*, p.24.

29 See the booklet accompanying the *Biograph* collection (Columbia, 1985), p.34.

30 Paul Williams, *Bob Dylan Performing Artist 1974–1986: The Middle Years*, p.30.

31 Michael Gray, *Song and Dance Man III: The Art of Bob Dylan*, p.181.

32 Quoted by Larry Sloman in the essay that accompanies *Tell Tale Signs: The
Bootleg Series Volume 8, Rare and Unreleased 1989–2006* (Columbia, 2008),
p.22.

33 Bob Dylan, sleeve notes to *World Gone Wrong* (Columbia, 1993), pp.8–9.

34 Nigel Williamson, *The Rough Guide to Bob Dylan*, p.159.

35 See Bob Dylan, *Chronicles Volume 1*, pp.148–53.

36 Bob Dylan, *Chronicles Volume 1*, pp.147–8.

37 Nigel Williamson, *The Rough Guide to Bob Dylan*, p.165.

38 Paul Williams, *Bob Dylan Performing Artist: 1974–1986: The Middle Years*, Preface,
p.xiii.

39 See Martin Scorsese, *No Direction Home: Bob Dylan* (International Film Finance
Ltd., Educational Broadcasting Corporation, Grey Water Park Productions, Inc.,
2005/Paramount Pictures 2008); this quote Disc 2, 23:14.

40 'A Conversation with Todd Haynes', this quote 38 minutes and 44 seconds (38:44)
into the 'conversation' with Haynes.

41 Bob Dylan, *Chronicles Volume 1*, p.147.

42 Nigel Williamson, *The Rough Guide to Bob Dylan*, p.183.

43 Larry Sloman in the essay that accompanies *Tell Tale Signs: The Bootleg Series
Volume 8, Rare and Unreleased 1989–2006*, p.30.

44 Quoted by Larry Sloman, ibid., p.30.

Chapter 9

1 Jon Collins, *Marillion/Separated Out* (Helter Skelter Publishing, 2003), p.175.

2 Steve Hogarth, sleeve note to the special edition of *Anoraknophobia* (Intact, 2001),
p.13.

3 Ibid., p.30.

4 Steve Hogarth, sleeve notes to *Brave* (EMI two-disc remaster, 1998), p.18.

5 Steve Hogarth, sleeve notes to *Afraid of Sunlight* (EMI two-disc remaster, 1999),
p.18.

6 *The Web UK Magazine* (volume 6, issue 4), December 2006, p.21.

7 Ibid., p.21.

8 *The Web UK Magazine* (volume 8, issue 1), March 2008, p.7.

9 *The Web UK Magazine* (volume 8, issue 4), December 2008, p.12.

10 Jon Collins, *Marillion/Separated Out* (Helter Skelter Publishing, 2003), p.183.

11 Reviews available at www.marillion.com/press/anorak.htm.

12 From 'The Meegan Files: Part 2', in *The Web UK Magazine* (volume 8, issue 2), June 2008, p.18.

13 Ibid., p.19.

14 From 'The Meegan Files: Part 3', in *The Web UK Magazine* (volume 8, issue 3), September 2008, p.25.

15 Ibid., p.30.

16 Ibid., p.25.

17 From Steve Hogarth's, interview with Alex and Joerg of the German fan club – The Web Germany – carried in *The Web UK Magazine* (volume 4, issue 4), Autumn 2004, p.8.

18 From 'The Meegan Files: Part 3', in *The Web UK Magazine* (volume 8, issue 3), September 2008, p.26.

19 Marillion, *Marbles on the Road*, (Racket Records, 2004).

20 From Steve Hogarth's, interview with Alex and Joerg of the German fan club – The Web Germany – carried in *The Web UK Magazine* (volume 4, issue 4), Autumn 2004, pp.12–13.

21 Ibid., p.13.

22 Ibid.

23 From 'The Meegan Files: Part 3', in *The Web UK Magazine* (volume 8, issue 3), September 2008, p.30

24 Ludgwig Wittgenstein, *Tractatus Logico-Philosophicus* (London: Routledge and Kegan Paul, 1961), trans. D.F. Pears and B.F. McGuinness.

25 Ibid.

26 Quoted by Ray Monk, *Ludwig Wittgenstein: The Duty of Genius*, p.505.

27 Source: www.steve-thorne.co.uk/.

28 E-mail circular to fans, 6 May 2009.

29 Paul Wilkinson, *Rat Salad: Black Sabbath the Classic Years 1969–1975* (Pimlico, 2007), p.2.

30 Jon Collins, *Marillion/Separated Out*, p.198

31 Phillip Wilding, *Happiness is the Road* review, Classic Rock magazine, issue 125, November 2008.

32 From the 'Make Mine a Double' band interview carried in *The Web UK Magazine* (volume 8, issue 3), September 2008, p.18.

33 Ibid., p.17.

Permissions

The author has made strenuous efforts to reference his work accurately and ensure that all essential permissions for lyric quotations have been obtained. Should any errors or oversights remain, the author will be pleased to address these quickly in advance of any further print runs.

Bigelf

The Gravest Show on Earth: written by Damon Fox and A.H.M Butler-Jones. Published by Evil Beatle Music /BMI. Lyrics used by kind permission.

Counting Sheep: written by Damon Fox. Published by Evil Beatle Music /BMI. Lyrics used by kind permission.

Black Sabbath

Black Sabbath: words and music by Terrance Butler, Tony Iommi, John Osbourne, William Ward. Published by Onward Music Ltd, Onward House, 11 Uxbridge Street, London W8 7TQ. Used by permission.

N.I.B.: words and music by Terrance Butler, Tony Iommi, John Osbourne, William Ward Published by Westminster Music Ltd. Used by kind permission.

Wicked World: words and music by Terrance Butler, Tony Iommi, John Osbourne, William Ward Published by Westminster Music Ltd. Used by kind permission.

War Pigs: words and music by Terrance Butler, Tony Iommi, John Osbourne, William Ward Published by Westminster Music Ltd. Used by kind permission.

After Forever: words and music by Terrance Butler, Tony Iommi, John Osbourne, William Ward Published by Onward Music Ltd, Onward House, 11 Uxbridge Street, London W8 7TQ. Used by permission.

Children of the Grave: words and music by Terrance Butler, Tony Iommi, John Osbourne, William Ward. Published by Onward Music Ltd, Onward House, 11 Uxbridge Street, London W8 7TQ. Used by permission.

Lord of This World: words and music by Terrance Butler, Tony Iommi, John Osbourne, William Ward. Published by Onward Music Ltd, Onward House, 11 Uxbridge Street, London W8 7TQ. Used by permission.

Into the Void: words and music by Terrance Butler, Tony Iommi, John Osbourne, William Ward. Published by Westminster Music Ltd. Used by kind permission.

Under the Sun: words and music by Terrance Butler, Tony Iommi, John Osbourne, William Ward. Published by Westminster Music Ltd. Used by kind permission.

Sabbath Bloody Sabbath: words and music by Terrance Butler, Tony Iommi, John Osbourne, William Ward. Published by Onward Music Ltd, Onward House, 11 Uxbridge Street, London W8 7TQ. Used by permission.

A National Acrobat: words and music by Terrance Butler, Tony Iommi, John Osbourne, William Ward. Published by Westminster Music Ltd. Used by kind permission.

Spiral Architect: words and music by Terrance Butler, Tony Iommi, John Osbourne, William Ward. Published by Westminster Music Ltd. Used by kind permission.

Hole in the Sky: words and music by Terrance Butler, Tony Iommi, John Osbourne, William Ward. Published by Westminster Music Ltd. Used by kind permission.

Symptom of the Universe: words and music by Terrance Butler, Tony Iommi, John Osbourne, William Ward. Published by Westminster Music Ltd. Used by kind permission.

Megalomania: words and music by Terrance Butler, Tony Iommi, John Osbourne, William Ward. Published by Westminster Music Ltd. Used by kind permission.

Thrill of it All: words and music by Terrance Butler, Tony Iommi, John Osbourne, William Ward. Published by Westminster Music Ltd. Used by kind permission.

The Writ: words and music by Terrance Butler, Tony Iommi, John Osbourne, William Ward. Published by Westminster Music Ltd. Used by kind permission.

It's Alright: words and music by Terrance Butler, Tony Iommi, John Osbourne, William Ward. Published by Westminster Music Ltd. Used by kind permission.

Gypsy: words and music by Terrance Butler, Tony Iommi, John Osbourne, William Ward. Published by Westminster Music Ltd. Used by kind permission.

All Moving Parts (Stand Still): words and music by Terrance Butler, Tony Iommi, John Osbourne, William Ward. Published by Westminster Music Ltd. Used by kind permission.

She's Gone: words and music by Terrance Butler, Tony Iommi, John Osbourne, William Ward. Published by Westminster Music Ltd. Used by kind permission.

Dirty Women: words and music by Terrance Butler, Tony Iommi, John Osbourne, William Ward. Published by Westminster Music Ltd. Used by kind permission.

Never Say Die: words and music by Terrance Butler, Tony Iommi, John Osbourne, William Ward. Published by Westminster Music Ltd. Used by kind permission.

Johnny Blade: words and music by Terrance Butler, Tony Iommi, John Osbourne, William Ward. Published by Westminster Music Ltd. Used by kind permission.

A Hard Road: words and music by Terrance Butler, Tony Iommi, John Osbourne, William Ward. Published by Westminster Music Ltd. Used by kind permission.

Shock Wave: words and music by Terrance Butler, Tony Iommi, John Osbourne, William Ward. Published by Westminster Music Ltd. Used by kind permission.

Air Dance: words and music by Terrance Butler, Tony Iommi, John Osbourne, William Ward. Published by Westminster Music Ltd. Used by kind permission.

Over to You: words and music by Terrance Butler, Tony Iommi, John Osbourne, William Ward. Published by Westminster Music Ltd. Used by kind permission.

Swinging the Chain: words and music by Terrance Butler, Tony Iommi, John Osbourne, William Ward. Published by Westminster Music Ltd. Used by kind permission.

Deep Purple

Child in Time: words and music by Blackmore/Gillan/Glover/Lord/Paice. Published by HEC Music Ltd. Used with permission of HEC Music Ltd.

Bob Dylan

Mr. Tambourine Man: words and music by Bob Dylan ©1964, 1965 by Warner Bros. Inc.; renewed 1992, 1993 by Special Rider Music. Used by kind permission of The Bob Dylan Music Company.

She Belongs to Me: words and music by Bob Dylan ©1965 by Warner Bros. Inc.; renewed 1993 by Special Rider Music. Used by kind permission of The Bob Dylan Music Company.

Love Minus Zero/No Limit: words and music by Bob Dylan ©1965 by Warner Bros. Inc.; renewed 1993 by Special Rider Music. Used by kind permission of The Bob Dylan Music Company.

Like A Rolling Stone: words and music by Bob Dylan ©1965 by Warner Bros. Inc.; renewed 1993 by Special Rider Music. Used by kind permission of The Bob Dylan Music Company.

As I Went Out One Morning: words and music by Bob Dylan ©1968 by Dwarf Music; renewed 1996 by Dwarf Music. Used by kind permission of The Bob Dylan Music Company.

All Along the Watchtower: words and music by Bob Dylan ©1968 by Dwarf Music; renewed 1996 by Dwarf Music. Used by kind permission of The Bob Dylan Music Company.

Wedding Song: words and music by Bob Dylan ©1973 by Ram's Horn Music; renewed 2001 by Ram's Horn Music. Used by kind permission of The Bob Dylan Music Company.

Tangled Up in Blue: words and music by Bob Dylan ©1974 by Ram's Horn Music; renewed 2002 by Ram's Horn Music. Used by kind permission of The Bob Dylan Music Company.

Simple Twist of Fate: words and music by Bob Dylan ©1974 by Ram's Horn Music; renewed 2002 by Ram's Horn Music. Used by kind permission of The Bob Dylan Music Company.

You're a Big Girl Now: words and music by Bob Dylan ©1974 by Ram's Horn Music; renewed 2002 by Ram's Horn Music. Used by kind permission of The Bob Dylan Music Company.

Idiot Wind: words and music by Bob Dylan ©1974 by Ram's Horn Music; renewed 2002 by Ram's Horn Music. Used by kind permission of The Bob Dylan Music Company.

You're Gonna Make Me Lonesome When You Go: words and music by Bob Dylan ©1974 by Ram's Horn Music; renewed 2002 by Ram's Horn Music. Used by kind permission of The Bob Dylan Music Company.

Lily, Rosemary and the Jack of Hearts: words and music by Bob Dylan ©1974 by Ram's Horn Music; renewed 202 by Ram's Horn Music. Used by kind permission of The Bob Dylan Music Company.

If You See Her Say Hello: words and music by Bob Dylan ©1974 by Ram's Horn Music; renewed 2002 by Ram's Horn Music. Used by kind permission of The Bob Dylan Music Company.

Shelter From The Storm: words and music by Bob Dylan ©1974 by Ram's Horn Music; renewed 2002 by Ram's Horn Music. Used by kind permission of The Bob Dylan Music Company.

Hurricane: words and music by Bob Dylan/Jacques Levy©1975 by Ram's Horn Music; renewed 2003 by Ram's Horn Music. Used by kind permission of The Bob Dylan Music Company.

Isis: words and music by Bob Dylan/Jacques Levy ©1975 by Ram's Horn Music; renewed 2003 by Ram's Horn Music. Used by kind permission of The Bob Dylan Music Company.

Man of Peace: words and music by Bob Dylan ©1983 by Special Rider Music. Used by kind permission of The Bob Dylan Music Company.

Roger Glover

Behind the Smile: words and music Roger Glover © 1975 British Lion Music Ltd, Used by kind permission.

Magnum

Sacred Hour: written by Anthony Clarkin. Published by Aviation Music Limited. Used by kind permission.

The Prize: written by Anthony Clarkin. Published by Aviation Music Limited. Used by kind permission

Breakdown: written by Anthony Clarkin. Published by Aviation Music Limited. Used by kind permission.

The Great Disaster: written by Anthony Clarkin. Published by Aviation Music Limited. Used by kind permission.

Vicious Companions: written by Anthony Clarkin. Published by Aviation Music Limited. Used by kind permission.

One Night of Passion: written by Anthony Clarkin. Published by Aviation Music Limited. Used by kind permission.

The Word: written by Anthony Clarkin. Published by Aviation Music Limited. Used by kind permission

Young and Precious Souls: written by Anthony Clarkin. Published by Aviation Music Limited. Used by kind permission.

Road to Paradise: written by Anthony Clarkin. Published by Aviation Music Limited. Used by kind permission.

Geoff Mann

For More Than a Day: written by Geoff Mann. Lyrics used by kind permission.

I Wouldn't Lie to You: written by Geoff Mann. Lyrics used by kind permission.

My Soul: written by Geoff Mann. Lyrics used by kind permission.

For God's Sake: written by Geoff Mann. Lyrics used by kind permission.

Flowers: written by Geoff Mann. Lyrics used by kind permission.

Creation: written by Geoff Mann. Lyrics used by kind permission.

Kingdom Come: written by Geoff Mann. Lyrics used by kind permission.

Afterwards: written by Geoff Mann. Lyrics used by kind permission.

Slow One: written by Geoff Mann. Lyrics used by kind permission.

Marillion

Chelsea Monday: words and music by Derek William Dick and Mark Kelly and Diz Minnett and Michael James Pointer and Steve Rothery and Pete Trewavas ©1983, Reproduced by permission of EMI Music Publishing Ltd, London W8 5SW.

Incubus: words and music by Derek William Dick and Mark Kelly and Steve Rothery and Pete Trewavas ©1984, Reproduced by permission of EMI Music Publishing Ltd, London W8 5SW.

Cinderella Search: words and music by Derek William Dick and Mark Kelly and Ian Mosley and Steve Rothery and Pete Trewavas ©1983, Reproduced by permission of EMI Music Publishing Ltd, London W8 5SW.

Runaway: words and music by John Helmer and Mark Kelly and Ian Mosley and Steve Rothery and Pete Trewavas and Steve Hogarth ©1993, Reproduced by permission of EMI Music Publishing Ltd, London W8 5SW/Imagem Songs Limited/Music Sales Limited, London W1T 3LJ.

The Great Escape words and music by John Helmer and Mark Kelly and Ian Mosley and Steve Rothery and Pete Trewavas and Steve Hogarth ©1993, Reproduced by permission of EMI Music Publishing Ltd, London W8 5SW/ Imagem Songs Limited/Music Sales Limited, London W1T 3LJ.

Estonia: words and music by Steve Hogarth and Mark Kelly and Ian Mosley and Steve Rothery and Pete Trewavas ©1997, Reproduced by permission of EMI Music Publishing Ltd, London W8 5SW/ Imagem Songs Limited/Music Sales Limited, London W1T 3LJ.

Map of the World: written by Steve Hogarth, Mark Kelly, Ian Mosely, Steve Rothery, Pete Trewavas and Nick Van Eade ©2001 Intact Records. Lyrics used by kind permission.

When I Meet God: written by Steve Hogarth, Mark Kelly, Ian Mosely, Steve Rothery and Pete Trewavas ©2001 Intact Records. Lyrics used by kind permission.

This is the 21ˢᵗ Century: written by Steve Hogarth, Mark Kelly, Ian Mosely, Steve Rothery and Pete Trewavas ©2001 Intact Records. Lyrics used by kind permission.

The Invisible Man: written by Steve Hogarth, Mark Kelly, Ian Mosely, Steve Rothery and Pete Trewavas ©2004 Intact Records. Lyrics used by kind permission.

Don't Hurt Yourself: written by Steve Hogarth, Mark Kelly, Ian Mosely, Steve Rothery and Pete Trewavas ©2004 Intact Records. Lyrics used by kind permission.

Fantastic Place: written by Steve Hogarth, Mark Kelly, Ian Mosely, Steve Rothery and Pete Trewavas ©2004 Intact Records. Lyrics used by kind permission.

Neverland: written by Steve Hogarth, Mark Kelly, Ian Mosely, Steve Rothery and Pete Trewavas ©2004 Intact Records. Lyrics used by kind permission.

Faith: written by Steve Hogarth, Mark Kelly, Ian Mosely, Steve Rothery and Pete Trewavas ©2007 Intact Records. Lyrics used by kind permission.

This Train is My Life: written by Steve Hogarth, Mark Kelly, Ian Mosely, Steve Rothery and Pete Trewavas ©2008 Intact Records. Lyrics used by kind permission.

Motörhead

Don't Let Daddy Kiss Me: written by Ian Kilmister. Published by Warner-Chappell Music Ltd. Used by kind permission

Saxon

Strong Arm Of The Law: words and music by Graham Oliver, Paul Anthony Quinn, Peter Rodney Byford, Peter Francis Michael Gill and Stephen Dawson © 1980 Carlin Music Corporation, London NW1 8BD – All Rights Reserved – Used by permission.

Heavy Metal Thunder: words and music by Graham Oliver, Paul Anthony Quinn, Peter Rodney Byford, Peter Francis Michael Gill and Stephen Dawson © 1980 Carlin Music Corporation, London NW1 8BD – All Rights Reserved – Used by permission.

Suzie Hold On: words and music by Graham Oliver, Paul Anthony Quinn, Peter Rodney Byford, Peter Francis Michael Gill and Stephen Dawson © 1980 Carlin Music Corporation, London NW1 8BD – All Rights Reserved – Used by permission.

Dallas 1pm: words and music by Graham Oliver, Paul Anthony Quinn, Peter Rodney Byford, Peter Francis Michael Gill and Stephen Dawson © 1980

Carlin Music Corporation, London NW1 8BD – All Rights Reserved – Used by permission.

Denim And Leather: words and music by Graham Oliver, Paul Anthony Quinn, Peter Rodney Byford, Peter Francis Michael Gill and Stephen Dawson © 1981 Carlin Music Corporation, London NW1 8BD – All Rights Reserved – Used by permission.

Twelfth Night

East of Eden: words and music by Twelfth Night. Published by Hit and Run Music Publishing Ltd. Used by kind permission.

Fact and Fiction: words and music by Twelfth Night. Published by Hit and Run Music Publishing Ltd. Used by kind permission.

We Are Sane: words and music by Twelfth Night. Published by Hit and Run Music Publishing Ltd. Used by kind permission.

Creepshow: words and music by Twelfth Night. Published by Hit and Run Music Publishing Ltd. Used by kind permission.

Love Song: words and music by Twelfth Night. Published by Hit and Run Music Publishing Ltd. Used by kind permission.

The Ceiling Speaks: words and music by Twelfth Night. Published by Hit and Run Music Publishing Ltd. Used by kind permission.

Sequences: words and music by Twelfth Night. Published by Hit and Run Music Publishing Ltd. Used by kind permission.

Index

A

AIIZ 64, 66
AC/DC 1, 2, 3, 52, 180, 182, 350
Adams, Bryan 257
Aerosmith 2, 27–28, 52, 93, 110, 196, 210, 350
A Genuine Freakshow 332
Airey, Don 103, 122
Åkerfeldt, Mikael 348
Allen, Daevid 169
Amos, Tori 93
Anselmo, Phil 342
Answer, The 339
Anthrax 77, 79, 194, 195, 203
Appice, Vinnie 65, 341
Argent 348
Ashton, Tony 106
Asia 331, 341
Audrey Horne 346

B

Bachman Turner 346
Bad News 193
Baez, Joan 46
Barden, Gary 70
B.B. King 48
Beard, Frank 343
Beatles, The 12, 47–48, 107, 168, 211, 339
Beck, Jeff 46
Benton, Glen 169
Bigelf 339, 340, 350

Big Leaves 83
Black, Jack 43
Black Label Society 342, 350
Blackmore, Ritchie 34–35, 46, 71–76, 80, 81, 95, 97, 98, 99, 100, 101, 102, 103, 105, 106, 108, 121–122, 133–134
Blackmore's Night 70, 106
Black Sabbath 2, 3, 5–6, 11, 13, 26–27, 46, 48, 52, 61–65, 66, 69, 96, 104, 110, 133, 134, 139, 142–158, 164, 170–173, 210, 332, 339, 341
Black Spiders 338
Blondie 95
Blue Öyster Cult 86
Bob Delyn a'r Ebillion 84–87
Bolan, Marc 339
Bolin, Tommy 34, 103, 105
Bonamassa, Joe 347–348
Bonham, John 24, 48
Bon Jovi (band) 52, 193–194, 195, 201, 203, 274, 350
Bon Jovi, Jon 27
Bower, Jimmy 346
Bowie, David 48, 129, 161, 339
Box, Mick 347
Bruce, Jack 210
Budgie 39–40, 46, 67, 73, 83, 109
Burgi, Chuck 75–76
Burnett, T-Bone 87
Burton, Cliff 80
Burzum 137
Bush, Kate 93, 109, 198

Butler, Geezer 65, 133, 144, 145, 147, 150, 151, 152, 153, 154–155, 156, 158, 210, 341
Byford, Biff 38, 55, 56–57, 58, 59, 176, 341
Byrds, The 247, 251

C

Cable, Stuart 297
Campbell, Phil 197
Carey, Tony 122
Carter, Neil 340
Castle, Ben 308
Catatonia 83
Cathedral 78, 340
Catley, Bob 89, 90, 127
Chumbawamba 49, 202
Cinderella 194
Clapton, Eric 46, 48
Clarkin, Tony 8, 89, 126, 127, 128, 129, 346
Clutch 347
Cohen, Matt 332, 344
Cohen, Rachel 344
Collins, Albert 48
Collins, Phil 48, 292
Cook, Paul 331
Cooper, Alice 33, 45, 46, 52, 230
Coverdale, David 102, 103, 105–106, 107
Cramps, The 44
Cream 210
Crowded House 274, 307
Cutting Crew 310

D

Daisley, Bob 67, 133–134
Damned, The 109
Darkness , The 5
Dead (Mayhem vocalist) 137
Deep Purple 2, 3, 4, 5–6, 33, 34–36, 42, 46, 52, 70, 71, 78, 80–83, 89, 94–107, 108, 109, 110, 121, 122, 133, 143, 339, 341
Def Leppard 193
Deicide 169
Demented Are Go 109

Denny, Sandy 88
Densmore, John 235 (ftn)
Devoil, Brian 168–169
Diamond, Neil 4, 95, 97
Diamond Head 70
Di'Anno, Paul 36–38
Dickinson, Bruce 36
Diddley. Bo 48
Dio (band) 70, 109, 194
Dio, Ronnie James 3, 13, 64–65, 107, 134, 143, 151, 341–342, 343, 344
Dire Straits 48, 108, 273
Dissection 137
Doors, The 2, 3, 21–23, 51, 93, 100, 210, 212–245, 272, 308
Dorrian, Lee 78, 340, 346
Doves 309
Down 342, 346
Downes, Geoff 331
Down 'n' Outz 348
Dream Theater 295, 342
Dumpy's Rusty Nuts 202
Dunbar, Aynsley 145
D'Virgilio, Nick 331
Dylan, Bob 2, 8, 12, 18–20, 31, 46, 48, 51, 87, 89, 147, 151, 161, 168, 209, 247, 250–257, 257–258, 262–273, 275–289

E

Eagles, The 94, 132
Earth 145, 152
Elliot, Joe 348
ELO 135, 339
ELP (Emerson, Lake and Palmer) 343, 349–350
Emerson, Keith 350
Euronymous 137
Europe 274
Evans, Rod 103

F

Fairport Convention 52, 88
Fish 40–41, 115, 119–121, 205–207, 213, 215, 293, 296, 297, 349
Flanagan, Fiona 267

Focus 94, 339
Foreigner 70, 108, 340
Four Minute Warning 201
Fox, Damon 339
Free 52

G

Gabriel, Peter 292, 331
Genesis 52, 120, 294, 331, 346
George Thorogood and the Destroyers 48
Gibbons, Billy 343
Gillan (band) 33 (ftn), 46, 69, 106, 109
Gillan, Ian 2, 33, 34, 35–36, 42–43, 80,
    81, 82, 94, 95, 98, 99, 100, 101, 102,
    103, 106, 122
Girl 66
Girlschool 66
Glitter Band, The 197
Glover, Roger 34, 71, 73, 74, 75, 76, 80,
    82, 95, 99, 102, 103, 107, 122
Gong 27, 169 (ftn), 181
Gorham, Scott 33
Gorky's Zygotic Mynci 47, 70, 83, 85, 295
Grateful Dead 284
Guns N' Roses 27
Guthrie, Woody 267–268
Guy, Buddy 265
Gwilym, Tich 83

H

Hackett, Steve 346
Hagar, Sammy 108
Halford, Rob 135
Hammerfall 340
Hammett, Kirk 29–30
Hanoi Rocks 2
Harris, Emmylou 253
Harris, Steve 36–37, 38, 54, 207
Harrison, Gavin 331
Hawkwind 31
Heaven and Hell 3, 13, 341–342, 343
Helmer, John 304
Hendrix, Jimi 23, 34, 46, 51–52, 57, 83,
    201, 213, 239 (ftn), 263–264, 343
Hetfield, James 29–30, 78

High on Fire 346
Hill, Dusty 343
Hogarth, Steve ('h') 41, 207–208, 209,
    293, 296, 297, 298, 299, 304, 305, 306,
    307, 310, 311, 312, 313–319, 320–321,
    329, 334–335
Holst, Gustav 101, 152
Hughes, Glenn 34, 102, 103, 105–106,
    107, 122, 182, 341–342
Humphries, Edwin 86
Hunter, Ian 348

I

Ian Dury and the Blockheads 95
Ian, Scott 79
Icons of Filth 214
IGB (Ian Gillan Band) 106
Iommi, Tony 26, 46, 65, 144, 145, 147,
    148, 150, 152, 153, 341
IQ 109, 168, 192, 292, 294, 331
Iron Maiden 2, 3, 36–38, 39, 46, 52, 54,
    70, 79, 89, 106, 109, 132, 135, 207, 350

J

Jagger, Mick 48
James, Siân 83–84
Jett, Joan 33
Jethro Tull 52, 70, 109
Jilted John 95
John, Elton 109
Johnson, Brian 180
Jones, Brian 23
Jones, John Paul 24, 25
Joplin, Janis 23, 34
Journey 52
Jowitt, John 331
Judas Priest 2, 48, 109, 135

K

Kansas 109
Kelly, Mark 299, 304, 305, 310, 318, 319,
    349
King Crimson 184, 331
King Diamond 137
King Kurt 109

Kiss 2, 52, 200
KLF, The 106
Korbel, Nolwenn 86–87
Korea 197–198
Krauss, Alison 2, 87–88
Krieger, Robby 219, 220, 228–229, 235 (ftn), 236, 240
Kula Shaker 104

L

Lande, Jorn 341
Lapaj, Michal 107
La's, The 309
Led Zeppelin 2, 5–6, 23–25, 37, 47, 48, 52, 87–88, 93, 102–103, 104, 108, 139–142, 181–182, 197
Lee, Albert 75
Lee, Jake E. 68
Lees, Simon 40
Lemmy 31–33, 44–45, 54, 56
Lethargy 346
Levin, Tony 331
Limelight 55–56
Lord, Jon 4, 34–35, 80, 82, 95, 98, 99, 100, 101, 103, 104–105, 106, 107, 305
Lydon, John (Johnny Rotten) 350
Lynott, Phil 31, 33–34, 77, 340
Lynyrd Skynyrd 52, 86, 185

M

Mackey, Graham (Mackey+) 300
Magnum 8, 70, 89–91, 125–129, 192, 197, 201, 346–347
Malice 196
Malmsteen, Yngwie 105
Manic Street Preachers 201
Mann, Geoff 11, 93, 139, 159–173, 197
Manson, Marilyn 211
Manzarek, Ray 22, 214, 235 (ftn), 238
Marillion 3, 12, 15–16, 40–42, 46, 69, 70, 89, 109, 111, 115, 119–121, 178, 196–197, 205–207, 209, 292–301, 303–321, 326, 328–329, 329–335, 341, 342, 344, 346, 348–349, 350
Marsden, Bernie 106

Marshall, John 77–78
Mars Volta, The 295
Massive Attack 309
Masterplan 341
May, Brian 46, 53
Mayer, John 306
Mayhem 137
McBrain, Nicko 36, 132, 134
McCartney, Paul 48, 211
Meatloaf 109, 346
Metallica 3, 28–30, 39, 46, 52, 70, 77–80, 106, 109, 194, 195, 203, 340, 350
Michaels, Brett 348
Michael Schenker Group (MSG) 67 (ftn), 70, 110
Miles, Buddy 35
Misfits, The 78
Mitchell, Joni 97, 215
Mogg, Phil 345, 348
Moody, Mickey 106, 347
Moon, Keith 34
Moore, Christy 265
Moore, Gary 70, 82, 340
Moore, Vinnie 345
Morley, Luke 338
Morrison, Jim 12, 21–23, 40, 161, 183, 210, 212–245, 272–273, 292, 312
Morrison, Van 265
Morrissey 215
Morse, Steve 81, 82, 103, 104
Morys, Twm 84–85, 86
Mosely, Ian 299, 315
Motley Crüe 203
Motörhead 31, 32, 33, 38, 46, 58, 79, 109, 193, 197
Mott the Hoople 348
Murray, Dave 36
Murray, Neil 106
Mythology 145

N

Napalm Death 78
Nazareth 109
New Device 338
New Flames 83

Newsted, Jason 30 (ftn)
Nicks, Stevie 196
Nirvana 52
Nobacon, Danbert (Chumbawamba
    vocalist) 201
Nödtveidt, Jon 137
Nugent, Ted 34

O

Oliver, Graham 57
Opeth 295, 348
Orange Goblin 339, 350
Orford, Martin 331
Osbourne, Kelly 148
Ozzy Osbourne 26, 31, 32, 46, 48, 54,
    64–65, 66–68, 109, 133, 135, 143, 144,
    145, 146, 147, 148, 152, 153, 154,
    156–157, 158, 193, 210–211

P

Page, Jimmy 5, 24, 46, 47, 139, 140, 141
Paice, Ian 34–35, 75, 80, 82, 95, 99, 100,
    101, 103, 106
Pallas 73, 109, 168, 197, 292, 294
Palmer, Carl 341, 349–350
Pantera 342
Pearl Jam 52
Peart, Neil 295
Pendragon 168, 292, 294, 338
Perry, Joe 27, 28
Persian Risk 197
Petty, Tom 48
Pink Floyd 52, 135, 184, 294, 295, 339
Plant, Robert 2, 24, 25, 47, 87–88, 139,
    140, 141
Poison 348
Polka Tulk Blues Band 145
Pop, Iggy 161
Porcupine Tree 295, 331, 340
Portnoy, Mike 342
Psychedelic Furs 109, 308

Q

Queen 48, 52, 53, 90, 104, 108, 135, 339

Queensrÿche 70, 201, 295
Quireboys, The 344, 346, 348, 350

R

Radiohead 295, 309
Rainbow 65, 70, 71–76, 77, 82, 96–97,
    105, 106, 108, 109, 110, 111, 122, 133,
    134, 143
Reasoning, The 332, 344
Red Hot Chili Peppers 52
R.E.M. 52
Rhoads, Randy 66–67, 68, 69
Richards, Keith 32
Rivera, Scarlet 253
Riverside 107
Roberts, Gorwel 86
Rolling Stones, The 51, 104, 110, 132,
    201, 265, 350
Rose, Axl 21
Rosenthal, David 73, 74
Rose Tattoo 200
Rothery Steve, 299, 304, 305, 307, 310,
    313, 317, 318, 319, 335
Rush 52, 180, 295

S

Samhain 78
Satriani, Joe 70
Saxon 38–39, 46, 55–60, 65, 70, 106,
    109, 110, 115, 175–176, 178, 340–341
Sayer, Leo 274
Schenker, Michael 110, 143, 345
Schenker, Rudolf 143
Scorpions 52, 62, 93, 143, 193
Scott, Mike 210
Sentance, Carl 197
Seviour, Kim 337
Sex Pistols 95, 350
Shelley, Burke 40, 83
Simper, Nick 103
Slayer 137, 139, 181, 188, 203
Smith, Adrian 36
South, Joe 104
Spear of Destiny 115
Spike (The Quireboys) 344, 348

Spinal Tap 5, 46, 197
Spock's Beard 331
Springsteen, Bruce 257
Squeeze 274
Stanway, Mark 89, 90
Status Quo 48
Steel Panther 5
Stereophonics 297
St. Hubbins, David 46–47
Strawbs, The 347, 348
Stray Cats, The 257
Strymdingars 86
Stryper 136, 139
Styx 108, 135
Sullivan, Jim 75
Superclarks 83
Super Furry Animals 83, 85
Sykes, John 33

T

Tank 109
Tears for Fears 331
10cc 94, 339
Thin Lizzy 33, 70, 77, 109
Thomas, John 39
Thompson, Tony 48
Thorne, Steve 331
Thunder 338
Topper 83
Touchstone 337
Transatlantic 342, 346
Trewavas, Pete 299, 308, 331, 342, 349
Tufnell, Nigel 47
Turner, Joe Lynn 72, 73, 74, 81, 103, 122
Twelfth Night 11, 93, 109, 159–163, 164,
    167, 168, 169, 170–172, 197, 292, 294
Twisted Sister 196, 200
Tyler, Steven 27, 28, 210

U

UFO 70, 108, 110, 185, 340, 344, 345,
    346

Ulrich, Lars 28–30, 106
Union, The 338–339
Uriah Heep 339, 347, 348
U2 45, 48, 52, 123, 309

V

Vandenberg (band) 70
Vandenberg, Adrian 70
Van Eade, Nick 310
Van Halen 52
Venom 137, 139, 348
Vigilante 73
Vikernes, Varg 137
Violent Femmes 201

W

Wakeman, Rick 70, 347
Ward, Bill 144, 145, 146, 151, 155
Warlock 193
WASP 194
Waterboys, The 210
Waters, Muddy 265
Waters, Roger 295
Wells, Junior 265
Whitesnake 70, 82, 106, 109, 347
Who, The 48, 51
Williams, Steve 40, 73
Williams, Viv 83
Wings 94
Wishbone Ash 346
Wonder, Stevie 106

Y

Yes 52, 182, 294, 331
Yoakum, Dwight 257
Young, Neil 48

Z

Zappa, Dweezil 340
Zappa, Frank 340
ZZ Top 342–343, 350